Complying with Europe

What does EU law truly mean for the member states? Do they abide by it or don't they, and why? *Complying with Europe* presents the first encompassing and in-depth empirical study of the effects of 'voluntaristic' and (partly) 'soft' EU policies in the member states. The authors examine ninety case studies across a range of EU Directives and shed light on burning contemporary issues in political science, integration theory, and social policy. The book reveals that there are major implementation failures and that, to date, the European Commission has not been able to perform its control function adequately. While all countries are occasional non-compliers, some usually take their EU-related duties seriously (world of law observance). Others frequently put their domestic political concerns above the requirements of EU law (world of domestic politics). A further group of countries neglects these EU obligations almost as a matter of course (world of neglect). This innovative study answers questions of crucial importance for politics in theory and in practice, and suggests how implementation of EU law can be fostered in the future.

GERDA FALKNER is Head of the Department of Political Science at the Institute for Advanced Studies, Vienna and Associate Professor of Political Science at the University of Vienna.

OLIVER TREIB is Assistant Professor at the Department of Political Science, Institute for Advanced Studies, Vienna.

MIRIAM HARTLAPP is Researcher at the Social Science Research Center Berlin.

SIMONE LEIBER is Researcher in Political Science at the Institute of Economic and Social Research, Düsseldorf.

Themes in European Governance

Series Editors
Andreas Føllesdal
Johan P. Olsen

Editorial Board

Stefano Bartolini	Ulrich Preuss	Helen Wallace
Beate Kohler-Koch	Thomas Risse	Albert Weale
Percy Lehning	Fritz W. Scharpf	J. H. H. Weiler
Andrew Moravcsik	Philip Schlesinger	

The evolving European systems of governance, in particular the European Union, challenge and transform the state, the most important locus of governance and political identity and loyalty over the past 200 years. The series *Themes in European Governance* aims to publish the best theoretical and analytical scholarship on the impact of European governance on the core institutions, policies and identities of nation states. It focuses upon the implications for issues such as citizenship, welfare, political decision-making, and economic, monetary, and fiscal policies. An initiative of Cambridge University Press and the Programme on Advanced Research on the Europeanisation of the Nation-State (ARENA), Norway, the series includes contributions in the social sciences, humanities and law. The series aims to provide theoretically informed studies analysing key issues at the European level and within European states. Volumes in the series will be of interest to scholars and students of Europe both within Europe and worldwide. They will be of particular relevance to those interested in the development of sovereignty and governance of European states and in the issues raised by multi-level governance and multi-national integration throughout the world.

Other books in the series:

Paulette Kurzer   *Markets and Moral Regulation: Cultural Change in the European Union*

Christoph Knill   *The Europeanisation of National Administrations: Patterns of Institutional Change and Persistence*

Tanja Börzel   *States and Regions in the European Union: Institutional Adaptation in Germany and Spain*

Liesbet Hooghe   *The European Commission and the Integration of Europe: Images of Governance*

Gallya Lahav   *Immigration and Politics in the New Europe: Reinventing Borders*

Gary Marks and Marco R. Steenbergen (eds.)   *European Integration and Political Conflict*

Frank Schimmelfennig   *The EU, NATO and the Integration of Europe: Rules and Rhetoric*

Michael E. Smith   *Europe's Foreign and Security Policy: The Institutionalization of Cooperation*

Michael Zürn and Christian Joerges (eds.)   *Law and Governance in Postnational Europe: Compliance beyond the Nation-State*

Tables

1.1	The six sample Directives	*page* 8
2.1	Establishing the policy misfit of a Directive	29
2.2	The aggregation system applied to establish the total misfit	32
2.3	Viable types of enforcement as a prerequisite of successful compliance	39
3.1	The attribution of explicit social policy competences to the EU in formal treaty reforms	42
4.1	The Employment Contract Information Directive and misfit in the member states	60
4.2	Overview of the Employment Contract Information Directive and its implementation	70
5.1	The Pregnant Workers Directive and misfit in the member states	79
5.2	Overview of the Pregnant Workers Directive and its implementation	92
6.1	The Working Time Directive and misfit in the member states	100
6.2	Overview of the Working Time Directive and its implementation	116
7.1	The Young Workers Directive and misfit in the member states	125
7.2	Overview of the Young Workers Directive and its implementation	138
8.1	The Parental Leave Directive and misfit in the member states	146
8.2	Overview of the Parental Leave Directive and its implementation	156
9.1	The Part-time Work Directive and misfit in the member states	165
9.2	Overview of the Part-time Work Directive and its implementation	176

10.1 Three logics of reaction to flexible European law   179
11.1 Infringement procedures initiated by the EU
     Commission   209
11.2 Mismatch between compliance of a member state and
     infringement procedure initiated by the EU
     Commission   216–217
12.1 Potential Europeanisation effects on national
     public–private interaction   233
12.2 Forms of interest group involvement in labour law
     decision-making   235
12.3 Impact of Europeanisation on domestic public–private
     interaction I: the upstream phase   238
12.4 Impact of Europeanisation on domestic public–private
     interaction II: the downstream phase   243
13.1 Categories of potential costs arising from six labour law
     Directives   261
13.2 Overall costs triggered by six Directives in fifteen member
     states   262
13.3 Total misfit created by six Directives in fifteen member
     states   263
13.4 Different degrees of overall misfit arising in the fifteen
     member states   264
13.5 Different degrees of overall misfit created by six labour law
     Directives   265
13.6 Total delays until essentially correct transposition: country
     ranking (in months after deadline)   271
13.7 Effectiveness of national enforcement systems (1990s and
     early 2000s)   272
14.1 Degrees of misfit and transposition performance   290
15.1 Three worlds of compliance   322
15.2 Law-abidingness of administrative and political systems in
     the three worlds of compliance   325
16.1 Voluntarist and non-voluntarist standards contained in the
     six Directives examined   349

Preface

This book is the result of intensive teamwork over a couple of years. Funded by the Max Planck Society, a research group on 'New Governance and Social Europe: Minimum Harmonisation and Soft Law in the European Multi-level System' was established at the Cologne-based Max Planck Institute for the Study of Societies. We are grateful to the Institute's Directors, Fritz W. Scharpf (until 2003) and Wolfgang Streeck, for their support of our work. From October 1999 to September 2003, the research team collaborated face-to-face in Cologne. Co-operation has been continuing ever since then, with e-mails and phone calls serving to bridge the physical gap between the team members, who have all moved on to new jobs in different places all over Europe.

Directed by Gerda Falkner, the group of collaborators included three doctoral students who wrote their dissertation theses on specific aspects within the group's common theme. In his doctoral thesis, Oliver Treib examined the transposition of EU Directives. Focusing on Germany, the Netherlands, Ireland and the UK, he sought to establish the relative significance of the amount of policy misfit vis-à-vis other explanatory factors in determining domestic transposition performance (Treib 2004). After completing his thesis, he continued to work in the project team as a postdoctoral researcher. Miriam Hartlapp's dissertation analysed the transposition process and the enforcement structures in the southern and francophone member states, and the European Commission's enforcement policy (Hartlapp 2005). Simone Leiber's thesis, in turn, addressed the role of labour and industry in the implementation process and the impact of EU labour law Directives on domestic state–society relations. Her country studies included the Nordic states, Austria, Italy and Luxembourg (Leiber 2005). Gerda Falkner's work on the project concentrated on the quantitative development of EU social policy over time as well as on the theory and history of EU social policy (in addition to project design, group management and research supervision). The research team was supported by three successive undergraduate research assistants. We are indebted to Myriam Nauerz, Charlotte Buttkus and Tina Steinbeck for their support with the collection and managing of data and literature.

This book presents the overall final results of the research group. It focuses on interstate and inter-Directive comparison. Further details on subtopics can be found in various articles and papers published during recent years, and in the three dissertation theses, each of which focuses on specific aspects and particular countries. (See the project homepage: http://www.mpifg.de/socialeurope.)

in transposition processes did not really play a central role. An exception is Lampinen and Uusikylä's (1998) quantitative analysis of EU infringement data, which takes into account the degree of corporatism as one of four independent variables. Additionally, interest groups are sometimes conceived of in qualitative case studies as actor-centred factors supplementing the institution-based misfit hypotheses. Tanja Börzel (2003a: 36)[13] developed a 'push and pull model' in order to specify conditions that facilitate compliance with EU law despite a high degree of adaptation pressure. Reluctant member states, she argues, may be forced to comply with EU law through sanctions by the EU Commission ('push from above'), and/or through mobilisation by societal actors such as interest groups ('pull from below'). A similar approach can be found in Knill and Lenschow's work (2001: 124, 126). They use the rather broad notion of a 'supportive actor coalition' in order to extend their misfit-based explanation. While these studies focus particularly on the positive effects of societal actors on the implementation of EU Directives, others take into consideration their potential blocking power as well (Héritier 2001a, 2001b). Here, the direction of interest group influence depends on the expected advantages and disadvantages arising from the required adaptations. From this perspective, interest groups appear as factors potentially fostering, but also impeding or delaying, implementation in the context of what could be called an 'opposing actor coalition'.

Some studies recently began to tackle the issue of 'Europeanisation and public-private interaction' from an opposite perspective, conceiving of interest groups not as an independent but as the dependent variable, that is as the target of Europeanisation. Parallel to EU research in general, the focus of analysis on European public–private relations has moved on from a bottom-up to a top-down perspective. While initially the development of interest representation structures at EU level and the interaction of interest group networks with the European Commission were studied,[14] several recent works have taken into consideration the top-down effects of the European level developments on national public–private relations and/or the intra-organisational structures of interest groups (see Schmidt 1996c for France; Lehmkuhl 1999, 2000 for the transport sector in Germany and the Netherlands; Wilts 2001 for the Netherlands; Cowles 2001 for the effects of the Transatlantic Business Dialogue on business interests in Germany, France and the UK; and on a general level Falkner 2000c).

---

[13] See also Börzel (2000).

[14] As it is not possible at this point to provide a complete overview of the various works in this field, see, for example, Greenwood, Grote and Ronit (1992); Eichener and Voelzkow (1994); Eising and Kohler-Koch (1994); Kohler-Koch (1996) and Falkner, Hartlapp, Leiber and Treib (2005) for further references.

Francesco Duina's work (1999: 44–5) indicates that both perspectives – interest groups as independent and dependent variable – may be closely related when it comes to the implementation of EU Directives. As explained above, Duina conceptualises the organisation of the interest group system as one dimension of his misfit concept. According to this, misfit may come about if, for example, the implementation of a Directive requires state intervention where there was autonomous regulation by the societal groups before. Thus interest groups may, on the one hand, have an influence on implementation outcomes; on the other hand, their internal structures, mutual relations or relationship to public actors may be influenced themselves by the transposition of Directives.

This book will link up with these works and systematically study these two perspectives in the social policy field, where the interest organisations of labour and industry play a particularly important role. On the broad empirical basis of ninety qualitative case studies, we will be able to observe systematically whether (among other important variables, see below) different types of public–private interaction patterns will make a difference to transposition outcomes. At the same time (in a separate section, see Chapter 12) we will analyse how state–society relations in the fifteen member states are affected by the EU's social policy Directives.

2.3   Guiding hypotheses: a pluri-theoretical approach

Against the background of the scholarly literature outlined above, it seemed most promising initially to adopt a pluri-theoretical approach. Additionally, our problem-oriented starting point made the broad explanatory capacity of an (albeit complex) approach more important than parsimony. Therefore, we collected the factors named as significant in earlier studies and formulated an elaborate catalogue of factors potentially influencing compliance.

Given that our aim was to detect all potential sources of compliance problems, combining the insights of earlier work was much more fruitful than discarding important contributions and only focusing on one of several promising lines of enquiry. For instance, there is no evidence for the arguments put forward by the top-down school of implementation theory being any less important than those stressed by the bottom-up reaction to the former's over-simplification. So, we included both aspects concerning the chain of command-and-control in the member states, along with elements concerning the participation of potentially important domestic actors in the EU decision-making process, in our search for the reasons for non-compliance.

Among the factors facilitating national compliance according to the authors in the more recent implementation literatures on EU law, there is again no need to highlight any single one. The kind and/or degree of non-compatibility between European and national standards may matter, but the specifics of national decision-making in implementation processes could be as important (or, at least, another important aspect). Our list of potential factors, therefore, includes the degree and type of misfit as well as (not as an alternative to) the statist or corporatist style of a national implementation process and the number of veto points. In addition to factors stemming from the national level, EU-related reasons can also play a role, such as characteristics of the legal text in question or the style of the legislative process at the supranational level.

Our pluri-theoretical approach combines *inductive and deductive reasoning*.[15] In principle, we started from a deductive perspective (inference from general to particular), since we derived our first draft set of hypotheses from extant political science theory and our work aimed at (dis-)proving them. On the way, however, we came across empirical cases that suggested additional useful hypotheses. Therefore, we added elements to our approach inductively (see, in particular, our typology in Chapter 15). The great advantage of having chosen a medium-N set-up (and of working with a reasonably long time horizon) is that we can actually verify or falsify innovative hypotheses not just in later studies (which is typical for small-N research that often ends with a new hypothesis being 'aired'[16]) but with the rest of the rather many cases at hand. In actual fact, our work started on the theoretical level, proceeded to the empirical level, returned to theorising and adding abstract assumptions to our original catalogue of hypotheses, only to go back to field work, and so forth – just like the 'grounded theory' school suggests (Glaser and Strauss 1967; Strauss and Corbin 1990, 1997).

Our inclusive project design has led us to *four categories of variables for the transposition success* of an EU Directive in a particular member state. To obtain a heuristic tool, we sorted our factors along the two potential 'roads' to transposition failure[17] of an EU Directive (see Figure 2.3), that is inertia (i.e. the transposition process does not get going or it stops due to reasons other than opposition) and stalemate (i.e. the process fails due to opposition).

---

[15] Such efforts to analyse empirical phenomena in generalising form using various theoretical lenses have been called 'triangulation' or 'abduction' (see Schneider 2003: 311).

[16] More often than not, the new hypothesis is formulated in an over-generalised way, so that a circle results of over-generalised hypothesis by author 1, test by author 2 leading to criticism and a new hypothesis that is again over-generalised, to be later criticised by author 3, and so on and so forth (see Fritz Scharpf's contribution to Schmidt et al. 1999).

[17] The other forms of non-compliance (i.e. non-enforcement and non-application) are discussed separately in later parts of the book.

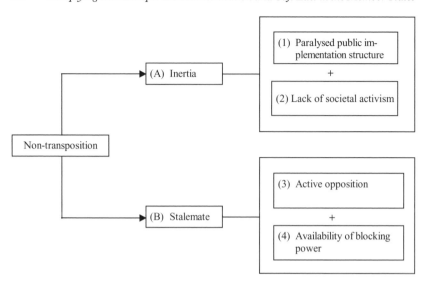

Figure 2.3 Possible 'roads' to transposition failure

Among the *country-related factors* for mal-transposition[18] (the first major subgroup of factors), potential reasons for non-compliance as discussed in the literature may fall into categories (1) to (4) (referred to in Figure 2.3).

(1) A *paralysed public implementation structure* can be due to a generally inefficient administration; to a particular misunderstanding or misinterpretation regarding the Directive (i.e. wrong interpretation in good faith); to administrative overload right at the time when a Directive has to be transposed; or to an extraordinary political situation such as the dissolution of parliament, elections or a government crisis. A potentially countervailing factor could be the existence of effective administrative 'watchdog' units that would monitor the individual ministries' performance in fulfilling their EU-induced duties.

(2) A *lack of societal activism* on the part of private actors who might successfully press for the transposition to be carried out may perhaps arise from the absence of policy entrepreneurs (see below at (3) for factors influencing this) or from the entrepreneurs not being granted access to the relevant policy network (e.g. in a political system that is extremely statist). At the same time, a chance to enforce the Directive's standards via the courts is a strong form of 'access'

---

[18] This includes non-transposition, incorrect transposition and delayed transposition.

to the implementation process since it opens up a path where private actors can even circumvent the state.[19]

(3) *Active opposition*, in turn, may stem from the administration, from the political system, from pressure groups or from the wider public. The decisive factors for political, administrative or societal opposition to EU Directives have made up the main part of theorising in recent implementation studies. We have specified the following questions as being relevant for our case studies: was the government outvoted in the Council of Ministers? How big is the qualitative and quantitative policy misfit? Must important national institutions and administrative procedures be adapted? How significant are the costs of adaptation for the state and for the economy? Were there any package deals during the implementation process counteracting its impact? Were the relevant societal actors in the implementation phase included in the national decision-making prior to the Directive? Are important actors opposed to the national procedure of transposition because they are sidelined, for example? Additionally, were the parties in charge of implementation already in office by the time of the Directive's adoption? And which is the government's dominant ideology (pro-interventionist or market-oriented in social affairs)?

(4) Finally, we look at whether the opposing actors have *blocking power*, either because they hold formal veto positions or because they are 'powerful players' (Strøm 2003) who can exert enough influence on the government to ensure that their concerns are taken into account. In certain member states, the unions and/or employers' associations may be among these powerful players. Relevant aspects in this category are, first, the way in which the social partners are involved in the transposition process (ranging from non-involvement to autonomous social partner implementation); second, if transposition is carried out (at least partly) by regional units; and third, how many veto positions are institutionalised in the national political system.

---

[19] Note, however, that Directives only have a vertical direct effect, i.e. they only affect the relationship *between an individual and the state* (or local authorities or public industries), not the relationship between private individuals. This implies that the state can be forced to apply non-transposed labour law Directives vis-à-vis state employees, but private employers cannot be forced to apply EU labour law Directives directly (i.e. there is *no horizontal direct effect* in the case of Directives, as opposed to EU primary law). To ensure a direct effect (after the transposition deadline has passed), Directives must not only grant individual rights, but also be clear, precise and unconditional (see, for example, case 41/74, *Van Duyn* v. *Home Office* [1974] ECR 1337). The *Francovich* case opened the possibility that individuals can sue the government for any losses as a result of a failure to implement a Directive (cases C-6/90 and C-9/90, *Francovich and Bonifaci* v. *Italian Republic* [1991] ECR I-5357). In this case, the Italian government had failed fully to protect workers whose firm had gone insolvent.

Since we study a whole set of different Directives, we have to go beyond a pure country-specific approach. After all, non-compliance could as well depend on *EU-related reasons* that differ from one law to another (the second major subgroup of factors). So, were the Directive's standards agreed by the social partners or by the governments in Council? How clear are the standards and how complex is the whole Directive? How many standards have to be transposed?

The empirical results presented in this book will demonstrate the usefulness of this pluri-theoretical approach. Simple arguments, which highlight the importance of one causal condition or a few individual causal conditions (such as the degree of misfit created by a Directive or the number of institutional veto players in domestic political systems), are unable to explain the implementation outcomes we observe. Instead, we find that a *combination of different factors* is needed to explain the diverse implementation performance in the fifteen member states (see especially Chapter 14). In contrast to the existing literature, our analysis furthermore reveals that the combinations of factors and the logic of their interplay vary fundamentally in different country clusters. We identify three different *worlds of compliance*, each with its own typical pattern of how the implementation of a piece of EU legislation is tackled procedurally (see Chapter 15).

In methodological terms, we try to bridge the gap between *qualitative and quantitative* research. According to conventional wisdom, 'qualitative' political science research is typically case-oriented and 'quantitative' research is variable-oriented – although recently some have suggested that qualitative research should become more variable-oriented (King et al. 1994), and quantitative research more case-oriented (Ragin 2000). We feel that both suggestions put forward very good reasons but, until now, have not been considered seriously enough when it comes to designing social science enquiries.

We tried to quantify as much as possible while still basically adopting a qualitative approach, that is we started out with our cases. This route had to be chosen since no adequate data was available to answer our research questions. We had to collect our data 'in the field' and to invest both an intensive and extensive effort in generating the data set on the implementation processes of six Directives in fifteen member states. Based on our expert interviews on each individual implementation process, in conjunction with both primary and secondary written sources, we knew our cases well enough to attribute viable values to our scales.

Operationalisation was, of course, a major challenge. Most importantly, we needed to specify the concept of 'misfit' and the costs created by specific Directives in such a way as to allow cross-country and cross-Directive comparisons.

2.4 What does a Directive mean for a member state? Operationalising misfit and costs

Misfit between EU demands and the given situation in a member state has been highlighted as the crucial explanatory factor for implementation performance in much of the recent literature on Europeanisation. The argument is based on the assumption that one can expect a smooth implementation process if a Directive requires only small changes to the domestic arrangements. Implementation problems, by contrast, are expected if considerable misfit must be rectified by a member state.

This strong emphasis on the category of 'misfit', even at the level of theory, adds to the great importance that needs to be attributed to this factor from a policy analysis perspective also: we can only estimate the practical effect of any EU policy if we know where the member states began their process of adaptation. In other words, establishing in a detailed manner both the status quo ante in the member states and the demands embedded in any European Directive is crucial. This is far from easy, at least in research practice, for a lot of EU regulation touches on intricate details of national legislation that no one but a national expert can know. The great effort needed explains why qualitative implementation studies have traditionally only analysed a few cases. Although the recent literature already goes far beyond what had been offered by earlier work, we found that for our study of six Directives in fifteen EU member states (i.e. ninety implementation cases in total) we needed a much more differentiated approach. While it is easy to state that there is some sort of misfit between a given EU policy and the domestic situation in a specific member state, it is much more difficult to conceptualise this misfit in such terms as to allow a direct comparison to be made between countries, and even between different policies.

Two steps are indispensable: categorising forms of potential misfit (which we will do here first) and operationalising the degree of misfit (see below). With regard to the forms, misfit can either be substantive, i.e. relate to content and so be policy-related ('policy misfit'), or apply to matters of procedure (i.e. affect domestic politics and/or the polity). *Policy misfit*[20] means that the contents of an EU Directive are not reflected in the relevant national law. This can relate to a gradual difference (e.g. two months of parental leave instead of three as a minimum) or to a matter of principle (e.g. there is no individual right to parental leave but the entitlement is restricted to mothers only). Hence Europeanisation can be of a quantitative kind (strengthening or weakening an existing policy) or a

---

[20] Several authors apply this term; see, e.g., Börzel (2000).

qualitative kind (the creation of completely new national institutions or structures or the replacement of existing ones).

Certainly, the policy misfit of a particular Directive may in some cases appear more important on paper than in practice. We try to capture the former aspect by the term *legal misfit*, and calculate a kind of discount in case the *practical significance* is comparatively lower. For example, a new right may not have been enshrined in domestic law, but it may have related to a large part of the workforce through collective agreements. Furthermore, it is important to include in the concept of legal misfit an evaluation of the *scope of application*. In other words, we look at the coverage of any newly attributed right. Such a right may, in some cases, seem very important at first glance, but may then be seriously limited by a narrow scope of application (e.g. when all atypical workers or important sectors of the economy are excluded). In short, our concept of substantive misfit takes due account of both the legal misfit and its practical significance.

No less difficult is attributing a size category to the misfit actually found in a specific case. We talk about a *high* degree of legal misfit if there are completely new legal rules, far-reaching gradual changes and/or important[21] qualitative innovations. Each of them will lead to a high degree of policy misfit in our system under the condition that all or a significant number of workers are affected and that there is no essential limitation on the level of practical significance. Otherwise, only a medium (or even low) degree of policy misfit will result in our classification.[22] Table 2.1 indicates how a similar logic is applied to medium and low degrees of legal misfit. Note that the basis of evaluation in terms of high/medium/low is the significance of the required changes in the context of the *national* labour law standards, while the comparison with other member states and other cases will take place on the basis of the degree of misfit established for each of the countries.[23]

---

[21] Our material includes no case where we assigned a large degree of legal misfit because of qualitative innovations alone. However, the individual right to parental leave was a qualitative change of medium-sized significance in Austria and Italy, where women earlier had systematically enjoyed precedence over men. And we attributed a low degree of adaptational pressure in Germany, where only the partners of housewives and students had been excluded from the right to take parental leave (see Ch. 8).

[22] Usually, limited practical relevance of legal misfit will only cause the degree of policy misfit to be diminished by one level (from high to medium or from medium to low). In one of our cases (Working Time in Denmark), however, the completely new legal provisions that had to be introduced as a result of the EU Directive were already available in practice to such an extent that we scaled down the adaptation requirements in the policy dimension by two degrees, from a high degree of legal misfit to a low degree of policy misfit (see Ch. 6).

[23] The following chapters explain in detail the empirical phenomena behind our classification of different degrees of misfit for all of our cases so that our categorisation can be

Table 2.1 *Establishing the policy misfit of a Directive*

Degree of legal misfit	Limited practical significance	Degree of policy misfit (total)
high	no	high
high	yes	medium
medium	no	medium
medium	yes	low
low	no	low
low	yes	low
none	–	none

Having thus established the overall amount of policy misfit of a particular Directive is not the end of our efforts to determine the degree of misfit in a given case of adaptation requirements. Beyond substantive rules, EU-level rules may also mismatch aspects of *politics and/or polity*.[24] In the area of environmental policy, manifold administrative routines at the domestic level are affected by European Directives. Sometimes even new bodies have to be set up to comply with procedural regulations stemming from the EU level.[25] In social policy, this is much less common, and in the particular area of labour law studied here, this has not been the case at all.[26] Nonetheless, public–private interaction patterns are sometimes affected by European integration. A shining example is that employee consultation patterns may be laid down in EU Directives. Our sample does not include any of these laws, but still we found misfit in the public–private field (i.e. in the politics/polity dimension). This is because even Directives that are concerned with substantive EU labour law have to be implemented in such a way as to conform to procedural European requirements. This refers notably to the fact that all workers included

controlled in an inter-subjective manner. Note that our misfit analysis refers to the time of adoption of the Directive. Subsequent changes, especially in the form of fundamental reinterpretations of a Directive by the ECJ, are not included in our analysis. In our view, the implementation of such far-reaching case law as the ECJ's *SIMAP* ruling (see Ch. 6), has to be analysed separately. However, such a separate analysis would have gone beyond the scope of the present book.

[24] This is often called 'institutional misfit' in the literature (see, for example Börzel and Risse 2000) but, since there are so many definitions of the term 'institution' (and many of them are very broad), we prefer a more specific label.

[25] There are many studies on the EU's environmental policy and its implementation (Jachtenfuchs and Strübel 1992; Knill and Lenschow 1998; Lenschow 1999; Börzel 2000; Jordan 2000; Knill and Lenschow 2000b; Heinelt et al. 2001; Knill 2001; Knill and Lenschow 2001; Holzinger et al. 2002; Lenschow 2002; Börzel 2003a).

[26] This refers to our six sample Directives only. New bodies had to be set up to comply with the 1989 Health and Safety Framework Directive, however.

in the field of application fixed in the Directive must be covered by the national transposition law. This demand, however, has proved impossible to meet on the basis of the established mode of autonomous social partner regulation in some areas of labour law in Denmark and Sweden. Consequently, European integration has forced some member states to adapt their institutionalised national ways of policy-making in the field of labour law, where the implementation of EU Directives is concerned (for details, see Chapter 12 and Leiber 2005).

We define it as a high degree of misfit in the politics/polity dimension if a crucial domestic institution or procedure is challenged (e.g. the 'Danish model' of social partner autonomy). A medium degree of this kind of misfit involves a less important, but still very significant, domestic institution or procedure (e.g. the freedom to derogate from working time regulation by collective agreement, as occurred in Sweden). The misfit in the politics/polity dimension is as important a part in our calculation of overall misfit as is the policy misfit (see Table 2.2 on our aggregation rules, below).

Finally, another crucial element of any estimation of misfit caused by EU regulation must be *costs*, i.e. the economic consequences (as opposed to, say, the citizenship dimension) of a required reform for the addressees on all levels. Costs should not be confused with any of the forms of misfit outlined above. A high degree of policy misfit can still only amount to small sums of money (e.g. if a new right is attributed to a group of people where hardly any take-up will occur) and, sometimes, small legal changes can add up to significant costs (e.g. in the field of working time standards).

Establishing the exact costs of adapting to an EU Directive for any specific country is virtually impossible. First, many types of actors are involved. Costs may fall on different units of the state, on semi-public and on private actors or companies.[27] If there is publicised data on the costs of adaptation at all, the data typically stems from interested actors. Note that even governments are interested actors in a wider sense, since adaptation costs can be used in the debate over the pros and cons of European integration, both in general and with regard to social policy in particular. The most detailed data on expected adaptation costs stems from the UK Department of Trade and Industry (Treib 2004). The real costs of adaptation in practice will never be known. It is even doubtful if they matter at all, at least when it comes to studying implementation performance. In

---

[27] Since the governments must be expected to protect themselves, the social insurance companies and the enterprises from additional costs wherever feasible (or to defend such costs for any actor if it suits their political purposes), we decided not to focus on the distribution on different actors.

this context, the costs of adaptation that can be realistically expected by the relevant national and international actors seem much more important. They, too, are difficult to establish. We consider a crucial step to be the defining of cost categories and the evaluation of their potential. With our field of labour law to hand, this indeed greatly facilitates the comparative assessment. Our first step was to establish the cost categories that a given Directive can potentially trigger in any member state. Secondly, we established empirically in interviews how many groups of workers and sectors are actually concerned in the fifteen member states. On the basis of our interviewees' cost estimates, which we compared with the costs mentioned for other countries and other Directives, we could categorise without too many problems the costs of adaptation triggered in a given member state, on a scale of low, medium, and high.

In the field of labour law, the costs created by any EU Directive are usually costs for private and public employers and sometimes for the social security system, too. The costs arising from the various labour law Directives studied in this book fall into six categories:

(1) *social security costs* (e.g. for improved income substitution);
(2) increased *wages per hour* as a result of higher protection standards (e.g. as a direct consequence in the case of working time reduction or as an indirect one in the case of restricting the use of comparatively cheaper child labour);
(3) costs *depending on the number of individual cases* to which a certain provision actually applies (e.g. exemptions from the duty for medical checks, which may vary a lot from enterprise to enterprise);
(4) costs for improved *health and safety protection* and for related assessments;
(5) once-only *conversion* costs for employers (e.g. for changing shift schedules);
(6) costs created by additional *administrative burdens* created by the EU Directive.

We categorise the first two types as creating high costs, at least potentially (obviously depending on the situation in a specific country); the third and fourth types will at best generate medium-sized costs, the fifth and sixth at most low costs. Note that, in empirical cases, the costs of even a potentially high-cost Directive may be small, and often the elimination of misfit will only require an administrative burden with rather insignificant costs. Beyond the short-term cost potentials, we also investigate the possible long-term consequences of our Directives in the member states and, at times, consider how a longer horizon may increase the potential costs.

Table 2.2 *The aggregation system applied to establish the total misfit*

Degree of policy misfit	Degree of politics/polity misfit	Costs	Degree of total misfit
high	high	high	high
high	medium	medium	high
high	low	low	high
medium	high	high	high
medium	medium	medium	medium
medium	low	low	medium
low	high	low	high
low	medium	medium	medium
low	low	low	low
. . .	. . .	. . .	. . .

The *aggregation of all dimensions of misfit* outlined above is, clearly, anything but trivial. We decided to rate high degrees of misfit in any one dimension (policy misfit, misfit in the politics/polity dimension, and economic costs) as a high degree of total misfit created by a particular Directive in a particular country. This follows the logic that no dimension of misfit can eradicate or soften adaptational pressure in another dimension. A high degree of misfit in terms of domestic state–society relations (or, alternatively, in terms of a specific new right granted to workers) cannot be outweighed by the fact that the costs, for instance, may be small. In turn, significant costs seem an important factor regardless of the abstract importance of the changes in terms of substance or politics. Consequently, our values for total misfit consist of the highest parameter values found in the three subcategories (see Table 2.2).[28]

Only on the basis of this elaborate system of operationalising misfit and costs can we, in the chapters that follow, analyse our ninety cases of implementation in a comparative manner, across both Directives and countries.

[28] We decided not to sum up the values for the different dimensions where, say, a large degree of policy misfit and a large degree of misfit in the politics or polity dimension would result in something like a 'super-high' degree of overall misfit. This is because we wanted to keep our classification scheme rather simple. Adding further intermediate categories would have been ill suited to the qualitative nature of the classification and the underlying empirical material. In order to avoid any potential loss of information caused by the aggregation of the different dimensions, Ch. 14 also addresses the question of whether specific types or dimensions of misfits have a systematic impact on implementation performance.

2.5   The difficult issues of national application and enforcement

Labour legislation without inspection is an exercise in ethics. (Francis Blanchard, General Director of the ILO 1974–1989)

After systematically studying the success or failure of correct and timely transposition, a further aspect of compliance with EU law needs to be taken into account: *are the EU's standards properly applied*?[29] To establish if EU law is actually applied in practice is probably the most challenging task in research on European integration. The many layers of compliance to be studied (transposition, monitoring, enforcement, and application) do not allow for a parsimonious research design. In fact, detailed ground-level surveys (in addition to the prior in-depth research on the political and legal aspects of transposition and inspection potential) would be needed to come up with fully reliable data. Such detailed micro-level analyses in fifteen member states, however, proved impossible to conduct within this project.

We opted for a comparatively slim but feasible mid-way design, by including questions in our in-depth interview series for each member state about whether particular application problems were known. Thus national experts provided us with information about major application problems in their countries. However, we cannot assume that the result is a complete picture of practical compliance. Nor can we be sure that the information is always fully correct. Biases might be due to the interviewees' attention, ideology, knowledge and analytical strictness in differentiating between EU-based rules and typical national problems. If the expert is more *attentive* to an issue he or she will note relatively more application problems (e.g. in the case of a completely new regulatory philosophy). Depending on his or her *ideology* he or she might weight application problems arbitrarily.[30] Moreover, some interviewees were comparatively *better informed* on application and enforcement issues because of their personal or professional background. Finally, it was often difficult to make the experts *differentiate* between problems connected to the Directive itself and application problems of any law (be it national or European) in the same issue area. For all these reasons, the data that we will present on application issues should be used with proper caution despite all our care in collecting and digesting this.

---

[29] By application we refer to the adherence to the rules by the addressees. In the case of the Directives studied here, the addressees are, typically, the enterprises or the state as an employer in public services.

[30] Thus even unions may be less critical if non-application of social standards occurs outside their core clientele's realm (e.g. atypical workers, etc.).

At the same time, it should be stressed that by tackling enforcement and application in our study we go far beyond the existing mainstream literature on the implementation of EU Directives. This makes our efforts seem worthwhile, notwithstanding the need for further research in this important area. On the basis of at least some systematically generated information on concrete application problems, on the one hand, and systematic information about the enforcement policy of a member state, on the other, we can progress towards a more balanced and empirically grounded answer than has hitherto been possible to the question of whether the EU standards are properly applied.

In order to balance the information on application problems from the expert interviews, we combined it with more systematic information on *enforcement policies in the member states*. This analysis is also partly based on interviews with national experts, while other sources such as the annual activity reports of enforcement agencies and a publication by the European Commission on structures and competences of national labour inspections (Kommission der Europäischen Gemeinschaften 1995) help to complete the picture. Our basic assumption is that an effective enforcement policy is one of several determinants of good compliance. More specifically, effective enforcement is one necessary condition for good compliance (but surely not a sufficient one). There is a close relationship between enforcement and application: the less voluntary proper application of EU standards is, the more enforcement will be needed to make the addressees comply and vice versa.

Every country has specific economic conditions (e.g. size of agricultural sector or number of small and medium enterprises) and geographical conditions (e.g. density of population, number of islands) that shape the task of putting EU law into practice. National enforcement structures have to correspond to these specific national realities. Moreover, regulatory styles, problem-solving approaches and legal cultures vary all over Europe. Thus enforcement in countries that do not have a good compliance culture (see Chapter 15) needs to satisfy different standards from those in countries where the law is generally upheld. Against this background, it should be emphasised that the EU is not a uniform area with regard to compliance with and enforcement of the law. 'Obedience differs. Not all Europeans are equally law-abiding citizens' (Waarden 1999: 96). The spectrum of law-abidingness can be illustrated by the following two quotations. While for Denmark, Biering (2000: 959) writes '[w]hen an act is issued it is obeyed, even if one has opposed its adoption and disagrees with its content', Putnam et al. (1993: 115) state in relation to Italy that here 'laws are made to be broken'.

Assessing the efficiency of institutions and actors involved in the enforcement policy (from here on referred to as the 'enforcement system') is therefore a cumbersome task. Absolute standards and measures can only serve as indicators since the character and the manner of enforcement have to address the problems and needs of a specific country. However, we argue that there are *some minimum requirements* that have to be fulfilled in every member state in order to guarantee that proper enforcement is at least possible. (Whether it actually takes place is another question.)[31] On an abstract level, we define these criteria as follows: (a) co-ordination and steering capacity, (b) pressure capacity, and (c) availability of information. If there are significant shortcomings for one or more of these criteria, effective enforcement is affected and application problems are more likely to occur.

2.5.1   Co-ordination and steering capacity

Enforcement systems differ in the number of institutions involved as well as with regard to their organisational form. State organisations (labour inspectorates), private–public organisations (e.g. equal treatment agencies), and non-state organisations (mostly social partner associations) often coexist in a non-hierarchical manner. In some countries, not only individual labour law standards but also health and safety standards are supervised by one state authority; in others they are administered by different state-run authorities. In addition, there are countries where health and safety aspects are enforced by a state body, while individual labour law is subject to enforcement by the social partners. We expect that there are national differences in the co-ordination of these structures, too.

Besides the number of institutions, the steering capacity of the enforcement systems differs. This can be explained to some extent by the uneven degree of devolution on the part of the competences for labour law enforcement. Only two of our fifteen member states have federal enforcement systems; in all other countries the central labour inspectorate has decentralised units. At these levels, resources and instructions from the central unit can be adapted to fit the previously mentioned economic and geographical intra-country diversity. Thus a certain degree of discretion is even necessary to avoid inflexibility. Hence we are not looking at the overall degree of independence of decentralised units. We are

---

[31] According to Article 10 of the EC Treaty every member state is responsible for actively taking 'all appropriate measures, whether general or particular, to assure fulfilment of the obligations' and to disapply 'any measure which could jeopardise the attainment of the objectives'.

interested rather in the extent to which the enforcement system as a whole is governable.

For successful enforcement of EU Directives, the responsibilities assigned to the different actors and institutions in the enforcement systems should be clear in order to prevent mutual obstruction. A coherent enforcement policy approach should be guaranteed by internal supervision and evaluation. Both co-ordination and steering ability are of crucial importance to assure effective and adequate reaction to known or assumed compliance problems.

2.5.2   *Pressure capacity*

This is the second minimum requirement for sufficient enforcement. Here, the probability by which breaking the rules will be punished and the severity of punishment are of importance. In combination, both have to outweigh the potential advantage the addressee would gain by non-application of a given rule. The probability of non-compliers being punished is shaped by the density and type of inspections, both of which determine the probability by which non-compliance is actually discovered. The resources allocated to the enforcement system give a rough indication of the density of controls. If the number of inspectors, calculated as a ratio for 100,000 dependent workers, is below the EU average (12.56), difficulties in enforcement seem a realistic danger from this perspective.

However, the number of inspectors is only part of the story. First, other actors in the enforcement system might function as equivalents, e.g. insurance companies that link company contributions to the accident rate or occupational physicians who assure the correct application of health and safety standards. Second, member states vary with regard to the proportion of *proactive and reactive* inspections carried out. Reactive inspections are a result of individual requests or complaints. Proactive inspections leave more room for systematic coverage and/or a (politically motivated) focus on specific questions or sectors, leading to an enforcement policy with more preventive character and long-term planning. The relationship of proactive and reactive controls is in most cases strongly influenced by whether an inspection authority has to follow all complaints or accidents at work or whether it is partially or totally free to decide whether it wants to inquire into a case. Third, the amount of time dedicated to field work, hence to inspections in the enterprises, differs considerably between member states.

In the sparse literature that exists, some importance is attributed to a fourth aspect, i.e. whether an inspection is of a general or a specialised type. Are inspectors responsible for all types of labour law (often including social security issues), or do they specialise in issues such as health and safety at work? It is normally assumed that generalists have a harder time meeting the requirements of the ever more complex regulatory rules, thus bearing out the adage 'jack of all trades, master of none' (Richthofen 2002: 42). Even though we do not think that the existence of such differences per se determines the available pressure capacity of an enforcement system, we expect specialised systems to have more difficulty ensuring that all of the standards studied here are actually enforced. In cases where public enforcement is limited to technical and medical issues, enforcement of both general and individual labour law should be assured by functional equivalents such as non-state actors (e.g. social partners). Conversely, problems are likely to occur when inspectors trained as generalists have to perform de facto as specialists in health and safety issues and feel ill equipped to do so. Put more generally, inspectors must be adequately trained in order to be able to fulfil their tasks properly. Moreover, some of the EU standards studied in this book require the support of specialists, such as when it comes to workplace assessment or to the control of maximal concentrations of certain substances listed in the Directives' annexes. Analytically, these experts have to be treated differently since they are application facilitators rather than enforcement actors. Without these supportive specialists, however, some of the standards could not be applied properly (even if the addressee were willing to allow it) because prior expertise is needed to make the standard fit to the specific workplace or employee.

The second crucial factor for successful pressure capacity, next to resources, is sanctions. Here the inspector must be able to make the addressees comply – even against their will – by exerting sufficient pressure. In an effective enforcement system, it is necessary that appropriate financial sanctions are available to an inspector who discovers non-compliance. In most enforcement systems administrative sanctions exist. Their scale corresponds to the severity of the offence, the number of breaches, potential repetition and, often, the size of the enterprise also. They can either be dealt with by the inspector or, at his or her request, by a senior official in order to guarantee comparability and objectivity. Appropriate punishment will be more difficult in those cases where no administrative sanctions exist and financial sanctions can only be imposed by the courts. Problems arise when the court system is overloaded and decisions are delayed for years. Often these difficulties in sanctioning procedures have led in practice to the adoption of enforcement strategies other than pressure (e.g. arbitration) or, in the worst instance, to outright non-enforcement. To sum up, the number of inspectors, the type of controls and the sanction capacity crucially influence the success or failure of enforcement – but not equally for all the labour standards studied in this book.

2.5.3   Availability of information

We argue that, for some standards, successful enforcement does not need pressure and monitoring (or only does so to a much lesser degree), but requires above all the availability of information. In those cases where the EU standard guarantees the employee a right he or she has to solicit individually. Hence, information and advice are of even greater importance than control and sanctions. It is only via information and advice that the employee is given the ability to exercise the new right. Since in most member states there is no proactive public enforcement of individual rights, NGOs and trade unions play an extremely important role in this regard.

The availability of information is the criterion that is most difficult to assess since many different actors come into play. However, only where state actors or motivated social partners proactively and permanently provide information for employees are employees systematically able to demand their rights. In countries with weaknesses in information provision, successful implementation of individual rights and, hence, the sound practical application of such EU standards will be impaired.[32]

2.5.4   Types of norms and corresponding types of enforcement

Table 2.3 lists different types of norms and the relevant type of enforcement needed to assure good compliance, together with examples from our social policy Directives. The second column features the type of enforcement matched to the type of norm in such a way as to allow, at least in principle, for successful enforcement. Note that the type referred to is a minimum requirement. More costly types (e.g. proactive inspections on top of reactive ones, or active enforcement by labour inspectorates on top of passive enforcement via court cases) and additional forms will always improve application.

---

[32] Another aspect of importance regarding the successful enforcement of individual rights is the availability of supportive institutions and the openness of the juridical system. Since they will also influence whether or not an employee will demand his or her right, open judicial systems with low thresholds for employees to file a complaint against the employer have a positive long-term effect on the uptake of individual rights. An empirical example is given in Ch. 9 but, for reasons of space, this aspect cannot be tackled in depth in this book (for more detailed accounts, see Tesoka 1999; Alter and Vargas 2000).

Table 2.3 *Viable types of enforcement as a prerequisite of successful compliance*

Type of norm	Appropriate type of enforcement (minimum)	Relevant EU standards
individual right	passive enforcement: citizens may sue (failure likely if no adequate information provision)	e.g. right to go on parental leave
general norm	active enforcement (reactive or proactive) (failure more likely if only reactive inspections, but depends on national law-abidingness)	e.g. maximum working hours and length of rest periods
general norm referring to technical standards	active enforcement with proactive controls (failure very likely if only reactive inspections, workplace assessments and expert knowledge indispensable for evaluation of good compliance)	e.g. adequate health and safety protection for pregnant, young or night workers

The enforcement of norms can ensue in a more or less active form. Passive enforcement generally takes place with respect to individual rights, as found in the Employment Contract Information Directive (e.g. right to receive a copy), the Pregnant Workers Directive (e.g. paid leave for ante-natal examinations), the Parental Leave Directive (e.g. entitlement to three months' parental leave) and the Part-time Work Directive (e.g. non-discrimination vis-à-vis a comparable full-time worker). As argued above, the criterion of pressure capacity is of less importance for these standards. For instance, a small number of inspectors does not diminish the probability that a worker will invoke his or her rights in court. Here the availability of information is of greater relevance for application success.

General norms can be found in the Pregnant Workers Directive (e.g. compulsory maternity leave) and both the Working Time and the Young Workers Directives (maximum working hours and minimum rest periods). Such norms exist independently of the demand of the individual. They are often regulated in collective agreements or in enterprise-level arrangements and may thus be respected without permanent inspections. If a culture of non-compliance exists, they will often be disregarded – unless proactive enforcement in the form of random inspections and reactive interventions exert pressure. For these standards, therefore, we expect more application problems where adequate pressure capacity is lacking.

More technical general norms in the Pregnant Workers, Young Workers and Working Time Directives (e.g. maximum concentration of certain harmful substances or special conditions for dangerous night work) require proactive inspections. They differ from the above-mentioned kind of general norm because they vary from worker to worker or from workplace to workplace. This means that employers often cannot establish proper compliance with a standard on their own. For the same reason, employees are often unable to judge the compliance or non-compliance of their employers. Therefore, the resources of the enforcement system dedicated to proactive inspections and workplace assessments are of major importance for correct implementation.

Thus one might speak of potentially equivalent pathways to good enforcement for different standards: via information, supportive institutions and the legal system, or via a well-staffed and well-organised labour inspectorate that actively controls. In other words, an evaluation of the three basic functions of any good enforcement system (co-ordination and steering capacity, pressure capacity, and availability of information) is needed if we are to establish good implementation of EU social law in the member states. Our result is not a full analysis of enforcement in the fifteen countries covered by our study, but we are in a position to identify those member states where grave shortcomings in this field cast fundamental doubts on the proper implementation of the social Directives studied in this book. The result of our work on domestic enforcement and application will be summarised in Chapter 13.

3   EU social policy over time: the role of Directives

Directives are one of several instruments that are used in EU social policy. This chapter puts them into perspective, outlining the wider context of the EU's social dimension over time and the important role played by Directives.[1] The main finding is that the role of binding regulative action has not been diminished, despite the debates on the open method of co-ordination (OMC). Therefore, we argue, studying social Directives is crucial not only for understanding the past, but also the present and, very likely, the future of European social integration.

3.1   Competences and decision modes

The 1957 EEC Treaty basically left social policy in the hands of the member states. The Treaty did not provide for an outright Europeanisation of social policies since too many national delegations had been opposed to such a move.[2] The dominant philosophy of this Treaty was that welfare would be provided by the economic growth stemming from the economics of a liberalised market, and not from the regulatory and distributive capacity of public policy (see, for example, Leibfried and Pierson 1995; Barnard 2000). It is indicative of the Treaty's pro-market bias that its only explicit legislative competence in the field of social policy related to the free movement of workers, which for the most part even allowed measures to be adopted on the basis of qualified majority voting (Articles 48–51 EEC Treaty).

However, the European Community's action capacity was incrementally increased in day-to-day politics. Where necessary or functional for market integration, the EEC Treaty implicitly allowed for social policy

---

[1] Thanks to Myriam Nauerz for her excellent research assistance.
[2] For a more detailed discussion of the historical background, see Falkner (1998: 56–77, 2003b).

Table 3.1 *The attribution of explicit social policy competences to the EU in formal treaty reforms*

Explicit community competence for . . .	EEC Treaty 1957	Single European Act 1986	Maastricht Social Agreement 1992	Amsterdam Treaty 1997	Nice Treaty 2001
'measures' to improve transnational co-operation under Art. 137	–	–	–	–	++
'incentive measures' to combat discrimination as defined by Art. 13	–	–	–	–	++
action against discrimination on grounds of sex, race, ethnic origin, belief, disability, age, sexual orientation (new Art. 13)	–	–	–	+	+
'measures' combating social exclusion	–	–	–	++	++
'measures' assuring equal opportunities and treatment of both women and men	–	–	–	++	++
employment policy co-ordination	–	–	–	++	++
funding for employment policy	–	–	+	+	–
social security and protection of workers	–	–	+	+	+
protection of workers where employment contract is terminated	–	–	+	+	+
collective interest representation, co-determination	–	–	+	+	+
employment of third-country nationals	–	–	+	+	+
working conditions (general)	–	–	++	++	++
worker information and consultation	–	–	++	++	++
gender equality for labour force integration in labour market	–	–	++	++	++
working environment (health and safety)	–	++	++	++	++
social security co-ordination	+	+	no impact	+	+
free movement of workers	++	++	no impact	++	++

– not mentioned
+ decision by unanimity
++ decision by qualified majority

interventions.[3] From the 1970s onwards, this opportunity was indeed used for social policy harmonisation at the supranational level. Unanimous Council votes were needed to do this, however. This meant high thresholds for joint action. Each government could veto social measures, which meant that the Community was caught in the so-called 'joint-decision trap' (Scharpf 1988). It was only from the mid 1980s onwards that changes to the European social policy provisions were successively introduced: by the Single European Act in 1986 and, later, by three EU Treaty reforms negotiated during the 1990s. Innovation affected both the level of competences (with the EC's powers being extended) and the level of procedures (qualified majority voting was first introduced in one aspect of European social policy and then extended to further areas).

In Table 3.1, we indicate when a competence was first attributed and whether it was maintained in later reforms. Unless indicated otherwise (for example, measures or co-ordination), this refers to the competence for binding regulative action. The understanding here is a wide notion of social policy, including issues such as the free movement of workers and the general principle of non-discrimination as defined by the new Article 13 ECT.

In 1987, the Single European Act came into force as the first major revision of the EEC Treaty. It formalised the internal market programme and was primarily an economic endeavour. However, social policy again constituted a controversial issue: how much social state building should go along with even more far-reaching market integration? In various so-called 'flanking' policy areas, notably environmental and research policy, EEC competences were formally extended.[4] In social policy, in contrast, the member state delegations were not willing to give the EEC a greater role. However, an important exception was made: Article 118a EEC Treaty on minimum harmonisation concerning the health and safety of workers would soon provide an escape route out of the unanimity requirement. For the first time in European social policy, it allowed member states to adopt Directives based on qualified majority voting in the Council. This was acceptable to all delegations because the field of occupational health and safety was closely linked to the internal market.

---

[3] This was laid down in the so-called subsidiary competence provisions. Laws in the member states which 'directly affect the establishment or functioning of the common market' could be approximated by unanimous Council decision on the basis of a Commission proposal (Art. 100 EEC Treaty). The Treaty also stipulated that in so far as 'action by the Community should prove necessary to attain, in the course of the operation of the common market, one of the objectives of the Community, and this Treaty has not provided the necessary powers, the Council shall, acting unanimously on a proposal from the Commission and after consulting the European Parliament, take the appropriate measures' (Art. 235 EEC Treaty).

[4] See Art. 130f–t EEC Treaty.

Neither the Thatcher government nor any other government, however, expected this seemingly 'technical' issue to facilitate social policy integration significantly in the decade to come. An extensive use of this provision was possible mainly because the wording and the definition of key terms of Article 118a were all but unequivocal: 'Member States shall pay particular attention to encouraging improvements, especially in the working environment, as regards the health and safety of workers.'[5] This provision was later used to adopt not only health and safety issues in a narrow sense, but also wider employment rights, for example in the Directives on Pregnant Workers, Working Time and Young Workers (see Chapters 5, 6 and 7).

The Maastricht Treaty extended Community competences to a wide range of social policy areas.[6] These include working conditions, the information and consultation of workers, equality between men and women with regard to labour market opportunities and treatment at work (in contrast to merely equal pay, as before), and the integration of persons excluded from the labour market. Some issues were, however, explicitly *excluded* from the scope of minimum harmonisation: pay, the right of association, the right to strike, and the right to impose lockouts. Additionally, unanimous decisions were restricted to social security and the social protection of workers; the protection of workers where their employment contracts are terminated; the representation and collective defence of interests of workers and employers, including codetermination; the conditions of employment for third-country nationals legally residing in Community territory; and financial contributions for the promotion of employment and job creation. Qualified majority voting was thus extended to many more issue areas than before, including, for example, the information and consultation of workers.

In the Intergovernmental Conference preceding the 1997 Amsterdam Treaty, social policy reform in a narrow sense was not a major issue, but employment promotion was. Because of the fierce resistance to social policy reforms from the UK Tory government (in office until May 1997), the Intergovernmental Conference decided to postpone the topic until the end, after a general election in the UK. The new Labour government immediately put an end to the UK's social policy opt-out. At the Amsterdam summit, therefore, the social provisions agreed upon in Maastricht

---

[5] The Article continues as follows: 'and shall set as their objective the harmonisation of conditions in this area, while maintaining the improvements made. In order to help achieve the objective laid down in the first paragraph, the Council, acting by a qualified majority on a proposal from the Commission, . . . shall adopt, by means of Directives, minimum requirements for gradual implementation' (Art. 118a EEC Treaty).

[6] Initially, these reforms did not apply to the UK. For details on the Social Protocol and Agreement, see Falkner (1998) and Hartenberger (2001).

could finally be incorporated into the EC Treaty. Apart from this, the only significant innovation (if compared with the status quo of the Social Agreement) was the new employment policy chapter of the EC Treaty (now Articles 125–30). While excluding any harmonisation of domestic laws, it provides for the co-ordination of national employment policies on the basis of annual guidelines and national follow-up reports. Furthermore, a new Article 13 on Community action against discrimination on grounds of sex, race, ethnic origin, belief, disability, age, and sexual orientation was inserted into the EC Treaty.

Finally, the Nice Treaty of 2001 did not bring much innovation in the social provisions chapter either. In some fields, the Council may in the future unanimously decide to render the codecision procedure (with qualified majority voting) applicable. This concerns worker protection where employment contracts are terminated, the representation and collective defence of collective interests, and the employment of third-country nationals (see Article 137.2 EC Treaty). Furthermore, the Community may now adopt measures encouraging co-operation between member states[7] with regard to all social issues, not just concerning social exclusion and equal opportunities, as was already the case in the Amsterdam Treaty.

3.2   The use of social competences over time

During the early years of European integration, social policy consisted almost exclusively of securing the free movement of workers and was rather non-controversial. In a number of Regulations,[8] the national social security systems were co-ordinated with a view to securing the status of internationally mobile workers and their families (for details, see for example Pierson and Leibfried 1995; Langewiesche and Lubyova 2000). The growth of decisions on this kind of directly applicable legislation was not a constant one. Nonetheless, this has always been, and still is, a very active field of EU intervention in the social sphere. Until now, there have been a total of sixty-five Council decisions on new or reformed Regulations in the area of the free movement of workers (see Figure 3.1).[9]

---

[7] 'The Council . . . may adopt measures designed to encourage cooperation between Member States through initiatives aimed at improving knowledge, developing exchanges of information and best practices, promoting innovative approaches and evaluating experiences' (Art. 137 EC Treaty).

[8] A Regulation is a legal instrument containing provisions that are directly binding in the member states so that no transposition into domestic law is needed (see Art. 249 EC Treaty).

[9] It goes almost without saying that the quantifying perspective applied in this chapter impedes conclusions concerning the quality of EU social law, in a wider sense.

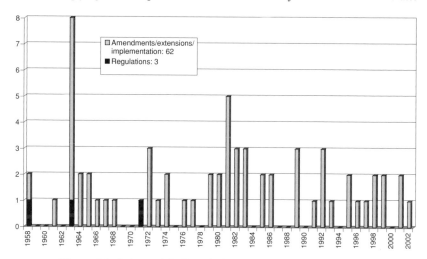

Figure 3.1 Substantial Regulations and amendments in the co-ordination of social security systems[10]

During the late 1960s, however, politicians started to discuss a *wider range of instruments and topics* in European social policy. At the 1972 Paris summit, the EC Heads of State and Government solemnly declared that economic expansion should not be an end in itself but should lead to improvements in the living and working conditions of citizens. They suggested a catalogue of social policy measures to be proposed by the Commission. Several of the legislative measures proposed by the ensuing Social Action Programme (OJ 1974 No. C13/1) were adopted by the Council up to the early 1980s, and further Social Action Programmes and many further Directives followed suit. Figure 3.2 shows the growth in social policy Directives from 1974 onwards.

The figure highlights that, since 1975, the EC has adopted social Directives almost every year. After 1986, some Directives updated older ones, or extended them to new geographical areas such as Spain and Portugal after their accession or the former GDR after German unification. By the end of the year 2002, fifty-five individual social Directives, seventeen amendments to existing Directives, and seven geographical extensions of

[10] Source: Celex (European Commission), last updated at the end of 2002. The data includes amendments, extensions and Regulations on implementation. The data excludes Regulations under the Euratom Treaty, on social statistics, on sampling surveys, on food for the needy from intervention stocks and on institutional details.

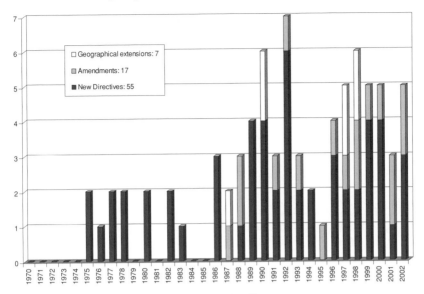

Figure 3.2 The EC's social Directives[11]

Directives had been adopted. The total number of decisions on social Directives was seventy-nine. These Directives typically fall within what is at the national level called labour law. EU legislation on social security issues, in contrast, is almost exclusively confined to the area of protecting workers who are moving from one member state to another.

1992 has so far been the most active year with six new Directives and one extension. Generally speaking, the 1990s were the most active decade. This may come as a surprise considering the initial fears that the internal market programme might not be accompanied by any social policy dimension at all (Steinkühler 1989). With each decade, the newly adopted social Directives have approximately doubled. If we only focus on materially innovative decisions on Directives (excluding geographical extensions), 61 per cent of all EC social Directives adopted before 2000 actually stem from the 1990s (see Figure 3.3).

[11] Source: own database from adjusted Celex data, last updated at the end of 2002. The data includes all Directives on 'social policy' and excludes Euratom Directives, Directives adopted by the Commission, Directives on the free movement of workers and on social statistics. Incorrect classifications were corrected. The date of adoption is according to the text of the Directive as published in the OJ.

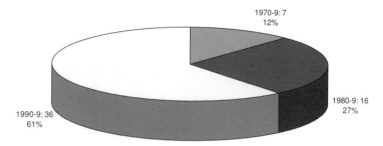

Figure 3.3 New EC social Directives and amendments to Directives, expressed in decades[12]

There are *three main areas of EC social Directives*: health and safety, other working conditions, and equality between women and men at the workplace (see Figure 3.4). The first is the most active field with twenty-eight Directives (plus eleven amendments to or extensions of Directives). Minimum standards on working conditions outside this area follow suit with twenty new Directives (and ten amendments or extensions). Finally, eight Directives belong to the field of non-discrimination and gender equality policy (plus three revisions or extensions).

Concerning *gender equality*, it should be mentioned that the European Court of Justice became a major actor since it interpreted Article 119 of the 1957 EEC Treaty on domestic measures to ensure equal pay in an extensive manner. From the 1970s onwards, this case law, which continued to proliferate considerably, was accompanied by legislation on matters such as equal pay for work of equal value, the equal treatment of men and women in terms of working conditions and social security, and even the burden of proof in discrimination lawsuits (Hoskyns 1996; Mazey 1998). In the field of other *working conditions*, a number of Directives was adopted during the late 1970s, for instance on the protection of workers in the event of collective redundancy, transfer of undertaking, or employer insolvency. Many more Directives followed suit during the 1990s, covering issues such as the right of workers to a written employment contract, the equal treatment of 'atypical' workers, the organisation of working time, and parental leave (Bercusson 1994, 1995; Blanpain and Engels 1995; Shaw 2000). With regard to *health and safety* (James 1993; Eichener 1997; Vos 1999), Community action was based on a number of specific

[12] Source: own database from adjusted Celex data, last updated at the end of 2002. The data includes all Directives on 'social policy' and excludes Euratom Directives, Directives adopted by the Commission, Directives on the free movement of workers and Directives on social statistics. Extensions of Directives are also excluded. Incorrect classifications were corrected.

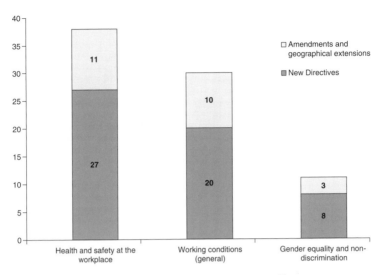

Figure 3.4 EC social Directives in different subareas[13]

action programmes. Directives included topics such as the protection of workers exposed to emissions and loads, as well as protection against risks at work from chemical, physical and biological agents (e.g. lead or asbestos).

3.3   A rise in non-binding acts?

The EU's social provisions also cover a number of non-binding provisions. By the end of 2002, the Community had adopted fifteen *Recommendations* (for instance on the fair participation of women and men in decision-making processes in 1996, on parking cards for handicapped persons in 1998, and on the implementation of employment policy in the member states in 2000, 2001 and 2002), fifty *Resolutions* (such as those on the social integration of young persons and on the equal participation of men and women in both family and professional life, both in 2000), sixteen *Conclusions* (such as those on the implementation of measures fighting sex tourism and child abuse in 1999), three *Declarations* (such as the one adopted at the end of the European Year of the Elderly in 1993) and

[13] Source: own database from adjusted Celex data, last updated at the end of 2002. The data includes all Directives on 'social policy'. It excludes Euratom Directives, Directives adopted by the Commission, Directives on the free movement of workers and Directives on social statistics. Incorrect classifications were corrected.

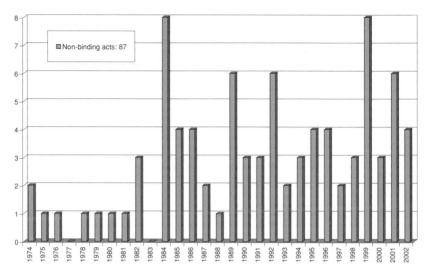

Figure 3.5 Non-binding social policy measures adopted by the Council[16]

three *Communications* (such as those on the European Social Agenda in 2000).[14] In sum, eighty-seven non-binding social measures were adopted between 1974 and 2002 (see Figure 3.5).[15]

Over time, non-binding social acts did increase in each decade – as suggested by the neo-voluntarism hypothesis (see Chapter 1). While the 1970s saw only seven such acts, the 1980s witnessed as many as thirty-two. Almost 50 per cent of all non-binding acts in EC social policy until 2003, however, were adopted between 1991 and 2000 (i.e. thirty-eight). Non-binding social acts were disproportionately numerous in two political phases: right after the Amsterdam Treaty from 1998 to 2002 (on average five per year) and from the Single European Act (1986) to the Maastricht Treaty (1992) (on average three and a half per year).

Among these non-binding acts, measures related to the 'open method of co-ordination' are quantitatively hardly important. In this context, the EU has a novel role as an engine and, at the same time, a corset for social reforms at the domestic level (for details, see Goetschy 2001; de la Porte and Pochet 2002). Under this new intervention style (developed incrementally as a follow-up to the European Council of Essen in 1994 and

---

[14] The choice of category does not always seem to follow a consistent logic.

[15] Before 1974, no such non-binding measures were adopted in the field of social policy.

[16] Source: own database from adjusted Celex data, last updated at the end of 2002. The data excludes Reports, Common Positions and Agreements in legislative procedures, ECSC and Euratom acts, and decisions on the free movement of workers, justice and home affairs, training and professional training and demography.

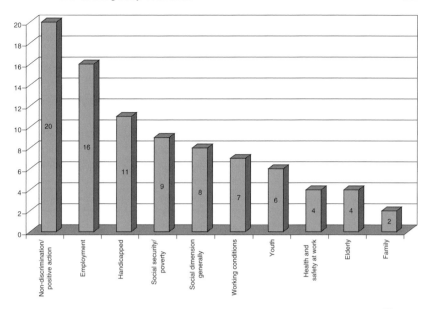

Figure 3.6 Issue areas covered by non-binding social policy acts[18]

formalised in the Amsterdam Treaty), the EU adopts annual employment policy guidelines (i.e. one formal act a year, which is legally non-binding and typically a Resolution). The actual specification of these guidelines in accordance with domestic policy legacies and ideologies is left to the actors at the national level. The member states must, however, present reports on how they have responded to the guidelines, and why they have chosen particular strategies in their 'National Action Plans'. They have to defend their options at the European level in regular debates on national employment policies, with the result that peer pressure can exercise a potentially harmonising effect on social policies in Europe. The open method of co-ordination has recently been extended to additional fields including pension reform, social inclusion, and education.[17]

As Figure 3.6 shows, most non-binding legal acts in EC social policy belong to the area of gender equality (23 per cent), followed by employment policy (18.4 per cent, with many acts being adopted even before the introduction of the OMC) and measures for the handicapped (12.6 per cent).

[17] However, its success cannot really be judged yet since we still lack reliable data on the practical effects in the member states.

[18] Source: own database from adjusted Celex data, last updated: end of 2002. The data exclude Reports, Common Positions and Agreements in legislative procedures, ECSC and Euratom acts, and decisions on the free movement of workers, justice and home affairs, training and professional training and demography.

To compare binding and non-binding forms of EU social policy, we should perhaps explain that, under the EC Treaty (Article 249), binding legal acts are Regulations, Directives and Decisions, while Recommendations and Opinions are referred to as non-binding instruments. Other non-binding acts such as 'Conclusions' and 'Declarations' do not show up in the relevant Treaty article; still they are frequently used in EU social policy. If we make a tally of all binding (and at the same time materially significant)[19] acts in EU social policy that were adopted up to 2003,[20] and all non-binding social measures that were enacted by the same date, the result is a rather large *acquis communautaire* of 159 adopted acts. This includes eighty-seven non-binding measures and seventy-two Directives (new ones or amendments).[21]

At first glance, one would assume that maybe the non-binding acts have slowly but surely increased at the expense of the binding ones (after all, the OMC has dominated much of the relevant discourse during recent years). As Figure 3.7 shows, the actual development has been approximately parallel. The non-binding social acts have very slightly dominated the binding acts ever since 1984 but have not grown faster than the binding ones in recent years.[22]

There is no space here to discuss in depth the interesting differences between issue areas in EU social policy. Suffice it to say that in *non-discrimination policy* there was no single Directive between 1987 and 1995. Afterwards, too, the growth in Directives was comparatively slow (seven decisions on Directives between 1995 to 2002, with a total of ten Directives being adopted by 2003). In contrast, the non-binding measures grew rather steadily and strongly (twenty in total). Most non-binding decisions fall in the subfield of gender equality, where the fundamental Directives

---

[19] This excludes decisions on the appointment of new members of certain committees and the like.

[20] This comparison excludes the Regulations on social security of migrant workers (i.e. many binding acts that can be understood as a part of EU social policy, in a very wide sense), since we are interested primarily in market-correcting policies here.

[21] These figures exclude extensions of Directives, which bring no innovation to content, since the comparison here is with non-binding acts, which are never formally extended to new member states.

[22] In cross-sectoral terms, the significance of non-binding measures seems to be considerably lower. Adrienne Héritier (2002) found that only about 10 per cent of all policy measures published in the Official Journal between January 2000 and July 2001 could be considered what she terms 'new modes of governance'. At closer inspection, this result is hardly surprising, since a very large part of EU policy measures adopted each year is formed by a multitude of highly technical Regulations and Decisions in the areas of agricultural and commercial policy, food aid and common customs and tariffs. These measures, which are uncommon in the area of social policy, are binding in character, but many of them have little significance in policy terms and expire after one or two years (see Page and Dimitrakopoulos 1997 for more details).

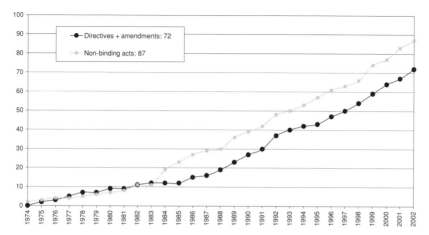

Figure 3.7 Stock of Directives and non-binding acts adopted by the EC Council in the field of social policy[23]

that established equal pay and equal working conditions in the 1970s and early 1980s were later accompanied by manifold non-binding initiatives and recommendations to facilitate the implementation.

This is quite different in the two other fields with significant numbers of non-binding acts, where the binding acts clearly outnumber the non-binding ones. In the area of *working conditions*, Directives (including amendments) increased significantly after 1990 (total: twenty-six) but non-binding acts remained quite rare (only seven in total). Binding minimum norms definitely dominate this field. This strategy seems quite appropriate considering that, for instance, the 1978 Recommendation on weekly working hours was never respected in practice. It was only in 1994 that the Working Time Directive brought about an approximation of the national rules and regulations on this aspect of working conditions, which is very important from the point of view of competitiveness (see also Chapter 6). This example may explain why the EU does not rely on a voluntary approach, but rather on binding minimum standards, in such cost-intensive working conditions. In this field, the argument of a potential distortion of competition in the EU's internal market due to a lack of common rules is particularly relevant (Scharpf 1999).

Against this background, it seems very plausible that the discrepancy between non-binding and binding acts is greatest in the sphere of *health and safety at the workplace*. While the *acquis communautaire* in this area includes thirty-six Directives (including amendments), there are only four

---

[23] Source: that of the figures on Directives and on non-binding acts.

non-binding acts. However, it should be mentioned that, without doubt, the character of the different subfields also explains some of the differences. While equal treatment is a cross-cutting matter that can be regulated for many professions and economic sectors in one piece of legislation, technical details of maximum exposure levels and the like cannot, the result being that the field of health and safety demands more specialised regulation for individual sectors and activities (seafarers, work with heavy loads, etc.).

Concluding the comparison between binding and non-binding acts in EU social policy, we should emphasise that both developed in parallel while there have been no indications so far that voluntary measures actually replace binding ones.[24]

3.4   Conclusions on the development of EU social policy

An analysis of the quantitative development of EU social policy from the 1950s up to the new millennium reveals two crucial points.

(1) From a quantitative perspective, *the development of EU social policy is quite impressive.* The EU has made use of its competences quite frequently, and the growth in social regulation (both binding and non-binding) has been significant. Despite all the ideological clashes in the Council of Ministers ever since the early 1980s, the 1990s was in fact the most active period in terms of binding regulative activity. With the benefit of hindsight, therefore, the argument that the internal market programme might not be accompanied by any significant social dimension, which was voiced by many observers in the early 1990s, has proven to be unjustified. A total of 57 per cent of all newly adopted social policy Directives (counted from 1957 to the end of 1999, without amendments) stems from the 1990s. The share rises to 61 per cent if we include Directives that amend older ones, and to 63 per cent if extensions are included too.

(2) The second conclusion concerns the character of EU social policy against the background of recent public debates on the open method of co-ordination and on neo-voluntarism. It may come as a surprise to learn that, in actual fact, *binding and non-binding decisions have developed approximately in parallel.* At least until the end of 2002, the data on adopted social acts does not indicate that soft measures actually supersede binding ones.

---

[24] Note that there is no space here to outline the redistributive dimension of EU social policy in the form of the European Social Fund.

It is true that during the late 1990s there were changes in the character of social Directives, just as predicted by the neo-voluntarism hypothesis. Some social Directives included many non-binding provisions and exemption possibilities while simultaneously containing fewer binding minimum standards than some of the previous Directives. But rather than seeing a complete replacement of the one by the other, we think it more appropriate to speak of a diversification of different elements contained in these Directives. Next to binding rules we now find provisions that allow for certain exemptions or further specification of details in the member states as well as non-binding recommendations.

But it is important to note that we do not observe a complete fading away of the binding rules. Nor is the trend towards diversification uniform across recent EU social Directives. In contrast, some recent Directives have again contained very detailed binding provisions (for instance, the Directives on the regulation of working time in sectors formerly excluded from EU intervention, and Directives in the health and safety field). We conclude therefore that the diversification of elements is one additional characteristic of some EU social policy measures but not a uniform feature of all social Directives.

To sum up, it is true that the 1990s brought about a number of non-binding elements in EU social policy, as described by the neo-voluntarism approach. Softer modes of steering can be seen both within the principally binding form of social policy legislation (i.e. Directives) and also in the new mode of governance known as the open method of co-ordination (OMC). It is crucial to note, however, that the proliferation of softer elements within Directives and non-binding instruments (alongside Directives) has not replaced 'hard' policy intervention by binding measures.

It seems that there are mechanisms that further the reproduction of the traditional elements in EU social policy, just as neo-institutional theory would predict: 'as we scan the institutional landscape, we find that institutional survival is often strongly laced with elements of institutional *transformation* that bring institutions in line with changed social, political and economic conditions' (Thelen 2003: 211, emphasis in original). There has been no fundamental change towards an exclusively 'soft' or 'neo-voluntarist' EU social policy, but rather an increasing differentiation of instruments and elements. This corresponds to a process of incremental 'institutional layering, which involves the partial renegotiation of some elements of a given set of institutions while leaving others in place' (Thelen 2003: 225). In the words of Adrienne Héritier and her collaborators (1994: 392) one could say that what we observe is an addition of policy elements rather than a substitution.

4 The Employment Contract Information Directive: a small but useful social complement to the internal market[1]

4.1 Aim and content of the Directive

The Directive on an employer's obligation to inform employees of the conditions applicable to the contract or employment relationship[2] will be referred to in this chapter as the 'Employment Contract Information Directive'. Its *general aim*, according to the explanatory considerations preceding the main part of the legal text, is to 'provide employees with improved protection against possible infringements of their rights and to create greater transparency on the labour market' (Consideration no. 2).

There is therefore a dual purpose to the Directive, one aspect being social (increasing the legal security of workers) and one economic (better flow of information on working conditions). Greater flexibility of labour markets affects not only the individual member state, but also the Common European Market: 'in the case of expatriation of the employee, the latter must, in addition to the main terms of his contract or employment relationship, be supplied with relevant information connected with his secondment' (Consideration no. 10; for details, see Article 4 of the Directive).

Hence the *compulsory minimum standards* of the Employment Contract Information Directive comprise six specific rules:

(1) that the workers are to be informed on essential aspects of the work or employment relationship;
(2) that the information must be given in written form;
(3) that expatriate employees should receive additional information;
(4) that any change of contract is to be notified in writing;
(5) that all employees who consider themselves wronged through failure to comply with the Directive may pursue their claims effectively;
(6) and that written information must be given upon request in the case of employment relationships pre-dating the Directive.

---

[1] Thanks to Charlotte Buttkus for her support in summarising the national interviews for this Directive.
[2] Directive 91/533/EEC of 14 October 1991, OJ 1991 No. L288/32–5.

All rights accorded by this Directive are therefore *information rights*. In other words, there is no obligation to change any detail of an employment relationship except the right to written information about its basic conditions in those cases where a corresponding right to written information did not exist before.

The information to be provided by the employer has to include the identity of the parties, the place of work, a description of the job, the date of commencement of the employment relationship, the amount of paid leave, the periods of notice to be observed if the employment relationship is terminated, the amount of remuneration and frequency of payment, the daily or weekly working hours, any relevant collective agreements, and, in the case of a temporary contract, its expected duration (Article 2).

This information has to be laid down in a written employment contract, in a letter of engagement, or in one or more other written documents which must be given to the employee within two months of commencing employment (Article 3). Employees required to work abroad for more than one month have to receive, prior to departure, a document containing additional information about the duration of their employment abroad, the currency to be used for payment of remuneration, any additional benefits in cash or kind, and, where appropriate, the conditions governing the employee's return (Article 4).

Furthermore, any change to the terms of the employment relationship must be recorded in writing and be brought to the attention of the employee within one month (Article 5). Employees who feel that their rights arising from the Directive have been violated must be able to pursue their claims by judicial process, after possible recourse to other competent authorities (Article 8). The duty to furnish information also applies to employment relationships established before the entry into force of the Directive. In this case, however, a request from the employee is required (Article 9).

There are four *possibilities for derogating from these standards*. Most importantly, member states may exclude from the scope of application (1) employment contracts lasting for less than one month, (2) workers with a weekly workload of less than eight hours, and (3) employees performing casual or specific work, if justified by objective considerations (Article 1.2). (4) Finally, access to the means of redress (before the court) can be restricted to cases where the employee has notified the employer and the employer has failed to reply within fifteen days (Article 8).

The policy scope of the Employment Contract Information Directive is therefore clearly specified and quite narrow. Unlike other EU Directives, it does not combine a group of ambitions, but focuses on one only (i.e. the right to written information on essential terms of employment).

Comparing this Directive with other EU social policy Directives (as discussed subsequently), the number of six binding standards is rather low (the upper extreme in our sample is the Pregnant Workers Directive with fourteen binding standards). Even more extraordinary is, however, the absence of any non-binding standards. While the Directives adopted more recently typically include a number of recommendations, this one does not. Finally, exceptions provided for in the Directive are comparatively few. Only four such allowances for derogations exist (compare the Working Time Directive with fourteen provisions on exemptions).

In a nutshell, the Employment Contract Information Directive is a comparatively short and straightforward piece of EU legislation, laying down standards that are limited in number but binding in character. The prescribed duty to supply information does not otherwise touch upon the terms of employment.

4.2   The European-level negotiation process

The Employment Contract Information Directive was the very first legislative project outside the health and safety field to be adopted under the 1989 Social Action Programme that had accompanied the EU's so-called 'Social Charter'. Point 9 of the Charter had actually stipulated that the employment conditions should be specified according to national tradition, by law, collective agreement or employment contract.

The specific economic background to the Directive, as outlined in its introductory considerations (see nos. 1–3), is that the development of new forms of work had led to an increase in the number of types of employment relationships. The relevant legislation of the member states was considered to differ considerably on such fundamental points as the requirement to inform employees in writing of the main terms of the contract or employment relationship. Differences in national legislation, however, were suspected to have a direct effect on the operation of the EU's common market (as expressed in Consideration no. 4 of the Directive as adopted in the Council).

This view was not actually shared by everyone. In its position paper on the Commission proposal, the EU-level employers' federation UNICE had argued that '[t]he Internal Market can function very well with these differences in legislation and practices'. In UNICE's view, the Commission's choice of Treaty basis was therefore not justified: 'The aim of the proposal is to harmonise the rights of workers and the choice of the legal basis should reflect this. Therefore, Art. 100 is not an appropriate legal basis' (UNICE 1991). This, however, did not mean a fundamental opposition in principle to the Directive. UNICE shared the view of all other relevant actors that workers should have a right to receive information on their employment conditions.[3] At the same time, UNICE would have preferred to leave all further details to national decision.

In overall terms, the Employment Contract Information Directive provoked little opposition, although Portugal seems not to have welcomed these rules in principle, agreeing to them only during the final night of the negotiations (Interview LUX1: 795–7; see also the section on partial non-transposition below). When the Commission aired its first plans to regulate this area, the Belgian government protested against any potential introduction of a right to a written employment contract. As in a number of EU member states, a formal employment contract was only known in a few special cases or sectors in Belgium (Interview B7: 691–705).[4] Other governments shared this concern and already the formal Commission proposal did not require an employment contract as such (European Industrial Relations Review – EIRR 206: 27). During the negotiations, even Ireland and, most notably, the UK were not opposed to this project since they fulfilled the crucial standards from the outset (an unusual situation in European social policy). Their workers were already entitled, unlike those in most of the continental states of the EU, to a written statement of the main terms and conditions of their employment (see, for example, EIRR 206: 27). In addition, the acceptance of the proposal by the UK's Conservative government was facilitated by the fact that the Directive's focus on the individual relationship between employer and employee fitted in with the Tories' anti-union policy (see below for more details).

Among the promoters of the Directive was Luxembourg. The smallest member state had already enjoyed a law on the right to a written employment contract since 1989 and had wanted the European partners to follow suit. Hence, the Luxembourg government pushed forward the dossier during its presidency in the first six months of 1991, and finally managed to reach a Common Position in the Council of Ministers in June 1991. During the negotiations in Council, some provisions were softened (the time for issuing the written information was extended from one to two months) and exceptions were added to the draft (most importantly, the possibility of excluding workers whose contract lasts less than one month). On that basis, the Directive was adopted unanimously under the Dutch Council presidency on 14 October 1991.

---

[3] It is important to underline again that the Directive is only about information on working conditions, not about any approximation of the terms of employment themselves.

[4] In the Belgian case, this was for fixed-term contracts, replacement contracts and part-time contracts.

Table 4.1 *The Employment Contract Information Directive and misfit in the member states*

	Degree of Legal Misfit	Limited Practical Significance	Degree of *Total Policy Misfit*	Degree of Politics/ Polity Misfit	Economic Costs	Degree of *Total Misfit*
A	medium	no	medium	–	low	medium
B	medium	yes	low	–	low	low
D	medium	yes	low	–	low	low
DK	medium	yes	low	–	low	low
E	medium	yes	low	–	low	low
F	low	no	low	–	low	low
FIN	medium	yes	low	–	low	low
GB	low	no	low	–	low	low
GR	medium	no	medium	–	low	medium
I	low	no	low	–	low	low
IRL	low	no	low	–	low	low
LUX	low	no	low	–	low	low
NL	medium	no	low	–	low	low
P	medium	no	medium	–	low	medium
S	medium	yes	low	–	low	low

4.3   Misfit in the member states: rather small but affecting all

If the Employment Contract Information Directive is a comparatively slim and non-intricate piece of legislation, does this imply that only few member states needed to adapt to its provisions?

In fact, our expert interviews in the fifteen capitals revealed that the Directive *confronted all EU members with policy misfit* (on the operationalisation of this concept, see Chapter 2). Even countries with comparatively advanced welfare and labour law systems, such as Austria, Germany, and Sweden, faced adaptational pressure that concerned more than just a few elements of the Directive. They actually needed to change their laws for each and every single standard set by this EU law. Only a few countries already had fully adequate levels of protection, at least in a number of aspects. These included, for example, France with regard to the means of written information and the defence of rights by judicial process, and the UK, Ireland, and Luxembourg, all with regard to written information on the modification of contract and the defence of rights by judicial process. While there is not a single case of complete fit with the Directive, there is no instance of large-scale misfit, either. *All fifteen member states fall into the categories of low or medium levels of misfit* (see Table 4.1).

That all cases show small- or medium-scale misfit is due to the fact that Ireland, the UK, France, Luxembourg and Italy already possessed a general legal rule requiring employers to issue a written document stating the essential terms of the employment relationship (albeit not all the detailed provisions of the Directive were guaranteed, accounting for some legal misfit nevertheless), so that the Directive in these countries only created a small amount of *legal misfit* from the outset. The other member states provided a right to written information on the employment conditions in exceptional cases or sectors. Therefore, we rated the legal misfit as medium-scale in Austria, Belgium, Germany, Denmark, Spain, Finland, Greece, the Netherlands, Portugal and Sweden. In several of these countries, however, the *practical* significance of the required legal adaptations was minor. Since extant collective agreements already guaranteed the same outcome in day-to-day practice, we made an allowance for this and ultimately attributed low *policy misfit* for Belgium, Germany, Denmark, Spain, Finland, the Netherlands and Sweden.

Hence, the Employment Contract Information Directive confronted only Austria, Greece and Portugal with more than small adaptational pressure, i.e. they had to deal with medium levels of policy misfit.

The Directive did not generate misfit in the *politics and polity dimension*. It did not require administrative reforms such as the creation of new administrative units or changes to existing administrative routines or responsibilities. Enforcement was simply left to the existing national court systems. The Directive did not prescribe any detailed organisational rules for this. Similarly, transposing the Directive did not challenge existing state–society relations in the member states, even in countries like Denmark or Sweden, which have strong traditions of autonomous social partner regulation in employment law. In fact, the rules governing employment contracts did not belong to the area of social partner autonomy at all (Sweden). Or they were not regarded as core social partner competence and therefore the shift of the regulatory instrument from collective agreement to law was considered negligible (Denmark). Hence, having to introduce legislation in this area did not constitute a problem for the specific brand of corporatism in these countries.

Finally, the *economic costs* of adapting to the Employment Contract Information Directive were minor everywhere in the EU – at least if one assumes that only a few employers had used the lack of written information duties as an instrument to set working conditions below the level defined by collective agreements or national legislation. Otherwise, an additional rise in labour costs would have to be calculated, since employees could easily challenge such unfavourable treatment with the aid of written statements about their working conditions. But since our empirical investigation did not reveal that this kind of practice was a widespread phenomenon, we consider the main cost implication of the Directive to be the imposition of an additional administrative duty on employers. This was comparatively more inconvenient for small and medium-sized enterprises, which tend to have (if at all) less professionalised and computerised personnel departments (see, for example, Interview F10: 1105–17; GR15).

4.4   Implementation in the member states

According to Article 9, member states had to incorporate the provisions of the Directive into their national legal order no later than 30 June 1993.

4.4.1   *Particularly interesting cases*

It may come as a surprise that Austria was among the countries with the comparatively largest misfit under the Employment Contract Information Directive. The misfit was, according to our operationalisation (see Chapter 2 above), medium-scale. Until recently, only white-collar workers were in the habit of receiving a written employment contract specifying the main conditions of their employment relationship. The large category of blue-collar workers, by contrast, typically had no written information on their terms of contract at all (Interview A1: 955–84, A2: 199–224).[5] Despite this misfit – which in terms of the Employment Contract Information Directive was comparatively rather severe – Austria adapted on time and essentially correctly.[6] Trade union experts are quite satisfied with the positive effects, especially with regard to blue-collar workers, and argue that without the Directive this innovation would not have been possible in Austria (Interviews A1: 955–84, A4: 98–301).

In Belgium, by contrast, a low degree of policy misfit (medium-scale legal misfit having in practice partly been covered by collective agreements) still led to an implementation delay of seven (and in some aspects even more than eight) years. The transposition was initially coupled with a much larger national reform project, aimed at simplifying the rather

---

[5] Although the Eurostat Labour Force Survey comprises data on occupational groups, it does not include the category 'blue-collar workers'. A reasonable proxy for this notion, however, can be constructed by cumulating the following three categories: 'plant and machine operators', 'craft-related trades workers', and 'elementary occupations'. In 1995, these three groups made up almost 40 per cent of all persons gainfully employed in Austria (Eurostat 1996: Table 044).

[6] The Commission's implementation report and our own expert interviews nevertheless revealed some minor aspects to be incorrect (see below).

complex bureaucratic administration of workers' social security coverage. The debates surrounding this project turned out to be very complicated, preventing adaptation within the deadline. After the Commission had issued a Letter of Formal Notice for non-implementation, Belgium gave notification of a draft legal project, which not only would have been insufficient to fulfil the requirements of the Directive, but also never made its way into the statute books in the first place. As a result of administrative sloppiness and the fact that Belgian actors in general did not seem to consider the Employment Contract Information Directive to be of great significance, non-transposition prevailed for a number of years.

Inertia was only overcome after the Commission issued an implementation report, which reminded the Belgian administration of its persistent breach of Community law. Ironically enough, however, the report only noted the material shortcomings of the original draft legislation, while the Commission had not realised for years that the project in question had never been adopted. Serious attempts to transpose the Directive were then made because in the run-up to the Belgian Council Presidency the government felt a need to act speedily to safeguard its reputation. As a consequence, the measures to implement the Directive were put into an 'omnibus legislation' project so as to speed up parliamentary approval. Hence, the haphazard supranational enforcement finally assured correct implementation where, before, compliance was obstructed by administrative inefficiencies and issue linkage.

Implementation in Germany was delayed for two years, albeit the country was faced with only minor adaptation requirements. This was due to conflicts between the two parties in government over whether or not part-timers working less than eight hours per week should be excluded from the scope of the implementation legislation. The smaller Liberal coalition party, and in particular its Minister of Economic Affairs, wanted to avoid 'unnecessary' burdens for business and thus demanded that these workers be excluded. The Christian Democratic Department of Labour and Social Affairs, traditionally representing the worker-friendly faction within the CDU (Zohlnhöfer 2001), argued against making use of this exemption because the exclusion of part-time workers would indirectly discriminate against women, who made up the largest proportion of part-time workers in Germany. The option to exclude this category of workers, though this was explicitly provided for in the Directive, would breach the relevant ECJ case law and should therefore not be used (Interview D6: 185–210). After protracted negotiations between the Departments and the coalition parties, it was finally agreed not to use the eight-hour exemption, but to create a threshold excluding all workers whose annual working time did not exceed 400 hours. This solution was in accordance with another derogation option of the Directive, permitting the exclusion of casual or specific work (see above). By the time this intra-coalition conflict was resolved, however, the implementation deadline had long since passed.

Spain's performance was even worse than Germany's. Correct implementation was not effectuated until five years after the EU deadline. A long-standing conflict on a related issue had shaken the polity right at the start of the 1990s. In 1991, a law was enacted stipulating that the employee representatives of a company were entitled to a copy of any new employment contract within ten days. This had been agreed bilaterally between the Socialist government and the unions, but raised serious opposition from the employers' side. The relevant political actors wanted to let things 'cool down' before the transposition of the Directive opened up this controversial issue again and so they opted for a rudimentary transposition that did not touch the contentious questions (Interview E4: 222–40). After a long while, full transposition was completed without any significant conflict. Hence, the assumed needs of domestic politics were given priority over European policies and the duties of EU membership.

Italy was almost as 'bad' an EU member as Spain in this case. It took four years beyond the implementation deadline and even a Reasoned Opinion from the Commission in an infringement procedure to make Italian law comply with the relevant EU provisions – all this for a case of small-scale policy misfit, as all relevant actors agreed (e.g. Interviews I8: 29–102, I6: 289–93). Italy already possessed a number of rules on written employment contracts from the 1980s. It only needed to adapt the scope of application and the details required to be included in the written information. In the end, Italy incorporated the provisions of the Directive almost word for word in a legislative decree (*decreto legislativo*). Since there were no signs of political conflict or opposition to the Directive, the delay was due entirely to administrative inefficiency.

Ireland was almost one year late in eliminating low-level policy misfit. The Directive was undisputed, but administrative bottlenecks, combined with higher priorities for other (domestic as well as European) legislative projects, which were ostensibly more important than the minor adaptations required by the Directive, prevented timely adaptation.[7]

The same can be said for Luxembourg, the prime candidate in our sample for administrative overload. Since a similar rule to the Employment

---

[7] In May 1992, the sponsoring Department of Enterprise and Employment was in charge of implementing a total of thirty EU Directives, primarily in the field of occupational health and safety (Dáil Deb., 27 May 1992, cols. 772–6). Moreover, the Department introduced no fewer than five major bills of national origin during 1993 (Dáil Deb., 9 December 1993, col. 208).

Contract Information Directive had already existed since 1989 (Interview LUX1: 768–89), implementation of the few adaptations required by the Directive appeared to be rather irrelevant in the eyes of the national policy-makers. Conditions of structural administrative overload necessitated that administrative action should follow the imperative of 'what is most important is to be done first'. It comes as no surprise, then, that the Directive was not transposed until two years after the deadline.

In Portugal, medium-scale misfit was created by this Directive, which was not welcome in principle. The transposing Portuguese legislative decree closely followed the text of the Directive – more specifically, the Portuguese text of the Directive. This version, however, lacked Paragraph c of Article 4.1 that guarantees posted workers information about the benefits in cash or kind attendant on their employment abroad, and so did the Portuguese transposition law from January 1994. This is a most curious story, especially given the fact that the Commission, apparently unaware of this inaccuracy in translation, criticised the lack of a provision relating to Article 4.1.c of the Directive in its implementation report (CEC 1999: 14). The EU's Babylonian diversity of official languages thus created a translation error which led to a situation in which the Portuguese transposition of the Employment Contract Information Directive is still not fully in line with the requirements regarding information for posted workers.[8]

Transposition in the United Kingdom was almost on time, which should not seem so surprising given the modest degree of adaptation

---

[8] It could not be established irrefutably whether this case was related to the highly contentious Posted Workers Directive. However, there is some evidence pointing in that direction. Although this Directive was only adopted in 1996, it had already been debated in a rather agitated way by the time the Employment Contract Information Directive had to be transposed. The Commission initiative on Posted Workers was triggered by an important ECJ judgment (Judgment of the Court of 27 March 1990, Case C-113/ 89, *Rush Portuguesa Lda* v. *Office national d'immigration* [1990] ECR I-1417) in a case involving a Portuguese construction enterprise (Rush Portuguesa). This judgment allowed the Portuguese firm to have its Portuguese workers build a railway track in France even before the freedom of movement of workers with Portugal came into force, referring to the freedom to provide services within the EC. Subsequently, the Commission presented a draft Directive in April 1991 aimed at guaranteeing a number of minimum working conditions (including wages) for posted workers on the basis of the standards applied in the country of their actual work. The object was to protect the social standards of the member states with higher pay, which were in competition with companies from other EU member states that could, if such protection was not in place, profit from the freedom to provide services in a way that was perceived to destabilise the former ('social dumping'). It is rather striking in the light of this that the very paragraph referring to *information regarding the benefits attendant on the employment abroad for posted workers*, as included in the other language versions of the Employment Contract Information Directive, should be missing in the Portuguese version of the Directive, especially given the fact that it reportedly took intensive negotiations up to the night before the final Council meeting to overcome Portuguese opposition to the Directive (Interview LUX1: 795–7).

required by the Directive. More surprising, however, was the fact that the neo-liberal Tory government accepted the Directive in the first place, even though it could have used its power of veto (which it had used on many other occasions before). The small degree of misfit for the UK tells only part of the story. When the Directive was presented by the Commission, the British Employment Secretary, Michael Howard argued that any European measure that disturbed the national status quo, as modest as it might be, was not welcome since it would nevertheless 'add to the burden on employers' (quoted in EIRR 206: 28). Why, then, did the British government change its mind and abstain in the final vote to let the Directive pass (*Financial Times*, 27 June 1991, p. 24; Hansard, HC, 18 October 1991, col. 265)? The answer is that the Directive's focus on the individual relationship between employer and employee squared well with the Conservatives' general anti-union policy.[9]

It was only consistent that the Directive was transposed as part of a larger legislative package whose explicit aim was to curtail trade union power further at the workplace. In its ideologically motivated struggle against trade union influence, the government even created more 'red tape' for employers than should have been required by the Directive (which was, ironically, criticised by the Labour opposition, see Ewing 1993). In fact, the transposition legislation was much more restrictive than necessary with regard to the possibility of referring to collective agreements as a means of information – the aim being to strengthen individual ties between employers and workers (*Financial Times*, 12 February 1992, p. 18).

4.4.2   Timeliness and correctness of transposition

Looking at the point in time at which the member states transposed the Directive *essentially correctly*,[10] only four member states were on time: Austria, Denmark, Finland and Sweden. The delay of the Netherlands and the UK was less than six months, Portugal's and Ireland's less than twelve. Two member states were between one and two years late: Greece and Luxembourg. Germany, Italy, Spain and Belgium were more than two years late in this case. At the time of writing, one member state still did not fulfil the standards of the Directive essentially correctly.

---

[9] That was also the tenor of an advisory report given to government by the Institute of Economic Affairs, a neo-liberal think tank, in the run-up to EU-level decision-making (*Financial Times*, 12 September 1990, p. 2, 29 November 1990, p. 15).

[10] That is the point in time at which the national rules and regulations satisfied the standards of the Directive almost completely, with only minor details missing or incorrect.

This means that the essentially correct transposition of the Directive was completed in timely or at least 'almost timely' fashion (i.e. delayed not more than six months) in six out of fifteen cases. Accordingly, the transposition of the Employment Contract Information Directive was *'significantly delayed'* (i.e. delayed for at least six months) by almost *two-thirds* of the member states.

By the end of our period of analysis, France had not implemented the Directive essentially correctly. At the end of April 2003, French legislation did not provide for information about the commencement date of the employment relationship and about the place of work. Moreover, the information for expatriate employees prior to their departure was not guaranteed, and only expatriate (but not 'normal') workers had to be notified in writing of modifications to employment conditions.

When we increase the standards for judging transposition performance and consider *completely correct transposition*, two additional cases of non-compliance come to light. In Austria, several smaller shortcomings existed. It seems that the province of Burgenland failed to adopt implementing regulations and so the provisions of the Directive are not guaranteed for civil servants working in provincial administration (CEC 1999: 7). Our interviews also revealed that apartment house caretakers (*Hausmeister*) have been excluded from the scope of the rules (Interview A2: 226–58). In addition, when conditions of the employment relationship are modified, the relevant Austrian law does not provide for an appropriate deadline within which the written information has to be issued, and the Austrian regulations do not contain a provision on the amount of paid leave or the notice period to be observed in the case of dismissal (CEC 1999: 9, 16). In Portugal, as has already been mentioned, the provision with regard to information rights for posted workers, which is not included in the Portuguese language version of the Directive, is still missing from the transposition law.

Figure 4.1 outlines the timing of the member states in terms of *essentially correct* and *completely correct* transposition of the Employment Contract Information Directive.

4.5   National problems with application and enforcement

As far as the practical compliance of national employers with the Directive's provisions is concerned, our interviews have revealed significant application problems in a number of countries, notably France (Interview F6: 460–5), Germany (Interviews D5: 1001–34, 1249–94, D8: 411–82), Greece (Interview GR9: 368–77), Ireland (Interview IRL5: 373–94), the Netherlands (Interview NL9: 919–71), and Portugal (Interviews

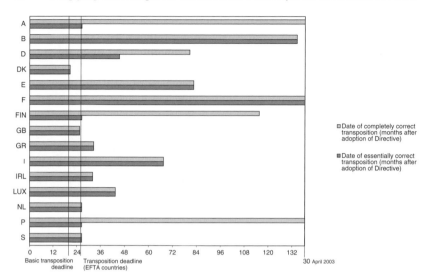

Figure 4.1 The Employment Contract Information Directive and timing of adaptation

P1: 684–8, P3: 318–20). For the most part, non-compliance concentrates on smaller establishments without specialised personnel departments (and usually with low union density). The main problem seems to be that both employers and employees often do not see the mutual benefits of writing down the essential terms and conditions of employment. Employers in Germany and Portugal in particular complained that the requirement permanently to inform workers about changes to their employment conditions was 'out of touch with reality' (Interviews D5: 1001–34; P4: 219–38). Workers, on the other hand, often lack awareness of their entitlement to written information when taking up a new job (see e.g. Interview IRL5: 376–83).

Under these circumstances, enforcement of the Directive through the court system is not an effective instrument with which to alleviate application problems. Nevertheless, breaches of the provisions have to be remedied in all member states by way of individual complaints to the courts. This is also true for the minority of countries, namely Luxembourg, France, Greece, and Spain, in which labour inspectorates are formally coresponsible for enforcement (Interviews LUX5: 170–95; F10: 548–57; GR3: 164–76, for Spain see CEC 1999: 15), because in reality no active inspection policy in relation to the standards in question is carried out in these countries either (Interviews F10: 1077–117; GR9: 368–77, E5).

One remedy for this situation could be improved information for employees so that they at least become aware of their rights and could, if need be, invoke them in court. As Austrian labour law experts have pointed out, however, in day-to-day practice it seems highly unlikely that someone would initiate a court case simply for not being given written information. This might, after all, invalidate the information by endangering (de facto) the employment relationship itself (Interview A6: 582–606). If enforcement via individual complaints to the courts cannot be expected to function effectively, member states should consider the possibility of actively controlling and enforcing the Directive through administrative authorities such as labour inspectorates.

In any case, the situation seems to differ from country to country. While no relevant case law is known in Austria, Danish employers have complained of a number of court cases that resulted in compensation having to be paid for non-fulfilment of the duty to furnish information (Interview DK3: 218–34). The altogether quite satisfactory application of the Directive in Denmark might also be due to the existence of a 'Labour Market Appeals Tribunal' (*Arbejdsmarkedets Ankenævn*), which, among other things, reacts to complaints arising from breaches of the Directive's standards (CEC 1999: 17).[11]

German disputes over the interpretation and application of the Directive have resulted in two ECJ decisions. The first one revealed the insufficient German transposition of a detail specified in the Directive and led to a subsequent revision of the German law.[12] The second ruling highlights the mutual benefits of the Directive's provisions in terms of legal clarity and transparency for employers and employees. It concerned the dismissal of an employee whose employer had argued that he was obliged to work a certain amount of overtime, which was refused by the employee. Since no overtime requirements were stated in the employee's job description, the Court held that the employee could not be obliged to work overtime and that, as a consequence, the dismissal was unlawful.[13]

A further problem in the day-to-day functioning of the Directive was witnessed in Austria, where experts from the labour side noted that some employers actually used the introduction of written information on

---

[11] Similar institutions concerned with the extra-judicial settlement of labour law disputes also exist, for example, in the UK and France.

[12] Judgment of the Court of 4 December 1997, joined cases C-253/96 to 258/96, *Helmut Kampelmann and others* v. *Landschaftsverband Westfalen-Lippe, Stadtwerke Witten GmbH* v. *Andreas Schade* and *Klaus Haseley* v. *Stadtwerke Altena GmbH* [1997] ECR I-6907.

[13] Judgment of the Court of 8 February 2001, case C-350/99, *Wolfgang Lange* v. *Georg Schünemann GmbH* [2001] ECR I-1061.

Table 4.2 *Overview of the Employment Contract Information Directive and its implementation*

Aim	Social: protection of workers' rights Economic: transparency of labour markets (national and international)
History	Commission Proposal 30 November 1990 Council Directive 14 October 1991 (Dutch Presidency)
Standards	6 binding standards (most importantly: written information on essential terms of employment relationship) 0 recommendations 4 exemption provisions
Degree of Misfit	High: 0 Medium: 3 Low: 12
Transposition problems	12 member states significantly delayed (at least six months) 1 member state has still not accomplished transposition essentially correctly

essential employment conditions as an opportunity to set down more employer-friendly conditions than practised before. It was difficult to protest at such a de facto lowering of standards, precisely because there had been no written proof before, and a number of conflicts were reported where the unions and works councils stepped in (Interviews A1: 1071–88, A6: 582–606). The Greek unions, too, were concerned about this possibility and it is thought to have occurred in some instances (Interview GR15). Trade unions in the Netherlands had been worried about similar problems during the transposition process (Interview NL12: 443–89), but in fact no large-scale abuse in this area could be discerned.

4.6   General assessment of the Directive's effects

On the level of common sense, the Employment Contract Information Directive has typically been judged to be a minor accomplishment within the EU's social policy Directives. A closer look confirms that no profound changes were brought about. However, some countries encountered not just low but, in overall terms, also medium degrees of policy misfit, according to our scale for inter-case comparison (see Table 4.2). Against this background of rather small-scale adaptation requirements, it may come as a surprise to note that the transposition of the Employment Contract Information Directive was '*significantly delayed*' (i.e. delayed for at least six months) in almost *two-thirds* of the member states. These results will be discussed in Chapter 14 in the context of the hypotheses presented in Chapter 2.

Aiming at an overall evaluation of this Directive's usefulness, a number of arguments should be taken into consideration. While it is true that the terms of the employment contract are not affected by the rule that written information must be issued, having a piece of paper pointing out a worker's rights and duties nevertheless provides for an improvement in terms of legal security. The individual may have better chances when claiming her or his rights than she or he would with an oral employment contract. This is why the majority of trade unions at the national level welcomed this Directive as an – albeit limited – improvement (see, for example, DGB 1991; Interviews A1: 955–84; B1: 401–12; DK1: 866–89; F6: 682–93; GB2: 565–613; GR9: 888–99; P3: 904–10; S3: 484–520).[14]

In particular, workers posted to other member states to carry out their duties are seen to have profited from the Directive (e.g. in Belgium, Interview B7: 1294–8). That they must possess a document stating their employment conditions is not only of importance at the individual level, however, but also beyond. The member state where they actually work has an easier task establishing what the posted workers' terms of contract are. This is of significance in fighting potential abuse of the freedom to provide services within the EU (e.g. in the construction sector).[15] It is significant in this context that the Directive's provision on compulsory written information for posted workers upon their departure was actually an innovation in all fifteen member states.

This leads us to the second goal of the EU's legislative initiative. As outlined above, the political aim of the Employment Contract Information Directive was not only social but also economic. Next to improving

[14] Some voiced a concern, however, that the new rules might initially lead to the specification of less employee-friendly conditions than pertained prior to the right to a written contract (on this transitory problem, see above). The Spanish trade unions seem to have been comparatively less interested in this Directive than they were about a potential individualisation effect. Spanish law had just introduced the obligation of the employer to give a copy of the employment contract to the employee *representatives* in the firm (E1: 462–5). In France, a number of union representatives felt that the Directive was superfluous (e.g. Interview F3: 867–95).

[15] Note that Directive 96/71/EC of the European Parliament and of the Council of 16 December 1996 concerning the posting of workers in the framework of the provision of services, OJ 1997 No. L018/1-6, was only adopted much later. According to this, the member states must ensure that, whatever the law applicable to the employment relationship, the undertakings must guarantee workers posted to their territory the terms and conditions of employment (covering, for instance, minimum pay and holidays) which are domestically laid down by law and/or by collective agreements. In any case, knowing the crucial terms of contract from a written document facilitates the supervision of respect for expatriate worker rights.

employee protection against possible infringements of rights, creating greater transparency on the labour market is also mentioned in the Directive (e.g. Consideration no. 2). While employer organisations typically complained about a certain amount of additional bureaucracy being created by 'Brussels' in this case, they rarely mentioned the effect of labour market transparency as a benefit arising from the Directive. By contrast, some employer representatives even explicitly stated that the Directive did not fall into their particular field of interest (e.g. Interview A5: 361–7, 90–127). This suggests that bureaucrats are actually more interested in labour market transparency than business is. One explanatory factor seems to be that fighting such aspects as the potential abuse of posted workers (see above) is primarily a task for national bureaucracies while it tends to serve the individual enterprise only indirectly.

When searching for a general guideline for evaluating and comparing the benefits of EU social Directives, two questions seem crucial. First, is a Directive useful in terms of the EU's internal market and/or its 'social dimension'? Second, is the Directive an improvement in terms of the social rights and standards applicable in the member states?

The first question is based on an EU-level oriented yardstick. In the case of the Employment Contract Information Directive, the answer is clearly positive. Even in purely economic terms, transparency on the cross-national labour market is crucial, for the optimal allocation of production factors depends on adequate information. In addition, this Directive favours the social dimension since transparency also makes for better control over the potential misuse of posted workers. This is of particular benefit for one of the socially weakest groups on the labour market.

The second question of improvements to national social standards and rights is oriented towards the de facto consequences of a Directive. Where the effects differ between member states, an aggregated answer is needed. It could be negative if more harm than good is done. In the case in hand, it seems that the legal security of workers has at least been somewhat enhanced in all member states, although no quantum leaps have been observed. In addition, there is no case where legal standards have been lowered, even though in some countries certain employers have appeared in practice to use the introduction of the Directive's information standards to fix less favourable employment conditions in the written statements.

The overall conclusion may be that the Employment Contract Information Directive is a small, but useful, step in terms of the EU's internal market, its social dimension, and the social standards in the member states.

5 The Pregnant Workers Directive: European social policy between protection and employability

5.1 Aim and contents of the Directive

The Pregnant Workers Directive[1] is one of the 'daughter Directives' enacted as a follow-up to the 1989 Framework Directive on Health and Safety.[2] While the Framework Directive introduced a general system of occupational safety and health, based on risk assessments, preventive measures, and the collaboration of employers, employee representatives and occupational physicians, the focus of the Pregnant Workers Directive is on new or expectant mothers, that is, on a particularly vulnerable group of workers who face specific risks at the workplace. The *general aim* of the Directive is 'to encourage improvements in the safety and health at work of pregnant workers and workers who have recently given birth or who are breastfeeding' (Article 1).

To fulfil this aim, the Directive includes a set of fourteen *compulsory minimum standards*. These can be divided into standards relating to occupational health and safety in a narrow sense, and into provisions belonging to the realm of employment rights more generally understood.

So far as health and safety issues are concerned, the Directive provides the following.

(1) Employers have to evaluate the potential risks to new and expectant mothers working in their establishments, taking into account a list of agents, processes and working conditions specified in the first annex to the Directive.

(2) Female workers and/or their representatives must be informed about the results of this assessment.

---

[1] Council Directive 92/85/EEC of 19 October 1992 on the introduction of measures to encourage improvements in the safety and health at work of pregnant workers and workers who have recently given birth or are breastfeeding (tenth individual Directive within the meaning of Article 16(1) of Directive 89/391/EEC), OJ 1992 No. L348/1–8.

[2] Council Directive 89/391/EEC of 12 June 1989 on the introduction of measures to encourage improvements in the safety and health of workers at work, OJ 1989 No. L183/1–8.

(3) Employers have to prevent women from being exposed to such risks by adjusting their working conditions, moving them to another job, or granting them leave for the necessary period.

(4) Pregnant and breastfeeding women may under no circumstances be obliged to perform tasks involving exposure to certain agents and working conditions listed in a second annex to the Directive.

(5) New or expectant mothers may not be forced to work at night but may, on the basis of a medical certificate, ask to be transferred by their employer to a daytime job or, if that is not possible, to be granted leave.

(6) Furthermore, the Directive calls on the Commission to draw up a set of guidelines which should serve as a basis for the risk assessment carried out by employers, and it requires member states to inform all employers and all female workers and/or their representatives of these guidelines.

The Directive provides the following as far as the wider employment rights are concerned.

(7) Every working mother is entitled to take at least fourteen weeks of maternity leave.

(8) This includes at least two weeks of compulsory leave.

(9) During periods of leave on health and safety grounds (see (3) above), an adequate allowance must be provided.

(10) During maternity leave, women are entitled to receive pay or allowance which must at least be equivalent to the benefits received during periods of sickness.

(11) Throughout maternity or health and safety leave, all employment rights have to be maintained.

(12) Moreover, pregnant workers are to be granted time off with pay for the necessary medical examinations.

(13) They may not be dismissed at any time during the period from the start of pregnancy to the end of maternity leave.

(14) Finally, member states have to provide judicial mechanisms or other means that enable women who feel that their rights have been violated to pursue their claims.

Compared with the other Directives in our sample, there are few *possibilities for derogating from these standards*. With regard to protection from dismissal, employers may indeed dismiss new or expectant mothers, but only in exceptional cases not connected to their pregnancy or maternity, and subject to the proviso that the employer produces a written declaration of the reasons for such a dismissal. Furthermore, member states may make the right to paid leave dependent on certain eligibility criteria, which in the case of a period of previous employment, however, may not exceed twelve months.

Finally, the Directive contains one *non-binding soft-law provision*. It stresses that the aim of protecting new and expectant mothers at work should be balanced against the goal of female labour market participation. Hence, 'the protection of the safety and health of pregnant workers, workers who have recently given birth or workers who are breastfeeding should not treat women on the labour market unfavourably nor work to the detriment of Directives concerning equal treatment for men and women' (Consideration no. 9).[3]

In sum, the Pregnant Workers Directive, despite its rather narrow focus on one specific group of workers, is quite wide-ranging in that it contains a comparatively large number of binding standards. In our sample, it is the Directive with the highest number of compulsory provisions. It also appears to be a relatively strict and clear-cut piece of Community legislation, since it contains only two opportunities to derogate from the binding standards and only one soft-law provision. But as we will see in the next section, the decision-making process leading to the adoption of the Directive was marked by two opposing regulatory philosophies. Since the conflict between these two approaches was never resolved, the Directive's provisions are somewhat Janus-faced, which has subsequently given rise to implementation problems.

5.2   The European-level negotiation process

When the Commission tabled its 'Proposal for a Council Directive concerning the protection at work of pregnant women or women who have recently given birth' (COM [1990] 406), public debates were dominated by controversies over the wider employment rights provision of the proposed measure. As often, the Conservative UK government was one of the most fervent opponents of the draft Directive. While the British government seemed to accept the health and safety standards (narrowly defined), it was opposed to the wider employment rights provisions laid down in the Commission proposal, especially with a view to the level of payment granted during maternity leave (EIRR 210: 13).

---

[3] In our analysis of the non-binding provisions enshrined in our Directives, we have also looked at the general considerations that usually precede the articles of a Directive. These general considerations, which have no binding legal force per se, usually do no more than rephrase the main standards of a Directive. But in some cases (as in the Pregnant Workers Directive), they also contain additional appeals to member states, and we have included such additional recommendations in our list of soft-law provisions.

The draft Directive was introduced on the basis of Article 118a, that is as a health and safety measure and so it only required a qualified majority of votes in the Council to be adopted. The draft provided for fourteen weeks of maternity leave on full pay, with the possibility of restricting eligibility to women who have enjoyed at least nine months' prior employment. This would have meant high costs for the UK, where maternity pay at the time was much lower and many women were completely denied the right to take maternity leave (EIRR 203: 19). In light of these considerable adaptation costs, the Tory government argued that the proposal would damage the job prospects of women rather than increase their protection levels. At the procedural level, the UK questioned the validity of the draft Directive's legal basis, arguing that the provisions on maternity leave belonged to the realm of labour law rather than to the sphere of health and safety, and thus had to be subject to unanimity rather than to qualified majority voting (*Financial Times*, 26 June 1991, p. 22). This criticism was shared by the Netherlands, Ireland, and Spain, although these countries seemed to accept the substance of the proposal (EIRR 210: 13).

The Dutch presidency finally reached a compromise which went quite some way towards accommodating the UK's objections. The compromise provided that the payment during maternity leave only had to be set at the level of sickness benefits. Owing to the low level of statutory sickness pay in the UK, this compromise meant that the overall level of maternity benefits of British women would only have to be raised very slightly. Moreover, the eligibility threshold was raised from nine months to one year, which further lowered adaptation costs for the UK (EIRR 217: 14–15). On the basis of this compromise, the Council reached political agreement on a Common Position in November 1991, with the British government abstaining (*Financial Times*, 7 November 1991, p. 2).

Adoption of the Directive was stalled for almost one year after the European Parliament proposed amendments to the Common Position, which would have considerably strengthened the draft. In particular, MEPs pushed for a substantial raising of maternity benefits to the level of at least 80 per cent of previous pay. The Commission supported this amendment and incorporated it into its revised proposal. According to the co-operation procedure, the Council could accept this proposal by qualified majority, but return to its Common Position only by unanimous vote. While eleven of the twelve member states agreed to return to the prior compromise, Italy, having already been discontent with the weak Common Position, refused to join the others, arguing that it favoured the proposal tabled by the Parliament and the Commission (EIRR 222: 2; *Financial Times*, 14 October 1992, p. 3).

In light of this strategic constellation, it is no surprise that the UK government, during its presidency in the second half of 1992, pressed for an adoption of the Directive, but only on the basis of the compromise agreed almost one year earlier (EIRR 225: 2–3). After protracted debates between the Commission, the Parliament and the Council, the UK presidency was finally able to convince the Italian delegation to abstain from the vote. This allowed the Directive to be passed on the basis of the diluted text agreed as a Common Position, without the strengthening proposals introduced by the European Parliament. The UK also abstained from the vote to demonstrate that it was still principally opposed to the Directive (EIRR 226: 2, 16–18).

But this highly politicised controversy over the level of pay during maternity leave was not the only point of disagreement between the member states. More or less unnoticed by the general public, there was a debate about the health and safety aspects of the Directive. The main focus here was on the question of how to strike the right balance between the principles of protection and employability. While countries like Germany or France wanted to upload their own systems of general, wide-ranging employment prohibitions to protect pregnant women, Ireland and the Netherlands favoured a system that focused much more on detailed risk assessments and individual medical requirements in order not to create unnecessary obstacles for women on the labour market (Interviews D2: 395–420; IRL3: 862–70; NL7: 599–605).

The clash between these two positions was not resolved during the negotiations in Council, but partly concealed by 'rhetorical' compromises. In Article 6, for instance, there is a clear discrepancy between the title, referring to '*cases in which exposure is prohibited*', and the actual content, which in fact only stipulates that pregnant and breastfeeding women 'may under no circumstances be *obliged* to perform duties for which the assessment has revealed a risk of exposure' to certain agents and working conditions (emphasis added, see also Vogel 1997). The following sections will reveal that this ambiguity, which in a similar fashion also applies to the provisions on night work, led to serious implementation problems in a number of countries.

5.3   Misfit in the member states: improving health and safety protection and removing general employment prohibitions

Despite these legal ambiguities, the Directive required significant adaptations in many countries. The provisions relating to the occupational safety and health of pregnant and breastfeeding women (risk assessment and measures to avoid exposure to these risks including paid health and safety leave) required reforms in all member states except Denmark. As far as the wider employment rights standards are concerned, the length of maternity leave had to be extended in Portugal (by one week) and Sweden (by two weeks) for all women, and in Germany and Luxembourg for women with certain types of premature births. In the UK, the existence of high thresholds with respect to previous employment requirements completely deprived many women of the right to take maternity leave and to receive maternity benefits. The Directive required these thresholds to be considerably lowered, thus allowing many more women to benefit from maternity protection. The provision relating to time off with pay for antenatal examinations required adaptations in no fewer than ten member states. Austria, Belgium, Denmark, Finland, France, Greece, Ireland, Luxembourg and Spain had to introduce such statutory entitlements and Germany was obliged to extend its existing scheme to women who were not covered by statutory health insurance.

Moreover, the provision protecting women from being dismissed on pregnancy or maternity-related grounds from the beginning of pregnancy to the end of maternity leave required changes to be made in five countries: Belgium and Germany had to effect only minor adaptations to the detail; Spain was obliged to specify its general constitutional clause prohibiting dismissals on discriminatory grounds so as to guarantee the detailed requirements of the Directive; the UK and Ireland were forced to eliminate the wide gaps existing in their dismissal protection schemes, which explicitly allowed the dismissal of women on grounds of pregnancy or maternity under certain conditions.

Surprisingly, all member states except Finland had to change their laws with regard to the Directive's provisions on night work. This standard, however, had a very varied impact at the national level. On the one hand, countries like Ireland, Spain and the UK did not have any statutory provisions protecting pregnant women from unhealthy night work.[4] In these countries, the Directive therefore required significant enhancements to the levels of protection for pregnant night workers. Minor improvements for this category of workers had also to be made in Denmark, the Netherlands and Sweden.

On the other hand, many countries had a complete ban on night work, either for all female blue-collar workers (France and Greece), specifically for pregnant women (Luxembourg and Germany, although with some

---

[4] The Spanish situation was characterised by a legal 'vacuum' which resulted from a 1992 ruling of the Constitutional Court in which the existing protective legislation enacted under the Franco regime was declared null and void.

Table 5.1 *The Pregnant Workers Directive and misfit in the member states*

	Degree of Legal Misfit	Limited Practical Significance	Degree of *Total Policy Misfit*	Degree of Politics/ Polity Misfit	Economic Costs	Degree of *Total Misfit*
A	medium	no	medium	–	low	medium
B	low	no	low	–	low	low
D	medium	no	medium	–	low	medium
DK	low	no	low	–	low	low
E	medium	yes	low	–	low	low
F	medium	yes	low	–	low	low
FIN	low	yes	low	–	low	low
GB	high	no	high	–	medium	high
GR	medium	no	medium	–	low	medium
I	medium	no	medium	–	low	medium
IRL	medium	no	medium	–	low	medium
LUX	medium	no	medium	–	low	medium
NL	low	no	low	–	low	low
P	medium	no	medium	–	medium	medium
S	medium	no	medium	–	medium	medium

exceptions), or for both female blue-collar workers in general as well as pregnant women in particular (Austria, Belgium, Italy, Portugal and Spain). All of these countries had the problem that their *general* night work bans were too restrictive and thus violated the general principle of the equal treatment of men and women. The Directive explicitly avoided such a restrictive approach since it only required member states to guarantee that new and expectant mothers 'are *not obliged to perform night work during their pregnancy and for a period following childbirth . . . , subject to submission . . . of a medical certificate* stating that this is necessary for the safety or health of the worker concerned' (Article 7 of the Directive, emphasis added). In these countries, the Directive therefore called for a less prohibitive system of protection which did not disadvantage women on the labour market. In countries that only had a general ban on night work for women in manufacturing, the downside of this over-restrictive approach to female blue-collar workers was that women employed outside the sector did not have any protection from dangerous night work at all.[5]

In sum, *all member states had to adapt their policies at least in some respect* (see Table 5.1). While six countries were in the relatively comfortable

---

[5] A partial exception to this is Belgium, where pregnant night workers employed outside manufacturing, but in the private sector, already had a system of protection equivalent to that provided for by the Directive. Thus, only female non-blue-collar workers in the public sector were affected by this gap in the system of protection.

position of having to enact merely small changes to their existing rules and regulations (Belgium, Denmark, Finland, France, the Netherlands and Spain), eight countries were confronted with medium levels of adaptational pressure (Austria, Germany, Greece, Italy, Ireland, Luxembourg, Portugal and Sweden). Finally, the UK was the only member state that had to deal with a high degree of policy misfit (see Chapter 2 for more details on the operationalisation of this concept). This is remarkable since the British government had successfully managed to achieve a considerable watering-down of the original Commission text. Nevertheless, the UK still faced large-scale adaptational pressure. Besides the points already mentioned above, the Directive called for a considerable enlargement of the scope of the UK's existing maternity leave scheme. Under the previous system, women had had to be continuously employed with the same employer for two years (part-time workers for five years!) before they had had the right to claim maternity leave and to receive maternity benefits. Part-time workers with fewer than eight working hours a week were completely excluded from maternity leave entitlements. Thus, before the Directive was issued, the right to maternity leave had been denied to about 40 per cent of pregnant women in the UK (Collins 1994: 10).

The Pregnant Workers Directive, like the Employment Contract Information Directive, did not cause misfit in the *politics and polity dimension*. It did not imply administrative reforms in the member states. The decision on how to organise the enforcement of the Directive's standards is entirely at the discretion of member states. All they have to do is provide for *any* kind of mechanism that enables women to assert their rights (see above). Likewise, the Directive did not touch upon the established relationship between the state and the social partners. Even in countries like Sweden or Denmark, with their tradition of autonomous social partner action, the protection of new and expectant mothers was a matter customarily governed by statutory rules.

Finally, the *economic costs* of implementing the Directive were low in most countries. This was due to the fact that the main changes required by the Directive consisted in the majority of cases either of largely cost-free qualitative adaptations, like the lifting of general employment prohibitions, or of a gradual improvement in health and safety standards. The 1989 Framework Directive had already brought about the potentially costly change towards a system of risk assessment. Nevertheless, in addition to this, some member states had to adjust their maternity leave schemes to a considerable degree, either by extending the duration of (paid) maternity leave or by widening the scope of the entitlements. As a result, the additional economic costs imposed by the Directive were medium-scale in Portugal, Sweden and the UK.

5.4   Implementation in the member states

5.4.1   *Particularly interesting cases*

From a misfit-oriented perspective, transposition of the Pregnant Workers Directive in the UK must come as a surprise. As we have seen above, the UK was the only country confronted with large adaptational pressure. Moreover, the significant extension of the scope of the existing maternity leave scheme, together with the other reforms required by the Directive, involved serious economic costs. According to government estimates, the additional annual costs caused by implementing the Directive amounted to between 160 and 220 million euros (HSC 1994, *Financial Times*, 17 October 1994, p. 14). Nevertheless, the UK was the second member state (after Denmark) to incorporate the provisions of the Directive correctly into national law, accomplishing this task only three and a half months after the deadline.

The reason for this seemingly astonishing outcome is that the Conservative government, in contrast to its stance on the Working Time or Young Workers Directives (see Chapters 6 and 7), did not in this case fight the rules to be enacted on ideological grounds. The statutory rules on maternity leave and the area of occupational health and safety had not been affected by the deregulation strategy of the Thatcher and Major administrations. After the provisions involving the highest costs had been successfully watered down in Brussels, it was no surprise that the Tory government did not use this Directive as an example to demonstrate its disagreement publicly with EC employment regulations, but instead complied with the rules. At any rate, this case demonstrates that large-scale misfit does not necessarily have to give rise to serious implementation deficits.

In contrast, the transposition of this Directive in several other countries reveals that even low or medium levels of adaptational pressure may result in considerably delayed or flawed adaptation. On the one hand, these cases demonstrate that the logic underlying the misfit-centred view in EU implementation research, i.e. the expectation that national governments and administrations are keen to protect their existing regulatory systems from fundamental changes imposed by Brussels, may also be activated by less far-reaching EU requirements. On the other hand, they also show that there are many other stumbling blocks to fast and correct adaptation besides the sheer degree of changes required by a Directive.

More than eight years after the end of the implementation deadline, Germany has still not managed to transpose the medium-level adaptation requirements of the Directive correctly. The reforms originally deemed necessary to comply with the Directive could only be enacted two and a half years after the expiry of the implementation deadline. Adoption of the measures was stalled because the parliamentary term ended before the Bill could be passed. Hence, the Bill had to be reintroduced in the aftermath of the 1994 elections. Moreover, a number of issues was added to the reforms necessitated by the Directive, causing controversial debates and thus further delays (Interview D3: 228–43).[6] The necessity of additional adaptation to the Maternity Protection Act only became obvious a few years later, after several court cases had been initiated by women who had not received the full entitlement of fourteen weeks of maternity leave because they had given birth prematurely (Interview D3: 474–522).[7] This problem was subsequently eliminated by a revision of the Act which came into force in June 2002.

Like many other member states, Germany has still not lifted its general ban on night work for pregnant and breastfeeding women, from which only women employed in a number of sectors like hotels and restaurants or entertainment are excluded. Here, the Directive's approach of stressing the employability of women clashed with the regulatory philosophy underlying the existing German system with its focus on general employment prohibitions. Officials from the Department of Family Affairs have so far openly refused to adapt the existing system to the Directive, claiming that the general ban on night work for pregnant women was more favourable to women than the Directive's system of avoiding dangerous night work on the basis of individual medical certificates. According to this interpretation, changing the system would constitute a lowering of protection levels, which was explicitly forbidden by the Directive (Interview D2: 275–326).

Interestingly, during the EU-level negotiations on the Directive, the Commission seems to have assured German negotiators that the general ban on night work for new and expectant mothers was in line with the Directive and could thus be upheld (Interview D3: 203–27, 356–65).

---

[6] The most controversial of these added issues concerned the protection of domestic servants from dismissal. Pressed by an interest group representing domestic servants, the government agreed to repeal a provision which allowed domestic servants to be dismissed after becoming pregnant, and provided them with state-financed compensation payments. This step, which was not called for by the Directive because domestic servants were generally exempted from its scope, caused resistance among many Christian Democratic and Liberal members of the parliamentary Committee on Economic Affairs, who considered it an unnecessary obstacle to the employment of domestic servants (Interview D3: 257–322; BT-Drucksache 13/2763: 12).

[7] This problem was due to the fact that maternity leave in Germany was divided into six weeks before and eight weeks after birth. For example, if the baby was born three days earlier than expected, these three days were not added to the eight-week postnatal leave, but lapsed (Interview D3: 474–522).

Given this informal 'okay' by the Commission, combined with the German actors' perception that their own system was superior to the Directive's approach, it is no surprise that the ban on night work was not tackled in the original reform initiatives. In the meantime, however, the Commission changed its mind. In its report on the implementation of the Directive published in 1999, the Commission criticised the general German ban on night work as contrary to EU law and announced that an infringement procedure was likely to be initiated (COM [1999] 100: 10). There are many indications suggesting that this change of mind was due to a reshuffling of responsibility for the Directive within the relevant Directorate-General of the Commission. While the EU-level negotiations were managed by the Directorate dealing with occupational health and safety, the implementation report was prepared by the Directorate on gender equality (Interviews D2: 366–85; EU1: 50–90), the latter being much more critical of general employment prohibitions for women than the former.

While not only the relevant administrative actors, but also the German centre-right government (in office until 1998) seemed to be opposed to lifting the general ban on night work, there have recently been signs of a change in this position under the 'red–green' government of Chancellor Schröder. In a recent parliamentary debate, the Greens in particular called for a lifting of the discriminatory ban on night work for pregnant women, and a government representative subsequently announced that a fundamental overhaul of the Maternity Protection Act will be carried out in the near future (BT Plenarprotokoll 14/234, 26 April 2002, pp. 23366–9).

Similar to Germany, the Austrian government has so far not succeeded in changing its rules and regulations so as to fulfil the medium-level adaptation requirements of the Directive. Administrative overload in the wake of Austria's accession to the EU delayed the enactment of the original transposition law for more than nine months (Interview A2a). Moreover, following claims from small and medium-sized enterprises that they would not be able to reorganise their health and safety procedures in time (Interview A2a), the government provided for a phased-in commencement of these rules, which was contrary to the Directive. According to this scheme, all companies were granted a two-year period of grace before they had to apply the new standards. At the end of this period, only large enterprises were obliged to put the new system into operation, while smaller enterprises only had to comply step by step. As a result, full coverage of all companies was not reached until 1 July 2000, more than five and a half years later than required. Finally, Austria still has not lifted its general ban on night work for pregnant and breastfeeding women. As in

Germany, the existing scheme is considered superior to the system provided for by the Directive. Hence, both government and administrative actors are opposed to lifting the general ban on night work and even seem to be ready to face an EU infringement procedure (Interview A2: 440–8), as has been announced in the Commission's implementation report (COM [1999] 100: 10).

In France, a small degree of misfit was followed by years of inertia. The reason again was that most French actors considered the existing statutory scheme of protecting pregnant and breastfeeding women sufficiently compliant with the EU Directive and partly even superior to what had been written into the European piece of legislation (Interviews F2: 523–6, F3: 175–9, 589–91, F5: 477–80, F9: 688–9). Hence, for several years the government refused to introduce specific leave for health and safety reasons connected to pregnancy, until the Commission initiated an infringement procedure. It was argued that, according to the existing French legislation, maternity leave could be extended for up to six additional weeks in cases of pathological pregnancies and on the basis of a medical certificate, and that therefore the national regulation and practice did not need to be changed. But the Directive required member states to guarantee that new or expectant mothers are given the right to paid leave not only for six weeks, but *for the whole period necessary to protect them* from dangerous substances or working conditions, provided that no suitable alternative employment is available. Even though trade unions had pointed to this incompatibility between the French regulation and the EU Directive, the French government stated that the national model provided sufficient or even better protection (Interview F6: 467–91). It was not until February 2001 that France gave in to European pressure and amended its legislation accordingly.

It took even more time before France correctly transposed the Directive's rules on night work. There were no specific statutory provisions regulating night work for new or expectant mothers, but France, like many other countries, had a general ban on night work for all female blue-collar workers, which was based on ILO Convention 89 adopted in 1948. This general ban on night work for women employed in manufacturing had been declared contradictory to EU equality law by the European Court of Justice in 1991.[8] As a result, France had to lift its general ban on night work. This process, however, turned out to be highly controversial since both left-wing and right-wing governments and even leftist trade unionists (see, for example, Interview F3: 888–9) supported the existing ban

---

[8] See the ECJ ruling in the *Stoeckel* case (Judgment of the Court of 25 July 1991, case C-345/89, *Criminal proceedings against Alfred Stoeckel* [1991] ECR I-4047).

as a measure that protected women from harmful working conditions and so lifting the ban was resisted for a long time. Under these circumstances, the need to transpose the night work rules pertaining to pregnant women was politically linked to this highly contentious issue (Interviews F3: 871–8, F7: 975–88). Hence, it could not be tackled successfully until the debates surrounding the removal of the general ban on night work for women had been resolved. In this case, issue linkage explains why the rules protecting pregnant women from dangerous night work were only enacted in May 2001, together with the decision to lift the general ban on night work for women in manufacturing.[9]

Similar resistance against the need to remove general night work prohibitions, again caused by the belief of national actors that the existing national systems were superior to the Directive's scheme, could be witnessed in Luxembourg and Italy. The Italian government has still not lifted its general ban on night work for pregnant women in manufacturing, which the Commission considers a breach of EU law (COM [1999] 100: 10). In addition, administrative inefficiency caused delays of more than two years in enacting the remaining (minor) adaptation requirements arising from the Directive.

Likewise, for almost four years after the implementation deadline had expired, Luxembourg's general lack of administrative resources prevented adoption of the original transposition legislation. However, the transposition Act adopted in 1998 was seriously flawed. Not only did Luxembourg still uphold its general ban on night work for pregnant women, but the Act also failed to comply with the risk assessment approach laid down in the Directive. These problems have to be ascribed at least partly to the unclear wording and the somewhat Janus-faced regulatory philosophy of the Directive (as outlined above). Prior to the Directive, there was a list of activities which were absolutely prohibited for pregnant women. The 1998 reform simply added the activities set out in the annexes of the Directive to this list, which resulted in a situation where pregnant women were debarred from doing almost any kind of work (Interview LUX2: 49–327).

It is interesting to note that, similar to the German case, the Luxembourg government had received an informal 'okay' from the European Commission for the first transposition law (Interview LUX2: 483–508), which included the night work ban and lacked the risk assessment. At a

---

[9] *Loi relative à l'égalité professionelle entre femmes et les hommes* (397–2001), Journal Officiel, 10 mai 2001. The night work rules for pregnant women became fully operational only one year later, when a legislative decree spelled out the details of how employers, workers and occupational physicians should proceed in practice (*Décret en Conseil d'Etat* 2002–792, Journal Officiel, 5 mai 2002).

later stage, however, the Commission no longer accepted this method of implementation. After it had initiated an infringement procedure against Luxembourg, these errors were corrected. As a result, Luxembourg only correctly managed to overcome the medium-scale misfit arising from the Directive about seven years after the expiry of the deadline.

In Spain, a mixture of issue linkage, unwillingness on the part of government to change the existing national policies, inadvertence, and the unclear wording of the Directive, led to a situation where some of the altogether minor adaptation requirements were only satisfied years after the deadline, while essential parts of what had to be changed still have not been transposed correctly. The first reform stage was delayed by more than a year since it was coupled with the very controversial transposition of the Health and Safety Framework Directive (Interview E3: 1216–308, 1479–658). This reform was considered insufficient in the Commission's implementation report (COM [1999] 100: 8 and 14). First, Spain only had a general constitutional clause prohibiting dismissals on discriminatory grounds, but no specific legislation making dismissals of new and expectant mothers unlawful. Spanish officials had thought the general constitutional clause to be sufficiently compliant with the standards. Second, Spanish legislation did not provide for health and safety leave. Contrary to the Directive, which explicitly stipulates that pregnancy should not be equated with illness (Consideration No. 18 of the Directive), pregnant or breastfeeding women who could not continue their work on health and safety grounds were simply sent on sick leave (Interviews E1: 625–32, E3: 812–17).

While these flaws were largely eliminated after the Commission's intervention, Spain still has not transposed the annexes of the Directive which list the dangerous substances and working conditions that have to be taken into account in any assessment of the risks to pregnant and breastfeeding women.[10] This gap had to be closed in response to the Directive, but the Spanish government was unwilling to do so. Despite union pressure, the government has so far failed to take any steps to transpose the Directive's annexes (Interview E1: 486–8, 636–53). In the original transposition process, the unclear wording of the Directive offered an elegant opportunity for the government to postpone the adaptation to the annexes. In Article 3 of the Directive, it was stipulated that the Commission would produce guidelines for the implementation of the annexes. Hence, the

---

[10] Since 1957, Spain has had a very comprehensive list of activities that are absolutely prohibited for new and expectant mothers. After the 1957 Decree was annulled by the Spanish Constitutional Court in 1993, because it was held to be contrary to gender equality principles, there was a legislative gap with regard to the health and safety protection of pregnant and breastfeeding women (Interviews E3: 608–27, 705–8, E3b).

government argued that it would wait for these guidelines to be drawn up before tackling the annexes. But it was not until 2000 that the Commission, in collaboration with national representatives, finally published them (COM [2000] 466). It turned out, however, that these guidelines were only a set of non-compulsory recommendations for employers and occupational physicians. Hence, the Spanish government only published a non-binding code of practice as a reaction to the Commission guidelines (Interview E3b) and continued to neglect the compulsory nature of the Directive's annexes. In this case, correct implementation would have been greatly facilitated if the original EU policy had been clearer and more demanding from the outset.

The Portuguese case shows the positive impact of the direct effect principle on proper implementation of EU Directives, especially when used as a threat by domestic interest groups. At the time of the Directive's adoption, Portugal did not meet the standard with respect to the length of maternity leave provided. During the national legislative process it became clear that the EU standards would only enter into force in Portugal once the transposition deadline had expired. Some women who became pregnant or gave birth after the transposition deadline would thus be deprived of eight days of maternity leave. When trade unions in coalition with the media picked up on the issue, the government saw itself forced to introduce the required extension of maternity leave retrospectively in order not to become subject to numerous ECJ rulings prompted by these workers (Interview P1: 1590–7, 1606–23). Hence, actual or threatened pressure from societal interests – which is unlikely in the typical Portuguese implementation processes – assured the timely implementation of this standard in this case.

In many of the cases mentioned so far, national governments and/or administrations openly refused to adapt to the Directive because they thought their existing policy models superior to the EU Directive's standards. While the thrust of this resistance in these cases was directed against having to relax systems of general employment prohibitions for new and expectant mothers, there is also one case in which a national government opposed transposition because it considered its existing scheme more conducive to female labour market participation than the system of the Directive. In Sweden, most parts of the reforms required by the Pregnant Workers Directive, including the extension of maternity leave by two weeks, were transposed without further problems and almost on time. The introduction of a two-week compulsory maternity leave, however, was not completed until August 2000, i.e. roughly six years after the end of the transposition period, and after the European Commission had instigated an infringement procedure. The Swedish government's official position was that the pre-existing twelve (later fourteen) weeks of *optional* maternity leave de facto guaranteed exactly the same level of protection. It argued that women in Sweden generally made use of the maternity leave for much longer than two weeks so that *forcing* them to stay at home for two weeks was neither necessary (Interview S8: 411–56) nor very conducive to female labour market participation. The contention that compulsory maternity leave was unnecessary had also prevented Sweden from joining the relevant ILO conventions on maternity protection (Interview S12). Only after the intervention of the European Commission did Sweden finally give in and introduce the compulsory leave required by the Directive.

5.4.2   Timeliness and correctness of transposition

Given widespread national resistance against the Directive and frequent misinterpretations of its provisions due to unclear wording, it is not surprising that only two member states – Denmark and the Netherlands – had *transposed the Directive essentially correctly* when the implementation deadline expired. Ireland and the UK were less than six months late, Belgium between six and twelve months. The delay in France, Greece, Luxembourg and Sweden amounted to more than two years, while the remaining six countries had not yet reached the stage of essentially correct implementation by the end of our period of analysis (end of April 2003).

As a result, only slightly more than a quarter of all member states managed to implement the Directive essentially correctly *on time or at least almost on time* (i.e. no more than six months after the deadline). This means that almost three-quarters of all member states did not accomplish this task without *significant delay*.

Austria and Germany are among the six member states that failed to fulfil the standards of the Directive essentially correctly by 30 April 2003. Both countries still had not lifted their general night work bans for pregnant and breastfeeding women. The same was true for Italy, where such a general night work ban existed for pregnant and breastfeeding women employed in manufacturing. Spanish legislation still lacked adequate transposition of the annexes on dangerous substances and working conditions. Without these two lists, the pregnancy-related risk assessment cannot be carried out properly. Furthermore, the health and safety leave created in response to the Directive did not apply to breastfeeding women. In Finland, the health and safety protection provided by the Directive was restricted to pregnant women, while breastfeeding women

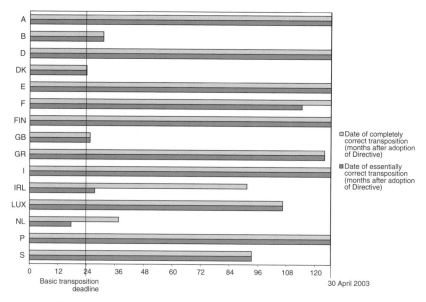

Figure 5.1 The Pregnant Workers Directive and timing of adaptation

were (and seemingly still are) not covered by these rules.[11] Finally, Portugal completely prohibited women from carrying out work involving the substances and working conditions listed in Annex 2, and it still maintained its general ban on night work for pregnant and breastfeeding women, although in a somewhat scaled-down version, prohibiting work at night for 118 days around the date of delivery.

If we look at completely correct transposition, one more case of non-compliance has to be mentioned. At the end of April 2003, France had not yet transposed the annexes to the Directive properly.

Figure 5.1 summarises the timing of the member states in terms of *essentially correct* and *completely correct* transposition of the Pregnant Workers Directive.

5.5   National problems with application and enforcement

As far as *practical compliance* with the rules on maternity leave and the health and safety protection of new and expectant mothers is concerned,

---

[11] We consider the protection of women against dangerous working conditions not only during pregnancy, but also during the (potentially much longer) period of breastfeeding an essential standard of the Directive.

the situation in most countries seems to be quite satisfactory. One problematic area in a number of countries is protection from dismissal. National experts from countries such as Belgium, France, Greece, the Netherlands, Spain and the UK have reported that legal disputes over unfair dismissals during pregnancy or maternity occur rather frequently (Interviews B7: 674–9; F10: 1182–209; E6: 61–79; NL10: 478–86, Petroglou 2000; James 2004: 26). However, there is no indication that these disputes are specifically related to the Directive. While in Spain the situation should be improving now that protection from dismissal has been made more explicit in response to the Directive, a Dutch expert has argued that the protection from unfair dismissal offered by the Pregnant Workers Directive is weaker than the one provided by sex discrimination legislation so that most of these cases have been dealt with under the latter rules (Interview NL10: 440–5).

Much more severe application problems have been reported in relation to compliance with the health and safety standards of the Directive. In Spain, there are general problems with the proper application of health and safety rules in smaller enterprises. In Greece, particular problems exist regarding the relatively large home-working sector, where predominantly women (and also pregnant women) are employed to produce textiles, leather goods or souvenirs, often under very unhealthy conditions. In this context, Agallopoulou refers to '*foyers cancérigènes*' (Agallopoulou 1999: 263–4). In Portugal, national experts report about general problems with applying health and safety regulations (Interview P1: 1452–61) and about resistance by employers to complying with these rules (Interview P3: 996–1000). One particularly problematic area in this respect seems to be the textiles and electronic industries in Northern Portugal, where many women are employed. Employers in this sector have to compete directly with low-cost producers from outside the European Union (in particular from Asia and Northern Africa, see Interviews P1: 1323–9, P5: 342–8; Cristovam 2001). This provides strong incentives to cut costs by circumventing strict health and safety rules.

At least some of the problems could be reduced by increasing enforcement efforts. In all member states, application of occupational safety and health regulations is actively monitored by labour inspectorates. But the resources available to the inspection authorities do not always seem to be sufficient, as the above-mentioned application problems clearly demonstrate. In many countries, the lack of adequately trained personnel undermines the correct implementation of the Pregnant Workers Directive, especially when it comes to the technical assessment of workplaces. Here, short-term non-compliance in the form of maintaining protection schemes based on absolute standards might even be better for the workers concerned than a half-heartedly implemented scheme that grants protection according to individually assessed needs – but without such assessments actually taking place.

Enforcement of the employment rights aspects of the Directive is dealt with in all countries by the courts. The problems regarding unfair dismissals do not appear to be related to systematic shortcomings in the institutional set-up of the domestic court systems. But there are differences between countries in relation to the availability of support and information for women who feel that they have been unlawfully dismissed on pregnancy-related grounds or have been refused their entitlements to maternity leave or benefits. Since these issues tend to have implications in terms of sex discrimination, supporting bodies which disseminate information and provide support to workers in equality-related claims also play a positive role here.[12]

5.6   General assessment of the Directive's effects

When trying to assess the overall effect of the Pregnant Workers Directive in the member states, the Janus-faced nature of the Directive has to be taken into account. The main goal of the Directive was to improve the health and safety protection of pregnant and breastfeeding women and to provide them with the necessary employment rights to avoid any disadvantages that might arise from this protection (see Table 5.2). In this respect, the Directive has actually improved the situation of new and expectant mothers in all member states to a certain extent – mostly by gradually tightening the health and safety standards, by requiring all member states to introduce a right to time off with pay for medical examinations during pregnancy (which had not been guaranteed in two-thirds of the countries), and by enhancing the previously insufficient dismissal protection rules obtaining in some countries. More importantly, the Directive closed considerable gaps in the maternity leave schemes: in the UK, where almost half of all employees had hitherto been excluded from the entitlements; in Portugal, where maternity leave had to be extended by one week for all working mothers; and in Sweden, where the length of maternity leave had to be extended by two weeks.

Apart from these moderate but noticeable enhancements to the social standards applying to pregnant and breastfeeding women, the Directive also had a second major impact on many member states. It necessitated

[12] One thinks of bodies like the Equal Opportunities Commission in the UK, the Equality Authority in Ireland, the Equal Treatment Commission in the Netherlands, or the gender equality ombudsperson in Sweden.

Table 5.2 *Overview of the Pregnant Workers Directive and its implementation*

Aim	To encourage improvements in the safety and health at work of pregnant workers and workers who have recently given birth or who are breastfeeding
History	Commission Proposal 11 September 1990 Council Directive 19 October 1992 (UK Presidency)
Standards	14 binding standards (most importantly: health and safety protection on basis of risk assessment, 14 weeks of maternity leave) 1 recommendation 2 exemption provisions
Degree of Misfit	High: 1 Medium: 8 Low: 6
Transposition problems	11 member states significantly delayed 6 member states have still not accomplished transposition essentially correctly

the removal of over-protective health and safety rules such as general night work bans or other blanket employment prohibitions applying to pregnant and breastfeeding women. As a consequence, the Directive also helped to overcome a number of serious impediments to the active participation of women in the labour market and thus promoted gender equality at the workplace. At the time that the Directive was debated at the European level, most observers and even some of the affected government representatives (see the German case described above) seem to have neglected the Directive's potential to bring about this second effect. As time went by, and as responsibility for the Directive within the Commission moved from the Directorate on occupational safety and health to the equality Directorate, the Directive turned out to be a 'Trojan horse', smuggled into member states' backyards, where it suddenly began to challenge the general employment prohibitions that were originally thought to be particularly favourable to women. This 'Trojan horse' strategy pursued by the Commission was facilitated by the fact that, during the negotiations, member states like the Netherlands and Ireland had taken great pains to ensure that the Directive was not modelled on the prohibitive approach of Germany, France or the southern member states but left enough room for individual assessments and the wishes of female employees. As a result of this, the Directive was worded so as to allow the Commission to challenge systems of general prohibitions operating at the national level.

It can be interpreted as a late victory of the 'employability faction' among national governments that the general night work bans for pregnant women (or all women in manufacturing) have already been lifted either completely or partially in Belgium, France, Greece, Luxembourg and Portugal, and will have to be removed in Austria, Germany and Italy in the near future – provided that the Commission pursues the respective infringement procedure against Italy or will actually initiate such proceedings against Germany and Austria, as already announced. Similarly, prohibitive health and safety rules have been turned, or will have to be turned, into more employment-friendly schemes based on individual risk assessments in Austria, Belgium, France, Greece, Italy, Luxembourg, Portugal and Spain. In this way, many of the Continental and Southern European systems of protection have been forced to diminish their 'prohibitive' elements and have moved further in the direction of the Scandinavian model of protecting new and expectant mothers with employability-compatible means. The drawback of this 'Trojan horse' strategy has been that many member states have resisted rather persistently and created huge delays in the case of this Janus-faced and, in many respects, loosely worded Directive.

We can therefore conclude that leaving political disputes over the fundamental goals of a Directive unsettled during the decision-making phase, and instead concealing them behind 'rhetorical' compromises, is a bad foundation for smooth implementation. In the long run, such a Directive leaves ample room for the Commission and the ECJ, as watchdogs over the proper implementation of EU law, to exploit unclear wording in order to push through far-reaching changes at the national level, which had originally not been considered part of the Directive by many of the affected member state governments.

6   The Working Time Directive: European standards taken hostage by domestic politics

6.1   Aim and contents of the Directive

The *general aim* of the Working Time Directive[1] is to improve the health and safety of workers by laying down minimum standards for the organisation of working time (Article 2 of the Directive). The Directive is based on a wide interpretation of occupational health and safety which assumes that working long hours is harmful to workers' health and thus has to be limited.

The Working Time Directive applies in principle to both public and private sectors. It includes twelve *compulsory minimum standards.*

(1) As a general rule, workers may not work longer than forty-eight hours per week, averaged out over a period of four months.
(2) Every worker has to be granted a consecutive daily rest period of eleven hours.
(3) Every worker has to be granted a consecutive weekly rest period of thirty-five hours, averaged out over a period of two weeks.
(4) Every worker has to be granted a break if the working day is longer than six hours.
(5) Moreover, employees are entitled to at least four weeks' paid annual leave.
(6) The four weeks' paid annual leave may not be replaced by an allowance.
(7) Night workers may not work more than eight hours per day (averaged out over a period to be defined by national law or collective agreement), while night workers whose job involves 'special hazards or heavy physical or mental strain' (Article 8) must work no more than an absolute limit of eight hours per day.
(8) Furthermore, employers have to keep records on the regular use of night workers so that these may be brought to the attention of labour inspectorates if requested.

---

[1] Council Directive 93/104/EC of 23 November 1993 concerning certain aspects of the organisation of working time, OJ 1993 No. L307/18–24.

(9) Night workers are entitled to a free health assessment before being employed on night shift and at regular intervals thereafter.

(10) Workers suffering from health problems related to night work have to be transferred 'whenever possible' (Article 9) to suitable day work.

(11) Night and shift workers must enjoy health and safety protection commensurate with the nature of their work, and the relevant protection and prevention facilities must be equivalent to those of other workers and must be available at all times.

(12) Finally, employers who organise work in accordance with a certain time schedule must 'take account of the general principle of adapting work to the worker' (Article 13), especially in the case of monotonous tasks and work at a predetermined work rate.

Member states are offered a total of fourteen *exemption and derogation possibilities*. (1) Certain sectors and activities may be totally excluded from the scope of the provisions. This applies to the transport sector, activities at sea and doctors in training.[2] (2) The Directive allows member states to adopt general derogations (without compensation) from the provisions on daily and weekly rest periods, breaks, night work limits, reference periods and maximum weekly working hours for activities 'where the duration of the working time is not measured and/or predetermined or can be determined by the workers themselves' (Article 17.1). This applies in particular to managers, family workers and clergymen. (3) Further derogations from the rules on daily and weekly rest periods, breaks, night work limits and reference periods may be agreed between the domestic social partners at all levels, but only if the workers concerned are granted equivalent rest periods. In particular, collective or workforce agreements may extend the basic reference period for averaging out the forty-eight-hour week up to twelve months.

If compensatory rest periods are granted, member states may also vary the rules on daily and weekly rest periods, breaks, night work limits and reference periods (up to six months) for the following sectors or activities: (4) jobs involving long travel distances (e.g. activities where the worker's place of work and his or her place of residence are distant from one another); (5) security and surveillance activities; (6) activities involving the need for continuity of service or production (such as work done in hospitals or prisons, agriculture, press and information services);

---

[2] Meanwhile, five Directives, partly based on sectoral European social partner agreements, have been adopted to cover these 'excluded sectors': Directives 1999/63/EC, 1999/95/EC, 2000/34/EC, 2000/79/EC and 2002/15/EC. Since the implementation deadlines of these Directives were too late for us to include them in our study, our analysis is restricted to the original Directive.

(7) areas where there is a foreseeable surge of activity (e.g. in agriculture or tourism); (8) if exceptional or unforeseeable circumstances occur; (9) or in cases of accident or imminent risk of accident. Derogations from the provisions on daily and weekly rest periods can also be adopted (10) to take account of the specific requirements of shift work (in particular in case of change of shifts); (11) and in the case of activities where work is split up over the day (e.g. in cleaning). These latter derogations are also allowed only if compensatory rest periods are granted. (12) Furthermore, if justified by 'objective technical or work organization conditions' (Article 5), the weekly rest period may be reduced from thirty-five to twenty-four hours.

(13) Member states may also provide for an individual opt-out from the forty-eight-hour week. Hence, workers who voluntarily agree to do so may work longer than an average of forty-eight hours per week. This derogation was set to be reviewed seven years after the expiry of the implementation deadline. (14) Finally, with a view to implementing the provisions on annual leave, member states are granted a transition period of three years during which they only have to provide for three weeks of paid annual leave.

The Directive, moreover, includes two *non-binding soft-law provisions*. First, member states are urged that Sunday should 'in principle' be included in the weekly rest period (Article 5). This provision was annulled by the European Court of Justice in 1996 (see section 6.2 for more details). Second, it is suggested that member states may go beyond the minimum health and safety provisions for night workers laid down in the Directive, by making the work of night workers who incur specific risks to their health or safety subject to 'certain guarantees' (Article 10).

In sum, the Working Time Directive is a rather encompassing piece of Community legislation. It regulates a wide range of important matters related to the organisation of working time. The comparatively large policy scope of the Directive is corroborated by the fact that it contains twelve compulsory standards. This is only two standards short of the Pregnant Workers Directive, which in our sample has the highest number of binding provisions. Perhaps even more significant are the fourteen exemption and derogation possibilities offered by the Directive – the highest number in our sample. The large number of derogations available not only significantly diminishes the Directive's otherwise rather ambitious level of protection, it also makes the Working Time Directive a very complex piece of legislation. This increases the likelihood of misinterpretation at the implementation stage. Finally, compared with the Directives on Parental Leave or Part-time Work, soft-law provisions do not play a major role in this Directive.

6.2 The European-level negotiation process

The draft Directive concerning certain aspects of the organisation of working time (COM [1990] 317) was presented by the Commission in July 1990. It turned out to be one of the most contentious social policy proposals of the 1990s because the proposal touched upon a politically and ideologically highly salient (and in economic terms also potentially very costly) issue. Especially after the French government and the European Parliament had successfully pressed for the inclusion of an average maximum weekly working time of forty-eight hours, the draft Directive provoked highly controversial debates in the Council of Ministers.

As many times before, this draft Directive too was vociferously opposed by the British Conservative government. The UK's tradition of voluntarism, together with the deregulation policies of Margaret Thatcher, meant that there were neither any statutory annual leave entitlements nor any legal provisions on working time limits or rest periods in the UK prior to the Directive. This lack of state intervention in the area of working time was coupled with a pronounced 'long-hours culture' (Interview GB4: 187), which meant that a large number of workers regularly worked longer than forty-eight hours per week. Hence, the draft Directive would have required major reforms entailing considerable economic costs in Britain. Nonetheless, the outright hostility with which the British government reacted to the draft was not only caused by the high adaptation costs anticipated, it was also a consequence of the specific blend of Euro-scepticism and neo-liberal economic thinking prevalent in the Conservative Party at the time.[3] The turmoil caused by the Directive in the UK was fuelled by the fact that the Commission, as in the case of the Pregnant Workers Directive (see Chapter 5), had tabled the proposal as a health and safety measure which could be adopted by qualified majority. It was quite clear that this step was part of the Commission's 'treaty-base game' (Rhodes 1995: 99) employed to circumvent the notorious British veto against any attempt of social regulation at the European level.

Although the UK government vigorously protested against the choice of this legal basis, it could not get round the threat of being outvoted in the

---

[3] In a speech delivered in April 1992 to the annual meeting of the Institute of Directors, an association of UK business leaders, Prime Minister John Major claimed that under no circumstances was he prepared 'to let Brussels intervene in areas which Westminster had decided to leave alone'. More specifically, he characterised the European working time proposals as 'unnecessary interference with working practices', adding: 'They are not for us. No one should be in any doubt. A Conservative government will strongly oppose such damaging regulation wherever it is found, and we will not readily acquiesce in any attempts to impose these costs on our industry' (quoted in *Financial Times*, 29 April 1992, p. 14).

Council. During the protracted negotiations in the Council of Ministers, therefore, the UK's strategy was marked by the 'desire to have a Directive that applies to as few people as possible and gives them as few rights as possible' (Interview GB4: 588–9). So the UK successfully pressed for the exclusion of sectors and activities for which the Directive would have meant very significant transformation, in particular doctors in training and activities at sea, including work performed on offshore oil platforms (*Financial Times*, 29 May 1993, p. 2, 2 June 1993, p. 1). The exemption of activities at sea was also supported by Greece, which wanted to protect its large maritime sector (*Agence Europe* 5991, 2 June 1993, p. 7).

Since the forty-eight-hour maximum weekly workload was the most worrying aspect for British industry, the most important success of the UK government in watering down the Directive was the fact that it pushed through the opportunity for individual workers to opt out of the forty-eight-hour week voluntarily (*Financial Times*, 25 June 1992, p. 1). The individual opt-out, as well as the exemptions for doctors in training and work at sea, were also supported by Ireland (*Irish Times*, 25 June 1992, p. 5, 23 November 1993, p. 2, 8 November 1996, p. 2). The Irish government also tried to soften the (considerable) impact of the Directive on its economy but it was not opposed in principle to the Commission's proposal and agreed to it in the final vote (*Irish Times*, 2 June 1993, p. 1).

A further point of contention among governments concerned the question of derogations from the core provisions by social partner agreements. France and Belgium wanted to allow such derogations only on the basis of national or sectoral collective agreements, while the UK and Ireland supported the idea that such derogations should also be possible by means of plant-level agreements between management and workers in order to take account of the decentralised collective bargaining structure in both countries (*Financial Times*, 1 May 1992, p. 1, 13 June 1992, p. 3; *Irish Times*, 2 June 1993, p. 1). Interestingly, the Dutch government supported the British and Irish claims, since decentralisation of collective bargaining on working time issues was at the heart of a parallel national reform process taking place in the Netherlands (Interview NL9: 997–1002). Finally, the decentralisation camp managed to have its way, with the final Directive allowing derogations by social partner agreements of all kinds, from national collective agreements to plant-level agreements, without the need even for union involvement.

In light of the considerable resistance on the part of some member states against the whole Directive or certain parts of it, it is not surprising that it took more than six years before the Directive could be adopted. When the Directive was finally put to the vote in the Council of Ministers, the UK government, unlike all the other member states, did not approve of the final compromise (*Financial Times*, 2 June 1993, p. 1; EIRR 239: 2). The fact that the UK government abstained from the vote, despite the wide-ranging concessions it had gained before, was a sign of protest against the allegedly improper legal basis on which the Directive had been tabled.

The British government argued that the introduction of working time limits was not a health and safety measure but an employment issue. Hence the Directive could not be based on Article 118a of the EC Treaty but only on Articles 100 or 235 of the Treaty, both of which required unanimous approval by the member states (*Financial Times*, 25 June 1992, p. 12, 4 November 1993, p. 2; see also Gray 1998). The UK's abstention has to be counted as a de facto vote against the Directive, therefore, not least because the Tory government stated its firm intention to challenge the legal basis of the Directive subsequently in the European Court of Justice (*Financial Times*, 24 November 1993, p. 2).

In March 1994, the UK did indeed bring an action before the European Court of Justice, seeking to annul the Directive on the grounds of its legal basis. The Court's decision was delivered more than two and a half years later, on 12 November 1996, and it rejected the UK's claims almost entirely.[4] There was only one concession to the argument of the UK government. The Court held that the (non-binding) provision suggesting that Sunday should 'in principle' be included in the weekly rest period had to be annulled, since no health and safety reasons could be construed that would justify such a provision in a Directive based on Article 118a (for more details about the case, see Gray 1998).

6.3   Misfit in the member states: considerable legal and procedural innovations with varying practical significance

In view of its encompassing and detailed character, it comes as no surprise that the Directive called for reforms to the existing rules and regulations in all member states (see Table 6.1).[5] In legal terms, four countries had to cope with large adaptation requirements. The UK had to begin from scratch since, prior to the Directive, there were neither any statutory annual leave entitlements nor any legal provisions on working time limits or rest periods. The starting point in Ireland was only slightly more

---

[4] Judgment of the Court of 12 November 1996, case C-84/94, *United Kingdom of Great Britain and Northern Ireland* v. *Council of the European Union* [1996] ECR I-5755.

[5] As has already been noted in Ch. 2 (note 23), we did not include the effects of the ECJ's *SIMAP* ruling in our analysis here since this judgment represents a largely unforeseeable reinterpretation of the Directive and thus would have to be studied separately. For more details on the background of the *SIMAP* case, see note 19 below.

Table 6.1 *The Working Time Directive and misfit in the member states*

	Degree of Legal Misfit	Limited Practical Significance	Degree of Total Policy Misfit	Degree of Politics/ Polity Misfit	Economic Costs	Degree of Total Misfit
A	high	yes	medium	–	medium	medium
B	medium	no	medium	–	medium	medium
D	medium	yes	low	–	low	low
DK	high	yes	low	high	low	high
E	low	no	low	–	low	low
F	medium	yes	low	–	low	low
FIN	medium	no	medium	–	medium	medium
GB	high	no	high	–	high	high
GR	low	no	low	–	low	low
I	medium	no	medium	–	medium	medium
IRL	high	no	high	–	high	high
LUX	low	no	low	–	low	low
NL	low	no	low	–	low	low
P	medium	no	medium	–	medium	medium
S	medium	yes	low	medium	low	medium

advanced. Although legislation on working time already existed, these rules did not apply to a number of important sectors; most of the standards enshrined in them were much less stringent than those required by the Directive[6] and, above all, they had been enacted in the 1930s, which was so long ago that they had become virtually irrelevant to contemporary practice within Irish companies (Interview IRL4: 263–7). Denmark only enjoyed legislation with regard to rest periods, annual leave, and the health and safety of night workers (Interview DK7: 151–285). In Austria, the maximum weekly working time limit was set at fifty hours, and a significant part of the health care sector (where very long working hours are a common phenomenon) was not covered by any statutory limit to weekly working time. Moreover, the standards on working time limits and health and safety provisions for night workers called for significant revisions of the existing Austrian legislation (Interviews A2: 626–746, A6: 164–70).

In the UK and Ireland, the large number of legal reform requirements were not reduced to any significant degree by collective agreements, resulting in large-scale *policy misfit* (on the operationalisation of this

---

[6] In particular, the maximum weekly working time limits ranged from fifty-four hours in retail, to sixty hours in industry, and sixty-one hours in hotels and the catering trade. Moreover, statutory entitlements to paid annual leave, although applicable to all workers, had to be extended from three to four weeks.

concept, see Chapter 2). However, the practical relevance of the considerable legal reform requirements was reduced significantly by existing collective agreements in Austria and Denmark (Interviews A6: 513–27, A8: 369–408; DK7: 277–84). Austria was thus left with medium policy misfit, while in Denmark the content and coverage of the existing collective agreements actually guaranteed most of the Directive's requirements for almost all of the country's employees and so the de facto policy misfit in Denmark was only small-scale.

A further seven countries – Italy, Portugal, Belgium, Germany, France, Finland and Sweden – were confronted with medium-scale legal reform requirements, but in the last five member states, the practical relevance of these law-based adaptations was curbed by the existence of collective agreements which already provided for most of the required changes. Hence, these five countries joined the remaining four member states in that they only faced minor changes to their existing policies. Considering the total policy misfit, therefore, the Directive confronted two countries (Ireland and the UK) with a high degree of adaptational pressure, four member states (Austria, Finland, Italy, and Portugal) with medium-scale reform requirements, and the remaining nine countries with low degrees of misfit.

If we look at individual standards, surprisingly, many countries had to change their rules and regulations on maximum weekly working time. In this context, it is worth recalling that the Directive's forty-eight-hour standard does not refer to normal weekly working time, which was already lower than 40 hours in most countries, but to total weekly working hours *including overtime*. With this in mind, our empirical analysis has shown that the statutory rules prevalent in nine countries all told did not fully guarantee the forty-eight-hour week for all relevant workers, although the de facto effects were often more limited than a focus on the legal level would suggest. In Portugal, Italy and Finland the statutory maximum weekly working time was within the limits set down by the Directive, but it was possible to undertake much more overtime than allowed by the Directive (Interviews FIN3: 219–43, FIN8: 463–517; P2: 93–6, P8: 662–4; Barreto and Naumann 1998: 405; Ferrante 1998; Treu 1998: 135). Finally, Sweden too had weekly working time limits that were below forty-eight hours, but allowed unlimited derogations from this statutory provision by way of collective agreements (Interviews S7: 479–84, S10: 196–9).

Almost half of all member states had to adapt their legislation with regard to paid annual leave. In the UK, no statutory annual leave entitlement existed, while in Ireland and Germany, the entitlement had to be extended from three to four weeks. However, collective agreements already granted most German workers more favourable annual leave (BR-Drucksache 507/93, 66), while the practical effect in Ireland was much greater (Dáil Deb., 26 November 1996, cols. 56–7). In Italy, no explicit minimum duration of annual leave was laid down by law and there was also no provision guaranteeing that the leave could not be replaced by payment (COM [2000] 787: 18). This latter aspect also had to be changed in Greece and Portugal (Interviews GR2: 182–96; P8: 615–54). In Belgium and Greece, finally, many fixed-term workers were de facto excluded from eligibility for annual leave. In Greece, the entitlement to annual leave was subject to a qualifying period of one year's continuous employment. Similarly, Belgian workers were not allowed to take any leave during the first calendar year of their employment (Interview B12; COM [2000] 787: 17–18).[7]

If we look at the *polity and politics dimension*, it turns out that the Working Time Directive, like all the other Directives in our sample, did not call for any administrative adaptations, since the choice of how to enforce the provisions is left to the discretion of member states. State-society relations, however, were significantly affected by the Directive in two countries (see Chapter 12 for more details). Most importantly, the regulation of working time, in particular the definition of maximum weekly working hours, was traditionally one of the core areas of autonomous social partner regulation in Denmark. Since this system of collective agreements could not guarantee coverage of all the workers affected by the European measure, the Directive called for the replacement of social partner autonomy by state intervention in the form of generally binding legislation. The effect was a bit less severe in *Sweden*, where legislation on working hours did exist prior to the Directive but the social partners were allowed to agree on unlimited derogations from the statutory standards. As a reaction to the Directive, these general derogation possibilities, and hence the contractual freedom of the social partners in this area, had to be limited.

The potential *economic costs* of implementing the Directive were comparatively high since limitations on weekly working hours, paid annual leave entitlements and minimum requirements with regard to daily and

---

[7] It should be noted that it was not entirely clear from the outset that the Belgian and Greek annual leave systems were inconsistent with the Directive since the Directive allowed member states to introduce or uphold certain conditions for entitlement to annual leave (Article 7 of the Directive). A judgment by the European Court of Justice in a British case has since made it entirely clear that a system making entitlements to annual leave dependent on a given period of prior employment is inconsistent with the Directive since it debars particular categories of employees such as fixed-term workers from the right to take annual leave (see text to note 11 below).

weekly rest periods all directly affect production costs. This is particularly obvious in the case of paid annual leave, but it is also true for shorter working hours, which might require the hiring of additional staff. At any rate, the two countries that were confronted with large-scale policy misfit, i.e. the UK and Ireland, also had to bear very significant economic costs. According to government estimates in the UK, implementing the Directive entailed additional annual costs of £1.9 billion, equalling more than €3 billion (DTI 1998: Annex E3). In view of the broadly similar starting position in Ireland, the economic costs created by the Directive are likely to have been equally severe. Medium-sized costs had to be borne by the economies of Austria, Finland, Italy and Portugal, while the remaining nine countries, owing to their already wide-ranging compliance with the main standards of the Directive, were only confronted with low costs.

6.4   Implementation in the member states

6.4.1   Particularly interesting cases

An empirical analysis of how the fifteen member states transposed the Working Time Directive casts serious doubt on the view that the fit or misfit between a Directive's standards and pre-existing domestic policies and institutions largely determines implementation performance and highlights the importance of national policy processes and interests.

First of all, we find two clear-cut examples of 'opposition through the backdoor' where the respective national governments fought hard against the Directive (or specific aspects of it) in Brussels and, after having lost the battle at the European level, tried to regain the advantage at the implementation stage. As will become clear though, this deliberate opposition was not primarily caused by the sheer size of the adaptation requirements, but rather by domestic party politics. This was particularly obvious in Germany. The key to an understanding of the German reaction to the Working Time Directive is not the slight policy misfit created by the Directive, but the fact that the European negotiations interfered (and in some important respects even collided) with a parallel domestic reform effort. There had already been several attempts by the German centre-right government in the 1980s to increase considerably the flexibility of the rather rigid statutory working time scheme from 1938. These initiatives repeatedly foundered on the resistance of the churches and the trade unions. Both had powerful allies within the christian democratic party in government (see Zohlnhöfer 2001: 129–36).

Nevertheless, a new effort was made in 1992 and became intermingled with the EU-level negotiations on the Working Time Directive. Under the national reform, one main tool for giving companies more flexibility in arranging their working time regimes consisted in a considerable extension of the reference period used to calculate maximum weekly working hours. While the existing legislation only allowed for minimum flexibility in this respect, it was above all the Liberal Minister for Economic Affairs, Günther Rexrodt, who pressed for an increase in the reference period. Through this initiative, companies were to be allowed to have their employees work much longer in periods of high demand than the customary maximum of forty-eight hours a week, provided that the overtime was compensated for within a certain time by shorter weekly working hours (*Frankfurter Allgemeine Zeitung*, 15 June 1993, p. 15; 13 July 1993, p. 11).

In view of these domestic plans, the German government called for the draft EU Directive to provide maximum flexibility by allowing reference periods of up to twelve months. However, the Germans could not push through their demands in the EU negotiations due to resistance by France and a number of other member states (EIRR 222: 2; *Financial Times*, 1 May 1992, p. 1; ArbuR 1993). Hence the final Directive provided for a basic reference period of only four months, which could be extended to six months in certain sectors and to twelve months on the basis of collective agreements. This defeat in Brussels placed the German government in the uncomfortable position of having to reduce the reference period of six months that had hitherto been laid down in the respective national draft legislation. Even though the need to adapt the domestic plans was well known within the Department of Labour and Social Affairs (Günther 1993: 20), and despite the fact that there would still have been enough time for such a move in the ongoing legislative process, the centre-right government upheld the original six months reference period. In addition, the final version of the German Working Time Act allowed the social partners to lay down longer reference periods on the basis of collective or company agreements without any upper ceiling, whereas the Directive defined a maximum reference period of twelve months for such cases.

The centre-right government thus openly refused to let its political goal of considerably increasing flexibility be restricted by more stringent European rules. The result of this political decision, which was predominantly caused by the Liberal coalition partner's pressure towards deregulation and flexibilisation, is that the German working time legislation has now been in serious violation of the European Working Time Directive for more than six years. This has been noted in the European Commission's official implementation report (COM [2000] 787: 15). So far, however, the Commission has not initiated legal proceedings against Germany.

The same pattern of party political opposition against complying with the Directive was to be witnessed in the UK. As has already been noted above, the UK Conservative government sought to annul the Directive in the European Court of Justice on the grounds that it had been issued on an improper legal basis. The government moreover announced that it would not take any steps to implement the Directive until the Court had issued its ruling (*Financial Times*, 2 June 1993, p. 1). Indeed, no preparatory work had been done when, a few days before the end of the implementation deadline in November 1996, the European judges handed down their decision in which they rejected all major points of the UK challenge.[8] Even then the Tory government's opposition continued. It openly refused to accept the Court ruling and demanded that the Treaty be revised in the ongoing Intergovernmental Conference so that the UK would not be covered by the Directive (Hansard, HC, 12 November 1996, cols. 152, 155). As a result, the government continued to prolong the implementation of the Directive until the end of its term in office in May 1997 (Interview GB4: 285–300).

Subsequently, the Labour government held true to its pre-election manifesto commitment to transpose the Directive (Interview GB3: 532–4). As a consequence of the delaying tactics of its Conservative predecessors, however, the Blair government could not help exceeding the implementation deadline by almost two years. The very different positions of the Tory government and its Labour successors show that the considerable transposition delay was not primarily caused by the significant reform implications of the Directive in the UK but by the different party political 'lenses' through which both governments looked at these reform requirements, provoking fundamental opposition on the one hand and support, or at least acceptance, on the other.

Despite the Labour government's much more positive stance vis-à-vis the Directive, strong pressure from employers' organisations, combined with the business-friendly turn in economic and employment policy following the election of Tony Blair as party leader, prompted a very minimalist transposition of the Directive. This minimalist transposition, however, was contrary to the Directive in some of the minor details.[9] Moreover, the fact that the UK made use of the individual opt-out facility led to serious abuse in practice (see section 6.5 below). In order to reduce

---

[8] See note 4 above.
[9] In particular, overtime was excluded from calculating night work hours. After Amicus, a British trade union representing manufacturing workers, had lodged a complaint with the Commission, the latter issued a Letter of Formal Notice in March 2002, arguing that this was not in line with the Directive (*Financial Times*, 29 April 2002, p. 2). As a reaction, the government amended its legislation so as to remedy the matter. This amendment came into force in April 2003 (the Working Time (Amendment) Regulations 2002 (SI 2002 No. 3128)).

the costs of the new annual leave provisions, the government also introduced a thirteen-week qualification period before a worker's entitlement to paid annual leave could become effective. The question of whether or not this threshold was in line with the Directive, however, was a matter of interpretation which in the end had to be decided by the European Court of Justice. While the Directive seemed to allow such eligibility requirements at least in principle,[10] the British trade union BECTU (representing workers in the broadcasting, film, theatre and cinema sector) initiated proceedings against the thirteen-week threshold because it completely debarred many of its members on short-term contracts from being eligible to paid annual leave. The case was subsequently laid before the ECJ for interpretation and in June 2001 the European judges finally argued that such an eligibility requirement was contrary to the Directive because it completely excluded certain fixed-term workers from the universal right to annual leave.[11] As a consequence of the Court's authoritative clarification of this issue, the UK government swiftly (i.e. in October 2001) amended the law so as to remove the thirteen-week threshold.

Party politics also played a decisive role in Ireland. Despite the huge misfit between the Directive's standards and the existing domestic rules and regulations, the centre-left government coalition of Fine Gael, Labour, and the Democratic Left, in charge of transposing the Directive, firmly supported its goals. The government hoped that a significant diminution of working hours would help reduce unemployment, which was still a serious problem for Ireland in the mid 1990s. Among the most enthusiastic supporters of this strategy was the Labour Party. It played a crucial role in the process since it held responsibility for labour market affairs within the government. When the respective Minister of State, Eithne Fitzgerald, put forward her plans to transpose the Directive, she followed her party's line and refused to take advantage of the clause allowing workers individually to sign opt-out agreements exempting them from the forty-eight-hour week. The Minister of State justified her decision by pointing out that the widespread use of such an individual opt-out facility would seriously hamper the positive labour market effects of the reform (*Irish Times*, 15 November 1996, p. 4; Dáil Deb., 26 November 1999, cols. 53–68). This attempt to go beyond the minimum

---

[10] Article 7 reads as follows: 'Member States shall take the measures necessary to ensure that every worker is entitled to paid annual leave of at least four weeks *in accordance with the conditions for entitlement to, and granting of, such leave laid down by national legislation and/or practice*' (emphasis added).

[11] Judgment of the Court of 26 June 2001, case C-173/99. *R.* v. *Secretary of State for Trade and Industry ex parte Broadcasting, Entertainment, Cinematographic and Theatre Union (BECTU)* [2001] ECR I-4881.

requirements of the Directive was endorsed by Irish unions but met with fierce resistance by employers' organisations and opposition parties. The opponents argued that such a step would have negative consequences for Ireland's competitive position vis-à-vis the UK in attracting direct foreign investments from the United States (*Irish Times*, 22 November 1996, p. 4, 25 February 1997, p. 16; Dáil Deb., 10 April 1997, cols. 784–5, 792–4). Confronted with these massive protests, the government agreed to allow employees to opt out of the 48-hour week individually, but only under very restrictive conditions and only for a transition period of two years (Interview IRL4: 888–938). The controversial debates about this issue and the protracted process of finding a compromise, however, meant that the transposition legislation was enacted only with considerable delay.[12]

In France, transposition of the Working Time Directive was delayed for almost four and a half years because the (comparatively modest) reforms called for by the Directive were linked to two very contested national processes. At the same time it has been convincingly argued by national experts that it was only due to this linkage that transposition was envisaged at all, since the government and administrative actors showed no great interest in complying with the EU standards (Interview F9: 931–2). The main part of the necessary adaptations was added onto the thirty-five-hour week flagship reform of the left-wing Jospin government. Concealed behind the controversial principles and details of this landmark reform, which aimed to fight unemployment by significantly cutting overall working hours and increasing flexibility of working time, the EU standards did not evoke any serious trouble or opposition. Rather, transposing the European demands was delayed because of the functional linkage with the complex and politically highly contested thirty-five-hour reform enacted by *Loi Aubry I*, adopted in June 1998, and *Loi Aubry II*, passed in January 2000 (see, for example, Interview F4: 148–310; Bilous 1998a, 1998c; EIRR 320: 28–31).

Full implementation of the Directive was further delayed by another case of issue linkage which was even more controversial than the thirty-five-hour reform: the lifting of the general night work ban on female blue-collar workers, which had been declared inconsistent with EU equality law by the ECJ's famous ruling in the *Stoeckel* case in 1991.[13] Although the Working Time Directive itself did not require the

---

[12] The provisions on the health and safety of night workers, which were handled in a separate process by the Irish Health and Safety Authority, were only incorporated into Irish law on 1 February 1999. The reason for this delay was administrative overload on the part of the Health and Safety Authority, which in Ireland is a rather common phenomenon in this policy area (Interview IRL3: 819–31).

[13] As to this case, see Ch. 5, footnote 8.

lifting of the ban on female night work, it called for the introduction of working time limits and health and safety provisions for night workers, which hitherto had not existed in France – neither for men nor for women. Besides the functional proximity, politically these issues were closely linked to the highly contested question of lifting the general night work ban on women, and it was decided that both would be regulated in one go. As a result of this linkage, the Act incorporating the night work rules of the Working Time Directive into French law was only adopted in November 2000, exactly two days before the ECJ would have decided on imposing a fine of €142,000 on France (Interviews F2: 1023–6, F4: 193–212, F6: 598–605).[14] Thus national reform resistance was valued higher than compliance with EU rules up to the point where the supranational level threatened to impose financial sanctions.

Similar problems of serious transposition delays due to issue linkage were to be witnessed in Italy. The Directive required significant changes to the existing working time legislation enacted in 1923. Not only did Italy have to reduce considerably the maximum average weekly working time (including overtime) from sixty to forty-eight hours. It was also forced to introduce legal provisions guaranteeing minimum daily rest periods, breaks and night work limits, as well as specific health and safety protection for night workers, and at least four weeks' paid annual leave. Even in view of the fact that many workers already enjoyed similar entitlements on the basis of collective agreements, these reform requirements were still substantial.

Following an accord laid down in the tripartite social pact of 1993, in which the government had agreed to give the social partners a more active role in the implementation of EU social policy Directives, the centre-left Prodi government agreed with the social partners in 1996 that the Working Time Directive should be implemented on the basis of a deal to be hammered out between both sides of industry. Given that the Directive required some serious changes to the existing rules and regulations, the three trade union federations, CISL, UIL and CGIL, and the employers' organisation, *Confindustria*, concluded with surprising speed an accord which delineated the social partners' plans for implementing the Directive. In view of this agreement, all the government had to do to comply with the Directive was to give legal effect to the social partners' deal by transforming it into a legislative decree (Interview I6: 329–77, I9: 61–113; Trentini 1997).

But that did not happen. While the Prodi government was willing to accept the social partners' arrangement, the plan was thwarted by the Communist Party (*Rifondazione Communista* – RC), whose parliamentary

---

[14] This piece of legislation came into force in May 2001.

support was required for Prodi's minority government to survive. As a result of controversial budget plans tabled by the government, the RC threatened to withdraw its parliamentary support. The government could only resolve this crisis by committing itself to a radical working time reduction along the lines of the French thirty-five-hour legislation, which was one of the central demands of the Communist Party (*Centro di Studi Economici Sociali e Sindacali* 1997a, 1997b). Consequently, the social partner deal was dropped and, instead, the government introduced a bill aiming to establish a statutory thirty-five-hour week in Italy (Ferrante 1998; Paparella 1998b).

This move was met with fierce protests not only by employers' organisations but also by trade unions, with both sides feeling let down by this unilateral imposition of very tight rules on working time that allowed for only limited flexibility. In the end, this highly controversial reform was never adopted by parliament. The RC finally withdrew its support for the government in the course of a further government crisis in October 1998. The reshuffled government coalition under Massimo D'Alema no longer had to rely on the Communist Party's support and the contested thirty-five-hour proposal was taken off the agenda (Pedersini 1997; Bilous 1998b; Paparella 1998a; Verzichelli and Cotta 2000). Besides the adaptation to the night work rules, which was enacted in a separate process in November 1999,[15] all that had been done by spring 2003 to comply with the Directive was the initiation of a partial reform that gave legal force to the social partners' proposal to bring the rules on maximum weekly working time into line with the Directive. However, the respective law (adopted in November 1998) only applied to workers in the industry (Ferrante 1998; Paparella 1998c).

The lion's share of the adaptation requirements created by the Directive was only incorporated into Italian law by a Decree that came into force in April 2003, no less than six and a half years after the end of the deadline. In the meantime, pressure from Brussels had increased considerably, after Italy had been convicted by the ECJ for non-transposition of the Directive[16] and the follow-up proceedings for non-compliance with the first ruling under Article 228 ECT, involving the threat of financial

---

[15] Similar to the French case, in Italy transposing the night work rules of the Directive was also linked to the process of lifting the general night work ban on women in manufacturing, which had become necessary after the ECJ had declared the Italian ban at odds with EU equality law (Judgment of the Court of 4 December 1997, Case C-84/94, *Commission of the European Community* v. *Italian Republic* [1997] ECR I-6869). Although this issue was not as contested as in France, the whole process had its own timing, which meant that the night work standards of the Working Time Directive were only transposed after a delay of more than three years.

[16] Judgment of the Court of 9 March 2000, Case C-386/98, *Commission of the European Communities* v. *Italian Republic* [2000] ECR I-1277.

sanctions, had already been transferred to the ECJ (see also Chapter 11). Similar to the French case, therefore, in Italy non-compliance (here boosted by diverging national policy interests) prevailed up to the point where the supranational level seriously threatened financial sanctions.

Another case where the misfit hypothesis cannot shed light on the reasons for implementation difficulties is Greece. Misfit was slight, but nevertheless the Directive was transposed with more than three years' delay. As in most of the other Greek cases studied in this book, the implementation process can by and large be characterised by a lack of interest on the part of the government and other political or societal actors. While working time flexibilisation was controversially discussed before, during and after the transposition process,[17] transposition was concluded rather quickly once the process had been triggered by rising enforcement pressure from Brussels. It was effected by a presidential decree which reproduced the text of the Directive almost word for word and thus remained almost completely isolated from the heated national working time debates. The significant delay was predominantly due to more than five years of inertia after the Directive had been adopted by the Council in 1993.

As outlined above, the transposition processes in Denmark and Sweden are cases of particular interest as well because here the European rules affected not only the policy contents but also the national state–society relations. This topic will be further discussed in Chapter 12.

6.4.2   Timeliness and correctness of transposition

In view of the massive domestic politicisation provoked by the Directive in many countries, the frequent linkage of implementation with contested and time-consuming national reform processes, and the complex nature of the Directive itself, it is no surprise that the member states' transposition performance for this Directive is the worst in our sample. When the implementation deadline expired on 23 November 1996, only one member state, Spain, had *transposed the Directive essentially correctly*, while a further two member states, Finland and the Netherlands, were less than six months late. The UK's delay was between one and two years. Austria, Denmark, France, Greece, Ireland, Italy and Luxembourg were more than two years late (some of them even four or five years). By the end

---

[17] In 1993 the conservative ND government had first tried to introduce elements of flexibilisation into the statutory working time rules but failed, just as the PASOK government that succeeded it. Within a year after Brussels had been notified of the transposition, a national reform tried to overhaul the established system again, since basic conflicts of interest had remained unsolved (Interviews GR9: 523–31, GR15).

of our period of analysis, four countries had not yet reached the stage of essentially correct transposition.

As a result, only one-fifth of all member states implemented the Directive essentially correctly *on time or at least almost on time* (i.e. no more than six months after the deadline). In other words, four-fifths of all member states accomplished this task no better than *significantly delayed*.

Belgium is among the countries that had not transposed the Directive essentially correctly at the end of our period of analysis. On 30 April 2003, the Belgian legislation debarred certain fixed-term workers from eligibility to annual leave. Moreover, several categories of workers were not properly covered by the standards enshrined in the Directive (especially doctors, veterinary surgeons and dentists, see Interview B7: 285–491, COM [2000] 787: 6). In Germany, the reference periods allowed for averaging out the forty-eight-hour week were being exceeded when the Directive was incorporated into German law. Hence, the general reference period was set at six instead of four months, and no upper limit was defined for the extension of the reference period (see above). For hazardous night work, moreover, no absolute daily working time limit of eight hours was defined (COM [2000] 787: 20).

In Portugal, the law provided that night work should be calculated without including overtime hours, and it did not guarantee that annual leave might not be replaced by pay. Moreover, the Portuguese legislation failed to specify the detailed criteria for defining hazardous night work and the practical details necessary to carry out health checks for night workers. (Interviews P3: 420–39, P8: 607, COM [2000] 787: 21.) In Sweden, transposition was achieved by incorporating a mere reference to the Directive in the Swedish working time legislation. This is an insufficient instrument of transposition because it lacks legal clarity and thus may lead to application problems (see below).

If we increase the standards for judging transposition performance and look at *completely correct transposition*, further cases of non-compliance demand our attention. By the end of April 2003, some of the Austrian federal states had not issued legislation guaranteeing the forty-eight-hour limit for their civil servants (Interview A6: 99–140). Greece failed to guarantee that the entitlement to four weeks of annual leave might not be replaced by pay (Interview GR2: 182–96). The Irish legislation did not ensure that employers should keep records on the regular use of night workers so that these could be checked by the labour inspectorate (COM [2000] 787: 24). In Luxembourg, it was not guaranteed that daily rest periods were consecutive, and no absolute eight-hour daily working time limit was provided for night workers performing particularly hazardous tasks (Interview LUX7: 386–424, COM [2000] 787: 21). The

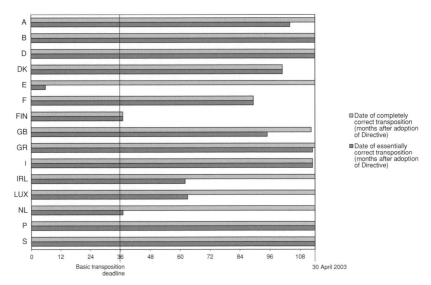

Figure 6.1 The Working Time Directive and timing of adaptation

latter problem also applied to the Netherlands, whose legislation, moreover, allowed employers to reduce the weekly rest period to thirty-two hours once in every five weeks, but failed to ensure that this possibility was restricted to shift workers and that these workers received compensatory rest periods (COM [2000] 787: 14 and 21). Finally, the Spanish rules and regulations lacked the required absolute eight-hour limit for hazardous night work, and there were problems with medical staff working for state-owned hospitals in some autonomous regions, who were not covered by the Spanish working time law (COM [2000] 787: 6 and 20).

Figure 6.1 summarises the timing of the member states in terms of *essentially correct* and *completely correct* transposition of the Working Time Directive.

6.5   National problems with application and enforcement

In terms of practical compliance with the standards of the Directive, our interviews revealed a number of problems in many of the member states. It seems that working time is an area in which violations of the law are quite widespread. We can distinguish between application difficulties arising from the way member states transposed the provisions of the Directive; problems associated with violations of working time rules in specific sectors; and non-compliance with working time provisions as a more general phenomenon in multiple sectors of the economy.

As to application problems resulting from *transposition peculiarities*, two countries stand out. First, Sweden transposed the Directive by way of simply referring employers and workers to the Directive to find out which working patterns are or are not allowed. This caused widespread application problems. In fact, the forty-eight-hour standard especially was widely ignored in practice since it is difficult to make sense of the very complex and loosely worded text of the Directive (Interviews S3: 912–25, S5: 90–148, 385–95, S10: 280–310). These problems still persist, but Sweden promised to remedy the matter after the Commission had issued a Letter of Formal Notice in March 2002 (see also Chapter 12).

The UK witnessed some of the most serious application problems, which was partly caused by the fact that it was the only country that did not have any statutory working time restrictions prior to the implementation of the Directive. For example, quite a number of employers refused to grant their employees the right to paid annual leave. In many cases, this seems to have been due to deliberate non-compliance on the part of employers seeking to avoid the associated costs of granting paid annual leave (NACAB 2000: 1). However, a large part of the practical non-compliance with working time rules was caused or at least facilitated by the way the UK transposed the Directive.

On the one hand, the UK was the only country that allowed employees in all sectors and occupations to opt out individually of the forty-eight-hour week by way of a written statement.[18] While the Directive stressed that these individual opt-out declarations have to be *voluntary* (Article 18 of the Directive), it turned out that employees are often pressurised by their employers to sign an opt-out agreement, especially in non-unionised workplaces and low-skilled jobs. In many cases, such opt-out clauses are already part of the employment contract and employees are willing to accept such clauses because long hours are seen as necessary to increase low rates of basic income (Edwards and Burkitt 2001: 3). Moreover, according to both employer and union representatives, application problems arose from the very complex nature of the UK legislation transposing the Directive. Since the government took advantage of all possible exemptions and derogations offered by the Directive, the resulting legal text is hard to understand and frequently gives rise to interpretation problems (Interviews GB4: 804–15, GB5: 740–59).

---

[18] As has been noted above, Ireland made use of the opt-out as well, but only for a transition period of two years. Austria allowed the individual opt-out only for employees working in hospitals. A few other member states took advantage of this clause as well, but again restricted its application to specific sectors (see Chapter 10).

With regard to application problems arising in *specific sectors*, many countries witnessed serious non-compliance with maximum working time and night work restrictions in hospitals and nursing homes. For example, violations of the forty-eight-hour limit in hospitals could be observed in some Austrian hospitals under the jurisdiction of federal states. Since the maximum working time limit had to be newly introduced in these hospitals, some of the state governments openly refused to comply with the new rules in order to avoid the resultant costs (Interviews A2: 1634–54, A6: 197–219). This problem was aggravated since the law does not provide for proper sanctions against public employers. While employers in the private sector can be heavily fined for violating the working time rules, there are no equivalent sanctions that can be imposed on public employers (Interview A6: 197–219).

Some violations of the rules on weekly working hours and night time work in hospitals were also reported in Belgium, where shortage of staff makes long overtime and night work necessary (Interview B7: 548–98). Serious compliance problems exist in German hospitals in the form of a shortage of rest periods and excessive overtime. Owing to a severe lack of personnel, many doctors and nurses are regularly forced to work for twenty-four or even more than thirty hours without interruption and without compensatory rest periods. Moreover, many employees in this sector are forced to work unpaid and undocumented overtime, and some cases were reported in which working time records were manipulated in order to conceal these illegal practices (see extensive newspaper coverage of the problem in, for example, *Süddeutsche Zeitung*, 25 May 2001, p. 2; 10 November 2001, p. 1; *Frankfurter Allgemeine Zeitung*, 21 May 2001, p. 17; 23 May 2001, p. 3). A more general problem in Germany seems to be that employers do not keep proper working time records so that the labour inspectorates cannot check whether or not the standards of the law have been complied with (Interviews D8: 581–625, D10: 387–458). Finally, the huge problems in the health care sectors of a number of countries could only be solved by a considerable increase in the number of staff working in hospitals and nursing homes. As long as hospitals in Austria, Germany, Belgium and a number of other countries continue to be plagued by serious staff shortage, violations of the working time rules seem to be almost inevitable.

Concerning the third type of non-compliance, i.e. disrespect for working time standards as a more *general phenomenon* to be found in many sectors of the economy, a number of countries have to be mentioned. In Ireland, many employees violate the forty-eight-hour standard, most of them voluntarily, since working excessive overtime is often the only way for them to supplement their low wages. This seems to be a general phenomenon, but it appears to be particularly severe in the area of security services (Interview IRL5: 419–32). Even an employer's representative admitted that a lot of Irish companies violate the provisions on rest periods and weekly working hours (Interview IRL7: 310–30). Similarly, rather widespread violations of the forty-eight-hour standard were reported in Portugal, especially in industry, but also in the service sectors, e.g. in banking or insurance (Interviews P2: 94–5, P3: 1007–53; see also Freyssinet and Michon 2003).

In Spain, working too much overtime also seems to be a general problem, and compliance with working time provisions is especially poor in certain service sectors such as cleaning (Interviews E4: 466–75, E5: 1148–50). General abuse of the maximum working time standards, especially with regard to night work, was also reported in Greece, in particular in small and medium-sized companies (Interview GR3: 238–50; EIRR 336: 8). In Luxembourg, widespread application problems to do with illegal overtime have been reported. Companies have to obtain explicit permission from the relevant authorities to let their workers perform overtime hours. Owing to a lack of administrative resources, the permission procedure is very time-consuming for companies. In order to avoid long delays, many companies therefore simply ignore the law and it is estimated that about half of all overtime is worked illegally (Freyssinet and Michon 2003), and it is reasonable to assume that some of the ensuing practices also violate the standards of the Working Time Directive.

At least some of these application problems could be improved by the member states. First of all, the problems stemming from the way member states transposed the Directive could easily be remedied by enhancing the legal certainty and clarity of the respective transposition laws, or by simply disallowing an individual opt-out that is plagued by widespread fraud as in the UK. Further violations could at least be reduced by intensified enforcement efforts. It is clear that proper application of working time rules will be hard to achieve in sectors or countries where both employers and employees have strong economic incentives to break these rules: in the one case to save money, in the other to increase low income levels. Some of the enforcement systems, however, seem to be inefficient in dealing with the given amount of non-compliance (see Chapter 13).

6.6   General assessment of the Directive's effects

What were the effects of the Directive in the member states? Did it only cause a huge amount of trouble for domestic political actors or were there real benefits? In trying to reach an overall assessment of the Directive's usefulness, two dimensions should be taken into account. First, the

Table 6.2 *Overview of the Working Time Directive and its implementation*

Aim	To improve the health and safety of workers by laying down minimum standards for the organisation of working time
History	Commission Proposal 25 July 1990
	Council Directive 23 November 1993
Standards	12 binding standards (most importantly: average weekly working time of 48 hours and 4 weeks' paid annual leave)
	2 recommendations
	14 exemption provisions
Degree of misfit	High: 3
	Medium: 6
	Low: 6
Transposition problems	12 member states significantly delayed
	3 member states have still not accomplished transposition essentially correctly

Directive indeed brought about some *notable improvements in the working conditions of employees in the European Union.*

The degree of changes required by the Directive was medium or even high in nine out of fifteen countries (see Table 6.2). A high proportion of all workers in Ireland and the UK benefited significantly from the Directive since hitherto these countries had no, or only very minimal, working time standards, both legally and in practice. Furthermore, the Directive improved (or could improve, if fully implemented) the situation of specific groups of workers. For example, the health protection and working time limits of night workers had to be advanced in most countries. Moreover, the Directive contributed to extending the coverage of the existing working time systems to a number of 'forgotten' groups or sectors, such as employees working in public hospitals in Austria or agricultural workers in Germany. The Directive also extended coverage of existing working time rules to a significant minority of Danish workers who had previously been left out in the cold by the corporatist system of autonomous social partner regulation.

Furthermore, the Directive, especially as interpreted by the European Court of Justice in the *SIMAP* case,[19] raised awareness for the poor

---

[19] The Spanish Trade Union of Doctors in Public Service (*Sindicato de Médicos de Asistencia Pública*) had asked the ECJ in a preliminary ruling for interpretation on the question of whether on-call duties had to be counted as working time. In October 2000 the ECJ decided in favour of the doctors. See Judgment of the Court of 3 October 2000, case C-303/98, *Sindicato de Médicos de Asistencia Pública (Simap) v. Conselleria de Sanidad y Consumo de la Generalidad Valenciana* [2000] ECR I-7963. As a consequence, working a normal day shift after on-call duty at night would violate the EU standards on rest periods.

working conditions of many employees in the health care sector, in particular with regard to excessive working hours and the lack of rest periods. Since real improvements in this sector have so far been thwarted by the unwillingness or inability of member states to ensure proper compliance with the law and to put into practice the *SIMAP* ruling of the ECJ, exploiting the Directive's potential will depend on further case law, on Commission intervention against non-compliant countries as well as on the outcome of the negotiations on revising the Directive that are currently underway.[20]

The second benchmark for assessing the Directive's effects relates to the amount of convergence it has brought about among the member states of the European Union. Here, our conclusion must be much more sceptical. It is true that some of the extreme outliers were forced to move towards the centre, while some of the countries with previously very rigid standards considerably relaxed and flexibilised their systems (e.g. Germany, the Netherlands, Austria, see Chapter 10 for more details). In this sense, there was indeed some kind of convergence in terms of levelling some of the differences.

However, national diversity still remains very significant. Hence, the Dutch working time provisions, even if considerably more flexible than before, are still much tighter than the minimalist system operating in the UK, especially taking into account the provision of an individual opt-out from the forty-eight-hour standard for British workers. If we add the progress of France towards the thirty-five-hour week to this picture, it becomes evident that companies are still confronted with (or can choose from) very diverse working time regimes across Europe. What they do not have any longer, however, is a place where there are generally no binding working time limits to be respected at all.

This leads to the conclusion that full convergence of working time regimes in the EU's internal market is still not in sight. At the same time, EU labour law has definitely set its mark, even on this field of great cost impact.

---

[20] One option that is currently debated in this context is to amend the definition of working time so as to avoid on-call duties having to be counted as working time.

7   The Young Workers Directive: a safety net with holes

7.1   Aim and contents of the Directive

The *general aim* of the Young Workers Directive[1] is to protect young workers from work involving dangerous or harmful employment conditions. To this end, it seeks to prohibit child labour, strictly to regulate and protect the work done by adolescents, and to ensure 'that young people have working conditions which suit their age' (Article 1). In order to achieve these goals, the Directive comprises thirteen *compulsory minimum standards*. They fall into standards relating to the area of occupational health and safety more narrowly understood, and into provisions belonging to the field of employment rights defined in a wider sense.

(1) With regard to the former, the Directive (Article 6.1) imposes a general duty on employers to 'adopt the measures necessary to protect the safety and health of young people' working in their establishments.

(2) More specifically, employers are required to carry out an assessment of the potential risks to young people before the actual take-up of work and each time there is a major change in working conditions.

(3) If this assessment reveals any risk to young people, the employer has to provide for a free assessment and monitoring of their health at regular intervals. Such a free health check-up also has to be granted to adolescents working nights, both prior to the assignment and at regular intervals thereafter.

(4) Moreover, employers are required to inform young workers and, in the case of children, their legal representatives of any possible risks and of the measures taken to prevent these risks.

(5) In particular, young people have to be protected from any risk arising from 'their lack of experience, of absence of awareness of existing or potential risks or of the fact that young people have not yet fully

---

[1] Council Directive 94/33/EC of 22 June 1994 on the protection of young people at work, OJ 1994 No. L216/12–20.

matured'. A detailed list of dangerous agents and work processes is given in Article 7.2 and in the two annexes to the Directive.

(6) In order to protect the health and safety of children further, the Directive generally prohibits the work of children, i.e. all young persons who are under fifteen years of age or are still subject to compulsory schooling. However, the Directive does permit a number of specific exemptions from this general ban on child labour (see below).

(7) For the exceptional employment of children in the context of cultural, artistic, sporting or advertising activities, the Directive lays down a separate system requiring that such employment be authorised by the competent authorities (usually the labour inspectorates) in individual cases, and that the working conditions in these cases are not detrimental to the safety, health and development or the education of the children involved.[2]

(8) As to the wider employment rights standards, the Directive defines a number of daily and weekly working time restrictions. As a general principle, if young persons are employed by more than one employer, their working hours have to be accumulated. For children who perform work on an exceptional basis, the general limit during term time is two hours on a school day, seven hours on a non-school day, and twelve hours per week. During school holidays, a maximum of seven hours a day and thirty-five hours a week may be worked by children. For children working in the context of a combined work/training scheme or an in-plant work experience scheme, the limits are eight hours a day and forty hours a week, but the time spent on training also counts as working time. For adolescents, i.e. sixteen- and seventeen-year-olds, the general working time limit is eight hours per day and forty hours per week.

(9) Furthermore, a minimum daily rest period of fourteen consecutive hours (for children) and twelve consecutive hours (for adolescents) has to be guaranteed,

(10) and all young persons have to be granted a minimum weekly rest period of two days

(11) as well as a break of thirty minutes where the working day exceeds four and a half hours.

---

[2] Note that, under the Directive, the employment of children in the context of cultural, artistic, sporting or advertising activities is governed solely by the individual authorisation system, while all the other provisions of the Directive (such as the minimum age for employment or the standards on maximum working hours and minimum rest periods) do not apply to this category of activities.

(12) In addition, the Directive lays down a general ban on night work for young persons. For children, the restricted period is between 8 p.m. and 6 a.m., while adolescents are not allowed to work either between 10 p.m. and 6 a.m. or between 11 p.m. and 7 a.m.

(13) Finally, with regard to enforcement, the Directive requires member states to lay down 'effective and proportionate' measures in the event of non-compliance with the provisions of the Directive.

In order to account for individual circumstances, the Directive altogether allows eleven *exemptions and derogations* from the above-mentioned standards. (1) While in general all persons under eighteen years of age with an employment contract or employment relationship are covered by the Directive, member states may exclude occasional or short-term work involving domestic service in a private household or non-dangerous work in a family business. (2) As regards the list of forbidden activities for young persons, member states may exceptionally allow adolescents to perform work involving some of these dangerous activities if this is indispensable to vocational training and provided that the work is supervised by a competent person. (3) Moreover, there are a number of exemptions from the general ban on child labour. Hence, children of at least thirteen years of age may be exceptionally allowed to perform 'light work' (a term which is further specified by the Directive), and children of at least fourteen years of age may be allowed to work under a combined work training scheme or an in-plant work-experience scheme.

(4) In addition, member states may derogate from the individual authorisation system pertaining to the employment of children in the context of cultural, artistic, sporting or advertising activities. And so children who have reached the age of thirteen may be employed in such activities without individual authorisation. Member states that have a specific authorisation system for modelling are allowed to retain this system. (5) The Directive, furthermore, allows some derogation from the working time restrictions. For children, the maximum working hours can be raised to eight hours on a non-school day during term time and to eight hours a day and forty hours a week during school holidays in the case of fifteen-year-olds. With regard to children employed under a combined work/training scheme or an in-plant work experience scheme and adolescents, derogations from the respective working time limits may be made 'either by way of exception or if there are objective grounds for doing so' (Article 8.5).

(6) The two days' weekly rest period may be reduced to thirty-six hours if 'technical or organisational reasons' justify such a step. (7) Moreover, the (consecutive) daily and weekly rest periods can be interrupted in the case of activities that are split up over the day or are of a short duration. (8) Member states are also allowed to vary the daily and weekly rest periods

of adolescents in certain sectors (shipping and fisheries, armed forces and the police, hospitals, agriculture, tourism, hotels and catering, and activities involving periods which are split up over the day), provided that there are objective grounds for doing so and that appropriate compensatory rest time is granted. (9) Employers may generally disregard the provisions on working time, night work, rest periods and breaks in relation to adolescents if unforeseeable circumstances (such as an accident) immediately require a temporary variation in the usual working pattern. In these cases, however, equivalent compensatory rest must be granted.

(10) Furthermore, there are exemption possibilities in relation to the rules on night work. The general prohibition of night work may be completely disregarded with regard to the work performed by adolescents in the shipping or fishing sector, the armed forces or the police, hospitals, or cultural, artistic, sporting or advertising activities, provided that compensatory rest time is granted. In other sectors to be specified by the member states, the period of prohibited night work can be reduced to the time between midnight and 4 a.m. in the case of adolescents, provided that they are supervised by an adult, assuming such supervision is necessary for their protection. (11) Finally, the Directive grants the UK a transition period of four years from the end of the normal implementation deadline, during which the latter is not required to implement the provisions relating to the maximum weekly working hours for children during term-time, or the maximum daily and weekly working hours and night work restrictions for adolescents. After the expiry of this transition period, the Council, on the basis of a report prepared by the Commission, may decide whether this temporary opt-out should be renewed.

Further to these compulsory minimum standards and exemption possibilities, the Directive also includes three *non-binding recommendations*. As to the first two soft-law provisions, the Directive stipulates that the two days' weekly rest period should be consecutive 'if possible' and that it should 'in principle' include Sunday (Article 10.2). With respect to the third, member states that allow children still subject to compulsory full-time schooling to perform work at all are called upon to ensure that 'a period free of any work is included, as far as possible, in the school holidays' of these children (Article 11).

In sum, the Young Workers Directive, albeit targeting a comparatively small category of workers, is rather encompassing in its policy scope. It covers the full range of relevant standards that are important for protecting young workers from harmful working conditions. It lays down detailed standards not only on the prohibition of child labour and the general health and safety of young workers, but also on daily and weekly working time, night work, daily and weekly rest periods, and breaks. This broad policy scope is underlined by the large number, i.e. thirteen, of compulsory standards, which is the highest number among the Directives in our sample. A corollary of this is the almost equally high number of eleven exemption and derogation possibilities, which in this dimension ranks the Young Workers Directive in second place behind the Working Time Directive. Finally, the comparatively small number of three non-binding recommendations indicates that soft-law provisions do not play a central role in this Directive.

7.2   The European-level negotiation process

When the Commission tabled its proposal for a Council Directive on the protection of young people at work (COM [1991] 543), the plan to improve the level of protection of workers below the age of eighteen was promoted in particular by countries like Luxembourg, France, Italy, and Spain (Interviews LUX1: 768–89; F4: 903–6; EIRR 238: 2, 239: 2).

Among the more critical countries, the most outspoken protest came from the Conservative UK government. The UK was the only country to have objections of principle to the Directive. Initially, the British government was especially opposed to the fact that the Directive 'threatened to outlaw the British paperboy and papergirl' (*Financial Times*, 15 November 1991, p. 10).[3] This issue touched upon a culturally deeply rooted British tradition, which even provoked opposition from the British Labour Party. Allegedly, it was Tony Blair, Labour's shadow employment secretary at the time, who intervened with Commission officials and thus secured an amendment of the Directive allowing for the maintenance of early-morning paper delivery by school children (*Financial Times*, 15 November 1991, p. 10).

After this problem had been eliminated, which was before the Commission had even presented its official proposal, the UK still remained the most fervent opponent to the Directive. The main argument this time was that Community intervention in this area was unnecessary and that the regulation of young people's working hours, rest periods and night work restrictions in particular should be left to member states (EIRR 243: 2). The UK government was only ready to accept the health and safety standards in a narrower sense, while all the other provisions were seen as an illegitimate interference with British practices. In order to understand the UK's opposition to these provisions fully, it has to be acknowledged that

---

[3] It is a widespread phenomenon in the UK that school children deliver newspapers. According to the National Federation of Newsagents, in 1991 there were about 500,000 paperboys and papergirls in the UK (*Financial Times*, 3 December 1991, p. 11). Many of them do their job in the morning, before school. A clause in an early draft of the Directive would have outlawed this practice, stipulating that school children were not allowed to perform work either before or during school hours.

the previously existing domestic restrictions on working time, night work and annual leave for sixteen- and seventeen-year-olds had been removed by Margaret Thatcher's government only a few years earlier, in 1988–9 (EIRR 220: 18; *Financial Times*, 23 November 1988, p. 14, 2 December 1988, p. 14). Thus, the Directive would have compelled the Conservative UK government to reverse its deregulatory measures and re-regulate the working time of young workers.

As blocking the Directive altogether was not possible, since adoption only required a qualified majority in the Council of Ministers, the UK tried to secure as many exemptions and derogations as possible. These efforts largely succeeded when the government was granted a six-year derogation from implementing the provisions on working time and night work for adolescents and the weekly working hours for children (EIRR 238: 2). This concession gave rise to objections from a number of member states. When the Council agreed on a Common Position, Spain and Italy abstained in protest. The two countries were particularly opposed to the fact that the six-year derogation should also apply to the weekly working hours of children (EIRR 239: 2).

In its second reading, the European Parliament called for a total removal of the UK derogation, and the Commission accepted the removal of exemptions for children in its revised text. As a consequence, unanimity was required for the UK to return to the text of the Common Position, which included the derogations for children. In this situation, the Greek presidency signalled its unwillingness to vote in favour of the Common Position, apparently because it was dissatisfied with the UK's opposition to a draft programme on social exclusion which was debated at the same Council meeting (EIRR 244: 2; *Financial Times*, 20 April 1994, p. 7). In the end, the UK got its way and the Council returned to the Common Position's text, thereby allowing all derogations originally granted to the UK (EIRR 246: 2).

Besides the fundamental British opposition, which could only be overcome in the end by substantial derogations and by the threat of majority voting, there were a number of minor national objections regarding specific provisions of the Directive. France pressed for an exemption that allowed its specific authorisation system for the employment of teenage models in Paris fashion shows to be upheld (Interviews F4: 567–72, F10: 1496–7). Denmark wanted to extend the exemptions from the ban on child labour so that Danish children below the age of 15 would be able to continue to perform auxiliary jobs in family businesses, such as harvesting strawberries (Interview LUX1: 791–834). These objections were not of a fundamental nature and could be dispelled relatively easily by granting specific derogations or exemptions to these countries, finally allowing the Directive to be passed by the Council in June 1994.

7.3   Misfit in the member states: modest reforms for a small group of workers

The Young Workers Directive, like the one on Employment Contract Information, caused only small or medium-scale adaptation requirements in the member states. This is mainly due to the fact that all countries, even the UK and Ireland, already had some sort of legislation protecting young workers. With regard to maximum working hours, minimum rest periods and night work restrictions, moreover, the Working Time Directive had already defined a certain minimum level of protection for all workers. In addition, the Directive only affected a rather small proportion of the total workforce (see below for more details).

Finally, it has to be noted that the amount of changes necessitated by the Directive was significantly reduced by anticipatory implementation in two countries. Five weeks before the adoption of the Directive, Spain enacted a reform Bill which eliminated a large part of the otherwise existing adaptation requirements. In Portugal, an anticipatory reform was enacted much earlier, at the end of 1991, but still a clear link to some of the Directive's standards can be discerned. At any rate, the reform agenda of the actual transposition process would have included a range of additional issues if the 1991 reform had not found its way onto the statute books.

The results of our empirical analysis reveal that six countries were confronted with medium degrees of *policy misfit* (Austria, Belgium, Denmark, Ireland, Portugal and the UK), while the remaining countries only had to come to terms with minor reform requirements (see Table 7.1; on the operationalisation of the concept of 'misfit', see Chapter 2).

Despite the general modesty of the policy misfit created by the Directive, many individual revisions of existing statutory provisions were called for. For instance, five countries had to increase the scope of their existing legislation so as to include all young workers covered by the Directive. Most importantly, the UK had no statutory rules for sixteen- and seventeen-year-olds (EIRR 220: 18; *Financial Times*, 23 November 1988, p. 14, 2 December 1988, p. 14). The Irish legislation excluded youngsters employed in the shipping and fishery sectors as well as in the army (Protection of Young Persons (Employment) Act 1977, s. 3). Moreover, the relevant statutory provisions of Belgium and France did not cover pupils performing work in the context of their education (Interview B3b; CEC 2001b: 32) and, in Greece, young workers employed in a private household or a family business in the agricultural or forestry sector were completely excluded from the legislation, whereas the Directive only

Table 7.1 *The Young Workers Directive and misfit in the member states*

	Degree of Legal Misfit	Limited Practical Significance	Degree of *Total Policy Misfit*	Degree of Politics/ Polity Misfit	Economic Costs	Degree of *Total Misfit*
A	medium	no	medium	–	low	medium
B	medium	no	medium	–	low	medium
D	low	no	low	–	low	low
DK	medium	no	medium	–	low	medium
E	low	no	low	–	low	low
F	low	no	low	–	low	low
FIN	low	no	low	–	low	low
GB I	low	no	low	–	low	low
GB II	medium	no	medium	–	low	medium
GR	low	no	low	–	low	low
I	low	no	low	–	low	low
IRL	medium	no	medium	–	low	medium
LUX	low	no	low	–	low	low
NL	low	no	low	–	low	low
P	medium	no	medium	–	low	medium
S	low	no	low	–	low	low

permits the exclusion of occasional or short-term work performed on such premises (Interview GR1b).

The general principle prohibiting child labour was already guaranteed in all countries but the details were not in line everywhere. In particular, Denmark allowed children to do light work from the age of ten onwards and thus had to raise this limit at least to the age of thirteen (Interview DK6: 873–931). Austria was forced to raise the age limit for youngsters allowed to do anything other than light work from fourteen to fifteen (Interviews A2: 858–1098, A8: 410–45). The same applied to the agricultural sector in Italy (Blanpain et al. 1997: 469).

In terms of the health and safety provisions of the Directive, all member states had to adapt at least some details of their respective regulations. As in the case of pregnant workers, it should be noted that the requirement for employers to carry out a risk assessment in relation to their workers had in principle already been provided for by the 1989 Framework Directive on Health and Safety. Against this background, the Young Workers Directive only called for a gradual improvement to the existing systems, in particular by obliging employers to carry out a *specific* risk assessment with regard to young workers. Moreover, the Directive contained a detailed list of dangerous activities which young persons are not allowed to perform, and it prescribed specific protective measures such as the provision of free health check-ups for young workers employed in potentially dangerous workplaces.

Such a specific system of health and safety rules for young workers, including explicit employment prohibitions and health provisions, had to be introduced in the UK and Ireland. The other thirteen countries already had statutory schemes aiming to protect young workers specifically and so only had to improve certain aspects of these rules and regulations. Of these, nine countries had to expand or adapt the applicable list of forbidden activities for young persons. This was the case in Austria, Belgium, Denmark, Germany, Greece, Italy, Luxembourg, Portugal and Spain.[4] Moreover, five member states were forced to adapt their regulations so as to guarantee free health check-ups for youngsters performing certain dangerous activities, especially in relation to night work. These were Austria, Belgium, Finland, Luxembourg and Portugal.[5]

With regard to the wider employment rights provisions of the Directive, the most important changes were required in the UK, where small adaptations to the working time of children had to be enacted in conjunction with completely new regulations on the working hours and night work limits of adolescents as well as on the weekly rest periods of all young workers (COM [1991] 543; Hepple and Hakim 1997: 664).

As to the working time standards, only three countries, Greece, Spain and Luxembourg, were fully in line with the detailed provisions of the Directive. The others had to enact some (mostly minor) changes. The Directive also required a number of more wide-ranging adaptations: Denmark, for instance, had to reduce daily working hours for adolescents from ten to eight hours and was forced to introduce for the first time a maximum weekly ceiling of forty hours (Blanpain et al. 1997: 267). Similarly, Ireland had to reduce considerably the working hours allowed for adolescents from nine hours a day and forty-five hours a week to eight hours and forty hours (Protection of Young Persons (Employment) Act 1977, s. 9). Belgium was also required to reduce the daily working hours of adolescents by two hours (Blanpain and Engels 1997: 225), and Sweden had to cut the maximum weekly working time of adolescents by five hours (Interview S13).

---

[4] For Spain, see Decree of 26 July 1957, published in *Boletín Oficial*, de 26 de agosto 1957. See also Interviews A2: 858–1098; B5: 343–63; DK6: 248–393; GR1: 508–669; I3: 251–379; LUX1: 360–515; P2: 731–1007; Schlüter 1997: 18.

[5] See Interviews A2: 858–1098; B2: 392–410; LUX1: 360–515; P2: 890–906; CEC 2001b: 75.

Besides the UK, the night work rules had to be tightened up in six other countries. Most notably, Portugal was forced to extend the restrictive provisions on night work to all non-industrial sectors of the economy (COM [1991] 543: 6). France had to extend the restricted period of night work for children by two hours (Interview F4: 535–683). Belgium had to extend the same period for adolescents by one hour (Labour Act 1971, Art. 35).

Moreover, only the regulations of Greece, the Netherlands, Spain and Sweden were completely in accordance with the Directive's standard on young workers' minimum weekly rest periods. All other countries had to improve their rules gradually with a view to guaranteeing that all youngsters are provided with a rest period of two days per week. Most notably, the UK and Finland had to introduce this standard for all young workers (see above and Interview FIN6a), while Germany had not guaranteed this standard for children before this Directive had to be implemented (Schlüter 1997: 17). In addition, the weekly rest periods had to be extended from one to two days in Denmark, France, Ireland, Italy and Portugal (Interviews DK6: 248–393; F4: 535–683; P2: 731–1007; Blanpain et al. 1997: 469; and see the Protection of Young Persons (Employment) Act 1977, s. 13 (Ireland) and the Conditions of Employment Act 1936, s. 49 (Ireland)).

Turning to the *politics and polity dimension*, the Young Workers Directive did not call for any administrative reform in the member states. Even though the Directive explicitly contains a provision on enforcement, this provision does not prescribe a specific enforcement system. It only requires member states to take 'effective and proportionate' measures in the event of non-compliance with its standards (see above). Likewise, the Directive did not interfere with the established relationship between the state and the social partners. Even in countries like Denmark or Sweden, the protection of young workers was a matter traditionally subject to statutory rules rather than to autonomous social partner agreements.

Finally, the *economic costs* of implementing the Directive were small in all countries. While the Directive did include some cost-relevant provisions, such as working time limits or free health check-ups, the total costs for employers were tempered by the fact that the Directive only concerned a rather small group of workers. Although exact figures for employees in the age group between thirteen and seventeen years are not available, Eurostat data includes figures on the share of workers between fifteen and nineteen years of age. In 1995, the proportion was below 5 per cent, even in the UK, which had the highest share of young workers (Eurostat 1996: Table 14).

7.4   Implementation in the member states

7.4.1   *Particularly interesting cases*

Perhaps surprisingly, Denmark was among the countries on which the Directive had the greatest effect. The Directive called for the considerable reduction of the working hours allowed for sixteen- and seventeen-year-olds and for a significant extension of the weekly rest period for youngsters from one to two days (Interview DK6: 248–393; Blanpain et al. 1997: 266–7).

Moreover, Denmark was the only member state whose legislation allowed children below the age of thirteen to perform light work. Children aged ten and upwards were allowed to work for a few hours, and they did so mostly in the context of newspaper delivery. Debates about raising this very low age limit had already begun in the early 1970s, when ILO Convention 138 Concerning Minimum Age for Admission to Employment was passed, which provided for an age limit of thirteen. But since newspaper publishers opposed any changes to this limit, and many politicians, especially from the Conservative and Liberal parties, a number of whom had themselves worked as paperboys in their youth, did not consider this kind of work harmful, there were no changes to the age limit (Interview DK6: 873–931). This blocking coalition at the domestic level only fell apart when the Commission tabled its draft Directive on Young Workers, which also provided for a higher age limit. Supported by the unions, but opposed by the employers, the Danish centre-left government took the opportunity to break the domestic deadlock and voted in favour of the Directive in the Council (Interviews DK3: 733–44, DK6: 832–53).

When the Directive was set to be implemented, however, the government's multi-level game almost failed, since it had lost its parliamentary majority in the elections of September 1994 and so the three governing parties of the social democrats, the Centre Party and the Radical Liberals had to seek support for their reform among opposition parties (Damgaard 2000). In this situation, it was the opposition Liberals (*Venstre*) in particular who expressed their strong reservations about raising the age limit, and set in train a controversial public debate over the pros and cons of this measure. Since the opposition parties held effective veto power, this conflict could not be resolved until after the social democratic Minister of Labour had offered a number of concessions to the opposition – although these did not affect the substance of what had to be transposed (Interview DK6: 564–613, 832–53). It says a lot about the importance of complying with EU law in Denmark that, despite these fierce debates, the government managed to implement the Directive in time.

Party political resistance was also crucial in the British case. This time, however, it came from within the government itself. As we have seen above, the UK was the most fervent opponent of the Directive at the European level. And despite having won a transition period of six years for some of the most important standards of the Directive, the Conservative government was very reluctant to comply with the remaining parts of the Directive. Owing to this ideological defiance, only a few relatively insignificant parts of the adaptation requirements had been implemented when the Conservative government was replaced by Labour in the elections of May 1997, almost a year after the expiry of the deadline. Under the Labour government, the process gathered momentum, but since there were many other employment reforms that Labour had announced in its election campaign and which therefore appeared more pressing than the Young Workers Directive, it still took some time until the transposition could be completed.

In June 2000, the six-year transition period ended, and the Labour government, reacting to union pressure, did not seek a renewal of this transition period, even though the employers' organisation, the Confederation of British Industry (CBI) had lobbied hard to gain a further exemption.[6] Hence, the UK now had to comply with the more significant rules on working time and night work for sixteen- and seventeen-year-olds. At the end of the 1990s, no specific legislation existed in this area in the UK due to the deregulation of the Thatcher government. But since the Working Time Directive had been implemented in the meantime, youngsters were at least covered by the rules applying to adults.

Despite its general support for the Directive, the Labour government was in no apparent hurry to comply with the remaining parts of the Directive. Again, other reforms appeared more important so that administrative resources in the responsible Department of Trade and Industry were directed towards these projects (Interview GB4: 365–73). As usual, employers pressed hard for a minimalist implementation, especially of the night work provisions, whereas the unions supported a stricter transposition of the Directive (Interviews GB3a, GB4a). Since young workers are not part of the core membership of unions, however, the young workers issue did not figure particularly high on their agenda. Thus, there was no one who would have pressed for swift adaptation, and therefore the second part of the transposition process was only completed in April 2003, almost three years after the end of the transition period. At least by then it brought some notable improvements, especially for

---

[6] See Interviews GB4: 117–20, GB5: 409–17; 784–6 and the Commission's report on the end of the UK opt-out (COM [2000] 457).

sixteen- and seventeen-year-olds who had fallen victim to Margaret Thatcher's deregulation policy at the end of the 1980s.

Besides these two rather positive examples, there were also some countries in which the improvements required by the Directive were at least partly counterbalanced by moves to lower the existing level of protection for some groups of young persons. In Germany, implementing the lesser reform requirements of the Directive as such did not pose any problems. However, controversies arose over the decision of the centre-right government to use the transposition process to exclude adult apprentices from the scope of the young workers legislation. Previously they had been covered by the stricter standards applying to young workers. This step had been called for by employers' organisations, especially from small craft employers who perceived this provision as an impediment to vocational training. The unions were fiercely opposed to this lowering of the level of protection and tried hard to stop these plans. Although their efforts failed in the end, union resistance and the heated debates surrounding this issue caused delays of more than eight months in transposing the Directive.

In Austria, exactly the same lowering of standards for adult apprentices was envisaged by the ÖVP/SPÖ grand coalition and, just as in Germany, the unions were heavily opposed to this action. The controversy could only be resolved by coupling the transposition to a larger reform package which had the aim of boosting vocational training (Interview A3: 137–58, 246–83). Moreover, employers were fiercely opposed to extending the continuous weekly rest period from forty-three to forty-eight hours, as required by the Directive. Previously, youngsters could be required to work a few hours on Saturday morning, but this was no longer possible with two full days off per week. This primarily affected bakeries, butchers' shops, dairies and retail outlets and so employers from these sectors advocated a minimalist implementation of this standard and struggled to make use of the available derogations. But since these were not very clearly worded in the Directive (see above), severe problems with interpretation occurred – at one point, it was not even clear any longer that two days' weekly rest meant forty-eight hours (Interview A2: 858–1098).

As a result of these two controversial issues, the revised young workers legislation could only come into force in July 1997, one year after the end of the implementation deadline. Following protests by negatively affected employers, the rules concerning the weekly rest period, which initially did not make use of the derogation options, were relaxed shortly after so as to allow the rest period to be reduced in some of the sectors that were most affected by this reform (Interview A3: 619–39; Gächter 1997). However, *full* transposition of the Directive was not completed until three years later. The minor adaptations to the employment restrictions applying to young workers had only come into force in January 1999, since this reform was used to update and consolidate the existing regulations (Interview A2: 858–1089; *Bundeskammer für Arbeiter und Angestellte* 1999). Finally, in mid 2000, a minor omission concerning health check-ups for youngsters working at night was remedied (Interview A2: 858–1098). Here, however, the existing night work restrictions for young people working in hotels and restaurants were relaxed so as to make full use of the flexibility allowed by the Directive. Compared with the situation before the Directive, this also meant a lowering of standards, even though this did not occur in the context of the original transposition process, but three years later.

The transposition of the Directive in the Netherlands was also marked by deregulation. The existing Dutch legislation was already largely in line with the provisions of the Directive. Only some gradual improvements were required to comply with the European standards. But instead of simply closing the remaining gaps, the government, reacting to employer pressure, decided to lift some of the general employment prohibitions applying to young workers and to replace them with a system of work under the supervision of an adult. The unions vociferously protested against what they perceived to be a lowering of the level of protection, but the government nevertheless proceeded with its plans.[7] The unions argued that the new system was contrary to the Directive, which in their view required full prohibition of the activities in question, and they even sent an official complaint to the European Commission (Interviews NL6: 112–73, NL12: 295–397). But a thorough analysis of the Directive and the corresponding Dutch legislation[8] reveals that the system of expert supervision is indeed in line with the Directive, which might also be the reason why the Commission so far has not reacted to the unions' complaint. The debates surrounding this issue, along with the fact that this reform was embedded in a wider reform that sought to consolidate the huge body of individual health and safety regulations (Interview NL7: 179–86), caused a delay of one year in adapting to the health and safety provisions of the Directive.

While the system of expert supervision did not breach the provisions of the Directive, the deregulatory agenda of the government which, despite being led by the social democrats, had assumed power with an explicit programme of deregulation and flexibilisation, did indeed come into conflict with other provisions of the Directive (see below for more details).

---

[7] The government not only seems to have been motivated by deregulatory goals, but also argued that the new system would allow young people to familiarise themselves gradually with working life. Under the rigid system of general prohibitions this was almost impossible (Interview NL6: 170–3).

[8] Especially Art. 7 of the Directive and Art. 1.37 of the so-called '*Arbobesluit*'. See Staatsblad 1997: 60.

In Portugal, transposition of the Directive had been preceded by a fundamental reform enacted in 1991. This reform had been triggered by ILO pressure to reduce the high rate of child labour in Portugal (Interviews P3: 1010–46, P8: 675–6, 960–83). By way of anticipated adaptation, the government also tried to incorporate the provisions of the draft Directive, which had been tabled by the Commission shortly before (Interview P2: 760–2, 1098–104). This reform was highly controversial since employers lobbied hard against the government's attempts to restrict cheap child labour. When the Directive was finally adopted in Brussels, the impact on Portugal had already been considerably reduced by the 1991 reform. Nevertheless, the reform requirements still reached medium-sized levels.

Against the background of the contentious reform enacted only a few years earlier, the centre-right government that was in office until November 1995 was reluctant to reopen Pandora's box and thus did not take any steps to transpose the Directive. The process only started after the Socialist minority government had assumed power. But the required adaptations were again fiercely contested between employers and unions. In particular, the extension of night work restrictions to all sectors (where, previously, night work limits had only existed in industry) was heavily opposed by employers' organisations. They lobbied for a full use of the flexibility granted by the Directive. However, this meant that the quite strict rules applicable in industry would be relaxed, which was opposed by the unions, who argued that this was a lowering of the level of protection (Interviews P2: 877–88, 1172–90, P8: 729–51). In the end, the employers prevailed. As a result of the initial inactivity and the subsequent controversies, the Directive was only transposed essentially correctly with a delay of more than six years.

In the third group of countries, factors like government negligence and administrative inefficiency caused serious delays in adapting to the Directive despite (or maybe even because of) low levels of misfit. Luxembourg managed to transpose the Directive only five years after the end of the deadline. Again, the main problem was a lack of administrative resources, combined with the bureaucratic logic of focusing on the most important issues and setting aside apparently minor reforms until the pressure from Brussels reached serious levels. In this case, the Luxembourg *malaise* was even slightly aggravated by the need for interministerial co-ordination. At any rate, transposition could only be completed once the ECJ had condemned Luxembourg for non-notification in 1999.[9]

---

[9] Judgment of the Court of 16 December 1999, case C-47/99, *Commission of the European Communities v. Grand Duchy of Luxembourg* [1999] ECR I–8999.

Finally, in France it also took an ECJ ruling of non-notification[10] before the government took the necessary steps to close the small gaps that prevented the existing French law from complying fully with the Directive. But in this case, it was resistance rather than inability that explained the surprising outcome. The French government considered the existing French rules sufficient to fulfil the requirements of the Directive (Interview F2: 1011–18). Despite being aware of the fact that some small changes would be necessary,[11] the government nonetheless refused to set its legislative machinery in motion. This resistance was definitely not caused by the (modest) effects of what had to be changed, but by the contention that the national model by and large was sufficient to comply with the European rules. Hence, it was only after European pressure had increased considerably – when, shortly after the ECJ ruling, the Commission even initiated a second infringement procedure under Article 228 ECT, which involved the credible threat of serious financial sanctions – that the French ceased to adhere to their national model and transposed the missing provisions of the Directive.

7.4.2   Timeliness and correctness of transposition

In view of the rather modest reform requirements caused by the Directive in the majority of member states, it is remarkable that only two countries, Denmark and Spain, had managed to *transpose the Directive essentially correctly* by the end of the transposition deadline in June 1996. Ironically, Denmark was among the countries that were confronted not just with small but also with medium-sized levels of policy misfit. One further member state, Sweden, was less than six months late, while the delay of Germany was between six and twelve months. Greece managed to transpose the Directive essentially correctly less than two years after the expiry of the deadline. The remaining ten countries were more than two years late. At the time of writing, two of them had even failed to implement the Directive in an essentially correct fashion. As a consequence, only one-fifth of all member states implemented the Directive essentially correctly *at least almost on time* (i.e. no more than six months after the deadline). In other words, four-fifths of all countries accomplished this task no better than *significantly delayed*.

[10] Judgment of the Court of 18 May 2000, case C-45/99, *Commission of the European Communities v. French Republic* [2000] ECR I–3615.

[11] According to the Court's judgment (see note 10 above), the French authorities had replied to the Commission's Letter of Formal Notice 'that the French legislation in force already contained most of the legislative provisions of the Directive'. Nevertheless, they 'acknowledged that that legislation still had to be supplemented in order to ensure satisfactory implementation'.

By the end of our period of analysis, two countries had not yet fulfilled the requirements of the Directive essentially correctly. On 30 April 2003, the law in Finland granted young workers only a weekly rest period of thirty-eight instead of forty-eight hours. It seems that this shortcoming was also partly caused by the unclear wording of the respective standard of the Directive, which has given rise to interpretation problems in Austria as well (see above). Furthermore, the principle that the working hours of young workers employed by more than one employer have to be added up when calculating maximum working hours was not being complied with, and young people assigned to night work were granted a free health check-up only once rather than at regular intervals. The Dutch implementation legislation also contained three breaches of the Directive. The weekly rest period only amounted to thirty-six instead of forty-eight hours. Moreover, young workers were generally allowed to do temporary overtime for up to nine hours per day and forty-five hours per week, provided that the working hours were averaged out to eight hours a day and forty hours a week.[12] Finally, fifteen-year-olds were only granted a daily rest period of twelve rather than fourteen hours, as required by the Directive.

Further to this, a number of minor violations of the Directive come to light if we apply even stricter standards and look for completely correct transposition of the Directive. On 30 April 2003, French legislation only protected the health and safety of young persons by means of a comprehensive set of prohibited activities, but did not require employers to carry out a risk assessment taking into account the specific risks to young workers (Interview F11). The list of prohibited activities for young people contained in Spanish legislation did not fully correspond to the annexes of the Directive (CEC 2001b: 27). In Greece, youngsters working in family businesses in the agricultural or forestry sector were completely excluded from the relevant provisions of domestic legislation, while the Directive only allows the exclusion of occasional or short-term work performed on such premises. This has a considerable impact on incorrect application since the primary sector is still comparatively large in this country and work is particularly dangerous there (Interview GR1: 685–9, Petroglou 2000).

In Italy, young workers assigned to night work were not granted regular health check-ups (CEC 2001b: 46). In Sweden, the schooling hours of young persons working under a combined work/training scheme were not counted as working time, and the health checks for youngsters working nights were not granted by generally binding legislation, but could only be

---

[12] The Directive, however, prescribed a total maximum of eight hours and forty hours respectively, from which derogations were only allowed in exceptional cases.

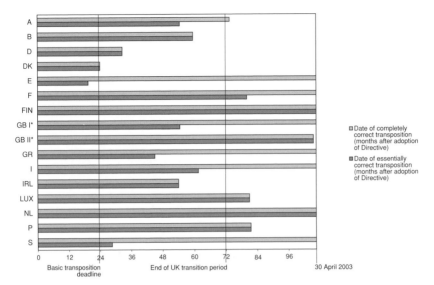

Figure 7.1 The Young Workers Directive and timing of adaptation

ordered by a supervisory authority (CEC 2001b: 82–3). Finally, the UK lacked a statutory provision guaranteeing children a weekly rest period of forty-eight (instead of only twelve) hours as well as a daily rest period of fourteen (instead of only twelve) hours.

Figure 7.1 summarises the timing of the member states in terms of *essentially correct* and *completely correct* transposition of the Young Workers Directive.

7.5   National problems with application and enforcement

With regard to practical application of the standards, our research uncovered a number of street-level compliance problems. First of all, there seem to be a certain number of violations of the child labour restrictions in many countries. Even in member states with rather efficient enforcement systems (see Chapter 13), such as Germany, the Netherlands or the UK, there were reports of illegal child labour, especially with regard to school children who take on work for which they are too young or which they are otherwise not allowed to perform (e.g. employment in industrial enterprises). Moreover, the working time restrictions are frequently abused, too. In Germany, for example, the federal government prepared a report on child labour in 2000 (BT-Drucksache 14/3500). On the basis of data gathered by the enforcement authorities of the *Länder*, the report reveals that almost a quarter of pupils in the state of Thuringia violated the legal rules on child labour. A researcher who carried out a project on child labour in the *Land* of North Rhine-Westphalia at the beginning of the 1990s argued that illegal child labour was a 'mass phenomenon'. According to his estimates, about half of all children with a job do not comply with the law (*Die Zeit*, 20 July 1998). Similar reports exist for the Netherlands (Interview NL1: 480–508; Lamers 1997) and the UK (Hepple and Hakim 1997: 683–4).

Given the relative effectiveness of the enforcement systems in these countries, it is likely that these types of violations of child labour restrictions are also widespread in many of the other member states. Dutch experts argued that illegal child labour is generally hard for enforcement agencies to prevent since many children *voluntarily* violate the rules in order to earn money to spend on mobile phones, CDs, clothes and the like (Interviews NL1: 480–508, NL6: 774–810).

Apart from this more general phenomenon of frequent 'self-exploitation', a number of countries face special problems with practical compliance. In Portugal, illegal child labour seems to be a particularly pressing issue. For example, children are forced to work not only in the production of shoes and other leather products in the north of Portugal, but also in agriculture and in hotels and catering. In recent years, considerable efforts have been undertaken to alleviate this problem. Partly as a reaction to rising international pressure, a number of public campaigns have been launched to raise awareness among parents and employers, and the active monitoring and enforcement activities have been significantly improved (Interviews P3: 652–75, P6: 587–732; Cristovam 1998b). Governmental and administrative actors seem to be aware of the problem and have taken steps to improve the situation.

In Ireland, a huge amount of non-compliance occurs in relation to unlawful employment of young persons in pubs and bars, where many adolescents earn extra money by serving drinks. In this context, many of them violate the night work restrictions by working beyond 11 p.m. There was consensus among our interview partners that this was a serious problem for which no solution has been found to date (Interviews IRL4: 351–407, IRL5: 360–71, IRL8: 1095–112). A code of practice was drawn up by the Department of Enterprise, Trade and Employment in collaboration with trade unions, restaurant and hotel associations, and vintners' organisations in order to alleviate this problem (Interview IRL4: 351–407; see also *Irish Times*, 25 July 2001, p. 7), but it needs to be accompanied by intensified enforcement activities. However, the labour inspectorate is still seriously understaffed and thus unable to carry out a sufficient number of inspections (see also Chapter 13).

A specific problem also seems to exist in Germany with regard to the working conditions of apprentices. Trade union representatives reported that the government's decision to exclude adult apprentices from the scope of the young workers legislation has given rise to a partial erosion of compliance with the more general rules on apprentices. Adult apprentices may now be required to work after a day spent at vocational school, but some employers have taken the reform as an invitation to stop counting as working time the time spent on vocational school with regard to all of their apprentices. As a consequence, the latter are sometimes required to work for forty-eight hours a week or more (Interview D7: 108–30, 236–74). So the government's legislative deregulation has partly functioned as a magnet inducing practical non-compliance more generally.

7.6   General assessment of the Directive's effects

In general, the Directive targets a particularly vulnerable group of workers, and hence might be seen as a helpful measure for improving the levels of protection of children and adolescents from harmful working conditions. The legislative intervention in favour of young workers appears to be even more important if one considers that the young are a classical 'outsider group'. They usually do not belong to the core membership of trade unions, and thus defending their interests may not always be top priority in union campaigns.

If we look at the actual effects of the Directive in the member states, however, we must note that, taken as a whole, the *improvements achieved were rather modest*. This was predominantly due to the fact that all countries already had some kind of statutory protection for young workers, many of them guaranteeing comparatively high levels of protection even before implementing the Directive. Thus the overall degree of misfit created by the Directive was comparatively modest (see Table 7.2). Having said that, it should not be overlooked that there were *some notable exceptions* to this general observation. At least in some cases, the Directive did lead to a significant improvement in the protection levels, mostly by closing gaps in the existing domestic schemes. Most notably, the Directive reversed the deregulation carried out by the UK government under Margaret Thatcher in the 1980s and thus provided sixteen- and seventeen-year-olds in particular with much improved working conditions. Moreover, the binding force of European law finally enabled the Danish government to raise considerably the minimum age of employment, i.e. from ten to thirteen years – action which the ILO had called for unsuccessfully for many years. In addition, the Directive caused some

Table 7.2 *Overview of the Young Workers Directive and its implementation*

Aim	To protect young workers from harmful or dangerous working conditions
History	Commission Proposal 15 March 1992 Council Directive 22 June 1994
Standards	13 binding standards (most importantly: prohibition of child labour and night work by young persons as well as strict daily and weekly working time limits for adolescents) 3 recommendations 11 exemption provisions
Degree of Misfit	High: 0 Medium: 6[a] Low: 9
Transposition problems	12 member states significantly delayed 2 member states have still not accomplished transposition essentially correctly

[a] The UK is a special case in relation to this Directive for there were two phases of implementation with rather different reform implications. Since our interest here lies in the overall picture, we have summarised all reform requirements of both phases in this table, resulting in medium-scale misfit for the UK.

notable improvements such as the extension of weekly rest periods or enhanced health and safety conditions for young workers in many countries.

At the same time, however, analysing the actual implementation of the Directive at the domestic level revealed that these improvements were considerably counterbalanced by the fact that quite a number of countries used the transposition process to lower some of their previously existing standards. Austria and Germany excluded adult apprentices from the specific protection hitherto offered by their young workers legislation. In Austria, the government relaxed the night work limits in hotels and restaurants in a second reform move after the original transposition process, so as to lower the standards to the level of the Directive. In the Netherlands, the government swam against the tide in that it curtailed the weekly rest period from forty-eight to thirty-six hours, thereby creating a breach of the Directive which would not have existed before. In Portugal, the government was forced to extend to all sectors the scope of the night work restrictions obtaining in the industrial area, but, in doing so, relaxed these rules considerably and thus lowered the level of protection for young workers employed in industry.

The non-regression clause of the Directive could not prevent these moves to weaken existing standards, largely due to the fact that it is worded very loosely.[13] Hence, it is doubtful that individual deregulation steps, which might be balanced by improvements in other areas (such as in Portugal), would actually be outlawed by the clause. Moreover, the clause only prohibits a lowering of the levels of protection in the context of implementing the Directive. But what if countries decide to lower their standards some years after the original transposition process, as was the case in Austria? It seems that such steps are also only incompletely covered by the non-regression clause as laid down in the Directive. Finally, the clause only refers to the level of protection afforded to young people (i.e. those below the age of 18). Hence, the exclusion of adult apprentices from the young workers protection legislation in Austria and Germany would not seem to fall within the scope of the clause. To be sure, this latter weakness could hardly be otherwise, as outlawing domestic deregulation *outside* the scope of a European Directive would entail a wide-ranging restriction of national autonomy, which would often reach beyond even the EU's competences. Nevertheless, the problems analysed here for the particular case of the Young Workers Directive have wider implications, since the general handling of the non-regression clause remains an issue which has so far been almost unnoticed both empirically (e.g. in the context of the Commission's enforcement policy) and analytically (in EU implementation research or legal analysis).

In sum, therefore, a mixed picture emerges. On the one hand, the Directive did indeed bring about some improvements in most countries. On the other hand, it led to the lowering of standards in some member states – or at least it could not inhibit such domestic developments. In a few countries, like the Netherlands or Germany, where the implementation of the Directive only entailed smaller enhancements but at the same time was accompanied by deregulation, the net effect of the Directive even tended to be slightly negative. While the overall effect of the Directive in all fifteen member states certainly was positive, the lesson to be drawn from the few cases where it actually had rather negative consequences is that the idea of a gradual improvement in social protection levels by means of European minimum standards depends heavily on the effectiveness of the non-regression principle. If the principle remains a 'dead letter', as in some of the above-mentioned cases, EU social policy could potentially become as much a motor for deregulation as a driving force for social improvement. To be sure, this pattern of EU social policy Directives as a 'deregulation magnet' was only of marginal importance among our total cases.

---

[13] 'The implementation of this Directive shall not constitute valid grounds for reducing the *general level of protection* afforded to young people' (Art. 16 of the Directive, emphasis added).

8 The Parental Leave Directive: compulsory policy innovation and voluntary over-implementation

8.1 Aim and contents of the Directive

The Parental Leave Directive[1] was the first EU-level social policy measure to be based on a framework agreement by the major European federations of management and labour (UNICE,[2] CEEP,[3] and ETUC[4]). The Parental Leave Directive did no more than give general legal force to the social partners pact. None of the latter's substantive provisions was modified, which is best illustrated by the fact that the agreement was attached, unchanged, to the Directive.

The *general aim* of the Directive is, according to the preamble preceding the main text of the social partners agreement, 'to set out minimum requirements on parental leave and time off from work on grounds of force majeure, as an important means of reconciling work and family life and promoting equal opportunities and treatment between men and women'. The purpose of the agreement is therefore to enable working parents to take a certain amount of time off from work to take care of their children. In this context, particular emphasis is put on enabling and encouraging men to take on a greater share of childcare responsibilities.

The *compulsory minimum standards* of the Directive thus encompass seven provisions:

(1) workers must be granted the right to at least three months' parental leave;
(2) this entitlement is to be an individual right of both male and female workers;
(3) parental leave has to be provided not only for parents with children by birth, but also for those who have adopted a child;
(4) workers may not be dismissed on the grounds of exercising their right to parental leave;

---

[1] Directive 96/34/EC of 3 June 1996 on the framework agreement on parental leave concluded by UNICE, CEEP and ETUC, OJ 1996 No. L145/4–9.
[2] The Union of Industrial and Employers' Confederations of Europe.
[3] The European Centre of Enterprises with Public Participation.
[4] The European Trade Union Confederation.

(5) after the period of leave, workers must be able to return to the same job, or, if that is not possible, to an equivalent or similar job;

(6) rights acquired by workers before the beginning of parental leave are to be maintained as they stand until the end of the leave period and must continue to apply thereafter;

(7) and, finally, workers have to be granted the right to 'force majeure leave', i.e. a certain amount of time off from work for unforeseeable reasons arising from a family[5] emergency that makes their immediate presence indispensable.

These binding provisions notwithstanding, establishing the access conditions and modalities for applying the right to parental leave and leave for urgent family reasons is left to the national governments and social partners. Hence, the Directive includes five *exemption and derogation possibilities*. (1) The entitlement to parental leave may be made subject to workers having completed a certain period of work or length of service, which, however, may not exceed one year. (2) Furthermore, a worker planning to take parental leave may be required to notify his or her employer of the dates at which the period of leave is to start and finish. It is up to the member states to decide upon the length of the period of notice. (3) Moreover, employers may be allowed to postpone the granting of parental leave for 'justifiable reasons related to the operation of the undertaking' (clause 2.3.d of the framework agreement). (4) In addition, member states can establish special parental leave arrangements for small businesses. (5) Finally, the conditions of access and detailed rules for applying parental leave may be adjusted to the special circumstances of adoption.

In addition to these binding standards and derogation possibilities, the Directive contains nine *non-binding soft-law provisions*. Hence, the Directive recommends (1) that the entitlement to parental leave should not be transferable between the parents, thereby increasing the incentives for men to take the leave; (2) that workers should continue to be entitled to social security benefits during parental leave, (3) in particular to health care benefits; (4) that parents ought to be able to take parental leave until the child has reached the age of eight; (5) that parental leave should not only be granted on a full-time basis, but also part-time, (6) in a piecemeal

---

[5] The Directive does not define the term 'family'. This is explicitly left to the member states (Ministerrat 1996). It is crucial to note, however, that by using this term, force majeure leave cannot be restricted solely to sickness or accidents of children, but must at least cover unforeseeable emergencies of spouses, too (for a similar interpretation, see Schmidt 1997: 122).

way, (7) or in the form of a time-credit system; (8) that men should be particularly encouraged to take parental leave in order to assume an equal share of family responsibilities, e.g. by measures such as awareness programmes; (9) and that the social partners at the national level ought to play a special role in the implementation and application of the European framework agreement.

Compared with the other Directives in our sample, both the number of binding standards (i.e. seven) and the number of derogation possibilities (i.e. five) in the Parental Leave Directive is below average. What makes this Directive stand out from most of the other ones is the rather high quantity of non-binding provisions. Among the social policy measures in our sample, the number of recommendations (i.e. nine) is only exceeded by the Part-time Work Directive, which comprises eleven such soft-law provisions. This large number of recommendations, relating to important features of the envisaged leave schemes, such as social security coverage during parental leave, flexible forms of exploiting the leave entitlement, or the maximum age of the child at which leave can be taken, seems to be due to the fact that trade unions and employers in the collective negotiations at the European level could not agree on definite standards on these issues. Hence, they chose devolution to the national implementation stage as a compromise strategy.

In sum, the policy scope of the Parental Leave Directive is rather narrow. It aims to establish a right for every worker, both male and female, to three months' parental leave and an entitlement to time off from work for urgent family reasons. Many details of these rights, however, are up to member states to define. In particular, the Directive includes a large number of non-binding recommendations which may or may not be taken on board by member states when implementing the Directive.

8.2   The European-level negotiation process

The first Commission proposal for a Directive on parental leave and leave for family reasons dates back to as early as 1983 (COM [1983] 686 final). On the basis of the argument that the quite diverse national provisions were thought to hamper the harmonious development of the Common Market, an approximation on the basis of Article 100 EEC Treaty was suggested. The minimum standards suggested were: three months of parental leave for either parent (to be taken up to the third birthday of the child), and an unspecified number of days off for family reasons to be decided by the individual member state. With regard to social insurance and pay, leave for *family reasons* was to be treated as time off with pay. In contrast, pay or indemnity for parental leave was only an option, to be met by public funds. The Commission advocated unequivocal non-transferability of these rights.

As a result of opposition by a number of member states, however, unanimous agreement on the draft was impossible. While the Conservative UK government was opposed to the Directive for ideological reasons, the Belgian and German governments were reluctant to accept the proposal because it would have interfered with ongoing domestic reforms. But party politics also played a role in triggering resistance from these countries. In Germany, debates on the establishment of a parental leave scheme were underway when the Commission tabled its draft. The scheme envisaged was relatively generous, but provided for the entitlement to parental leave to be transferable between mothers and fathers. The draft Directive, in contrast, included the principle of non-transferability, which meant that fathers would have stronger incentives to go on leave. This was not acceptable to the centre-right German government,[6] and therefore Germany was among the opponents of the Commission's parental leave proposal (Buchholz-Will 1990).

In Belgium, the Ministry for Social Affairs had tabled plans to introduce a national parental leave scheme in the early 1980s, but this motion encountered opposition within the centre-right government coalition. As a compromise, a more moderate (and more employer-friendly) scheme of career breaks was created which offered the possibility of up to one year off work, but relied on the employer's agreement and required a stand-in by an unemployed person. The draft Directive would have called for a significant upgrading of this compromise and was thus rejected by the Belgian government in 1985 (Interview B6: 30–7; Malderie 1997). Hence, the proposal was set aside for almost a decade.

Surprisingly, it was the Belgian Council presidency that put the Directive back on the agenda in 1993. This policy shift was caused by a change of government at home. The liberals had changed places with the socialists, who now formed a grand coalition with the christian democrats. Hence, the political climate for parental leave in Belgium was much friendlier than eight years earlier. Therefore, the Belgian presidency presented a new compromise proposal on parental leave. The new text no longer provided for non-transferability, which made the proposal acceptable to Germany, but British resistance continued. During the Social Council's November session, the UK reportedly tried in vain to obtain

---

[6] In September 1985, the German social democrats tabled an alternative proposal (BT-Drucksache 10/3806). Although it failed to include non-transferability, it provided for a prolongation of the leave period if both parents shared the leave. The government, however, refused to consider this idea and went ahead with its own transferable scheme, which was finally adopted in December 1985.

derogation from the Directive, and then restated its opposition.[7] Fruitless negotiations continued until autumn 1994. Despite consensus among eleven delegations in the last relevant Council debate on 22 September 1994, adoption of the proposal was still not possible due to a British veto (Ministerrat 1994; Hornung-Draus 1996).

This was the ideal situation for an application of the Maastricht Social Agreement, which by then had already been in force for almost a year. It excluded the UK from the social policy measures adopted by the other (then) eleven member states and allowed for the adoption of Euro-collective agreements between the major interest groups on social issues that could be implemented by the EC Council Directives (for details on the Social Agreement, see Falkner 1998). Hence, consultation of labour and management on the issue of 'reconciliation of professional and family life' was instigated by the Commission on 22 February 1995. The three major cross-sectoral federations of UNICE, CEEP and ETUC were keen to show that the Euro-corporatist procedures of the Maastricht Treaty could actually be put into practice.

The collective negotiations were successfully concluded after only five (out of a possible nine) months, on 6 November 1995 (*Agence Europe* 6600, 8 November 1995, p. 15). With a view to implementation, the ETUC, UNICE and CEEP requested that the Commission submit their framework agreement to the Council for a decision that would make the requirements binding in all the member states of the Union with the exception of the UK. Soon after the formal signing of the agreement on 14 December 1995, the Commission accordingly proposed a draft Directive to the Council (on 31 January 1996; cf. *Agence Europe* 6657, 1 February 1996, p. 7). Reportedly, the draft was a matter of controversy in the Social Affairs Council (cf. *Agence Europe* 6698, 29 March 1996, p. 8). For some delegations, the content of the framework agreement left too much room for interpretation, making proper application in the member states a difficult task. Others thought that the social partners had neglected the powers of the EU institutions by introducing a non-regression clause and a time limit for implementation. Nevertheless, a political consensus was reached on 29 March,[8] and the Directive was formally adopted without debate on 3 June 1996.

---

[7] At one point, a lowest common denominator solution seems to have emerged: the UK wished parental leave to be only granted to mothers, not to fathers. Reportedly, only the Irish delegation and the Commission were immediately against this 'awful' change (as one Commission official described it in an interview), which made the Commission threaten to bring in the ECJ against this discrimination on grounds of sex.

[8] Agreement was unanimous. Adoption, however, was postponed with a view to winning parliamentary approval in Germany (*Agence Europe* 6699, 30 March 1996, p. 7).

8.3   Misfit in the member states: policy innovation for some, qualitative improvements for many

Many scholars have argued that by the time of its adoption, the importance of the social partners agreement on parental leave lay in its existence rather than its substance. The symbolic importance of a first collective agreement at the EU level, to prove that the corporatist procedures of the Maastricht Social Agreement could be operational, was indeed great. At the same time, it was widely criticised that the agreed minimum standards were low (for example, see Keller 1997; Keller and Sörries 1999). Specialist journals such as the European Industrial Relations Review highlighted above all that the minimum three months of parental leave represented the shortest time allotted in any of the countries with a statutory right to parental leave, i.e. in Greece (EIRR 262: 15). One had the impression that legal changes would only be required in a very small number of countries. As to urgent family leave on the grounds of *force majeure*, the Directive's provisions were initially thought to improve the status quo only in Ireland and the UK, the latter originally being outside its remit (EIRR 263: 23).

In the light of these sceptical assessments, it might come as a surprise that our in-depth analysis of the Directive's reform implications reveals a slightly different picture. In fact, *adaptational pressure was created in all fifteen member states*. Four countries did not have any generally binding legal provisions on parental leave when the Directive was adopted (Belgium, Ireland, Luxembourg and the UK). In Belgium, the practical relevance of this considerable legal misfit was softened by the fact that a scheme of career breaks already existed. It was used by many as an equivalent for parental leave, although taking such a career break depended on the consent of the employer.[9] Nevertheless, there are three countries for which the Directive meant a considerable innovation even de facto, and thus resulted in significant *policy misfit* (for more details on this concept, see Chapter 2).

The remaining member states all had some kind of parental leave system in place, but in a considerable number of them this leave was not an individual right of male and female workers alike. The Directive thus

---

[9] In Luxembourg, employees had also been able since 1988 to take a career break and receive an allowance during this time. But these regulations did not include a right to return to the same or a similar job. A parent taking advantage of this career break always had to run the risk of not being re-employed. This is a very important difference from parental leave as defined by the Directive, and therefore we (and the political actors in Luxembourg as well) considered the introduction of parental leave as a complete innovation.

Table 8.1 *The Parental Leave Directive and misfit in the member states*

	Degree of Legal Misfit	Limited Practical Significance	Degree of *Total Policy Misfit*	Degree of Politics/ Polity Misfit	Economic Costs	Degree of *Total Misfit*
A	medium	no	medium	–	low	medium
B	high	yes	medium	–	low	medium
D	low	no	low	–	low	low
DK	low	no	low	high	low	high
E	low	no	low	–	low	low
F	low	no	low	–	low	low
FIN	low	no	low	–	low	low
GB	high	no	high	–	low	high
GR	medium	no	medium	–	low	medium
I	medium	no	medium	–	low	medium
IRL	high	no	high	–	low	high
LUX	high	no	high	–	low	high
NL	medium	no	medium	–	low	medium
P	medium	yes	low	–	low	low
S	low	no	low	–	low	low

demanded the introduction of qualitative improvements to the existing schemes. In Austria and Italy the parental leave regulations were mainly focused on women, whereas fathers were entitled to take the leave only if the mother refrained from using her right. Less significantly, the Austrian, German, Greek, and Portuguese systems excluded single-income families, that is, the typical male breadwinner could not take parental leave if his partner was not employed but worked at home as a housewife.

Moreover, the majority of member states needed to change their legislation in regard to *force majeure* leave. While Denmark, Ireland, Luxembourg, and the UK did not have generally binding legal rules on absence from work for urgent family reasons, Finland, France, Greece, Spain and Sweden had to adapt their existing regulations, mostly by including emergencies relating to family members other than children in the scope of the leave.

Altogether, there is not one country whose rules and regulations were already completely in line with the Directive. Seven member states had to cope with slight policy misfit, five with medium degrees of policy misfit, and three countries were confronted with large-scale policy misfit (see Table 8.1).

As far as *adaptational pressure in the politics and polity dimension* is concerned, the Directive did not require administrative reforms such as the assignment of new tasks to existing administrative units or the establishment of new ones. Enforcement of the provisions was left to the existing national (court) systems without the stipulation of any explicit institutional rules. Similarly, state–society relations were left untouched by the Directive in all but one country. This exception is Denmark, where the implementation of the Directive only demanded limited adaptation in policy terms (specific to *force majeure* leave) though it called for the introduction of generally binding legislation, instead of autonomous regulation by the social partners, to achieve these reform requirements, thereby challenging the established relationship between the state and the social partners (see Chapter 12).

The overall *economic costs* of implementing the Directive were modest in all the member states. This was mainly due to the fact that the Directive neither prescribed any payment nor demanded any social security coverage during either parental leave or *force majeure* leave. All that employers had to cope with, therefore, were the costs of replacing a worker during his or her absence from work.

8.4   Implementation in the member states

The Parental Leave Directive had to be incorporated into national law by 3 June 1998. A maximum additional period of one year was granted 'if this is necessary to take account of special difficulties or implementation by a collective agreement' (Article 2 of the Directive).

Since the British Conservative government had secured an opt-out from the European Treaty's Social Chapter at the Maastricht summit, the UK was not initially covered by the Directive. After Tony Blair's Labour government had assumed power in May 1997, the UK signed up to the Social Chapter and declared its willingness to implement the Directives that had been enacted during the opt-out period (EIRR, 282: 2, EIRR 284: 2). As a consequence, the UK's transposition deadline was later than that of the other member states. The UK had to comply with the Directive by 15 December 1999.

8.4.1   *Particularly interesting cases*

The first striking point when looking at the national transposition of this Directive is that the three countries with high degrees of policy misfit performed comparatively well, at least in terms of timing. The UK and Ireland both had to introduce completely new parental leave systems and managed to do so relatively fast. However, they initially transposed the Directive incorrectly. The governments of both countries were generally favourable to the family-friendly aspirations of the Directive. Pressurised by employers' organisations, though, they decided to introduce a 'cut-off date' limiting the parental leave entitlement to parents whose children were born after the coming into force of the Directive (in the case of Ireland) or the implementation legislation (in the British case). The trade unions in both countries considered this contradictory to the Directive, which was denied, however, by the employers' organisations (Interviews GB2: 184–95, 531–52; IRL1: 250–63).

The dispute between the two sides of industry played a decisive role in these cases since the Parental Leave Directive was based on an agreement between the chief organisations of business and labour at the European level. Hence, the same actors that had negotiated the parental leave deal in the first place now had conflicting views about the interpretation of their own agreement.[10] Since the Irish and British governments had decided to follow the employers' interpretation, the trade unions turned to the European level in order to clarify the matter. The Irish Congress of Trade Unions filed a complaint with the European Commission, who in turn initiated an infringement procedure against Ireland (Interview IRL1: 880–921). In the UK, the Trades Union Congress brought a case against the government in the High Court in London, which was subsequently referred to the European Court of Justice for a preliminary ruling (Interview GB6: 270–7; *Financial Times*, 16 May 2000, p. 6, 24 May 2000, p. 10). At the same time, the Commission also initiated an infringement procedure against the UK.

Since the European-level social partners had explicitly requested in their agreement that 'any matter relating to the interpretation of this agreement at European level should, in the first instance, be referred by the Commission to the signatory parties' (Clause 4.6 of the agreement), the Commission consulted representatives of UNICE, CEEP, and ETUC in order to clarify the matter. The foremost European organisations of business and labour finally supported the Commission's interpretation that the cut-off dates introduced in Ireland and the UK were contrary to the parental leave agreement.[11] On the basis of this clarification, and given the pressure which the EU infringement proceedings were causing, the Irish and British governments subsequently agreed to amend their legislation so as to repeal the cut-off date.

---

[10] Despite the UK's opt-out, the British TUC was included in the trade unions' delegation as a member with full voting rights. On the employers' side, the CBI also took part in the negotiations, but only as an observer (Falkner 1998: 118; Hartenberger 2001: 108).

[11] The text of the Reasoned Opinion issued by the European Commission against Ireland is reprinted in Clauwaert and Harger (2000: 117–18). This document also describes the process of consultation with the European-level social partners.

Lacking any real statutory parental leave entitlements, Luxembourg too was confronted with large-scale policy misfit. Nevertheless, the government not only transposed the Directive comparatively fast, i.e. within the extended implementation period,[12] but also went far beyond the minimum standards. The comparatively fast transposition of the Directive is even more astonishing given the fact that Luxembourg is very often among the countries transposing with significant delay. Being a small country with limited administrative capacities, implementation of EU Directives is frequently hampered by administrative overload. As a consequence, complying with European measures that demand only minor reforms appears less urgent a task than transposing Directives requiring the introduction of completely new rules like e.g. the Parental Leave Directive (Interview LUX1: 1000–34).

Further to the administration's unusually smooth functioning in this case, compliance was facilitated by the Luxembourg government's firm political support for the Directive. Parental leave was seen as a measure which could help reduce unemployment. It was expected that unemployed persons could replace employees on parental leave and would thus have the chance to reintegrate into the labour market. Hence, the government proposed a parental leave scheme which was not only longer than required (six instead of three months) but also very generously rewarded, and even pushed it through in the face of massive opposition by employers to 'unnecessary gold plating' of the Directive (Interviews LUX6: 143–87, LUX11: 570–634). However, in striking similarity to the UK and Ireland, a cut-off date was introduced, restricting eligibility to parents whose children were born or adopted on or after 1 January 1999, i.e. the date on which the law came into force. It is for this reason that the European Commission initiated a second infringement procedure against Luxembourg, this time for incorrect transposition, which has since even reached the stage of referral to the ECJ.

As already noted above, Belgium was one of the opponents of the Directive when the Commission put forward its first proposal in 1983. But after a change of government had improved the political climate for parental leave in Belgium, and after the creation of a system of career breaks along with a proliferation of parental leave schemes in collective agreements (Interview B6: 38–40) had reduced the adaptational pressure

---

[12] Although the transposition deadline could be extended for one year, which would have been enough for Luxembourg to complete implementation on time, member states had to apply to the Commission formally for such an extension. Apparently, Luxembourg failed to do so, which is why the Commission issued a Letter of Formal Notice (in August 1998) and a Reasoned Opinion (in February 1999) because Luxembourg had not by then given notice of its implementation measures.

of the Directive, the Belgian government supported the deal struck by the EU-level social partners and pressed for swift implementation.

An 'implementation race' between the social partners and the Labour Minister Miet Smet even accelerated the process. The former wanted to transpose the Directive by means of a generally binding collective agreement, which would make payment during leave dependent on additional state intervention. Since Minister Smet insisted on implementation under the existing system of career breaks, which she had introduced in Belgium and to which she therefore was personally attached (see Vanderhallen 1998), the social partner scheme was not backed financially. Under the Minister's scheme, which followed the logic of the career breaks system, the leave would be paid, but could be refused by the employer in businesses with fewer than ten employees (Interview B9: 302–14). Both sides went ahead with their plans and realised their aims long before the end of the transposition deadline, leading to the curious situation where Belgian employees can now choose between two systems: a rather minimalist one created by the social partners and a more generous (and, above all, paid) statutory one (Interview B9: 302–14). Since the Belgian system of social partnership enables both sides of industry to act autonomously, the diverging interests between the government and the social partners in this case actually furthered the swift implementation of the Directive rather than obstructing timely transposition.

Unlike Belgium, Italy was more than two years late in overcoming medium-scale adaptational requirements. In November 1999, an infringement case was even referred to the European Court of Justice on the grounds of non-transposition of the Directive. After adoption of appropriate legislation in Italy, the case was finally dropped in June 2000 (COM [2001] 309: 31). The belated introduction of this piece of legislation was mainly down to strong opposition from the employers' side (Interviews I6: 294–327; I9: 114–34). Interestingly, these conflicts were not so much focused on the compulsory adaptations as primarily due to the centre-left government's decision to over-implement the Directive significantly, above all by raising the length of (state-financed) parental leave from six to ten months, as well as to the fact that transposition was part of a broader act on reconciling working time and family care (Interview I5: 398–474).

In Germany, even small-scale misfit resulted in a significant delay in implementation of two and a half years. Although the existing parental leave scheme in general was much more generous than the Directive's standards, it had to be adapted so as to include single-income couples. The conservative-liberal government in power until 1998 was totally opposed to such a step since this was at odds with its conservative family-policy preferences (Interview D9: 143–50). When the European Commission issued a Letter of Formal Notice as a result of not receiving German transposition notification in 1998, German officials swiftly countered that there was no need for a change to the German legislation (Interview D3: 538–635). Despite the insufficiency of existing German legislation, the Commission seemed to be content with this reply and took no further action. Only after the new centre-left government had assumed power in October 1998 was transposition of the Directive accomplished. This reform not only eliminated the reform demands from Brussels, but even outstripped the minimum requirements of the Directive. In particular, it introduced a legal right to work part-time during parental leave and allowed parents to take parental leave simultaneously. Here, favourable political interests at the national level in the end brought about a more favourable outcome than supranational enforcement would have been able to produce on the basis of the binding provisions of the Directive.

France fulfilled the requirements of the Directive essentially correctly from the outset, but still has not reached the stage of full compliance. Here, it seems that the small number of changes required – only the provisions on *force majeure* leave had to be adapted somewhat – was one of the main causes of the lengthy inertia. A generous, state-financed parental leave system had existed in France since the 1970s. Only two years before the adoption of the Directive, this scheme was updated, thereby removing the main shortcoming of the existing legislation with regard to the standards of the Directive: the need to receive the employer's consent as a precondition for taking parental leave in small and medium-sized enterprises (EIRR 262: 18–19). Given this recent reform, combined with the general superiority of the French scheme, all actors felt that no adaptation was required.[13]

The Directive, however, called for a revision of the rules on *force majeure* leave so that workers would be able to take time off to care not only for children, but also for other family members. This adaptation requirement was ignored by French actors. In 2000, the *force majeure* regulations were even revised in the context of a wider reform with predominantly national origins, creating a right to paid leave of up to twelve months in order to take care of sick children. But this reform did nothing to close the gap between the existing scheme and the Directive, since the perception of a superior national scheme prevailed amongst national actors.

In Greece, a law enacted in 1998 eliminated only the most obvious part of the medium degree of misfit. This reform primarily dealt with

---

[13] Even trade unionists argued that no reforms were necessary since the Directive in essence only replicated the French system: '*Donc, la Directive n'a fait que prendre le droit français et le mettre au niveau européen*' (Interview F9: 675–6, similarly Interview F3: 552).

an improvement in maternity rights while at the same time repealing the exclusion of workers in small establishments (fewer than fifty employees) from the right to take parental leave. According to our interviews with national experts, interpretation problems, it appears, have so far prevented national actors from realising that one of the major demands of the Directive was also the inclusion of single-income couples in the parental leave scheme. This is not the case under current Greek law (Interviews GR2: 277–86; GR6: 71–7, GR14). This lack of awareness is typical for Greece and was especially obvious in this case. The debates surrounding the 1998 reforms show that even trade unions focus predominantly on furthering maternity rights, while (unpaid) parental leave lacks strong interest group support. Hence, there was nobody to push for full compliance with the Directive. This has recently changed since the EU Commission now finances an equal treatment think tank in Athens (KETHI), which has just begun to discover the issue (Interview GR14).

Two further interesting cases are Denmark and Luxembourg due to the role the national social partners played in the transposition of the Directive (see Chapter 12).

8.4.2   Timeliness and correctness of transposition

With regard to the point in time at which member states had *essentially correctly fulfilled the demands arising from the Directive*, only four member states were completely punctual: Belgium, Finland, the Netherlands and Sweden. The delay in Austria ranged between six and twelve months, in Portugal and Spain between one and two years. France, Germany, Ireland, Italy and the UK were more than two years late. By the time of writing, Denmark, Greece and Luxembourg had failed to meet the requirements of the Directive essentially correctly. Hence, almost *three-quarters of all member states* transposed the Directive *significantly delayed*, that is, more than six months later than required.

By the end of our period of analysis, three countries had not transposed the Directive essentially correctly. On 30 April 2003, Denmark's implementation by collective agreement could not guarantee that all workers have a right to *force majeure* leave. Greece failed to comply fully with the individual-rights standard of the Directive since single-income couples were still not entitled to take parental leave. Moreover, part-time workers were excluded from the *force majeure* leave scheme. In Luxembourg, the introduction of a 'cut-off date' unlawfully restricted the right to parental leave to parents whose children were born on or after 1 January 1999. Furthermore, *force majeure* leave could only be invoked in the case of a

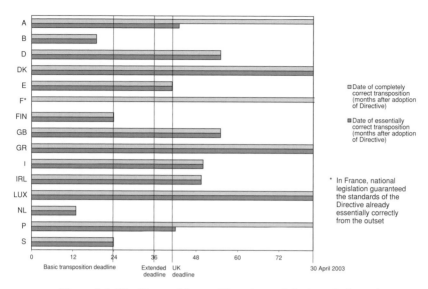

Figure 8.1 The Parental Leave Directive and timing of adaptation

child's sickness, but not with regard to other family members such as spouses.

Analysis of an even stricter benchmark for compliance, i.e. the accomplishment of completely correct transposition, reveals three more noncompliant countries. In Austria, the revised law actually granted both mothers and fathers roughly the same rights to parental leave, but there was still a small advantage for the mother: Since parental leave cannot be taken simultaneously by both parents, it is up to the parents to agree who should take the leave. If there is disagreement, the mother automatically takes precedence over the father (Interview A2a). In France, as in Luxembourg, *force majeure* leave could not be taken in connection with sick family members other than children (see above). In Portugal a specific legal provision protecting leave-takers from being unfairly dismissed was still lacking.

Figure 8.1 summarises the timing of the member states in terms of *essentially correct* and *completely correct* transposition of the Parental Leave Directive.

8.5   National problems with application and enforcement

When it comes to assessing the practical application of the Parental Leave Directive's standards, as transposed by the member states, our interviews suggest that only relatively few application problems in a narrower sense exist, i.e. cases where employees are unlawfully denied their right to take parental or *force majeure* leave, or where exercising the right is difficult due to interpretation problems.

In Belgium, application of the rights seems to be hampered by the confusing coexistence of the statutory scheme on the one hand and the system based on the social partners agreement on the other. This is especially so since the more favourable statutory scheme partly depends on the approval of the employer. Therefore, the less generous social partner scheme remains of central importance. Moreover, Belgian experts reported that there were general problems for employees in the health care sector with actually taking parental leave since there is a great shortage of labour in this sector and thus employers have trouble finding appropriate replacements (Interview B6: 242–56). Even though these problems are serious and worth mentioning, parental leave is generally accepted in Belgium and in many cases financial support is granted.

In Greece, invoking the right to parental leave is particularly problematic for workers employed in small and medium-sized enterprises (SMEs), mostly without union presence (Interview GR3: 305–20). While poor application of labour law in small workplaces is a common phenomenon not only in Greece but also in other countries, the bad application record of SMEs appears to be of particular relevance in this case. First of all, Greece is among those countries with an especially high proportion of SMEs – about 90 per cent of all companies have fewer than ten employees (Zervakis 1999: 660). Moreover, extending parental leave rights to employees in small companies was one of the main demands implied by the Directive.

In Portugal, the trade unions report employer resistance to workers who want to make use of their statutory employment rights as a general problem (Interview P3: 996–1000). In the parental leave case, employer opposition in the everyday operation of the law might even be stronger than usual. During the transposition process, the government rejected employers' calls to make eligibility to parental leave depend on a certain length of prior employment (Interviews P1: 1980–5, P4: 89–93).

In Ireland, problems occurred in relation to *force majeure* leave. The government had transposed the relevant provisions of the Directive almost literally. As these were worded very loosely, however, quite a number of disputes between employees and employers arose over the interpretation. They had to be settled by the courts. Employers were very reluctant to grant *force majeure* leave because the government had decided that employees would continue to receive 80 per cent of pay during their absence from work. As a result of these disputes, a very narrow definition of '*force majeure*' has been established which stresses the unforeseeable nature of the events that require the employee's absence from work. For example, a child's appointment in two weeks for hospital treatment is not covered since this is not an unpredictable emergency (Interview IRL1: 521–65, 1105–54; DJELR 2002: 83–4). This interpretation nevertheless seems to be in line with the vague stipulations of the Directive.

In Sweden the concept of 'time off from work on grounds of *force majeure*' caused application problems as well. In order to ensure fully correct transposition, the Swedish government incorporated the unclear term of the Directive into their domestic regulations. As a result, transposition was formally correct, but difficult for national actors to apply (Interview S12).

Increased national enforcement efforts could alleviate some of these problems. In most countries, breaches of the legal provisions on parental or *force majeure* leave have to be settled by the courts. Even in countries where labour inspectorates are formally responsible for ensuring compliance with the law (Belgium, France, Greece, Italy, Luxembourg, Portugal and Spain), it appears that no active inspection policy is carried out. This lack of active monitoring is certainly due to practicalities, because requesting and granting (or rejecting) parental leave happens in a haphazard way and on an individual basis. This means that it cannot be monitored as easily and efficiently as compliance with working time regulations can, through routine inspections. Nevertheless, if problems in certain sectors are known, as in the small company sector in Greece, specific monitoring efforts could certainly improve the situation. Moreover, a proliferation of specific support institutions in this area, such as the Equal Opportunities Commission in the UK, the Equality Authority in Ireland, the *Instituto de la Mujer* in Spain or, more recently, the KETHI in Greece, which inform employees about their legal rights and sometimes also provide aid in the event of legal proceedings, could improve the overall level of compliance with the Directive.

8.6   General assessment of the Directive's effects

Given the sceptical assessments of the Directive at the time of its adoption (see above), the domestic effects are definitely more far-reaching than expected. The Directive thus gave rise to medium or even high degrees of misfit in nine countries (see Table 8.2).

First of all, there are three countries in which the Directive led to *considerable policy innovation* since there had been no parental leave scheme before. This group of countries not only comprises the 'usual suspects' of Ireland and the UK with their voluntaristic, intervention-adverse

Table 8.2 *Overview of the Parental Leave Directive and its implementation*

Aim	To improve workers' ability to reconcile work and family life To enable and encourage men to assume a greater share of childcare responsibilities
History	Commission Proposal 18 November 1983 Council Directive 3 June 1998 (Italian Presidency) Extended to the UK 15 December 1997 (Luxembourg Presidency)
Standards	7 binding standards (most importantly: individual right to three months' parental leave) 9 recommendations 5 exemption provisions
Degree of Misfit	High: 4 Medium: 5 Low: 6
Transposition problems	9 member states significantly delayed (at least six months) 3 member states have still not accomplished transposition essentially correctly

traditions in labour law. It also covers a Continental EU country (Luxembourg), which is usually thought to have a well-developed welfare state and a generous labour-law system but has nevertheless had to install a new system of parental leave.

What hitherto seems to have been completely overlooked by most observers is the significant *qualitative improvement* that the Directive has meant to a number of countries that already had rather generous parental leave systems. In particular, the Directive put an end to rules that gave women priority over men in accessing parental leave, excluded single-income families from the schemes or required the approval of the employer before parental leave could be taken. Consequently, the Directive has indeed substantially improved workers' rights that aim to reconcile work and family life in a number of countries.

If we turn from legal effects to *practical outcomes* in the member states, a more cautious conclusion seems to be appropriate. Considering *actual take-up rates* of parental leave, the limits of the Directive become evident. On the basis of the small amount of data available, apparently the highest take-up rates are to be found in countries where parental leave is paid, such as in Sweden, Finland, Germany and Austria (Bruning and Plantenga 1999: 200–3). In countries offering unpaid leave only, take-up rates are much lower (EIRR 262: 15). This is particularly severe in countries like Greece and Portugal (Interviews GR14; P1: 1868–75), where average wages are very low and so employees cannot afford to go on leave without any supplementary financial aid. Since the Directive does not require the provision of payment during parental leave, no decisive improvements to this situation have been achieved.

A look at the countries in which parental leave was newly introduced corroborates this impression. In Ireland, where a rather minimalist scheme without any payment for parental leave is in operation, take-up rates are rather low. Research commissioned by the government revealed that only about 20 per cent of eligible employees actually made use of their entitlement in 2001 (DJELR 2002: 119). No data is available so far for the UK but it is very likely that it would point in a similar direction. In contrast, much higher take-up rates have been reported from Luxembourg (Interview LUX11), where the government chose to over-implement the Directive considerably by providing generous state benefits for workers on parental leave. Hence, positive outcomes in terms of take-up rates may only be observed where national governments considerably improve on the minimum standards of the Directive.

If we turn our attention to *gender disparities among leave-takers*, women still make up the vast majority in almost all countries. The likelihood of fathers taking parental leave appears to be lowest if entitlements to parental leave are transferable between the parents and/or if payment is low or non-existent. In Germany or Austria, for example, only between 1 and 2 per cent of leave-takers are men (Bruning and Plantenga 1999: 200; Vascovics and Rost 1999). Where parental leave is generously compensated, ideally on an earnings-related basis, take-up rates for fathers are higher. The most striking example in this respect is Sweden, where parents receive 75 per cent of their previous earnings during the largest part of their leave. Here, about 50 per cent of all fathers take some period of parental leave, even though women still take much longer periods of leave (Bruning and Plantenga 1999: 200).

Even though there is no indication that the Directive has led to a fundamental overhaul of this situation, it has brought about some slight improvements. First of all, the Directive has considerably strengthened the legal rights of men to take parental leave. In countries where men had previously been legally disadvantaged in their access to the leave schemes, the Directive has removed one of the most obvious stumbling blocks for increased male take-up rates.

Moreover, the Directive has stimulated reforms in some countries, which might turn out to have positive effects on the share of male workers involved with childcare. Provisions on the non-transferability of parental leave entitlements and on part-time or flexible forms of take-up, albeit only non-binding in character, did have an effect in some countries.

Belgium, Ireland, Luxembourg and the UK all made entitlement to their new leave schemes non-transferable. In Portugal, the government introduced a new non-transferable parental leave scheme in addition to the existing transferable system. Indeed, the share of men who take parental leave is comparatively high in some of these countries. Available data reveals that about 15 per cent of all leave-takers in Belgium are men (Clauwaert and Harger 2000: 24). In Ireland, this figure rises to 16 per cent (DJELR 2002: 120). A number of other voluntary reforms likely to have a positive effect on male take-up rates, such as the considerable widening of flexible leave forms, have been implemented in some countries.

However, it is still too soon to assess the practical effects of these steps. In this context, we should not forget that the low rate of fathers on parental leave is in large part the result of deeply entrenched role definitions in society which, in so far as they are malleable by political intervention at all, will only change through a gradual process whose extent will have to be measured in decades rather than in months or years.

In sum, the Parental Leave Directive considerably advanced the legal rights of male and female workers in many countries. In particular, fathers were put on a more equal footing with mothers when it comes to reconciling work and family life. While equality in practice is still nowhere in sight in the EU, the Directive's binding and non-binding rules had some positive effect (the latter maybe even more than the former). In countries that implemented the provisions in a minimal way, overall take-up rates of parental leave remained largely unchanged or, if the scheme had to be newly introduced, only reached moderate levels. The Directive also stimulated a significant number of voluntary reforms that had a positive effect in particular on the willingness of men to take on a greater share of childcare responsibilities (for an assessment of these voluntary reforms, see also Chapter 10).

9   The Part-time Work Directive: a facilitator of national reforms

9.1   Aim and contents of the Directive

Following the arrangement on parental leave, the Part-time Work Directive[1] was the second EU social policy measure that stemmed from a framework agreement drawn up by the European-level social partners UNICE, CEEP and ETUC. Like its predecessor, the Directive rendered the social partner agreement generally binding without changing the substance.

The *general aim* of the Part-time Work Directive is twofold. On the one hand, it aims to 'provide for the removal of discrimination against part-time workers and to improve the quality of part-time work', while on the other hand it seeks to 'facilitate the development of part-time work on a voluntary basis and to contribute to the flexible organisation of working time' (clause 1). Hence, the agreement combines classical social aspirations (to outlaw discrimination against part-time workers and to improve their working conditions) with a wider economic objective (to improve the flexibility and performance of the labour market by stimulating the use of part-time work).

The Part-time Work Directive lays down one broad *compulsory minimum standard*. It stipulates that with regard to working conditions, part-time workers may not be treated less favourably than comparable full-time workers unless such unequal treatment is objectively justified. Where appropriate, the benefits of part-time workers are to be determined on a *pro rata temporis* basis (clause 4). For example, employers are required to offer their part-time workers at least such entitlements to pay, holidays or occupational pensions as is equivalent to the proportion of hours that they work in relation to a comparable full-time worker.

This principle of non-discrimination is further specified by two important definitions. Part-time workers are understood to be all workers whose

---

[1]   Directive 97/81/EC of 15 December 1997 concerning the framework agreement on part-time work concluded by UNICE, CEEP and ETUC, OJ 1998 No. L14/9–14.

normal hours of work are less than the normal hours of work of a comparable full-time worker. More significantly, the term 'comparable full-time worker' is defined on the basis of an 'onion skin model', which provides for the working conditions of a part-time worker to be compared with 'a full-time worker in the same establishment having the same type of employment contract or relationship, who is engaged in the same or a similar work/occupation'. If no such comparable full-time worker exists in the same establishment, the comparison must be based on a relevant collective agreement. Where no such collective agreement exists, it has to be made 'in accordance with national law, collective agreements or practice' (clause 3).

Since drawing proper comparisons is at the heart of any non-discrimination clause, this 'onion skin model' ensures that part-time workers are able to prove that they are being discriminated against, even in the absence of a comparable full-time worker at their own workplace. This is particularly important as a considerable number of part-time workers are employed in establishments such as cleaning companies or retail outlets, where often no full-time worker with a comparable job exists. Establishing discriminatory practices solely on the basis of comparison within the same workplace will often be impossible (see, for example, Interviews D1: 177–216; GB6: 153–9).

The Directive leaves member states four *possibilities for derogating* from the principle of non-discrimination. (1) Part-time workers working on a casual basis may be excluded from the scope of the non-discrimination principle (clause 2.2). Moreover, member states can make the access of part-time workers to particular working conditions depend (2) on a certain period of service, (3) a certain minimum amount of working time, (4) or a certain level of earnings, as long as such restrictions are justified by objective grounds (clause 4.4).

Furthermore, the Directive includes no fewer than eleven *non-binding soft-law provisions*. (1) In a general fashion, the Directive urges national governments and social partners to eliminate legal, contractual or administrative obstacles to part-time work and to facilitate access to part-time jobs. (2) If a worker refuses to transfer from full-time to part-time work or vice versa, this should not be a legitimate reason for dismissal. (3) 'As far as possible' employers should accept requests from employees to transfer from full-time to part-time work (4) and vice versa. (5) To that end, employers are called upon to provide timely information on vacant full-time or part-time jobs in their enterprises. (6) Moreover, the access to part-time work should also be facilitated for employees in skilled and managerial positions, (7) and steps ought to be taken to enhance the access of part-time workers to vocational training. (8) In addition, the

Directive recommends that employers provide workers' representatives with appropriate information about part-time working in the enterprise.

(9) Besides this, the EU-level social partners encourage member states to remove potential disadvantages for part-time workers arising from the organisation of their statutory social security systems. (10) In so far as they make use of the possibility of excluding casual workers from the scope of the non-discrimination clause or of restricting access to particular working conditions on the basis of a certain period of service, working time or level of earnings (see above), member states should periodically review these exclusions and restrictions so as to ensure that the objective grounds which they were based on still remain valid. (11) Finally, the major European associations of management and labour call on member state governments to allow the national social partners to play a special role in the implementation and application of their framework agreement.

The Part-time Work Directive is perhaps the most neo-voluntarist EU measure in our sample. It comprises only one (albeit rather broad) binding standard and allows member states to use a number of potentially far-reaching possibilities for derogation. Above all, it contains a total of eleven non-binding recommendations, which is the highest number of soft-law provisions in our sample. As we will see below, the very soft regulatory approach of the Directive is a result of both employers' organisations and some national union federations resisting the move to render the provisions in question binding.

9.2 The European-level negotiation process

The origins of the Part-time Work Directive reach back as far as December 1981, when the European Commission put forward its first draft Directive on voluntary part-time work (COM [1981] 775). This aimed at protecting part-time workers from discrimination by granting proportional claims on remuneration and holiday/redundancy/retirement payments. Furthermore, an obligation to conclude written labour contracts and preferential treatment for part-time workers in the event of there being any possibility of them taking up full-time employment was provided for. Another Directive was proposed on temporary employment and fixed-term contracts (COM [1982] 155), suggesting that such atypical work be used in exceptional cases only. It provided for social protection to be equal to that of permanent employment. These proposals encountered an extremely hostile climate in the Council and had no chance of being adopted.

Nevertheless, the Commission followed up on the issue. In the context of its action programme implementing the 1989 Social Charter, the

Commission proposed a package of three draft Directives on 'atypical work'. The main reason for suggesting three legislative projects instead of one was the Commission's 'treaty-base game' (Rhodes 1995: 99). In other words, this was a tactical move with a view to employing various legal bases, two of them allowing for majority voting. In the short run, however, only one of the proposals was adopted by the Council of Ministers. It guaranteed proper health and safety protection for fixed-term and temporary agency workers.[2]

The other two drafts were much more controversial since they impinged on the more costly issue of giving 'atypical' workers *pro rata temporis* entitlement to statutory social security benefits and to important employment conditions such as pay, annual leave and occupational pensions (see COM [1990] 228 and COM [1990] 228 – SYN 280). In particular the proposal which the Commission had based on Article 100a ECT, arguing that national differences in the costs of employing 'atypical' workers might lead to distortions of competition, was met with hostility, especially from the UK Conservative government (EIRR 203: 11). Opposition was also voiced from countries like Germany, where a significant share of part-time workers was excluded at the time from social security coverage (Interview D1: 777–819, *Financial Times*, 14 June 1990, p. 24, 27 November 1990, p. 2).

Finally, the Commission announced its intention to reintroduce the proposal under the procedures of the Social Policy Agreement, that is without the participation of the UK (EIRR 252: 28). After two rounds of Commission consultations, the European-level chief associations of management and labour agreed to enter into negotiations on 'flexibility of working time and security for workers'. Both sides had rather antagonistic positions. The employers wanted to restrict the scope of the negotiations to 'permanent part-time work' only, and they tried to limit the impact of the principle of non-discrimination by introducing thresholds, such as, for example, a certain company size. Moreover, the employers' side was fundamentally opposed to including anything related to statutory social security in a potential agreement. The ETUC wanted to cover all forms of atypical work (i.e. part-time, temporary, casual and agency work), housework and teleworking (although not necessarily all within

---

[2] Council Directive 91/383/EEC of 25 June 1991 supplementing the measures to encourage improvements in the safety and health at work of workers with a fixed-duration employment relationship or a temporary employment relationship, OJ 1991 No. L206/19–21. At the time of writing, a further proposal on temporary agency workers is being debated in Council (COM [2002] 149) after the European social partner negotiations foundered on the insurmountable differences between both sides (Broughton 2001).

the framework of these negotiations). The employees' side recognised that it would not be possible to deal with statutory social security in the agreement but nevertheless pressed for a recommendation on social security to be attached to the agreement (Interview with ETUC official; see also Dürmeier 1999).

Owing to the different positions on the scope of a potential agreement, it took a long time before it was agreed that the negotiations would be restricted to (all kinds of) part-time workers, but that the other forms of flexible employment should be tackled in subsequent negotiations.[3] But both sides also had to overcome a number of other difficult controversies. In any case, the part-time work negotiations were 'far more complicated technically than the first negotiation between the social partners' (*Agence Europe* 6900, 25 January 1997: no. 35). Besides the almost inevitable haggling between unions and employers over the right balance between worker protection and management flexibility, one major cross-cutting split in the negotiations was between trade unions, especially those from Southern low-wage countries such as Greece and Portugal, which considered part-time work a precarious type of employment that employees took on mostly involuntarily and only as a second-best solution in the absence of full-time employment. On the other side, both unions and employers from countries such as the Netherlands, Germany or the Nordic member states were having positive experiences with part-time work as an instrument by which to increase labour-market flexibility, enhance the quality of life and allow more people (especially women) to participate actively in the labour market.

As a result of these diverging interests, an extension of the original nine-month deadline granted by the Commission was necessary to reach an agreement. The final 'draft European framework agreement on part-time work' was accepted during the final plenary negotiations on 14 May 1997. It was submitted to the decision-making bodies of UNICE, CEEP and the ETUC for signature (*Agence Europe* 6974, 15 May 1997: no. 29). All three organisations endorsed the draft agreement, but considerable criticism of the weak results was voiced by both German ETUC members, and by the Luxembourg federation of Christian unions, the French *Force Ouvrière*, and the ETUC's Women's Committee (Dürmeier 1999: 34–5; Falkner 2000a). Nevertheless, the draft agreement was adopted with a qualified majority by the ETUC Executive Committee. The final

---

[3] Indeed, the EU-level social partners later reached an agreement on fixed-term workers, which was then transformed into a generally binding Directive: Council Directive 1999/70/EC of 28 June 1999 concerning the framework agreement on fixed-term work concluded by ETUC, UNICE and CEEP, OJ 1999 No. L175/43–8.

agreement was then formally signed on 6 June 1997. In order to render the agreement generally binding, the Commission subsequently proposed a Directive, which was adopted without any change by the Council on 15 December 1997.

9.3   Misfit in the member states: legal innovation for many, modest practical relevance for all

In the light of the harsh criticism voiced by some unionists, the overall level of domestic adaptation required by the Directive, although comparatively moderate in overall terms, seems quite remarkable. In legal terms, seven member states had no statutory provisions guaranteeing the principle of non-discrimination against part-time workers with regard to their employment conditions (Denmark, Finland, Ireland, Italy, Portugal, Sweden and the UK). These countries were thus confronted with a high degree of *legal misfit* (for more details about our operationalisation of this concept, see Chapter 2). The practical relevance of these reform requirements, however, was diminished by the fact that female part-time workers, who usually make up the largest share of all part-time workers, were already protected to some extent against less favourable treatment on the basis of European and national sex discrimination legislation and case law. Belgium, France and Greece already had non-discrimination legislation for part-time workers in place, but these laws did not cover important sections of the relevant workforce (the public sector in Belgium and Greece, and part-time workers working more than 80 per cent of normal weekly working hours in France). This accounts for medium-scale legal misfit, the relevance of which was further diminished by the existing protection of female part-timers against discrimination, based on principles of sex equality.

The remaining countries already had legislation that provided for non-discrimination against part-time workers with regard to their working conditions, but had to adapt some minor details, mostly to fulfil the Directive's 'onion skin model' for comparing part-time and full-time workers. Only the Netherlands already complied fully with the Directive and thus did not have to enact any legal changes to its regulations. Otherwise, seven countries were faced with medium levels of *policy misfit* and seven member states had to cope with low levels of policy misfit (see Table 9.1).

However, a look at the *politics and polity dimension* of misfit reveals that the situation described above tells only part of the story. While the Part-time Work Directive, similar to the other Directives in our sample, did not call for administrative adaptation at the domestic level, it challenged the existing relationship between the state and the social partners in Denmark

Table 9.1 *The Part-time Work Directive and misfit in the member states*

	Degree of Legal Misfit	Limited Practical Significance	Degree of *Total Policy Misfit*	Degree of Politics/ Polity Misfit	Economic Costs	Degree of *Total Misfit*
A	low	no	low	–	low	low
B	medium	yes	low	–	low	low
D	low	no	low	–	low	low
DK	high	yes	medium	high	medium	high
E	low	no	low	–	low	low
F	medium	yes	low	–	low	low
FIN	high	yes	medium	–	medium	medium
GB	high	yes	medium	–	low	medium
GR	medium	yes	low	–	low	low
I	high	yes	medium	–	low	medium
IRL	high	yes	medium	–	medium	medium
LUX	low	no	low	–	low	low
NL	–	–	–	–	–	–
P	high	yes	medium	–	medium	medium
S	high	yes	medium	high	medium	high

and Sweden. In both countries, the social partners traditionally regulated the working conditions of part-time workers autonomously. The Directive challenged this tradition of 'free collective bargaining' in this area in that it required state intervention in the form of generally binding legislation to guarantee full coverage of the workforce (see also Chapter 12). Hence, the Directive called for medium-scale policy adaptation but gave rise to large-scale misfit with regard to the existing state-society relationship.

Finally, the *economic costs* of implementing the Directive were low in most countries, either because discriminatory practices with regard to the employment conditions of part-time workers had already been outlawed or because the largest share of part-timers had already been protected from discrimination by sex equality legislation. However, the extent of de facto discrimination especially in terms of wages or occupational pensions was large enough to let the economic costs of adaptation reach medium-scale levels in Denmark, Finland, Ireland, Portugal and Sweden. In these countries part-time workers had not as yet been provided with statutory rights to equal treatment in terms of their employment conditions. Especially in the Nordic countries, although in Portugal too, discrimination was not only a phenomenon which depended on the company policies of individual employers, but often stemmed from discriminatory clauses included in collective agreements. Hence, they affected all part-timers employed in a particular sector.

Moreover, there are national differences in the extent to which discrimination against part-timers had de facto already been removed on the basis of European sex discrimination litigation. Taking as an indicator the number of national court cases from the field of social policy that were transferred to the ECJ for a preliminary ruling, it emerges that Denmark, Portugal and Ireland belong to the group of low-level litigiousness, whereas the UK, along with Germany and the Netherlands, have been particularly active in this area.[4] Similar to the countries with low levels of litigiousness, it is reasonable to conclude that EU sex discrimination claims had not significantly removed discrimination against part-time workers in Sweden and Finland, since these two countries only joined the EU in 1995.

As these context conditions were very different in the UK, the economic costs of adaptation were altogether low, despite the fact that completely new legislation had to be introduced. First, British women's groups were among the most active in pushing through sex discrimination claims on the basis of European non-discrimination rules (Tesoka 1999; Alter and Vargas 2000; Caporaso and Jupille 2001). Hence, unfavourable treatment of part-time workers had already been eliminated to a large extent on the basis of gender equality principles (Interview GB6: 314–16). Second, the Directive's 'onion skin model' was next to useless in the UK context. Under the conditions of a very decentralised industrial relations system such as the British one, it effectively failed to extend the point of reference for finding a comparator beyond the level of the individual company since the vast majority of all collective agreements only apply to single companies or establishments (Interview GB6: 132–88).[5]

9.4   Implementation in the member states

The Part-time Work Directive had to be incorporated into national law by 20 January 2000, with the possibility of a maximum period of one year being added 'to take account of special difficulties or implementation by a collective agreement' (Article 2 of the Directive). As in the case of parental leave, the UK was initially not covered by the Directive due to the Conservative government's social policy opt-out. The Labour government put an end to the opt-out and, as a result, the UK's transposition

---

[4] Data collected by Stone Sweet and Brunell for the period between 1961 and 1995 reveals that there were forty preliminary reference procedures in the field of social policy stemming from the UK, fifteen from Denmark, five from Ireland, and none from Portugal (Stone Sweet and Brunell 1998: 75).

[5] In 1990, only 10 per cent of all employees in the private sector were covered by a collective agreement that applied to more than one company (Edwards et al. 1999: 20).

deadline ran out a few months later than the one applying to the other member states. The UK had to implement the Directive by 7 April 2000.

9.4.1   Particularly interesting cases

In the UK and Ireland, the process and outcome of transposing the Directive was characterised to an unusually large extent by the incommensurable interests of the two sides of industry. In both countries, the fact that the Directive was founded on a European-level social partner agreement seems to have significantly increased the political salience of the issue on the part of domestic employers' organisations and trade unions.

In Ireland, the relevant government department sought to increase the role of the social partners in the transposition of the Directive in order to reflect the important role the social partners had played in the European-level decision-making process. Contrary to normal practice in the preparation of employment legislation, therefore, the Department of Enterprise, Trade and Employment established a tripartite working group, bringing together representatives of employers, trade unions and affected ministries to discuss the way in which the Directive should be implemented (Interview IRL4: 425–549).[6] Instead of facilitating the transposition, however, this intensive involvement gave rise to long delays due to protracted battles between both sides of industry over the interpretation of the main concepts of the agreement.

Disagreement centred on the definition of 'casual workers', a category of employees which could be excluded from the non-discrimination principle, and on the question of whether non-discrimination against part-time workers with regard to their 'employment conditions' should cover pay and occupational pensions. It took a long time before these disputes were finally settled within the tripartite working group. The results could be interpreted largely as a victory for the unions. Following the ICTU's line of argument, pay and pensions were fully included in the scope of the non-discrimination principle. Moreover, although the casual worker exemption was used, the term was defined rather narrowly and the exclusion only referred to occupational pensions (Interview IRL1: 645–56, 834–49, Dáil Deb., 21 November 2001, cols. 1032–3). But, owing to the long debates, the end of the basis implementation deadline had almost been reached when the working group finished its talks in October 1999 (Interview IRL1: 295–300). As a consequence, the government made use of the one-year extension option provided by the Directive. However,

---

[6] Usually, the social partners are consulted thoroughly on domestic employment legislation, but on a bilateral basis.

administrative overload on the part of the departmental unit in charge of preparing the transposition bill and on the part of the central government service responsible for drafting all Irish legislation, coupled with the rather long parliamentary process, further delayed developments (Interview IRL4: 1062–94, 1115–37, 1680–98). As a result, even the extended deadline was exceeded by almost a year before the transposition law could be adopted in late December 2001.

In the UK, the Labour government was confronted with a similar situation. On the one hand, it was pushed hard by the unions to comply with the standards of the Directive and even to go beyond the minimum requirements while, on the other, the CBI vociferously urged it to keep the burden on business to a strict minimum and, specifically, to avoid any 'gold plating' of the Directive. Pressurised by the CBI, the government made use of all possible restrictions in the definition of the comparator (such as the need to have the same type of contract, the same qualifications, etc.) and, in particular, limited comparisons to the level of the individual employer. Altogether, this meant that about five million of the six million part-time workers effectively could not benefit from the non-discrimination principle since they lacked a comparable full-time worker in the same company (DTI 2000b). The TUC protested against this restrictive approach and argued that the Directive required comparisons to be made on the basis of collective agreements as well. But since the practical effect of such a step would have been very limited in the UK (see above), the trade unions did not pursue this point with any great enthusiasm.

Consequently, the government did not change the definition as initially proposed, even if that meant that the UK legislation was legally in breach of the Directive and could thus be challenged in court. The reasons why the TUC has so far not acted against this breach are twofold. First, the practical benefits of such a challenge would be marginal and, second, the government already made an important concession to the unions in return for its employer-friendly stance in the comparator issue: while the government had planned to apply the part-time work legislation, like most other UK employment law, only to 'employees', the TUC demanded that the scope be extended to 'workers', a category which under UK law not only includes people with an employment contract or relationship but also 'quasi employees' like freelance or agency staff (Interview GB10: 177–203, Burchell et al. 1999: 5–19, 90–1). In the end, therefore, the outcome was a package deal in response to fierce pressure from both sides of industry. In substantive terms, the package deal meant that the Directive was somewhat over-implemented and slightly under-implemented at the same time. The protracted political debates surrounding these issues, together with certain problems of administrative overload resulting from the relevant Department having to deal with a large number of new employment proposals after the Labour government came to power, caused a short delay of three months in transposing the Directive (Interview GB6: 666–92).

In contrast to the moderate (but nevertheless hard-fought) policy improvements in Ireland and the UK, which mostly stuck to the minimum standards of the Directive, a much larger effect was brought about in countries where governments also took into account the wide array of soft-law provisions of the European social partner agreement. The most striking example in this respect is Germany. Here, the centre-left government under Chancellor Gerhard Schröder considered the stimulation of part-time work an effective instrument by which to reduce unemployment (Interview D6: 628–48). In order to reach this goal, it took almost all of the soft-law provisions of the Directive into account and turned them into binding 'hard law', which meant that the modest minimum requirements of the Directive were considerably 'gold-plated'. For example, the German government turned the recommendation on stimulating part-time work into a *binding legal right to work part-time* for all workers employed in establishments with more than fifteen employees. Hence, an employer can only refuse requests by workers to reduce their working-time on the basis of 'business-related reasons' that would make such a step economically unfeasible.

German business organisations were vociferously opposed to what, in their view, placed an unnecessary and damaging burden on employers. In order to contain these massive protests, the government tied the transposition of the Part-time Work Directive to the implementation of the Directive on Fixed-term Contracts, the latter being a matter of interest for employers' organisations. This package deal facilitated the timely transposition of the Part-time Work Directive, which otherwise would have been highly problematic. Even with the package deal, the negotiations were complicated and time-consuming enough to force the German government to make use of the option laid down in the Directive of extending the implementation deadline by one year to take account of special difficulties (Interviews D1: 957–65, D5: 397–413, 729–79, D6: 750–83).

The Directive was transposed under similar circumstances in Spain. This time, however, it was a conservative government that aimed to improve labour market performance by boosting part-time work. While the binding standard of the Directive only required a certain reformulation of the already existing non-discrimination principle, so as to incorporate the Directive's 'onion skin model' of comparison, the Spanish government took on board many of the soft-law provisions and went far beyond the European minimum requirements. In the course of this ambitious reform, however, the government revised the previously correct definition of a part-time worker so as to restrict it to employees working up to 77 per cent of normal working hours. In this respect, the Spanish government swam against the tide by moving the domestic standards away from, rather than in the direction of, the European standards. It appears that this action was triggered by the desire to avoid the excessive costs that would have arisen if the specific supporting measures for part-time workers' pension entitlements had been extended to all part-time workers (even those who work only slightly less than full-time workers). Although understandable, this reform nevertheless clearly violated the terms of the Directive. This violation persisted until the government enacted a further reform in March 2001, which restored the correct definition of part-time work already applicable before 1998 and which correctly implemented the Directive's 'onion-skin model' (Miguélez Lobo 2001). The correct transposition of the Directive was therefore ensured only 14 months after the expiration of the deadline.

A broadly similar picture emerges from the transposition of the Directive in Portugal. In contrast to Spain and Germany, Portugal previously had no legislation governing part-time work and so the Directive's minimum standard required significant reforms. Implementation was facilitated by the fact that there were already national plans to regulate part-time work when the Directive was adopted at the European level. As in Spain and Germany, the aim of this reform was job creation by boosting part-time work. This time, it was a coalition between a social democratic minority government and employers' organisations which pushed this reform through. Left-wing trade unions especially were sceptical because they considered part-time contracts as second-class employment with very low salaries. The new law was nevertheless passed in July 1999, half a year before the expiration of the deadline.

In substantive terms, the Portuguese legislation not only provided for non-discrimination against part-time workers but also took up many of the non-binding recommendations of the Directive that sought to facilitate the use of part-time work. The core of these measures consisted of social security incentives for recruiting part-time staff. As in Spain, it seemed useful to restrict the eligibility of these incentive measures to part-time workers whose working hours were significantly below the working hours of a full-time employee. As a result, the definition of a part-time worker was restricted to workers with a weekly working time of no more than 75 per cent of the usual working time of a full-time worker. Instead of limiting this restrictive definition to the incentive measures scheme, it was also applied to the non-discrimination principle, which was contrary to the Directive. Furthermore, the comparator provision was transposed incorrectly, restricting comparisons to the level of the individual company and thereby ignoring the 'onion skin model' that provided for comparisons outside the company also.

In Italy, transposition of the Directive was also regarded as an opportunity to improve labour market performance by increasing the number of part-time workers. Traditionally, the Italian approach to part-time work had been a restrictive one since the unions especially regarded part-time work as a precarious form of employment to be avoided where possible. The existing legislation explicitly allowed the social partners to limit the percentage of part-time workers that could be employed in an enterprise. Part-time workers were not allowed to perform overtime. Since the government was determined to boost part-time work, the transposition process was not only used to give effect to the non-discrimination principle, but also to take up many of the soft-law provisions of the Directive and thus to over-implement the Directive significantly. As in Portugal and Spain, social security incentives for increasing part-time work were created, but without wrongfully excluding any part-time workers from the scope of the legislation (EIRR 313: 8, 314: 8–9, 316: 9; Pedersini 2002). The government attached unusually high importance to the swift realisation of this reform, from which it expected positive labour market effects. While Italy is often among the laggards in implementing EU Directives, transposition in this case was completed only slightly more than two months after the expiration of the deadline.

The Danish and Swedish cases were also interesting, since transposing the Directive in these countries touched upon the relationship between the state and the social partners (see Chapter 12 below).

9.4.2   Timeliness and correctness of transposition

Looking at the point in time at which governments had complied with the requirements of the Directive *essentially correctly*, it emerges that only five member states were entirely punctual: Austria, Germany, Greece, Luxembourg and the Netherlands. Germany, however, had to make use of the one-year extension to achieve this status, while Austria, Luxembourg and the Netherlands fulfilled the Directive essentially correctly from the outset. Denmark, France, Italy and the UK were less than six months late; Ireland was between six and twelve months late. The delay in Belgium, Finland, Sweden and Spain was between one and two years. At the time of writing, Portugal did not fulfil the standards of the Directive essentially correctly. As a consequence, *more than one-third of all member states* transposed the Directive *significantly delayed*, that is more than six months later than required.

As already mentioned above, by the end of our period of analysis, one country had still not transposed the Directive essentially correctly. On 30 April 2003, the Portuguese transposition legislation, which had already been adopted at a very early stage, excluded part-time workers with a weekly working time of more than 75 per cent of the usual working hours of a full-time worker.

When we increase the standard for judging transposition performance and enquire into *completely correct transposition*, our attention is drawn to more cases of non-compliance. In Austria, no transposition process was ever initiated even though trade unions argued that adaptation was required (Interview A1: 955–84). By 30 April 2003, therefore, the Austrian part-time work legislation did not fully conform to the standards of the Directive. It excluded certain categories of employees (managers, agricultural workers) from the principle of non-discrimination. Moreover, the definition of a comparable full-time worker did not appear to be fully in line with the 'onion skin model' laid down in the Directive. Both of these shortcomings have been criticised by the European Commission's implementation report (CEC 2003: 8, 12–13). In a similar vein, Luxembourg had not changed its legislation despite the fact that the need to extend the level of comparison beyond the company level in accordance with the Directive's 'onion skin model' was not recognised in Luxembourg either. The regulations of Finland, Greece and the UK also lacked a proper definition of the term 'comparable full-time worker' (CEC 2003: 13–16, see also above).

Figure 9.1 summarises the timing of the member states in terms of *essentially correct* and *completely correct* transposition of the Part-time Work Directive.

9.5   National problems with application and enforcement

Since most of the transposition laws have come into force only very recently (some of them even after we had completed our interviews), it is in many cases too soon to detect problems in practical compliance with the new rules. Hence, we can only present a very patchy picture of domestic application problems. On the basis of the available evidence, however, it appears that practical compliance with the Directive's non-discrimination principle is altogether rather satisfactory. This does not mean, however, that no problems exist at all. Trade unionists in Austria reported that there were still clauses in some collective agreements which

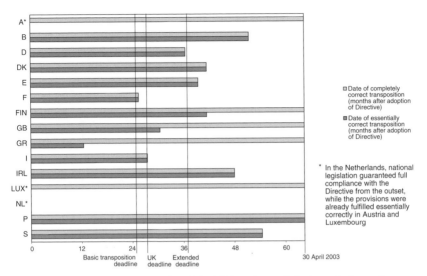

Figure 9.1 The Part-time Work Directive and timing of adaptation

discriminate against part-time workers, e.g. taxi drivers (Interview A1: 808–44). The existence of such discriminatory practices is all the more severe if it is taken into account that the Austrian government, despite union pressure, so far has refused to initiate any reform to adapt to the Directive's provisions.

A more general problem is that the Directive's non-discrimination principle is not strong enough to improve the poor working conditions of part-time workers who lack an appropriate comparator to establish that they were being discriminated against. In the UK this problem is most pressing. The most severe restriction on finding a comparator is that it is practically impossible to extend the level of comparison beyond the individual company. Owing to the virtual absence of cross-company collective agreements, this would still be true even if the Directive's 'onion skin model' were finally implemented legally. Hence, many part-timers working in branches such as cleaning or retail, where most of the workers are employed on a part-time basis, would not be able to establish that they were being treated in a discriminatory way. While this weakness might be specific to the UK, the Directive admits further restrictions on the comparator issue (i.e. comparison may be restricted to somebody with the same type of contract and performing the same or broadly similar work), and these might lead to problems with finding an appropriate comparator in other countries as well.

Another problem is related to ensuring that part-time workers who are treated less favourably than a comparable full-time worker can actually assert their rights. In some countries, the labour inspectorates are responsible for ensuring practical compliance in that area (e.g. in Belgium, France, Greece, Spain and Portugal). In France and Greece, employers even have to inform the labour inspectorate about the hiring of part-time workers. While this is potentially an effective instrument for labour inspectorates to keep track of possible infringements of the law,[7] it turns out that de facto active inspections concerning the rights of part-time workers are rare (see e.g. Interviews B4: 386–96, F10: 1742–50). Hence, the main onus for ensuring compliance with this Directive is on individual employees, who have to become active in asserting their rights in court. As there are well-known obstacles for workers who wish to resort to the court system (above all, a court case will negatively affect the mutual trust between employees and employers), extrajudicial mechanisms of conflict resolution are a very effective way to improve law enforcement in this area.

The most striking example among our cases demonstrating the effectiveness of such mechanisms is the enforcement of the part-time legislation in the Netherlands. Here, the Equal Treatment Commission plays a very positive role in ensuring compliance with the rights of part-time workers. The Commission is an independent body originally set up to deal with disputes in the area of sex discrimination. Subsequently, the area of responsibility of the Commission has been widened. Nowadays, the Commission is also responsible for discrimination against part-time workers. It is very easy to lodge a complaint with the Commission. No lawyer has to be hired, and an employee only has to present prima facie evidence of discrimination. Although the decisions of the Commission are not legally binding on the parties involved, in practice most employers and employees abide by the decisions of the Commission. This may be due to the fact that judges normally follow the opinion of the Commission. Thus, chances are very low that a court decision would lead to a different outcome (Interviews NL8: 421–81, 664–705, NL10: 473–535).

9.6   General assessment of the Directive's effects

If we want to draw conclusions regarding the Part-time Work Directive's impact in the member states, we first have to consider the varying importance of part-time work within the domestic labour markets. In 2000, the

---

[7] It might also act as an administrative obstacle to part-time work, though, and thus work against the goal of facilitating the use of part-time employment.

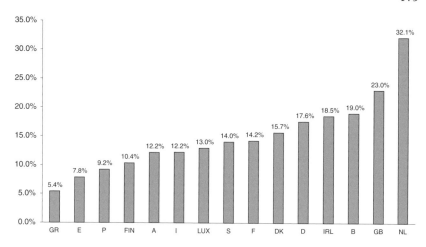

Source: OECD Labour Force Statistics

Figure 9.2 Part-time workers as a share of total employment (2000)

percentage of part-time workers as a share of total employment ranged from 5 per cent in Greece to 32 per cent in the Netherlands (see Figure 9.2). Hence, the Directive with its dual aim of improving the levels of protection of these workers and facilitating access to part-time work had a very different meaning in the member states. For some countries with comparatively large numbers of part-time workers but little protection, the Directive did have a considerable effect in terms of improving the situation of a significant group of workers (like the UK and Ireland, and to a lesser extent also Denmark or Sweden). It is true that the impact on these countries is tempered by the fact that female part-time workers, who represent the vast majority of part-time employees in all member states, had previously been able to take legal action against discriminatory employment conditions on the grounds of indirect sex discrimination.

Nevertheless, the improvements brought about by the Directive should not be underestimated. Not only does the Directive ensure that male part-time workers are covered by non-discrimination legislation for the first time in many countries (Denmark, Finland, Ireland, Italy, Portugal, Sweden and the UK), in countries that had no general non-discrimination legislation before the Directive was implemented, finding a comparator should now also be easier for women.

Merely looking at the effects of the binding standards, however, is only part of the story (see also Chapter 10). The Directive also included eleven

Table 9.2 *Overview of the Part-time Work Directive and its implementation*

Aim	Non-discrimination against part-time workers with regard to their employment conditions Facilitation of part-time work and improvement in the flexible organisation of working time
History	Commission Proposal 13 June 1990 (first draft December 1981) Council Directive 15 December 1997 (Luxembourg Presidency) Extended to the UK 7 April 1998 (UK Presidency)
Standards	1 binding standard (principle of non-discrimination against part-time workers) 11 recommendations 4 exemption provisions
Degree of Misfit	High: 2 Medium: 5 Low: 7 None: 1
Transposition problems	6 member states significantly delayed (at least six months) 1 member state has still not accomplished transposition essentially correctly

non-binding recommendations (see Table 9.2). A total of eight countries reflected some or all of these soft-law provisions in their transposition legislation. The most significant cases were Germany, Italy, Portugal and Spain, where taking up the non-binding provisions was seen as an opportunity to create additional jobs. On the one hand, Germany already started out with a fairly high share of part-time workers, which it aimed to increase even more, taking the Netherlands as its role model. On the other hand, Italy, Portugal and Spain all had comparatively low levels of part-time employment, mostly due to a traditionally very restrictive approach towards such 'atypical' forms of work. They took the Directive as an opportunity to rethink their traditional regulatory philosophies fundamentally. Instead of restricting part-time work, they followed the recommendations laid down in the Directive, by removing obstacles to part-time work and by creating legal as well as financial incentives for full-time workers to transfer to part-time jobs.

Hence, we can distinguish between countries in which the Directive predominantly had the effect of improving the situation of part-time workers, countries in which the Directive primarily led to measures facilitating the access to part-time work, and finally countries in which no effect could be observed since no transposition processes were initiated.

In sum, we can conclude that the Directive, while certainly not revolutionary in its impact, did bring about some modest but noteworthy improvements for part-time workers in terms of increased social protection. Moreover, the Directive's non-binding recommendations inspired a number of governments to enact significant reforms aimed at facilitating and stimulating part-time work (see Chapter 10 for more details).

10   Voluntary reforms triggered by the Directives

The preceding chapters have dealt with the compulsory reforms related to our six EU Directives. However, the domestic impact of EU policies is not necessarily confined to such obligatory adaptations. Member states may use the transposition process to push through voluntary reforms that go beyond the minimum level required by European Directives. On the one hand, this can be a *reaction to European soft law* and, in fact, recent social policy Directives have included a considerable number of concrete but legally non-binding recommendations. On the other hand, member states might also decide to *surpass the level of the EU's minimum standards* (say, by creating a parental leave scheme which offers six instead of the required three months of leave).

From an abstract point of view, three different logics of treating the binding and non-binding parts of a Directive can be specified: minimalism, maximalism and a logic of domestic politics (see Table 10.1). The most frequently discussed assumption in the competitiveness-oriented literature is that the reaction of member states to potentially costly EU policies is driven by a *logic of minimalism*. According to this view, only binding law has the potential to harmonise the different domestic working conditions. In the absence of obligation, no additional costs to the national enterprises or the administration would be accepted in response to European policies. Hence, we should expect member states to strive for a most minimal transposition which disregards soft-law provisions, avoids any other form of over-implementation, and even tries to lower higher domestic standards, if they exist, to the European level.

Some of the more recent writing on the 'open method of co-ordination' starts from the opposite direction and expects member states to react to EU Directives according to a *logic of maximalism*. In this view, soft law comes close to binding law in its effects, the contention being that the carrots of 'learning processes' and the sticks of public 'naming and shaming' will drive governments to go with the recommended 'best practice'. Thus governments become inclined to follow the EU's recommendations systematically and transform them into hard national provisions. Moreover,

178

Table 10.1 *Three logics of reaction to flexible European law*

Logic	Result	Underlying mechanism
Minimalism	No lifting of standards beyond binding minimum; soft law is disregarded; lowering of existing standards to minimum floor	Avoiding unnecessary economic costs (social dumping orientation)
Maximalism	European recommendations are systematically adopted; previously higher standards are upheld; minimum level of the binding standards is surpassed	Learning and diffusion of 'best practice'
Domestic politics	Case-to-case decision whether or not to follow recommendations, to surpass otherwise the minimum standards, or to uphold or lower previously higher standards	Not a matter of principle but of specific national political priorities

member states can be expected to uphold existing standards even beyond the required minimum and at times even surpass the minimum level of binding standards to give full effect to the general thrust of European Directives, according to this logic.

The third type of reaction follows a *logic of domestic politics*. Here, the preferences of domestic actors, their relative influence and the character of the decision-making process determine whether soft-law provisions are incorporated into national law, whether the binding minimum floor is otherwise surpassed, or whether existing higher standards are upheld or lowered to the European minimum level. Rather than being a matter of principle, therefore, the domestic reaction depends on situational factors such as the (party) political preferences of the government in office or the concerns and influence of interest groups.

10.1 Soft-law elements in the Directives: valuable or in vain?

The view that recent social Directives have tended to contain many non-binding elements has been one trigger of the neo-voluntarism debate (see Chapter 1). In actual fact, the number of soft recommendations included in the six labour law Directives studied in this book range from eleven (Directive on Part-time Work) to zero (Directive on Employment Contract Information).[1] According to the logic of economic minimalism, member states should ignore these non-binding recommendations if they

---

[1] See Chs. 4–9.

wish to avoid unnecessary costs. In contrast to this sceptical assessment, our empirical results show that soft law may indeed have an effect in the member states.

10.1.1   *The individual Directives: any follow-up to soft law?*

10.1.1.1   Employment Contract Information Directive: lack of soft law   Since the Employment Contract Information Directive does not contain a single soft-law provision, it is not possible to come to a conclusion as to soft-law effects and, most importantly, the question of minimalism in the implementation of EU Directives. That some member states were willing to do more than required is nevertheless clear from the fact that there was over-implementation in six cases (see section 10.2.1.1 below).

10.1.1.2   Pregnant Workers Directive: no soft-law effect   The binding standards of the Pregnant Workers Directive forced a number of member states to improve protection standards while removing obstacles to female labour market participation. One additional recommendation in this legal act is that maternity protection should not adversely affect the job opportunities of women. However, this provision did not cause any significant voluntary action to be taken in the member states.

Two voluntary reforms which at first sight point in this direction seem in fact to be of national origin. In Germany, the transposition process was used to revise an existing scheme that helped small companies bear the costs of employee replacement for pregnancy or maternity-related reasons. Funded by employers' contributions from all sectors, this scheme previously only assumed 80 per cent of the costs. As a reaction to criticism by a number of small crafts employers, who argued that the limited extent of refunding was not sufficient to protect them from economic overburdening, the scheme was extended to guarantee reimbursement of all costs. There are no indications, however, that the recommendation of the Directive played a decisive role in this (Interviews D2: 430–88, D3: 257–322; BMFSFJ 1999: 29–30). Likewise, Spain, using money from the unemployment insurance scheme, created a system that subsidised the hiring of workers as a replacement for women on maternity leave (Interview E3: 825–31). The general resistance of the Spanish government and administration to implementing the Directive properly, along with the fact that the subsidisation scheme was created in the context of a wider national reform on the reconciliation of work and family life, does not, however, support the interpretation that this reform was triggered by the recommendation of the Directive.

At the same time, it should be noted that some member states had a general ban on night work for all female blue-collar workers or, more specifically, for pregnant women. Some of these countries were rather reluctant to lift these bans and only did so with considerable delay. In particular, this concerns France, Greece and Luxembourg. By the time of writing, Austria, Germany, Italy and partly also Portugal are still upholding such provisions which have a negative bearing on the employability of women. Debates on the content of the recommendation, i.e. that 'protection' should not impinge on employability, have been the result in Belgium and Greece. French discussions to the same effect, however, seem to be related to the general night work issue rather than to this Directive.

10.1.1.3 Working Time Directive: two recommendations without much effect Looking at the two non-binding recommendations of the Working Time Directive, it seems fair to say that they did not play a major role in the domestic implementation processes. With regard to *prohibiting Sunday working*, countries that already had a general ban on Sunday working (with exemptions) either left their existing regulations intact or actually extended the possibility of working on Sundays (as happened in Germany, the Netherlands and Austria). On the other hand, countries where no such ban had been in place before, especially Ireland and the UK, could not be induced by the Directive's recommendation to change the situation.

Looking at the effect of the soft-law provision on *specific measures to protect the health and safety of night workers*, roughly the same picture emerges. Although some of the national laws contain specific measures to protect the health and safety of night workers even beyond the standards explicitly laid down in the Directive, most of these provisions have not been introduced in the course of implementing the Directive (but were simply upheld). This applies to most of the measures protecting particularly vulnerable groups, such as young or pregnant workers, from night work, even though the Commission's implementation report lists these as national provisions implementing the Directive's recommendation (COM [2000] 787: 23–4).

10.1.1.4 Young Workers Directive: soft law implemented as soft law The Young Workers Directive includes three non-binding recommendations. As to the first two soft-law provisions, the Directive stipulates that the two days' weekly rest period should be *consecutive* 'if possible' and that it should 'in principle' include *Sunday* (Article 10.2). As to the third soft-law provision, member states that allow children still subject to compulsory full-time schooling to perform work are called on to make sure that 'a period free of any work is included, as far as possible, in the *school holidays*' of these children (Article 11; emphasis added). On this basis, some limited effects could be observed.

In Belgium and Finland, the recommendation with regard to consecutive weekly rest periods was made a compulsory provision. In the Finnish case, however, this over-implementation was partly offset by the fact that the length of the weekly rest period is only thirty-eight instead of forty-eight hours. Not all remaining countries completely disregarded this recommendation: in Austria, Denmark, Germany, Italy, Ireland, Luxembourg, Portugal, Spain, Sweden and the UK,[2] the soft-law provision was implemented as soft as it was, that is the law in these countries now *recommends* to employers that the forty-eight-hour weekly rest period should be consecutive if possible.

The same pattern could be observed in relation to the inclusion of Sunday in the weekly rest period. In the course of implementing the Directive, no single country introduced a compulsory ban on Sunday working for young workers. But Austria, Denmark, Luxembourg and Sweden at least took over the soft version contained in the Directive, according to which employers should, in principle, include Sunday in the weekly rest period of children and adolescents. The recommendation that children still subject to compulsory full-time schooling, to the extent that they are allowed to work at all, should be granted a certain leave period which 'as far as possible' should be included in their school holidays was disregarded by many countries, either because their rules and regulations did not allow these children to perform work at all or because they already provided for a minimum period of annual rest during school holidays. Among the few potential target countries, the UK took on board this recommendation, guaranteeing children a minimum period of two consecutive weeks free from work. In Ireland, the respective period was voluntarily extended from two weeks to three weeks.

10.1.1.5 Parental Leave Directive: soft law with effect in a majority of member states One of the most striking observations made when examining the implementation of the Parental Leave Directive is that the nine non-binding recommendations did not turn out to be of purely symbolic value. On the contrary, no fewer than ten member states reflected one or more of these soft-law provisions in their transposition measures. Only Denmark, Finland, France, Greece and Sweden totally ignored the Directive's recommendations.

---

[2] In the UK this only applies to young persons working on ships. See the Merchant Shipping and Fishing Vessels (Health and Safety at Work) (Employment of Young Persons) Regulations 1998 (SI 1998 No. 2411), reg. 6.

Belgium, Ireland, Luxembourg, Portugal and the UK made the entitlement to parental leave non-transferable. It seems that this recommendation was only implemented by countries which introduced completely new schemes. This was even true for Portugal. Although an entitlement to up to two years' 'special leave' already existed, the government introduced a new parental leave scheme in addition to the existing system. Interestingly, the new scheme was made non-transferable, whereas the 'special leave' system had been transferable. Apparently, this was done because Portuguese officials were convinced that this provision of the Directive was compulsory rather than optional (Interview P1: 1895–902).

The recommendation that taking leave should be possible until the child's eight birthday was reflected in the legislation of four countries. Austria and Germany retained their general age limits but provided for the option to take part of the leave until the child is seven (Austria) or eight years of age (Germany). In Italy, the age limit was raised from three to nine. In the Netherlands, the government originally wanted to raise the age threshold from four to six, but the trade unions pushed to let parents take the leave until the child has reached the age of eight.

With regard to flexible forms of take-up, Germany adopted a rather wide-ranging system which gives parents working in companies with more than thirty employees the legal right to work part-time during parental leave. Portugal went even further and endowed all employees with a legal right to work part-time during parental leave (Interview P9: 792–6). Belgium endowed mothers and fathers working in companies with more than ten employees with a legal right to part-time leave. In addition, provision was made for leave to be taken in a piecemeal way and on the basis of a time-credit system provided that the employer agrees (Clauwaert and Harger 2000: 21). Finally, the option to postpone part of the leave introduced in Austria and Germany implies that the leave here can also be taken in a piecemeal way. Furthermore, both countries created the possibility for mothers and fathers to take parts of the whole leave period alternately.

The provision that men should be encouraged to take on an equal share of the childcare responsibilities also had a substantial impact in some countries. In Germany, the measures relating to simultaneous leave and part-time working during parental leave were explicitly meant to make parental leave more attractive to men. In addition, the introduction of the new Act was accompanied by a public campaign sponsored by the Department of Family Affairs which aimed to encourage men to become more involved in childcare. A similar campaign was also conducted in Spain but was not supplemented with specific legislative measures. In Portugal, the introduction of a right to part-time leave was aimed at making parental leave for men more appealing. On top of that, the government created a specific incentive for fathers to avail themselves of their right to parental leave: while leave normally is unpaid, the first fifteen days of the leave taken by a male employee are paid by the state. Ministry officials considered this measure to be a direct reaction to the Directive (Interview P1: 1752–84, 2164–69). Finally, Italy provided fathers with the right to an extra month's leave if they take parental leave for at least three months.

10.1.1.6   Part-time Work Directive: soft law with effect in a majority of member states revisited   In terms of hard- and soft-law provisions, the Part-time Work Directive is the most neo-voluntarist EU measure in our sample. It comprises only one (albeit rather broad and significant) binding standard and eleven non-binding recommendations. During the national implementation processes, nine countries actually took on board some or all of these recommendations (while Austria, Denmark, France, Luxembourg, Sweden and the UK did not). Most importantly, the Directive comprises a number of recommendations for facilitating access to part-time work and for eliminating legal, contractual or administrative obstacles to this type of work. Moreover, it calls on member states to remove potential disadvantages for part-time workers arising from the organisation of their statutory social security systems (see Chapter 9 for a detailed list of all eleven soft-law provisions).

The most significant cases of national adoption of the recommendations are Germany, Italy, Portugal and Spain. The governments of these countries considered the soft-law provisions of the Directive a useful tool for boosting part-time work in order to create additional jobs. Hence, the national transposition laws reflected almost all of the Directive's recommendations, thereby creating powerful instruments with which to facilitate part-time work, such as the legal right to work part-time in Germany and Portugal or the generous financial incentive measures adopted in Italy, Spain and Portugal.

As has already been noted in the chapter on the implementation of the Part-time Work Directive, Germany incorporated almost all of the non-binding recommendations laid down in the Directive since the centre-left government aimed to cut unemployment by boosting part-time work. Most important in this context was the fact that the government created a legal right to work part-time. The Portuguese transposition legislation outlawed existing restrictions on the recruitment of part-time staff, such as the specification of a certain maximum percentage of part-timers (Interviews P3: 559–60, P8: 825–6; Cristovam 1998a). Similar to the regulation in Germany, it was stipulated that employers must, as far as possible, give consideration to requests by workers to transfer from full-time to part-time work. Most of the remaining recommendations were incorporated as well. The government, moreover, created social security incentives for recruiting part-time staff which were outside the scope of the Directive strictly speaking. Full-time workers transferring to a part-time job were granted reductions in social security contributions. Employers who hired a young job-seeker or a long-term unemployed person as a result of transforming full-time into part-time jobs were also rewarded with reduced social security contributions for the newly hired workers (CEC 2003: 35–6).

In Spain, the principle of non-discrimination was extended to statutory systems of social security, as recommended by the Directive. Part-timers with a working time of less than twelve hours per week or forty-eight hours per month had hitherto been excluded from these schemes. In order to counterbalance de facto discrimination in the pension scheme, the Spanish government even set the pension entitlements of part-time workers at a rate which was 50 per cent above the *pro rata temporis* level. In other words, a person who has worked for twenty years on a part-time basis will now receive a pension equivalent to thirty years (Interview E2: 234–8; Chozas Pedrero 1999: 411; Hutsebaut 1999). Moreover, the Spanish government took into account several other recommendations of the Directive that sought to improve the situation of part-timers and to stimulate the use of part-time work (Interview E4: 1104–67, 1216–22; EIRR 300: 30–1; Bundesarbeitsblatt 1999; Valdeolivas García 1999). These measures were agreed between the government and the unions, while employers' organisations walked out of the negotiations in protest against the sweeping over-implementation of the Directive proposed by the government (Interview E2: 166–71, 455–7, 762–70).

Italy removed two of the main obstacles to part-time work, namely restrictions on overtime and ceilings on the number of part-time workers laid down in collective agreements. The new law also took into account many of the other recommendations of the Directive. For example, it was provided that part-time workers have precedence when applying for full-time job vacancies offered by their employer. In the case of part-time vacancies, employees working full-time may ask to reduce their working hours so as to transform their job into a part-time position. Furthermore, like its Portuguese and Spanish counterparts, the Italian government created considerable social security incentives that aimed to promote the use of part-time work (EIRR 313: 8, 314: 8–9, 316: 9; Pedersini 2002).

Like Germany and Portugal, the parliament of the Netherlands adopted an Act in February 2000 which provided employees with a legal right to decrease (and also to increase) their working hours. It should be noted, however, that the process leading up to this reform had already been initiated in the early 1990s and thus had predominantly national origins (Interview NL8: 964–1037; Kamerstukken 1992–1993, 23 216, No.1–2).

A more limited effect was brought about by the soft-law provisions in a further four countries. In Ireland, employees are now protected against dismissal if they refuse to accede to a request by the employer to transfer from full-time to part-time work or vice versa. Moreover, the Irish legislation now calls on the Labour Relations Commission, a tripartite body aiming to improve the quality of industrial relations, to review potential obstacles to part-time work and to issue recommendations as to their potential removal (Dobbins 2002). So far, however, no positive steps have been taken in this direction. Similarly, the Belgian National Labour Council has taken the step of preparing a report on existing obstacles to part-time work (Interview B4: 227–323), but up to now no legal or contractual consequences have resulted from this report.

The Finnish legislation imposes a duty on employers to inform their employees about vacant part-time or full-time jobs, and an existing regulation has been tightened so as to guarantee that priority is given to part-time workers if an employer wants to fill full-time jobs (Interview FIN5: 127–76, FIN8: 289–303). In the UK, finally, although the recommendations were completely disregarded in the national transposition legislation, some of them were nevertheless included as examples of 'best practice' in a (legally non-binding) explanatory guide on the legislation (DTI 2000a).

10.1.2   *Patterns across countries and Directives*

The bird's-eye view of the implementation of EU soft-law provisions stemming from our six labour law Directives reveals clearly discernible patterns. Some countries and some Directives are indeed relatively successful when it comes to implementing soft law while others are not.

Among the Directives, it is the Part-time Work Directive's recommendations (eleven in total, but not all relevant in every state) that have most frequently been implemented in a binding way. We know about thirty-five such cases. This equals about 22 per cent of all 165 theoretically possible adaptation opportunities.[3] The Parental Leave Directive comes second

---

[3] Note that this number does not take into account the fact that the recommendations had, in some cases, already been fulfilled beforehand. Hence, the adaptation opportunities *actually possible* will be lower. Since it was empirically very hard to establish whether or not the goal of a specific recommendation had already been met fully or in part, we rely

with twenty-five cases (equalling about 19 per cent of all 135 theoretically possible adaptation opportunities). Far behind are the Directives on Young Workers (two out of forty-five theoretically possible cases – about 4 per cent), Working Time (one out of thirty theoretically possible cases – about 3 per cent) and Pregnant Workers (none out of a total number of fifteen theoretically possible adaptation opportunities). However, there are clear differences in take-up between different recommendations within the same Directive.

With regard to individual soft standards, it appears that those with potentially *the highest costs are the least complied with* (e.g. non-discrimination with regard to statutory social security for part-timers, continuity of social security cover for parents on leave). By contrast, those aspects that will entail hardly any significant costs to the state or business tend to be more frequent (e.g. awareness campaigns to encourage fathers to become more involved in childcare, part-time system for taking parental leave).

The one flexible recommendation that would have required a *major change in regulatory philosophy* did not have any effect, i.e. the one on protecting the employability of pregnant women who are, inter alia, hampered in several countries by a general ban on night work for women. We therefore conclude that, where soft law is at odds with deeply rooted principles of national labour law, a non-binding recommendation will hardly ever be a strong enough trigger for change. By contrast, these are typically the cases where the member states concerned have, by the time the Directive was adopted, strongly advocated that the provision should not be a binding but a non-binding one, and these member states will only in exceptional cases deviate from their stance during the implementation period (at best after a change in government).[4]

As far as the *member states* are concerned, we see that some countries rather frequently follow non-binding suggestions in EU law while others regularly ignore them. Above all, Germany has proven to be an over-implementer in the soft-law dimension. In ten cases, the soft-law elements in our Directives were transposed in a binding way in Germany. They all belong to the Part-time (six) and Parental Leave (four) cases, where the then new social democratic government's ideological preferences went hand in hand with the Directives' general thrust and recommendations.

---

here on the theoretically possible opportunities as a measure for comparing the different Directives.

[4] These findings fit in with the theoretical point made by Adrienne Héritier (2003), who argues that voluntary modes of governance are unlikely to work if redistributive, prisoner's dilemma or institutionally deeply entrenched problems involving a significant level of conflict between winners and losers are to be solved.

Second comes Italy (with seven recommendations on Part-time and two on Parental Leave having been adopted), where the respective reforms were also effectuated by centre-left governments whose ideological positions were in line with the goals of the recommended provisions.[5]

At the other end of the continuum, Denmark and Sweden *never* reacted to any soft-law provision, and the UK, Greece and France *hardly ever* responded. This seems to be a matter of principle: Denmark and the UK are fervent defenders of national competence in social affairs and try to keep EU intervention levels as low as possible, while France and Sweden, it seems, are extremely strong defenders of their 'national models' in social policy, which they perceive to be superior.[6] Moreover, Denmark and Sweden are among the countries that are, for cultural reasons, particularly prone to comply with the compulsory parts of EU law. Against this background, it does not appear to be a reasonable strategy to raise the level of potential conflicts by incorporating soft law. Greece in general tends to neglect adaptation requirements stemming from the EU. Thus, it comes as no surprise that it also disregards those parts of the Directives that are legally non-binding in nature (see Chapter 15 for more details about the role of cultural factors in determining member states' typical modes of reaction to both hard and soft law).

10.1.3 *Recommending that soft law be complied with*

Quite often member states did not impose the recommendations from our six Directives in a legally binding way but recommended that the social partners should conclude agreements to the very same effect or that businesses should voluntarily comply with the relevant provisions. This occurred in twenty-five cases. Again, there are clear patterns with regard to the distribution of such phenomena across countries and Directives.

Interestingly, it is *not the corporatist countries* that lead the list, but the UK (with six cases, all concerning Part-time Work), as a result of the fact that the British government wanted to encourage enterprise-level agreements. Next comes Spain (three cases, two for Part-time Work and

---

[5] It should be noted that not only left-wing, but also centre-right governments sometimes incorporated EU recommendations if these were in line with their own political aspirations. For example, this was the case when the conservative Spanish government decided to take on board some of the soft-law provisions of the Part-time Work Directive in order to boost part-time jobs and thus to combat unemployment.

[6] For Denmark and Sweden, the low rate of incorporating soft law may also have been furthered by the fact that the transposition of our sample Directives was very rarely connected to a more far-reaching modernisation of the existing regulatory systems in these countries. In other member states, broader reform processes seem to have provided additional 'windows of opportunity' for the adoption of EU recommendations.

one for Young Workers). It is followed by a number of countries with either one or two examples. Only Greece and the Netherlands have failed to turn EU soft law into national soft law in a single case within the six Directives.

With regard to the Directives, both the Working Time Directive (with its two recommendations) and the Pregnant Workers Directive (with one recommendation) failed to account for a recommendation to comply with EU soft law in a single EU member state, while the eleven soft-law provisions of the Part-time Work Directive induced domestic soft law in ten cases. But, viewed as a whole, there is no unequivocal relationship between the number of recommendations in EU law and the likelihood of domestic soft-law adaptation. The Directive which caused the highest number of such optional transposition provisions (fourteen) was the Young Workers Directive (with only three soft-law provisions), whereas the nine recommendations of the Parental Leave Directive only occasioned one case of soft adaptation.

Again, our impression is that a logic of domestic politics is being followed in many cases. Hence, it depends on the preferences of domestic governments and/or social partners whether a specific recommendation is implemented as hard law, adopted in the form of a soft recommendation, or ignored completely. The country patterns also imply that cultural factors are at work when it comes to domestic reactions to EU soft law (see Chapter 15 for more details).

10.2   Over-implementation of compulsory minimum standards

Besides reacting to soft law, member states may also exceed the minimum level defined by the Directives by raising their domestic standards further than required. This form of over-implementation is explicitly allowed by the Directives under scrutiny, since they only define minimum standards and leave it up to member states to go beyond these standards. Hence, a member state which has to introduce three months of parental leave for the first time may also enact legislation providing for six or twelve months' leave. From a perspective of economic minimalism, such instances of voluntary over-implementation should not be expected to occur, since member states are deemed to fend off every unnecessary burden on their economies in order to improve their competitiveness in the Common European Market. Again, our empirical findings reveal a somewhat different picture, as the following short overview will make clear.

10.2.1   The individual Directives compared

10.2.1.1   Employment Contract Information Directive: one significant and four minor cases   In the case of the Employment Contract Information Directive, the only significant case of implementation exceeding the minimum standards was found in the Netherlands, where the trade unions successfully convinced the government to extend the scope of the transposition legislation to 'quasi-employees' such as freelance or home workers. In addition, provision was made for posted workers to be given more information than required by the Directive (Interview NL8: 547–78; STAR 1992: 4; Kamerstukken 1992–1993, 22 810, No. 3: 2–4). Furthermore, there are four minor cases of implementation exceeding the minimum standards of the Directive. In Austria, written information on the essential terms of employment must be given within a few days after the conclusion of the employment relationship (CEC 1999: 12). This period is shorter than the two months required by the Directive. Similarly, the period is one month in Denmark (CEC 1999: 11). In Luxembourg, information about contractual modifications has to be issued immediately instead of within one month (CEC 1999: 12). Portuguese law, finally, requires employers to inform their employees about *all* conditions of their employment relationship, whereas the Directive only requires information about the *essential* conditions (CEC 1999: 9–10).

10.2.1.2   Pregnant Workers Directive: one significant and three minor cases   The Pregnant Workers Directive also produced one significant case of implementation surpassing the binding minimum standards. In France, generous rules on remuneration during the newly created health and safety leave were established, with employees receiving benefits equivalent to 100 per cent of their previous pay, financed partly by social security funds and partly by the employer. Three more minor instances of implementation exceeding the binding standards could also be observed. In Ireland, the enabling legislation entitled women not only to time off with pay for medical check-ups before giving birth, but also afterwards. Moreover, fathers were given the option to take leave if the mother died in, or shortly after, childbirth. In Luxembourg, the protection against dismissal of pregnant women was set to apply even before the respective women had notified their employer of their pregnancy (Interview LUX2: 280–99). Finally, Portugal created a specific tripartite body in charge of authorising exceptional dismissals of women during pregnancy and maternity leave (say, in case of an employer's insolvency). Under the terms of the Directive, it would have been sufficient to place responsibility for this task on existing enforcement agencies (e.g. the labour inspectorate). Furthermore, employers were explicitly required to inform their employees in writing about the results of the pregnancy-related risk assessment.

10.2.1.3 *Working Time Directive: no significant, but four minor cases*   In the case of the Working Time Directive, it is difficult to establish the extent to which member states exceeded the minimum requirements of the Directive. It is clear that the standards in a number of countries are well above the minimum requirements laid down in the Directive. In France, for example, an average weekly working time limit of thirty-five hours is applicable (instead of an average forty-eight-hour weekly working time limit specified in the Directive). However, this reform was certainly not triggered by the European Working Time Directive, but had predominantly national origins. Similarly, the weekly working time limits in Belgium and the Netherlands are also more favourable to workers than the ones allowed by the Directive, but this was also the case before the Directive had to be implemented, which means that lowering the standards to the level of the Directive would have violated the Directive's non-regression clause (see Chapter 7).

Nevertheless, we found four clear-cut (albeit rather minor) instances of implementation exceeding the European minimum standards. In Belgium and France, all night workers have to respect an absolute daily maximum of eight hours, while the Directive would have allowed greater flexibility for non-hazardous night work. In Germany, night workers are entitled to be transferred to day work if they have a child to be taken care of or a person who is in need of nursing and is dependent on the worker (German Working Time Act 1994, s. 6.4). Finally, Greece laid down a consecutive daily rest period of twelve (instead of the stipulated eleven) hours (Interview GR2: 145–60).

10.2.1.4 *Young Workers Directive: two major and three minor instances*   When implementing the Young Workers Directive, two member states went significantly beyond the binding standards. France extended to all young workers the stricter working time standards that applied to children. Hence, the working time limits of sixteen- and seventeen-year-olds were voluntarily raised from eight hours per day and thirty-nine hours per week to seven hours per day and thirty-five hours per week. In Ireland, the Directive was used as part of an effort to improve the skill levels of young people by extending their school attendance. Hence, the minimum working age was voluntarily raised from fifteen to sixteen years, and the compulsory school leaving age was raised accordingly. Moreover, the enforcement mechanism was made more accessible

to young people and the sanctions were raised considerably (from about (€125 to approximately €1,900).[7]

Additionally, four minor cases of implementation that surpassed the compulsory minimum level could be witnessed. In Germany, the sanctions against violations of the young workers legislation were voluntarily raised from around €10,000 to approximately €20,000. Portugal also doubled the financial sanctions against non-compliance with the relevant law, although the absolute level still remained much lower than in Germany (ranging from €400 to €9,600 depending on the type of violation). Greece not only compelled employers to respect the general health and safety obligations laid down in the Directive, but introduced the statutory requirement to provide a competent person to supervise young workers during the initial period of their employment. In Luxembourg employers were required to inform young workers and their representatives *in writing* about the results of the required risk assessment, and a further restriction on the amount of work undertaken by school children was created, i.e. pupils are now only allowed to do two hours of work on a school day, while, additionally, the total duration of schooling and working hours may not exceed eight hours per day.

10.2.1.5   Parental Leave Directive: three significant and four minor cases   The Parental Leave Directive produced the most instances of surpassing adaptation. Most significantly, Luxembourg's scheme provides for six instead of three months' parental leave, which is, moreover, generously paid by the state and pertains to persons usually not considered employees, i.e. civil servants and the self-employed. Belgium also introduced paid parental leave financed by the state, although this special paid leave may be refused by the employer in small establishments with fewer than ten employees. Italy voluntarily extended the length of the leave period from three to six months and now grants self-employed women tax relief if they arrange to be replaced by another person. More

---

[7] While it could be argued that some of these measures to raise the level of sanctions were required by the Directive's provision that called for 'effective and proportionate' measures against violations of the standards (especially the raising of sanctions), the steps to increase accessibility to the judicial system for young workers certainly went beyond what would have been required by the Directive. Previously, young workers who felt that their rights were violated had to initiate legal proceedings before the High Court. The stringent legal formality of such proceedings, however, was an immense obstacle to young workers actually making use of this option. Therefore, the new Act allows young workers to file complaints with a Rights Commissioner in order to defend themselves against detrimental treatment by employers. It is common understanding that this procedure is much less formal and therefore much more easily accessible to employees than ordinary court proceedings (Interview IRL8: 574–619).

minor instances of this kind of over-implementation relating to the binding standards of the Directive can be observed in Austria (notice periods have been reduced and employees now enjoy the right to be informed about important events in their company during parental leave), Germany (option for parents to take parental leave simultaneously), Ireland (*force majeure* leave has to be paid by the employer) and Portugal (the right to take parental leave was partly extended to grandparents, who are now entitled to thirty days' special 'grandparents' leave').

10.2.1.6   Part-time Work Directive: two major, no minor instances
In comparison, the Part-time Work Directive only gave rise to relatively few cases of over-zealous adaptation, which, however, were significant in their policy implications. In Greece, the transposition process was used voluntarily to improve the situation of part-timers working on Sundays in that they were awarded 75 per cent of the Sunday work premiums of a full-time worker (EIRR 302: 25). Moreover, it was stipulated that employers have to notify the labour inspectorate of the hiring of part-time workers to facilitate enforcement of their rights (Interviews GR2: 485–92, GR8: 313–17).[8] The UK government, pressurised by trade unions, voluntarily extended the scope of the legislation on part-time work to 'quasi-employees' such as freelance or agency staff.

10.2.2   Patterns across countries and Directives

According to our information, national governments exceeded one or more of the European minimum standards in twenty-seven out of ninety-one cases. These were spread rather evenly across all Directives. Only the Part-time Work Directive prompted significantly fewer member states to go beyond its minimum standards. This is due to the fact that the Directive only contains one standard, which theoretically leaves less opportunity to rise above the strict minimum.

But while there are no unequivocal patterns across Directives, *clear country clusters* do emerge. Spain, Finland and Sweden have never exceeded the binding standards of our six Directives. Denmark, Italy, the UK and the Netherlands have also been rather reluctant in this respect (one case each). At the other end of the continuum, Luxembourg takes the lead with four out of six cases of over-zealous implementation, followed by Austria, Germany, France, Ireland, Greece and Portugal (three

---

[8] Note, however, that this notification requirement could be interpreted as an additional (bureaucratic) obstacle to hiring part-time workers. Hence, doing more to reach the first goal of the Directive, i.e. the protection of part-time workers, could mean in this case doing less to achieve the second goal, i.e. the facilitation of part-time work.

cases each) and Belgium with two cases. Hence, some of the country patterns discovered in the reactions to EU soft law can be found here, too. Denmark, the UK, Finland and Sweden are again among the fairly 'minimalist' group. And Germany once more is one of the most frequent over-implementers. Interestingly, Italy, while evidently quite responsive to soft-law recommendations, hardly ever exceeds the binding standards.

In sum, these findings yet again point to the importance of domestic politics as the major factor determining whether or not a country exceeds the strict minimum requirements imposed by the EU. In most of the cases mentioned above (and especially in the more significant ones), the reasons for surpassing adaptation were either domestic (party) politics or interest group pressure. However, it seems that some countries explicitly try to avoid such 'gold plating', while, in others, making use of European implementation processes in order to realise substantively related domestic goals appears to be a normal feature of the policy-making process. Therefore, cultural factors once again seem to play an important role here (see Chapter 15 for more details). At any rate, there is no general tendency towards a logic of economic minimalism caused by competitive pressures among the member states in the Common European Market.

10.3   'Minimalism' revisited

10.3.1   Exemptions: used or disregarded?

From a perspective of economic minimalism (as outlined above), one could expect that all exemption clauses of a Directive should be used in all member states. However, this is not the case. We could not carry out detailed legal research into all of the forty exemption provisions of our six Directives, but we systematically asked our interviewees about their use. In a total of 260 cases, it was brought to our attention that a member state made use of one of them. Out of a total number of theoretically possible cases of 600, this equals about 43 per cent. However, only a minority of 98 cases concerned newly introduced exemptions (16 per cent); the others already existed and were merely maintained (27 per cent). Since our numbers are less trustworthy in this respect than for the other areas of our research, some indicative examples have been introduced. They alone can sufficiently support the conclusion that sheer minimalism is not the underlying major principle in the implementation of EU law.

Under the Working Time Directive, the member states were allowed to provide for an individual opt-out from the forty-eight-hour week (as seen in Chapter 6). If required, workers who voluntarily agreed to do so could also work longer than an average of forty-eight hours per week. Ireland, along with the UK, had supported the clause during the negotiations. Nevertheless, not even the Irish ultimately used this 'backdoor route' out of the forty-eight-hour maximum on a permanent basis (but only for a transitional period of two years). In fact, none of the other states except the UK used this exemption in a general fashion. The fact that it was an *individual* opt-out seems to have made using this option unattractive outside the individualised industrial relations systems of Ireland and the UK.

However, a number of member states used this exemption for individual sectors with specific problems. Austria allowed the individual opt-out – though reluctantly – for hospital employees, after the government had been fiercely lobbied by hospital employers to ease the problems associated with extending the forty-eight-hour standard to the whole hospital sector (Interview A2: 2060–98). Luxembourg made use of the exemption with regard to the hotels and catering sector (COM [2003] 843: 16). The severe impact of the ECJ's *SIMAP* ruling, which meant that on-call duties had to be treated as working time rather than as rest periods, was the reason why France allowed certain employees in the health care sector to opt out of the forty-eight-hour week individually (see COM [2003] 843: 16). The same is true for Germany, where the opt-out possibility was recently applied to employees whose working time regularly involves time spent on call.[9] At the time of writing, similar debates were under way in Spain and the Netherlands (see COM [2003] 843: 16). Despite this increasing use of the individual opt-out possibility, it has to be said that the member states in general did not make use of the full range of exemptions and derogations offered by the Directive. For example, only the UK and Greece completely excluded from the scope of their working time legislation all sectors and activities endorsed by the relevant Directive.

With regard to the Pregnant Workers Directive (see Chapter 5), German domestic workers were fully covered by the dismissal protection scheme although they could be excluded from the scope of the Directive. In the case of the Working Time Directive, Austria included doctors in training in its newly-created working time legislation for hospitals, even though the Directive would have allowed them to be excluded (Interview A2: 747–83). When implementing the Young Workers Directive, Italy not only disregarded almost all exemptions relating to the prohibition of work by children below the age of fifteen, but even removed its previously existing exemptions. The only exemption that still remains is work in the

---

[9] See Art. 4b of the *Gesetz zu Reformen am Arbeitsmarkt vom 24 Dezember* 2003, Bundesgesetzblatt I, 2003, p. 3002.

context of cultural or similar activities. And, in the case of the Part-time Work Directive, Denmark did not make full use of the permitted derogations. Many Danish collective agreements excluded part-time workers with less than fifteen hours' weekly working time from eligibility to certain benefits. Although this threshold presumably would have been covered by the Directive's provision that allowed member states to make eligibility to specific working conditions contingent upon a certain level of working time (clause 4.4 of the framework agreement), the threshold fixed by law was lowered to ten hours (Interviews DK2: 109–39, DK4: 554–80).

10.3.2 Upholding higher national standards in the field of EU recommendations

A particular phenomenon which we wanted to focus on is the *upholding of prior standards* that go beyond the Directive's binding standards.[10] Since the six Directives studied here include a total of 119 provisions (binding and non-binding standards plus derogation possibilities), adding up to 1,785 individual cases in all fifteen member states, it was impossible to produce a scrupulous account of each and every of them. We had to practise a sort of 'positive selection', that is to concentrate on those examples mentioned as important by our interviewees. Furthermore, we could rely on an indicative subfield, i.e. the non-binding recommendations about which we included a series of questions in our expert interviews. Were higher national standards upheld even where the Directives did not manage to introduce binding standards?

We could establish such a stance in a total of 70 cases where, in the field of a Directive's non-binding recommendations (390 in total), the recommended measure had already been in place in a specific country and was then upheld. It is important to note, however, that this does not imply a lowering of standards in the other 320 cases (the latter occurred infrequently – see immediately below). Instead, this usually indicates that the relevant standards did not exist at all prior to the Directives. At any rate, since these provisions had not been incorporated into the Directive's floor of minimum standards, a minimalist logic should dictate that those standards were lowered to an even greater extent than in the field of binding minimum standards.

All countries where a substantial number of higher standards existed prior to the Directives upheld these higher standards in a considerable

---

[10] Please note that this is *not* included in our definition of over-implementation. Since EU Directives are not meant to lead to any lowering of standards, this seems more of a 'normal' way of implementation, the frequency of which was unknown before our study.

number of cases. The same is true if we look at different pieces of legislation. Focusing on the two Directives (Parental Leave and Part-time Work) that had more than just a few soft-law provisions again reveals a considerable number of cases where previously higher standards were upheld.

From the viewpoint of economic minimalism, one would have expected the member states to have lowered the relevant standards rather than maintain them. Thus, our findings again suggest that the reaction of member states to flexible EU standards is not driven by a minimalist logic.

10.3.3   Lowering prior standards

Further to the upholding of previously higher standards, we wanted to find out whether existing standards are actually lowered during transposition. As already pointed out above, the sheer number of individual standards and exemption options enshrined in our Directives made a detailed analysis of this question unfeasible. Instead, we had to focus on those examples that were mentioned by our interviewees.

We only found eight cases (out of our 91) where this, or a similar phenomenon, occurred. They neatly fall into three groups.

(a) *Illegal lowering due to Directive* (four cases). In these cases, the Directive itself triggered a lowering of standards, although this is explicitly forbidden in the non-regression clause of all EU social policy Directives. Two cases concern the Young Workers Directive. Portugal was forced to extend to all sectors the scope of the night work restrictions applying in industry. By adopting new rules for all sectors which were considerably less protective than the old regulations in industry, the level of protection for young workers in this sector was lowered. Transposition of the Directive in the Netherlands even resulted in 'undercutting adaptation'. The government reduced the weekly rest period from forty-eight to thirty-six hours, thereby creating a violation of the Directive which would not have existed before.

Two further cases may also be assigned to this category of undercutting implementation. When transposing the Working Time Directive, Germany extended the reference period for averaging out weekly working hours from two weeks to six months (instead of four) and allowed the social partners to agree on reference periods without any maximum length, both arrangements being contrary to the Directive. In the Part-time Work case, Spain also (temporarily) moved some way against the direction specified by the EU Directive. The government changed the originally correct definition of a part-time worker so as to restrict the term to employees working up to 77 per cent of normal working hours. Interestingly, this step was an indirect by-product of substantial over-implementation. The Spanish government created considerable social security incentives for people who took up a part-time job. In this context, the new definition of part-time work was to prevent part-time workers who work almost as much as full-time workers from also benefiting from these subsidies. Nevertheless, it was contrary to the Directive. In a subsequent reform a few years later, the correct definition was reinstated.

(b) *Lowering for domestic political reasons, not directly due to Directive* (two cases). The second category comprises two cases in which domestic standards were weakened for domestic political reasons largely unrelated to the Directive in question. In this area, the Working Time Directive is again the problematic case in our sample, notably the implementation of this Directive in Austria and the Netherlands. However, both countries did not respond directly to the Directive, but lowered their standards either according to an earlier plan, as in the Netherlands, or in the aftermath of transposition, as occurred in Austria. Both cases fit a more general domestic pattern of incremental liberalisation and flexibilisation that is not directly related to the EU. In legal terms, the Austrian case does not seem to be a violation of the non-regression clause since it was only effected a few years after the end of the original transposition process, whereas the clause clearly refers to the process of implementing the Directive. The Dutch case, however, would at least appear to be problematic, since the lowering of standards (albeit causally unrelated to the Directive) was effected in the course of transposition. But since the wording of this particular clause in general is rather vague, it is impossible to make an unequivocal assessment.[11]

(c) *Lowering for potentially valid policy reasons* (two cases). The two cases in this group are marked by a lowering of previous standards that falls outside the scope of the Directive, at least in the legal sense. They relate to the transposition of the Young Workers Directive in Austria and Germany. Both countries lowered the protection level for apprentices aged over eighteen, arguing that employers should be encouraged to offer more apprenticeship places. Since the Directive's scope only covers workers below the age of eighteen, the level of protection for *young* workers (legally speaking) was not weakened.

---

[11] Article 18.3 of the Directive reads: 'Without prejudice to the right of Member States to develop, in the light of changing circumstances, different legislative, regulatory or contractual provisions in the field of working time, as long as the minimum requirements provided for in this Directive are complied with, implementation of this Directive shall not constitute valid grounds for reducing the general level of protection afforded to workers.'

In overall terms, it is important to note that lowering here refers only to the domain of a specific standard. It does not mean that this is the overall effect of the Directive in the country concerned. In all the cases we detected, other standards were raised at the same time. In no case where there was a need for domestic adaptation did one of our Directives exclusively create a negative effect.

10.4   Conclusions: less minimalism than expected

All forms of implementation resulting in levels above the minimum floor of EU standards seem unexpected under the logic of minimalism outlined above.

Given the large number of individual provisions to track down, our information on the follow-up to soft law, on the use of exemptions and on the fate of previously higher standards of necessity cannot live up to the ideal of a meticulous analysis covering all possible details. However, we asked our interviewees whether or not the Directives' recommendations were taken into account and whether or not the available exemptions were used, as well as noting all significant information from our interviews on formerly higher standards that were upheld. The latter is, however, very partial information, so that many of the figures presented in this chapter are, without doubt, seriously underrated.[12] Nonetheless, if we make a tally of all the information discussed above, the emerging picture should give some indication as to the potential effects of neo-voluntarist policies in the European multi-level system.

Fifty out of ninety-one implementation case studies resulted in our team observing one or the other sort of active over-implementation in the follow-up to the Directives (either by way of adopting recommendations or by enacting reforms that go beyond the binding standards). On top of this, a number of very striking non-uses of exemption possibilities were noted, such as in the case of the individual opt-out provision from the Working Time Directive in most member states. Great caution is called for in using these data, but still our results point in a clear direction: *the economic 'logic of minimalism' cannot account for the large majority of cases.* Neither does the logic of maximalism hold, since there are clearly many

---

[12] Note that our interviews were rather extensive since there are usually not many different national experts available to answer questions on the background and negotiations to each of our Directives. This gave rise to tight time constraints in a number of interviews, and the many binding standards to be discussed sometimes left little time to enquire about the upholding of prior national standards and the implementation of non-binding ones.

cases where exemptions were used or recommendations disregarded, and even a small number of instances where standards were lowered.

In most cases, the member states seem to be following a 'logic of domestic politics'. They pay tribute to political considerations, most often related to either the ideology or policy paradigm of the parties in government, and to other important interests of a party-political or interest-political kind. At the same time, various groups of countries show quite different but at the same time relatively stable patterns that seem to be based on cultural factors (see Chapter 15).

11 The EU Commission and (non-)compliance in the member states

It is obvious and has been argued throughout the book that the effect of EU social policy Directives depends on timely and correct implementation in the member states. This chapter will briefly outline which instruments the EU Commission can use to make non-compliant member states fulfil their European duties. The aim is to assess the phenomenon empirically and to confront the occurrence of relevant failures with the Commission's enforcement policy.

11.1 State of the art

Within the field of research on the EU, a number of authors have dealt with the question of how well member states follow their commitment to implement EU law. Generally speaking, these studies can be divided along two lines, i.e. the approach taken and the data used. Thus most of the literature could easily be sorted into a four-box matrix, where the x-axis distinguishes between quantitative and qualitative studies, and the y-axis differentiates between cases where the initiative lies with an individual complainant[1] or with the European Commission. In such a table we would find a first group of quantitative studies working with data from individual complainants (e.g. Golub 1996; Stone Sweet and Brunell 1998); a second group of studies that examine the phenomenon of, or differences between, preliminary ruling procedures from a qualitative angle (e.g. Tesoka 1999; Alter and Vargas 2000); a third group of qualitative studies that deal with the question of why states comply with a specific EU rule and what role Commission enforcement plays in this case (e.g. Duina 1997; Knill and Lenschow 1997; Knill 1998; Börzel 2000; Héritier 2001a; Knill 2001; Börzel 2003a); and finally a fourth group that analyses quantitative data about Commission enforcement. Below

---

[1] Note that this refers to preliminary rulings and not to those infringement procedures where citizens or public interest groups served as information sources in the run-up to a Commission infringement procedure, since the Commission is the master of the procedure in these latter cases.

we will focus on this last group of quantitative studies and will present their most important findings in order to discuss critically the approach taken and to complement this perspective with the less biased (but also less encompassing) information about compliance in the ninety-one cases studied here.

There are a number of studies that analyse the quantity and evolution of infringement processes initiated by the EU Commission.[2] One common conclusion is that member states perform differently when it comes to compliance with EU responsibilities. The southern member states as well as France and Belgium appear to perform significantly worse than their Scandinavian counterparts. This difference between countries is variably categorised into 'leaders, laggards and best performing' (Kassim 2001) or 'law abiding' and 'worst culprits' (Miles 2001: 154). In the same literature stream, variation by policy area is sometimes found to be even more pronounced than cross-country variation (for example see Mendrinou 1996).[3] Environment and consumer policy, as well as internal market legislation, rank highest among infringement procedures. Here implementation seems to be more controversial and compliance less likely.

However, it is not clear whether the categorisation used really refers to differing levels of compliance between countries or sectors or if it is simply the result of a differing Commission enforcement policy: the Commission might treat the typical latecomers more strictly, and policy priorities may guide its enforcement policy. Only a few authors within compliance research address in detail the role and the policy of the European Commission (mostly insiders such as Ehlermann 1987; Ciavarini Azzi 1988, 2000; but see also Tallberg 1999; and to a lesser degree Mendrinou 1996).

Recently published work has taken a more specific look at questions of non-compliance. Sverdrup (2002a, 2002b, 2003) for example uses the length of infringement procedures to address the question of whether or not there are differences between member states in the way they deal with a case once a procedure has been opened. Hence he focuses on member state reactions to enforcement. Sverdrup comes to the conclusion that

---

[2] See for example Ehlermann (1987); Mendrinou (1996); Lampinen and Uusikylä (1998); Ciavarini Azzi (2000); Mbaye (2001); Neyer and Zürn (2001); Börzel (2003b); Sverdrup (2003).

[3] Note that this does not contradict the finding of country patterns. It is simply another classification of the same material, which turns out to show even higher inter-group differences while, within a single policy field, country-specific differences in the level of compliance generally remain in place. This means that even if a country sometimes evinces a specifically good or bad performance in one sector (e.g. Spain is a laggard in implementing internal market Directives, while its performance in implementing employment and social affairs Directives is significantly better; Secrétariat Général 2001: 136) overall changes in the ranking from one policy field to another remain modest.

Nordic states[4] are in this sense more compliant (Sverdrup 2003). Somewhat contrasting findings are presented by Jensen. He uses a regression model to test the assumption that southern member states have greater compliance problems. The result is that '[m]embership in the "South" group of relatively poor, low-wage member states does not translate into increased seriousness of conflict with the Commission over implementation' (Jensen 2001: 31).[5] The results might be due to the differing and, in both cases, selective sets of cases: Jensen focuses on labour policy only, while Sverdrup's analysis covers all policy areas but is limited to a five-year range.

This leads to an important and so far neglected problem with the research on EU compliance: people do not talk about the same things. More precisely, even though the dependent variable is always compliance with EU rules, studies make use of different country samples (often without controlling for later accession dates, e.g. Ehlermann 1987; Mbaye 2001), policy sectors, time sequences (some starting in the late 1960s – Mendrinou 1996; others about thirty years later – Ciavarini Azzi 2000), length of time spans (ranging from decades – Tallberg 2002; to a couple of years only – Pridham and Cini 1994; Sverdrup 2003), policy instruments (treaty principles, Directives, fraud), stages to the infringement procedures (Letter of Formal Notice, Reasoned Opinion, Transferral to the ECJ, Judgment by the ECJ), reasons for the infringement procedure (non-notification, non-transposition, non-application) or length of the infringement procedure (either as a whole or between stages). Data is aggregated without accounting for multiple entries (Audretsch 1986; Tallberg 2002), averages are calculated on differing bases (EU 10, 12 or 15, sometimes disregarding smaller member states such as Luxembourg – Lampinen and Uusikylä 1998; or Austria – Mbaye 2001) and data flows of infringement procedures (e.g. Mendrinou 1996) are used alongside snapshots of specific points in time (e.g. Ciavarini Azzi 2000). On top of this, additional sources sometimes come into play (e.g. notification of national transposition measures, complaints registered). Owing to this multitude of criteria – which are not always clearly marked off – it comes as no surprise that the results are incongruous.

Therefore it is equally unsurprising that estimations of a perceived compliance problem (again measured against Commission enforcement data) range from the statement that 'rates of compliance with EU regulation are better or at least as good as compliance with regulations at

---

[4] By this he means Finland, Denmark and Sweden, as well as EFTA members Norway, Iceland and Liechtenstein.

[5] The 'South group' in his work comprises Italy, Greece, Spain and Portugal.

other [domestic or international] levels' (Neyer and Zürn 2001: 6)[6] to the argument that the (presumably low) level of compliance in the EU is a 'significant systemic phenomenon' (Mendrinou 1996: 1) or even 'a serious threat to the development of common European policies' (Lampinen and Uusikylä 1998: 249). Moreover, even though many authors doing quantitative research about compliance acknowledge that the data they work with does not depict the actual level of compliance in the member state, this bounded perspective at times does not keep them from at least implicitly assuming that the data is unbiased (e.g. Mendrinou 1996: 3).

In fact, studies that use data of official infringement procedures brought by the Commission against a member state often test – and reject or validate – hypotheses on how to explain compliance in a member state, even though the data do not allow for such kinds of conclusions. Similarly the frequent attempt to distinguish between outright opposition and inadvertent non-compliance (e.g. Tallberg 2002: 626) seems to be empirically impossible if merely a data set of this type is examined.[7] With regard to this subject, Krislov, Ehlermann and Weiler (1986: 73) rightly argued that '[a] correct evaluation is possible, if at all, only on the basis of a case-by-case analysis'. Three other popular working hypotheses (or even conclusions) in the literature are: over time, member states have become more reluctant to comply with EU legislation (Lampinen and Uusikylä 1998: 236); a significant share of non-compliance is the result of administrative inefficiencies (Mendrinou 1996: 8); or the Commission treats member states differently in order to avoid conflicts with those countries that make the most significant contributions to the EU budget and/or have considerable voting power in the Council, or where the population is very 'Eurosceptic' (Börzel 2001: 812; see also Neyer and Zürn 2001: 7).

We argue that there is a fundamental difference in analysing data on official Commission infringement procedures and in looking at actual non-compliance in the member states.[8] In other words, the tip of the

---

[6] However, this argument is extremely over-generalised since the underlying empirical basis is limited to only one case for each of the three areas covered: market making, regulative and redistributive policies.

[7] The attempt simply to measure the length of time passed between the Commission's initiation of a procedure and the correct transposition of the required standards does not sufficiently take into account that, even though willing, member states can still be inhibited by a number of other factors (e.g. veto points or administrative procedures).

[8] It is quite another task, which we cannot systematically tackle in this chapter, to determine the influence of Commission enforcement policy on the level of compliance or non-compliance of a member state. But see section 11.2.3 for further exploration of this issue.

iceberg does not necessarily say much about the size or the shape of those parts that remain below the waterline.[9]

In particular, insight about the interaction of supranational enforcement and domestic implementation remains a research desideratum. This holds true for the literature on compliance with EU legislation and EU enforcement policy in general. In part this is due to the fact that all these studies implicitly or explicitly measure compliance by looking at the number of infringement procedures initiated. Thus the research on compliance in the EU is almost exclusively research on the reaction to non-compliance (either on the part of individuals mediated via the national legal system or on the part of the European Commission). The much cited expression of Weiler (1991: 2465) that there is 'a "black hole" of knowledge ... regarding the true level of member state implementation' remains unmitigated, despite research and empirical interest in the question having increased greatly over time.

At least some of the expectations raised in the literature can be rejected or confirmed for the ninety-one cases studied here. In what follows, we will first describe, then analyse the official enforcement policy of the European Commission and, finally, compare the findings with the results from Chapters 4 to 9 on the timeliness and correctness of implementation processes in the member states. This will allow us to draw sound conclusions about the Commission's enforcement policy in relation to domestic violations of EU law.

11.2   Supranational enforcement

11.2.1   Competences

The ECT assigns the EU Commission the role of 'guardian of the Treaties' (Article 211 ECT). Articles 226 and 228 introduce the so-called infringement procedure, which allows the Commission to take action against a member state that does not comply with EU law. The use of this procedure in day-to-day policy-making is laid down in a number of 'internal procedure' documents.[10] It consists of four different stages: the 'Letter of Formal Notice', the 'Reasoned Opinion', the 'Referral to the

---

[9] Tanja Börzel has set up an impressive database that allows her to make a methodologically more sophisticated use of the Commission data. Drawing on this material she has published studies that explain the implementation process at the national level (Börzel 2003a) as well as a concept for analysing Commission data (Börzel 2001, 2003b). However, even her cross-sectoral database does not make it possible systematically to link Commission enforcement policy to the implementation processes.

[10] There were important reforms in the 1990s (1993, 1996, 1998) which partly evolved due to a competition between the Secretariat General and the Directorate General for

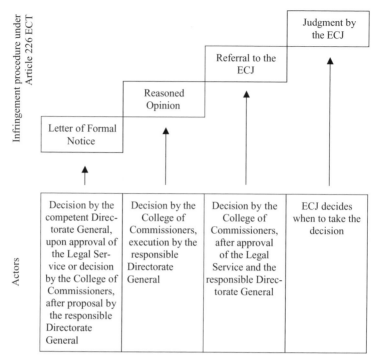

Figure 11.1   The EU infringement procedure

ECJ' and the 'Judgment by the ECJ' (see Figure 11.1). The first three stages are initiated by the EU Commission, the final stage is under the autonomous control of the ECJ. Nevertheless, they reflect an interaction of the supranational and national levels of governance. Behind the scenes, moreover, this is frequently a cumbersome interaction of different organisational units within the EU Commission. Who participates varies from step to step, and so it is important to understand the Commission as a 'multi-organisation' (Cram 1994). Below, we will shed light on these processes by explaining both the legal bases and the practical restrictions of supranational actors.

the Internal Market and which have been further accelerated by the growing external pressure from the European Parliament and the public (Interview COM2, Secrétariat Général 1993a, 1993b, 1996, 1998). The latest changes, published at the end of 2002, allow the EU Commission to prioritise infringements that undermine the foundations of the rule of law, that endanger the smooth functioning of the Community legal system or that consist in the failure (correctly) to transpose Directives. In the same document it is expressly stated that the Commission is free to use additional, non-legal and more promising instruments to bring member states behaviour into line with EU law (see COM [2002] 725).

The *first stage* is a 'Letter of Formal Notice'. Here the procedure still lacks an official character. The function of the letter is to make the member state aware that the Commission considers its behaviour in breach of a specific rule and to set a deadline for correcting the matter.[11] In cases where the letter is issued for failure to give notice of a transposition measure, it is almost always automatically sent out by the responsible unit (after approval by the Legal Service). However, when the letter is in response to cases of incorrect transposition, the College of Commissioners has to decide whether and when the procedure will be initiated as proposed by the responsible Directorate General (Interview COM1).

The *second stage* is labelled 'Reasoned Opinion'. If the member state does not remedy the breach of Community law admonished in the first stage, another letter follows. This is the first official (and usually publicised) stage of the procedure. Here, again, the decision is taken by the College of Commissioners, while the execution lies with the respective Directorate General. It is the first stage with official character and as such is often the subject of a press release by the EU Commission aimed at increasing the pressure by 'naming and shaming' the member state. By the same token it is a politically much more sensitive decision and the procedure, which in the initial stage often operates under a more or less automatic logic, may become subject to political, national or policy interests.

In the *third stage* the case can be referred to the ECJ. As in the preceding stage, the decision is taken by the College of Commissioners, but after the approval of the Legal Service and the responsible Directorate General has been given. Again, the decision to hand a case over to the ECJ increases the political pressure on the member state and is thus sometimes a politically delicate issue. How far the role as 'guardian of the Treaties' legally compels the Commission to make reference to the Court is discussed controversially in the legal literature (e.g. Krück 1997; Borchardt 1999: 1664; Karpenstein and Karpenstein 1999). It is obvious that, at least with regard to the timing, the political leeway is very large. Moreover, since things that the EU Commission does not know cannot be made subject to legal proceedings, ignorance might be a shield at any point within the procedure to unburden the supranational enforcement actors.

The *fourth stage* is the 'Judgment of the ECJ'. This is the only stage where the decision does not lie with the EU Commission, since it cannot directly influence the time and content of the judgment of the ECJ.[12] Interestingly, very few infringement procedures referred to the ECJ are

---

[11] Formally the time limit is set between one and two months. In practice, considerably more time passes, a full year being more the rule than the exception.

[12] Note that a judgment may even be made ex post, even though the member state has abrogated the breach of EU law by then.

decided in favour of the member states.[13] To put it differently, cases where uncertainty remains as to whether or not the member state is failing to fulfil its duty to comply with EU law normally do not make it to this stage; either they are not addressed officially or they are resolved on the way.

In cases of remaining opposition to the ECJ judgment, it is possible to recommence the procedure: a second 'Letter of Formal Notice' is sent, followed by a second 'Reasoned Opinion', etc. However, for many years the second infringement procedure did not significantly increase the pressure on the member state. This changed with the adoption of the Maastricht Treaty. In 1993, the possibility of financial sanctions was introduced in Article 228 ECT, although the use of this new instrument was impeded until 1997 by a lack of rules on how to calculate these sanctions.[14] Now, with more than five years having passed since this new emphasis was acquired, and unlike expected by some authors (e.g. Marks et al. 1996: 352), the financial sanctions have proven to be a well-functioning mechanism to increase the pressure on non-compliant member states. While in many cases the announcement of the Commission that sanctions were to be imposed already led to hectic activity at the domestic level with a view to finally ensuring compliance (e.g. in our sample concerning the Working Time Directive in Italy), there have been only two cases until now where sanctions were definitely imposed (penalising Greece for a dump in Korupitos/Crete and Spain for insufficient quality of bathing waters).[15]

It is important to note that, in all stages, a stringent and effective procedure does not just depend on a proper functioning of the Commission units mentioned so far. In addition, the Language Service has to assure that the letters are drafted in the language of the member state before the College of Commissioners decides. Quite often, it is not possible to judge the completeness of the measures notified and, in particular, understand properly whether or not they meet the standard requirements unless a translation is available. In these cases, recourse to external experts, e.g. national barristers in specialised offices in Brussels, is widely used and often of paramount importance (Interview COM2).

Following this general overview of the infringement procedure, we will

[13] Mbaye (2001: 268) even argues that between 1969 and 1995 no decision by the ECJ was made in favour of a (presumably) non-compliant member state. However, this claim is disputed by Mendrinou (1996: 12) and Ciavarini Azzi (2000: 60).

[14] The amount is composed of a lump sum and different coefficients (length and relevance of the contempt, as well as financial power of the member state). The sanctions can range from €500 per day (minimum penalty for Luxembourg) to €791,293 per day (maximum penalty for Germany). See CEC (1997b).

[15] See Judgment of the Court of 4 July 2000, case C-387/97, *Commission of the European Communities* v *Hellenic Republic* [2000] ECR I-5047; Judgment of the Court of 25 November 2003, case C-278/01, *Commission of the European Communities* v. *Kingdom of Spain*, (at the time of writing, this judgment had not been published in the European Court Reports).

Table 11.1 *Infringement procedures initiated by the EU Commission*[16]

	Letter of Formal Notice	Reasoned Opinion	Referral to the ECJ	Judgment by the ECJ
Employment Contract Information	**B, D, F, GB, GR, I, IRL, LUX, NL, P** F	**I**		
Pregnant Workers	**B, D, F, GR, I, LUX, P** A, D, E, F, FIN, I, IRL, LUX, S	**GR, LUX** E, F,[17] I, IRL, LUX, S	**LUX**	
Working Time	**A, F, GB, GR, I, IRL, LUX, P, F, I** B, D, DK, F, GB, GR, LUX, P, S	**F, GB, GR, I, LUX, P, I** DK	**F, I, LUX, I**	**F, I**
Young Workers	**A, F, GB, GR, I, LUX, P, S, F**	**A, F, GB, GR, I, LUX, P**	**F, I, LUX**	**F, LUX**
Parental Leave	**D, GB, GR, I, IRL, LUX, P** IRL, GB, LUX	**I, LUX, P** IRL, GB, LUX	**I** LUX	
Part-time Work				
Total	43 22	20 10	9 1	4
	65	**30**	**10**	**4**

Light face type indicates that the infringement has been initiated for non-communication of national transposition measures (in most cases this equals non-transposition).
Bold type signifies cases relating to incorrect transposition.
Shaded type denotes procedures following Article 228 ECT. These procedures are counted as separate processes, even though they concern implementation processes for which infringement proceedings under Article 226 ETC have already been conducted.

now look at the empirical picture that emerges from our study of compliance with six labour law Directives in the fifteen member states.

Table 11.1 reveals striking differences between Directives and member states with respect to the quantity and quality of infringement procedures

[16] Decisions for infringement procedures published by the EU Commission up to 9 July 2003, regarding the implementation of the six EU social policy Directives.

[17] In this case, a first Reasoned Opinion was addressed to France in 1999, but instead of a Referral to the ECJ, a second Reasoned Opinion followed in 2001 (see COM[2002] 324).

initiated by the European Commission. Most remarkable is the fact that procedures for non-notification (66 per cent at the first stage) more than double the number of procedures for incorrect transposition and that none of the latter has reached the ECJ so far. It is also worth mentioning that the Commission did not initiate a single infringement proceeding for incorrect application, even though the case studies in Chapters 4–9 have revealed that there are many shortcomings in practical compliance with our Directives.

There are sixty-five 'Letters of Formal Notice', thirty 'Reasoned Opinions', ten 'Referrals to the ECJ' and finally four 'Judgments by the ECJ'. About half of the cases were dropped after the first stage, and this number is halved again at the next stage. Two factors account for this: often the transposition process is delayed at the national level, but after one or two more years even slow and cumbersome law-making processes are accomplished. Additionally, the political costs of enforcement increase for the EU Commission incrementally (Mendrinou 1996: 9). As a result doubtful cases do not make it easily to the ECJ.

Comparing Directives, most of the infringement procedures have been initiated with a view to the Pregnant Workers Directive (sixteen) and the Working Time Directive (nineteen). Procedures relating to the latter have proved to display more conflict between the supranational and the national level, as the higher numbers of Referrals to the ECJ (four) and of Judgments by the ECJ (two) indicate. The absence of any infringement in the case of the Part-time Directive is also conspicuous. Here, the substantially later date when the Directive came into force has to be borne in mind. But, as we will see below, this can neither fully explain nor justify the absence of supranational enforcement.

When looking at the Employment Contract Information Directive it is interesting to note that ten out of the twelve member states of the time received a 'Letter of Formal Notice' from the Commission in July 1993. The Commission exercised its duty as a watchdog right at the end of the transposition deadline (30 June 1993). However, these infringement procedures were not followed up by further steps to ensure proper implementation of the Directive. Only Italy received a Reasoned Opinion in January 1996 (and reacted by adopting adequate legislation in May 1997), while it was several years later that France obtained a Letter of Formal Notice for incorrect application (2002). In no other case did the Commission adopt follow-up measures, even though a number of member states were identified as breaching parts of the Directive in the Commission's 1999 report on Monitoring the Application of Community Law (COM [1999] 301) and in an implementation report relating to the Directive issued by the Directorate General for Employment in the same year (CEC 1999).

As mentioned above, the Commission initiated numerous infringement procedures against non-compliant member states for the Pregnant Workers Directive. Seven Letters of Formal Notice were issued in 1995 due to non-notification, but only the proceedings initiated against Greece and Luxembourg were followed up by a Reasoned Opinion in June 1996 and, due to persistent non-notification in Luxembourg, by a Referral to the ECJ in December 1997.[18] Once Luxembourg had adopted its transposing legislation in July 1998 and had subsequently notified the Commission thereof, the proceedings ceased (COM [1999] 100: 5). In terms of pursuing substantive transposition flaws, the Commission's enforcement policy turned out to be comparatively rigorous. Nine member states received a Letter of Formal Notice, and six were issued with a Reasoned Opinion, due to wrongful implementation of several standards of the Directive. Despite this unusually tough monitoring of substantive correctness, numerous implementation shortcomings have still been left untouched (see Chapter 5).

The highest number of EU-level enforcement actions in our sample has so far been taken with regard to the Working Time Directive. In terms of *non-notification* of transposition measures, the Commission initiated the first stage of the infringement proceedings against eight countries soon after the end of the transposition deadline in spring 1997. Owing to persistent non-notification in most of the cases, six Reasoned Opinions followed in December 1997. While the UK, Greece and Portugal subsequently transmitted their transposition measures to Brussels in 1998, the Commission transferred the remaining three cases to the ECJ. In Luxembourg, constant administrative overload had kept the ministry from tackling the adoption but, given the advanced stage and the threat of an ongoing infringement procedure, it finally communicated its legislative provisions to the Commission and the case was closed soon afterwards. France and Italy, however, were condemned by the ECJ for non-transposition of the Directive in 2000.[19] In February 2003, the Commission even initiated the Article 228 procedure because both countries still had not complied. The procedure against France was terminated in December 2001 after the first stage, though, because the controversial *Loi Aubry* had since transposed important parts of the Directive. Italy, in contrast, only took the necessary steps to implement the Directive in April 2003, a couple of

---

[18] The remaining proceedings for other member states were dropped after transposition measures had been communicated to the Commission.

[19] See Judgment of the Court of 8 June 2000, case C-46/99, *Commission of the European Communities* v. *French Republic* [2000] ECR I-04379; Judgment of the Court of 9 March 2000, case C-386/98, *Commission of the European Communities* v. *Italian Republic* [2000] ECR I-01277.

days before a second ruling of the ECJ. A second judgment by the Court would have imposed – for the first time in the area of social policy – daily fines (here €238,000 per day; Muratore 2003) for failure to comply with the first ruling (see Chapter 6 for more details).

The Commission's activities against non-compliant member states in the working-time field also concerned cases of incorrect or insufficient transposition. A first procedure against Denmark was initiated in 1999 and was followed by a range of infringement procedures against altogether nine member states up to 2003. Only one of these procedures, the one against Denmark (which was also the first to be initiated), has so far reached the stage of a Reasoned Opinion. The subject of the Danish procedure was the transposition via collective agreements, which could not guarantee full coverage of all workers (see Chapter 12 for more details). Overall it seems that the Commission has a firm interest in improving compliance with the Directive but nevertheless appears far from willing, or able, to pursue all (or at least all major) violations.

Against this background, it is noticeable that the legal complexity of the Directive has so far given rise to two important ECJ rulings, *BECTU* and *SIMAP* (see Chapter 6). Both cases now allow for more certainty on the part of the Commission as to when a member state may be classified as violating specific standards of the Directive. By 2003, moreover, the EU Commission was waiting for the results of reports from national experts on compliance with the concept of effective working time in hospitals. The enforcement policy based on this report will be most interesting to follow since the question of implementation in this area is linked to substantial financial costs for the member states as employers. Similar to the Pregnant Workers case, the envisaged revision of the Directive might also influence the Commission's future actions against non-compliant member states. Thus compliance and enforcement are expected to be, politically, highly sensitive issues (Interview COM1b).

Until now all infringement proceedings initiated by the Commission concerning the Young Workers Protection Directive referred to non-notification. Eight Letters of Formal Notice were issued in the beginning of 1997, followed in all but the Swedish case by a Reasoned Opinion later the same year. In the following two years the infringement proceedings against Italy, Luxembourg and France reached the third stage. All three countries had long remained inactive at the national level, although for different reasons: in Italy there was strong controversy between the government and the social partners on the question of apprenticeship; the administration in Luxembourg continued to be constantly overloaded; and French actors simply considered the national regulation to be at least as good as the European standards, thus denying a need for transposition.

The last two countries were condemned by the ECJ in December 1999 and May 2000.[20] Since France did not adopt transposition measures until February 2001, the Commission again decided to initiate the Article 228 procedure to tackle persistent non-compliance in this country. With regard to the Young Workers Directive, therefore, the sequence of the enforcement actions against non-notification was swift and severe compared with the Directives discussed so far.

The picture of a comparatively stricter enforcement policy with regard to non-compliant member states appears to persist in the case of the Parental Leave Directive. Seven Letters of Formal Notice have been issued so far for failure to give due notice of the transposition measures, most of which were sent shortly after the end of the transposition deadline, in July or August 1998 (Germany, Greece, Ireland and Portugal) or at the end of the year (Luxembourg and Italy). The later commencement of the infringement procedure against the UK in July 2000 is attributable to the delayed transposition deadline (15 December 1999) as a result of the non-participation of the Major government in the Maastricht Social Agreement (as seen in Chapter 8). Most member states responded to the Commission enforcement policy with the notification of national transposition measures. However Italy, Luxembourg and Portugal did not react with notification, so stage two followed in 1998. It was then that the latter two provided notification and only in the Italian case, where the controversial transposition debate raged for two more years, was compliance not assured until 2000. Here the EU Commission transferred the procedure to the ECJ in 1999.

In three cases, the notified measures were allegedly incorrect since the parental leave entitlements were restricted to parents whose children were born after either the Directive or the implementation legislation came into force (Ireland, the UK and Luxembourg respectively). These countries were admonished by a Letter of Formal Notice and a Reasoned Opinion to bring their regulations in line with the standards of the EU Directive on parental leave. The warnings finally made the UK and Ireland comply and remove their cut-off dates (see Chapter 8 for more details), while the Luxembourg case reached the ECJ in July 2003. The Commission's actions against the UK and Ireland had been prompted by 'whistle blowing' from domestic trade unions.

At the time of writing, the EU Commission has not initiated a single infringement procedure with regard to the Part-time Directive.

---

[20] See Judgment of the Court of 21 October 1999, case C-430/98, *Commission of the European Communities* v. *Grand Duchy of Luxembourg* [1999] ECR I-7391; Judgment of the Court of 18 May 2000, case C-45/99, *Commission of the European Communities* v. *French Republic* [2000] ECR I-03615.

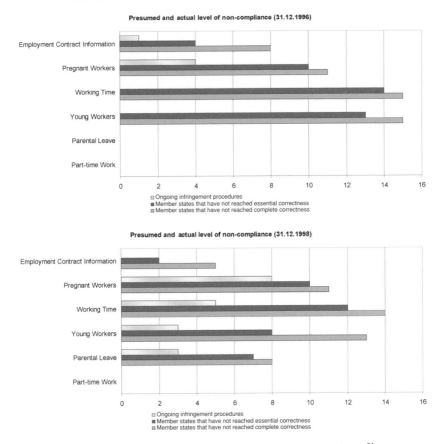

Figure 11.2 Presumed and actual levels of non-compliance[21]

Considering that there are still five member states in which certain details of the Directive are not yet completely satisfied, that one country breaches an important aspect of the Directive and that, moreover, adaptation has been considerably late in many member states, this is quite remarkable. There are no signs that this situation will change in the near future. Although the Commission's implementation report (CEC 2003) notes

---

[21] The intention of this figure is to disprove systematically the usefulness of a perspective that takes ongoing infringement proceedings as the only indicator of actual compliance with EU rules. Note that the information given in this figure represents snapshots of the situation at four different points in time. Therefore it is possible that some procedures mentioned in Table 11.1 above do not show up at all because they have been initiated and terminated between two snapshots. For example, this is true of the procedure against the UK's incorrect transposition of the Parental Leave Directive.

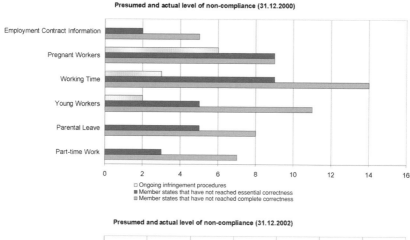

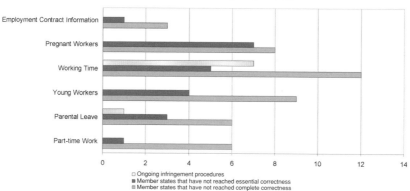

Figure 11.2 Continued

most of the national breaches of the Directive, there is no indication of imminent Commission intervention against these shortcomings.

11.2.2 Fit between transposition performance and the Commission's enforcement policy

It will have already become clear from the previous section that there are many cases where late or incorrect transposition of EU standards does not trigger an infringement procedure. Figure 11.2 demonstrates the discrepancies between the presumptive level of non-compliance, based on the ongoing infringement procedures initiated by the EU Commission, on the one hand, and the actual level of compliance at four different points in time, on the other.

Table 11.2 *Mismatch between compliance of a member state and infringement procedure initiated by the EU Commission*[22]

	Employment contract information (30/06/93)	Pregnant workers (19/10/94)	Working time (23/11/96)	Young workers (22/06/96)	Parental leave (03/06/98, 15/12/99)	Part-time work (20/01/00, 07/04/00)	Total inconsistencies per member state
A	–	inconsistent enforcement	inconsistent enforcement	inconsistent enforcement	–	–	3
B	inconsistent enforcement	consistent enforcement	inconsistent enforcement	no enforcement	–	no enforcement	4
D	inconsistent enforcement	inconsistent enforcement	inconsistent enforcement	–	inconsistent enforcement	–	4
DK	–	–	inconsistent enforcement	–	no enforcement	–	2
E	no enforcement	inconsistent enforcement	–	–	no enforcement	no enforcement	4
F	inconsistent enforcement	inconsistent enforcement	inconsistent enforcement	inconsistent enforcement	–	–	4
FIN	–	inconsistent enforcement	–	no enforcement	–	no enforcement	3
GB	consistent enforcement	–	inconsistent enforcement	inconsistent enforcement	consistent enforcement	–	2

Table 11.2 (*Cont.*)

GR	consistent enforcement	inconsistent enforcement	inconsistent enforcement	consistent enforcement	inconsistent enforcement	–	3
I	inconsistent enforcement	inconsistent enforcement	consistent enforcement	consistent enforcement	consistent enforcement	–	2
IRL	consistent enforcement	inconsistent enforcement	inconsistent enforcement	no enforcement	inconsistent enforcement	–	4
LUX	inconsistent enforcement	inconsistent enforcement	inconsistent enforcement	inconsistent enforcement	inconsistent enforcement	–	5
NL	consistent enforcement	–	–	no enforcement	–	–	1
P	consistent enforcement	inconsistent enforcement	inconsistent enforcement	inconsistent enforcement	consistent enforcement	no enforcement	4
S	–	inconsistent enforcement	inconsistent enforcement	consistent enforcement	–	no enforcement	3
Total inconsistencies	6	11	11	9	6	5	48

22 The data in this table stem from the Commission's annual reports on monitoring compliance with EU law: COM (1994) 500, COM (1995) 500, COM (1996) 600, COM (1997) 299, COM (1998) 317, COM (1999) 301, COM (2000) 92, COM (2001) 309, COM (2002) 324.

This clearly shows that looking at the infringement procedures initiated by the Commission at a certain point in time – a methodological approach taken by much of the existing literature – does not say much about the actual level of (partial or complete) non-compliance in a member state. While no constant bias can be observed, the 'degree of mismatch' varies considerably between different points in time and between Directives. To return to the image of the iceberg, it is striking with respect to the Directives studied here how great the submerged part is, and how its shape differs from the tip (while the latter also changes dramatically over time without the submerged part changing correspondingly). Thus a different approach is needed to measure the phenomenon under scrutiny and to explain its occurrence and effects.

In what follows, inconsistencies with the duties to enforce EU law have been quantified systematically (see Table 11.2). By operationalising the consistency of enforcement policy according to the Commission's own rules and then comparing it with the enforcement policy actually conducted, light is shed on the motivation for Commission action. Underlying questions, such as whether and why some member states have been spared or whether a pattern or a clear policy for enforcement exists, can be addressed more thoroughly than before. In order to avoid hypercritical benchmarks, the following analysis disregards smaller violations of EU law. Instead, only those cases where the stage of essentially correct transposition has not been reached are considered to be the cases in which Commission action would be required. In terms of timing, we use the Commission's own criteria. Hence, infringement procedures are considered inconsistent when a case of (significantly) incorrect transposition has not been answered by the Commission with a 'Letter of Formal Notice' within one year after the transposition deadline or when, after that, more than a year elapses before the subsequent stage is initiated (see Secrétariat Général 1993a, 1998: 4; and, even more ambitious, 1996: 3–4).

In contrast to existing studies, the matching of all official Article 226 and Article 228 procedures with the actual level of compliance has allowed the inclusion of cases in the analysis where (significant) non-compliance has taken place but which have not been subject to an infringement procedure by the Commission (twelve cases of 'no enforcement'). Together with those procedures that did not follow the above-mentioned stages within the appropriate time scale (thirty-six cases of 'inconsistent enforcement') they account for the total of forty-eight inconsistent cases. On the other hand, the twenty-nine cases where the member state transposed the respective Directive (essentially) on time and correctly are also included in the analysis (denoted by dashes), as well as those cases where the enforcement policy of the EU

Commission followed its own rules (thirteen cases of 'consistent enforcement'). Hence, enforcement often does not take place at all (20 per cent of all sixty-one cases in which enforcement would have been required) or only takes place in an inconsistent manner compared with the Commission's internal rules (59 per cent of all cases in which enforcement would have been required). In all those inconsistent cases, one could say that *the Commission itself is a non-complier.*

Hence, even though non-compliance is most likely to occur, at least for some time, it is not systematically addressed by means of infringement procedures. When and how the enforcement policy of the EU Commission comes into play is *not automatic*, but depends on institutional constraints and political decisions. These factors also explain why infringement procedures are not carried through step by step until compliance is assured, but are often terminated after the state has complied with the requirements in parts or at the surface only. To advance our knowledge beyond the statement that enforcement by the European Commission often does not take place (or does not take place within an appropriate period of time), we systematically looked at the enforcement policy of the EU vis-à-vis its member states and asked (a) what role administrative resources play; (b) whether there are differences in enforcement between Directives (c) or member states; (d) to what extent the enforcement policy takes the degree of misfit (e) or the general level of social protection into account; and finally (f) if outright opposition during negotiations is answered with more thorough enforcement.

(a) It is often assumed that *limited administrative resources* on the part of the Commission are at the heart of insufficient enforcement (e.g. Nugent 2001: 165). However, detailed Commission implementation reports (e.g. CEC 2001b) reveal that the knowledge about what is going on in the member states is greater than one might think when reading through the literature.[23] In these reports, many cases of non-compliance are critically described but nevertheless not addressed by an infringement procedure. Thus it seems useful to distinguish between resources employed to acquire knowledge and resources used to execute enforcement steps. Even though the EU Commission may be aware of non-compliance in a member state, the limited resources do not allow it to follow up all suspected cases and respond to all the non-compliance with Directives within a reasonable time span.

More precisely, and in addition to the above-mentioned need for linguistic and legal expertise, the *principle of equal treatment* of member states often hinders the timely execution of enforcement policies. This is so

---

[23] This is not to say that, in our view, the EU Commission knows everything.

because the Commission is very reluctant to accuse a member state of non-compliance until there is a clear picture of the situation in the other member states, which means that infringement procedures often have to wait until the last consignment of notified national transposition measures (which in labour law are often especially voluminous from countries with federal administrations, e.g. Austria and Germany) has been translated and analysed (Interview COM1). If limited resources to execute the enforcement policy do not allow the Commission to follow up all cases of non-compliance systematically, it is all the more interesting to see which Directives or member states are chosen.

The most striking result is the *heavy bias towards infringement proceedings due to non-notification* (see above, Table 11.1). Exactly two-thirds of the infringement procedures studied here dealt with non-notification. When comparing the Commission's reaction to non-notification and to incorrect transposition, we see that infringement procedures were initiated in 95 per cent of the cases (forty of forty-two) where member states had not notified the Commission of their transposition measures in time or within one year after the expiry of the deadline, while (significantly) incorrect transposition was only responded to by an infringement procedure in 51 per cent of the cases (twenty-two of forty-three). Moreover, infringement procedures for non-notification were in almost all cases initiated in time and were executed rather rigorously (thirty-one of forty, thus 78 per cent), while only one out of twenty-two infringement procedures for incorrect transposition followed the Commission's own rules.

This fits nicely with the argument that resources determine the Commission's enforcement policy. While the question of whether a member state has fulfilled its notification duties can easily be answered with a simple yes or no, establishing whether or not the notified measures are correct requires more resources and expertise, and is thus a much more laborious task for the responsible unit within the Commission.

In our sample this bias in social policy enforcement towards the monitoring of non-notification gave rise to a strategy of '*notification compliance*' in some member states. Knowing that the content of the national measures notified often escapes immediate scrutiny, some member states complied on a superficial level by giving notice of reform projects that were never adopted (e.g. Directive on Employment Contract Information in Belgium), laws that obviously did not correspond to the scope of the Directive (e.g. Working Time Directive in Belgium), or a hotchpotch of old legislation to keep the EU Commission busy while gaining more time for controversial national transposition processes (e.g. Young Workers Protection Directive in Portugal).

This also reveals that what might have looked like an improvement in transposition of EU policy over time,[24] when simply the number of notified national measures are taken into account, represents in some cases at least no more than what has been called 'tick the boxes implementation' where member states 'complete the appropriate monitoring forms in the manner "expected" by the supervising body, safe that it [i.e. the EU Commission] lacks the resources to check systematically whether what is on the completed form bears any relationship to reality' (Richardson 1996: 282).

(b) *Some Directives are more thoroughly enforced than others.* This was the case for the Pregnant Workers and Working Time Directives, while non-compliance with presumably less salient issues such as the Employment Contract Information Directive remained unresolved for years (Interviews E4: 1924–8; P1: 303–4).[25] In the case of the Pregnant Workers Directive, the increased interest in a pronounced enforcement policy may have been fostered by several factors. A central point is the renegotiation of the Pregnant Workers Directive (envisaged for 1997, but still pending at the time of writing), where prior evaluation of the effect of implementation is of utmost importance. Moreover, as described in Chapter 5, the responsibility for this Directive within the Directorate General has passed to the Equal Treatment Department. Supranational actors have proven in the past to be especially skilful in making the most of the latitude they enjoy with regard to equal treatment policy (e.g. Warner 1984; Mazey 1998) and seem to be keener to enforce such a Directive.

With regard to the number of infringement proceedings initiated from a perspective of policy interests, the Working Time Directive also seems to be high on the agenda of the EU Commission. This corresponds nicely to the tough negotiations and the remarkable effect of the EU standards in all member states. But even though enforcement policy has been far-reaching for the Working Time Directive, the infringement proceedings were rather late. This is certainly due to the complex nature of the Directive, the rather late initiation of a process of revising the Directive (ten years after its adoption) and the fact that compliance or non-compliance with relevant standards of the Directive was only clarified by important ECJ rulings years after the end of the transposition deadline.

The argument that policy interest on the part of the EU Commission is conducive to successful enforcement does not mean that the opposite is

---

[24] As argued by several authors, e.g. Tallberg (2002: 624) and Sverdrup (2003: 12).

[25] Thus, the Commission ignored no fewer than twelve cases of severe non-compliance with the other four Directives. In all of these cases, the Commision did not take any enforcement actions even though member states had not yet reached the state of essentially correct transposition.

also true, i.e. that limited enforcement equals limited interest. With regard to the Part-time Directive, a Commission official admitted that the systematic lack of enforcement was simply due to administrative difficulties. These difficulties had arisen due to the unequal use of the extension possibility for member states regarding the transposition period (see Chapter 9), which had prevented infringement procedures from being triggered quasi automatically (Interview COM1b). To sum up on this point, Commission enforcement does not systematically follow identical rules but, within the limited range of opportunities, Directives of particular interest are chosen for closer inspection.

(c) What about the observation that *some member states are more often the subject of infringement procedures than others?* As described in the introduction to this chapter, the number of infringements across all policy sectors varies between member states. Within social policy, in 1997, the then Commissioner Padraig Flynn announced that Luxembourg, France, Greece and Italy were 'lagging behind' in implementing social policy (CEC 1997a). On the basis of such a statement it seems at least realistic that supervising actors within the Commission would have responded to the bad implementation performances with a tougher stance on enforcement.

At first sight, the especially stringent Commission actions against Italy (Working Time, Young Workers and Parental Leave) and Greece (Employment Contract Information and Young Workers) in our sample fit neatly into the hypothesis of a tougher strategy vis-à-vis these latecomers. But when looking at the transposition processes in these member states in more detail, it transpires that this was usually simply a reaction to less compliant behaviour.[26] At the same time, our sample shows a number of cases in these member states where bad implementation was only addressed inconsistently with infringement procedures by the EU Commission (for instance the Directives on Employment Contract Information and Pregnant Workers in Italy or the Pregnant Workers and Working Time Directives in Greece). Hence our cases suggest that most of the time differences in the treatment of member states cannot be attributed to a systematic favouring of 'the good guys' over 'the bad guys'.

Generally speaking, differences in enforcement persist to the extent that the EU Commission is free to choose the instrument judged to be the most adequate to tackle the specific case of non-compliance. Thus, in a case of outright opposition, a stringent infringement procedure might

---

[26] This does not mean that infringement proceedings are a good indicator for the actual level of non-compliance in the member states since there are many violations that are not met with enforcement action by the Commission.

be the adequate instrument, while misinterpretation or administrative difficulties are better addressed in co-operative meetings (Interview COM2, see also COM [2002] 725). Such strategic choices can look like the favouring of some countries over others when taking Commission infringements as the only measure of EU enforcement policy. This again makes clear that infringement procedures depend heavily on the inter-action of the supranational and the national level and as such cannot be interpreted correctly by simply neglecting one level.

(d) Assuming that the EU Commission is interested in implementing as much of the policy content of EU Directives as possible, and taking the argument of limited resources into account, it would be reasonable to expect *infringement procedures in those cases where misfit with pre-existing national policies is high*.

The empirical data does not endorse this hypothesis for the cases stud-ied here. In 75 per cent (six out of eight) of the cases with large-scale policy misfit and (significant) non-compliance by member states, infringement procedures were initiated. 83 per cent (twenty of twenty-four) of the cases of (significantly) late or incorrect transposition of medium misfit were the subject of infringement procedures, and finally, 79 per cent (twenty-three of twenty-nine) of the cases of low degrees of misfit and (significant) domestic non-compliance have been addressed by an infringement pro-cedure.[27] Thus the results show no clear causal pattern. The characteris-tics and constraints of an infringement procedure described above clearly indicate that enforcement policy is complex and that there are many other factors that seem to be much more important (such as the internal organ-isation of the Commission or the policy interests in certain Directives).

(e) A further plausible assumption is that *enforcement policy tends to focus on those countries where the general level of labour law protection is low* in order to work towards a 'level playing field'. However, those countries that are most commonly assumed to have an overall lower level of labour law pro-tection (Southern Europe, Ireland, and the UK) do not reveal a clear pattern of EU enforcement policy directed towards them. Even though on average they are more often subject to Article 226 procedures than the other member states (5 per member state compared to the average of only 3.78 for the rest of the member states) and even though the EU Commission responds to non-compliance in a slightly higher percent-age of these cases with an (albeit most often inconsistent) infringement

---

[27] Those cases where the member state was already essentially or fully in compliance at the time of adoption of the Directive (four) or where the Directive was transposed essentially timely and correctly (twenty-five) are not included in these calculations because accord-ing to our above-mentioned operationalisation, there was no need for an infringement procedure.

procedure,[28] these are no signs of these member states receiving a similar treatment. On the contrary, there are large differences within the group. In our sample, there was only one infringement procedure against Spain, while Greece, Italy, Ireland and Portugal were subject to supranational enforcement with regard to all but one of the Directives studied here, with the UK being located between these two extremes (four procedures). At the same time, the remaining countries were quite often confronted with infringement procedures, e.g. Germany and France four times, and Luxembourg five times. Thus an enforcement policy that would focus mainly on the member states with assumed lower levels of labour law protection was not found in the empirical data.

Moreover we have come to the conclusion that, for several reasons, the general level of labour law protection cannot easily be assessed. Especially in the highly regulated southern European labour markets, the assessment of the level of protection very much depends on the benchmark used.[29] This observation has two implications. First, the above-mentioned group of assumedly 'low level countries' is more heterogeneous than generally thought and has to be constituted differently for different Directives. Second, and with regard to the assumption that the general level of labour law protection could indicate whether the Commission is more likely to initiate an Article 226 procedure, it has become clear that the Commission itself has to decide in each area if national regulations and practices can balance punctual deficits with a view to specific standards.

(f) Finally, we checked whether *outright opposition during the negotiations alerts EU Commission officials and thus leads to an especially attentive enforcement policy*. This working hypothesis has proven to be of some empirical relevance for our sample even though, again, it is as a trend rather than a causal effect. Our empirical studies have revealed three clear-cut cases where national governments openly rejected a draft Directive either wholly or in part during the EU-level negotiations and subsequently refused to transpose the unwanted measure at the domestic level.[30] In only one of these three cases did the Commission remain inactive in the matter of ensuring domestic compliance (Working Time Directive in Germany). However it has not been possible as yet to substantiate these observations with respect to a larger number of cases.

---

[28] Measured as the number of cases with incorrect or late transposition that were met by an infringement procedure for Spain, the UK, Greece, Italy, Ireland and Portugal on the one hand (83 per cent) and for the rest of the member states on the other (78 per cent).

[29] For example, these difficulties relate to the question of how extremely protective legislation for some groups (Pregnant Workers, Young Workers) is to be weighted in the broader picture. An associated aspect is the question of how to balance the need for protection for some groups of workers with the challenge of providing equal opportunities for all to participate in the labour market.

[30] For more details, see Chapter 14.

To sum up, the level of domestic non-compliance is significantly higher than that suggested by an exclusive focus on the official infringement proceedings. The Commission is well aware of this fact, but limited resources prevent it from adopting a more systematic approach to enforcement. Under these circumstances, the actual interventions are determined by the political preferences of the responsible actors within the Commission hierarchy. Nonetheless, the significant differences between member states are not the result of political favouritism but of the necessity to prioritise some cases over others. Our sample shows that these prioritisations often follow Directives. It seems that the choice is made largely by the responsible unit and depends on its workload, the complexity of the Directive, and the overall importance attached to the policy. Opposition during the negotiations also seems to influence positively the likelihood of an infringement procedure being initiated – however this trend is less clear than the prioritisation of Directives. Even if it were sensible to concentrate forces on instances of particularly severe non-compliance (and this is an explicit goal of recent changes in EU enforcement policy, see COM [2002] 725), the sample has shown that too often infringement procedures relate to non-notification instead of taking the correctness of the reported transposition measures into account. Finally, our analysis reveals that enforcement policy at the supranational level allows for the fact that different problems have to be treated differently, and that enforcement can only be properly understood as the interaction of two levels of governance.

11.2.3   Effect of infringement procedures on the implementation process

The remainder of this chapter tries to shed light, at least in an exploratory manner, on the specific effect of supranational enforcement activities on the implementation process in the member states. We differentiate between four effects. An infringement procedure may *kick-start* the domestic adaptation process, it may *accelerate* ongoing processes or lead to a *correction* of implementation mistakes, or it may have *no direct effect* at all. The frequency of occurrence was determined for a subgroup of five countries[31] and gives a first indication of the relevance of these four potential consequences of attempted enforcement.

One possible effect of a letter from Brussels is to *kick-start* the national transposition process. This is the case when the implementation process at the national level is characterised by persistent inertia (see Chapter 2 on this concept). Most of the time this accompanies a rather inefficient administrative structure that lacks any safeguard mechanism to assure

---

[31] Belgium, France, Greece, Portugal and Spain (for more details see Hartlapp 2005).

that transposition ensues quasi automatically when time runs out, e.g. administrative 'watchdog units'.[32] Since this kick-start effect is closely linked to specific national transposition problems, it comes as no surprise that this has turned out to be the dominant effect in some member states (Greece and France), while it has never appeared to be of any importance in others (e.g. Sweden or Finland). The significance of these country patterns is discussed in more detail in Chapter 15. In the cases that belong to the former group, transposition of the EU standards would not have occurred until today, most likely, had it not been for supranational activism. In the subgroup studied in more detail, the effect occurred six times in total, but all cases arose in either France or Greeece. It thus seems to be a very important explanatory factor in some cases, while it does not come into play in others.

Acceleration is the label most suited to describing the positive bearing of infringement procedures on the timeliness of political processes already under way at the national level. Here, two effects are conceivable: one is that, with mounting pressure from the EU, national opposition can be partly or totally neutralised. This means that controversies or blockages due to resistance against the EU standards in question or the envisaged way of incorporating them into national law are now counterbalanced by external pressure to reach a compromise. Supranational enforcement therefore brings about a change on the level of importance attached to concurring arguments. The other effect is that supranational enforcement policy is used by the government to induce the choice of a slimmer form of transposition to circumvent potential veto points. The result of supranational intervention is thus a change in the transposition instrument. This is clearly visible in the case of the Young Workers Directive in France, where the *Assemblée Nationale* gave its permission to use a decree (*ordonnance*) as the transposition instrument at a point in time when the transposition deadline had expired by almost five years and financial sanctions from the EU were becoming increasingly likely. For our subgroup sample, acceleration was observed in seven cases. In these cases the former type of acceleration (neutralisation of opposition) occurred less often than the latter (choice of instrument).

Infringement proceedings can also have a bearing on the implementation process in the form of *correcting* member state implementation. Again, two different groups have to be distinguished analytically. In one group, the letter from Brussels is the response to an obviously incorrect transposition. Hence, it does not change the perception of what has to be

---

[32] Such as the government commissioner appointed in Belgium in 1999 to assure better time management for transposition processes.

regarded as a correct or incorrect transposition measure. It is the infringe-ment procedure as an instrument that forces the member state to modify its measures. A perfect example of this is the very late adjustment of the French legislation in order to ensure finally that pregnant women who are unable or not allowed to perform their work due to their condition are provided with specific leave on health and safety grounds. In this case, the wording of the EU standard was clear enough from the outset and did not allow for differing interpretations. In the other group of cases, the letter from the EU Commission changes or clarifies the perception of the member state as to the correctness of a national transposition measure. Thus it is the content of the infringement procedure that decides on the correctness of national behaviour.[33] When compared with the other three categories of effects discussed, this is presumably the smallest group (four instances in the present sample) since the EU Commission tends to be reluctant to make real interpretative choices due to its limited competen-cies in the field.[34] Here, the bearing of supranational enforcement policy is on the content level.

In a remarkably large number of cases (50 per cent in our sample of five member states) there appears to be *no direct effect* attributable to the infringement procedures. Yet again, two forms have to be distinguished analytically. The first comprises infringement procedures that overlap with the end of the transposition process at the national level, where the letter was sent from the EU at a point in time when a reform law was about to be or had already been adopted, but notification of it had not yet been given. In these cases the action of the supranational level has no bearing and the implementation procedure would have had the same outcome without the letter being sent. The other group is made up of cases where national matters were held to be of greater importance than a reaction to the infringement procedure. To put it differently, in these cases the course of events remained dominated by the influence of national administrative and political procedures, actors, and preferences. Hence, here again, the process would not have looked any different with-out the infringement.

Finally, we come to the conclusion that, in overall terms, infringement proceedings as they are practised today are a rather inadequate instrument for assuring compliance, even though the situation would be worse if there were none at all. Thus, regardless of the concrete effect in a specific

---

[33] The cases of Parental Leave in the UK and Ireland, although outside the subsample discussed here, are good examples of this (see Ch. 8).

[34] The most important decisions of this type have been taken by the ECJ via the preliminary ruling procedure (see *SIMAP* and *BECTU* rulings in Ch. 6) and are thus not the type of effects discussed here.

case, the simple presence of EU enforcement policy increases the level of compliance with EU rules in the member states. To put it differently, implementation at the national level always takes place in the shadow of the infringement procedure; without it, compliance shortcomings would undoubtedly be even greater.

12 Beyond policy change: convergence of national public–private relations?

This chapter extends the study of Europeanisation from the sphere of policy content to policy-making patterns, specifically to public–private relations. Since the beginning of the 1990s, remarkable developments have taken place in EU social policy at this *procedural* level. Since this specific style of public–private co-operation is restricted to one policy area only, we prefer not to speak about 'Euro-corporatism' (Gorges 1996), but rather about a 'corporatist policy community' (Falkner 1998).

The EC Treaty's social provisions (see Articles 136–48) now[1] contain three layers of social partner participation in the policy process. First, a member state may entrust management and labour, at their joint request, with the implementation of social policy Directives. Secondly, the European Commission now has a legal obligation to consult both sides of industry before submitting social policy proposals. And thirdly, but most importantly, management and labour may, on the occasion of such consultation, inform the Commission of their wish to conclude social partner agreements instead of proceeding with traditional EU legislation. Such agreements may, at the joint request of the signatory parties, be implemented by a Council decision based on a proposal from the European Commission. Thus, since the 1990s, the social partners have been formal co-actors in EU policy-making.[2]

The member states of the European union are characterised by deeply rooted systems of public–private interaction that exemplify their respective processes of public policy-making. These systems are extremely diverse, ranging from countries usually labelled pluralist (like the UK)[3] to others (like Austria or the Scandinavian countries) normally ranked with high degrees of corporatism (see, for example, the comparative overview

---

[1] The Amsterdam Treaty introduced into the EC Treaty (which is binding for all) what had been, after the Maastricht Social Agreement, the rule among the member states with the exception of the UK (for details, see Falkner 1998), but it did not otherwise change the rules of this game.

[2] For the fate of various Euro-collective negotiations, see Falkner (2003a).

[3] Not so according to Schmidt (1999: 1), where the UK is used as a case of statism.

of Siaroff 1999). It is therefore useful to enquire whether stronger social partnership at EU level (as outlined above) will bring about similar developments domestically: *Are the national systems of public–private interaction affected by EU social policy? If so, how?*

The focus of this chapter is on changes in national public–private interaction patterns related to the negotiation and transposition of EU social policy Directives. The rationale is that one should expect any changes to occur primarily in the 'Europeanised' part of the national political systems, i.e. those connected to European policies and their trickling down within the multi-level system. In the following sections, we shall begin by explaining why it is reasonable to expect a certain degree of Europeanisation of national public–private relations. We will then outline a typology of public–private interaction patterns in public policy-making as a yardstick for detecting major changes, and then summarise the results of our fifteen country studies. In conclusion, we will discuss whether there is a convergence of public–private interaction patterns as a result of Europeanisation.

12.1   Operationalising Europeanisation effects on national public–private relations

Compared with EU-related policy implementation, top-down Europeanisation of policy-making patterns is so far a much less researched field.[4] Theoretical knowledge is still in its infancy. Some authors have extended the concept of misfit between the EU and the national level (as explained in Chapter 2) from policy change to the realm of politics or polity (Börzel and Risse 2000; Risse et al. 2001; Börzel 2005; with reference to interest groups: Cowles 2001). Here, an ideal-typical EU pattern (e.g. pluralism) is compared with the respective type at the national level (e.g. corporatism). The underlying assumption is that, when types differ, national adaptation is to be expected. If they match, the existing national patterns remain unchanged or are potentially reinforced. For several reasons we have chosen a different path. As will be further outlined below, establishing *the* ideal-typical public–private interaction pattern is not an easy task, either for the EU or for the national level as a whole.

---

[4] But see the growing number of books and articles examining, for example, EU-induced administrative change (Wessels and Rometsch 1996; Héritier 2001a; Knill and Lenschow 2001), the Europeanisation of regional structures (Börzel 2002b; Morlino 2002) and of national parliaments (Maurer and Wessels 2001; Scholl and Hansen 2002), national public–private relations (V. Schmidt 1996; Coen 1998; Lehmkuhl 1999, 2000; Cowles 2001; Wilts 2001; Beyers 2002; Knill and Lehmkuhl 2002), legal structures (Conant 2001), national identities (Risse 2001) or public discourses (Schmidt 2000b, 2002).

In addition, recent 'misfit-centred' literature reveals ambiguities in the potential effects of low and high degrees of misfit. In some studies, a high degree of misfit is conceptualised as both an obstacle[5] (inducing national opposition) and a driving force[6] (causing adaptational pressure) for Europeanisation. To consider misfit as the 'necessary condition' (Börzel and Risse 2000: 5) for all kinds of Europeanisation processes thus does not allow far-reaching conclusions to be drawn as to the actual effects of Europeanisation, which strongly depend on national 'mediating factors' (Risse et al. 2001: 9) and, as we assume, on the underlying transmission mechanism also. Irrespective of the degree of misfit, adaptational pressure via 'hard' binding EU law (e.g. via Directives, which have to be transposed and can even be enforced by ECJ sanctions) is likely to differ from 'soft' incentives such as a European best practice model of interest intermediation or state organisation. In the field of EU social policy, these soft incentives play a particularly important role.

As no existing theory provides any definite hypotheses with regard to such Europeanisation effects, we proceed in an exploratory way, looking at very concrete Europeanisation incentives that stem from EU social policy and their actual effects on national public–private relations. In this chapter we examine three different ways – with potentially contradictory effects – in which EU social policy might exert top-down influence on the public–private interaction in policy-making at the national level.

(1) On the one hand, *the upward shift of competences may impinge on the scope of public–private interaction*. The EU has taken on board a number of competences so that certain issue areas are withdrawn from the national political arena. Actors, in particular the social partners (where they play a major role), may experience this as a loss of influence vis-à-vis the government. The fact that the EU is increasing its legislative powers can potentially limit the scope of corporatist deals at the domestic level. The latter may certainly be replaced by EU-level corporatist deals (as has been the case in social policy recently). In this case, national actors again play a role as members in Euro-federations of interest groups, but that is a different story which does not directly counterbalance the loss of influence at the national level. Moravcsik (1994) argues that the role of national executives in the EU provides the latter with important additional resources

---

[5] See, for example, Cowles (2001: 162): 'if the domestic relationship does not resemble that found at the European level, one might expect problems in adaptation'.

[6] In a study on the effects of the Transatlantic Business Dialogue (TABD) on domestic business–government relations, Maria Green-Cowles argues: 'One would expect both the German and French industry associations [which do not resemble the EU pattern – authors' remark], therefore, to undergo considerable adaptational pressures as a result of the Europeanisation of business–government relations in the TABD' (Cowles 2001: 168).

(such as domestic agenda control or privileged access to information), enabling them to change the national balance of power to their advantage. Is this also the case for the relationship between governments and the social partners in the social policy field?

(2) On the other hand, much 'softer' EU incentives may lead to a strengthening of the social partners in the member states. *Article 137, para. 4 ECT invites member states to have their social partners implement EU Directives.* The member states are explicitly allowed to 'entrust management and labour, at their joint request, with the implementation of Directives' adopted under that heading.[7] This provision was initiated by the Danish Commissioner Henning Christoffersen (Hartenberger 2001: 146), who wanted to protect the Nordic model of policy-making in the area of labour law, which is based on extensive social partner autonomy.[8] Was this opportunity embraced by member states, in particular those where the social partners traditionally do not play a major role?

(3) In addition, we will analyse *whether the EU social partner Directives (which have been adopted via the negotiation procedure explained at the start of this chapter) have any particular effect on the national social partner relations.* The 'corporatist policy community' in EU social affairs (Falkner 1998) may, for example, be perceived as a best practice model for national systems. There might be process diffusion in the sense that national actors apply a logic of appropriateness and follow the much-quoted EU model. The role of 'framing' and of the 'diffusion' of policy paradigms and ideas has recently engaged much attention in European integration studies (Kohler-Koch and Edler 1998; Kohler-Koch 2000b; see also Knill and Lehmkuhl 1999; Radaelli 2000). The case of social partnership (or corporatism, which we consider to be synonymous here) reveals a national paradigm with a long-standing tradition in many EU countries, but which has now gained some currency at the supranational level and might therefore feed back again into the member states (be it into those that have already been practising social partnership or into others).[9] Table 12.1 summarises the potential Europeanisation effects on

---

[7] Governments have, at the same time, to ensure that management and labour introduce the necessary measures by agreement no later than the date by which a Directive must be transposed. Otherwise, the member states are obliged to take any action necessary to guarantee the results required by that Directive (Art. 137, para. 4 ECT).

[8] We shall point out below that, as a result of earlier European case law, which restricts this Treaty Article in a particular way, the desired effect was not achieved in the Danish case.

[9] We avoid introducing the notion of 'learning effects' here for there is no clear indication that corporatist co-operation in policy-making will invariably result in better solutions. Therefore, learning in the sense of cause-and-effect relationships cannot be expected to lead each time to more national public–private co-operation. National actors may also

Table 12.1 *Potential Europeanisation effects on national public–private interaction*

Direction of EU-generated stimuli		Source	Transmission mechanism
Restriction	Narrowing of scope for national public–private interaction	EU competences	*Hard*: binding law
Encouragement	*Explicit*: for corporatism in implementation of EU law	In EC Treaty	*Soft*: up to the member states if they take up or not
	Implicit	In recent EU practice: corporatist policy community might spread	*Very soft*: best practice diffusion

national public–private relations stemming from EU social policy since Maastricht.

To measure potential effects, we need a categorisation of social partner involvement in public policy-making.[10] Unfortunately, the academic literature on 'corporatism versus pluralism and statism' is far from uniform in its approach to categorising individual countries. In fact, there is *no single authoritative classification of the EU member states* with regard to their patterns of interest politics, and comparative studies do not always draw the same conclusions.[11] Recent papers by EU scholars, for example, have regarded France, Italy and Spain as statist polities, while Austria, Germany and the Netherlands are usually considered corporatist, notwithstanding partly differing definitions (Streeck and Schmitter 1994:

'learn' that exiting from corporatist patterns can at times lead to greater policy innovation or even to improved solutions (although the opposite may certainly be true as well; it all depends on the specific national conditions).

[10] We thus conceive the social partners as a particular type of interest group on both sides of the labour market. As far as the national level is concerned, we make use of the term 'social partners' in the way it is also used by the European Commission: it simply refers to the peak level organisations on both sides of industry in each member state (regardless of whether there is a weaker or stronger tradition of institutionalised partnership and co-operation between management, labour and the state).

[11] For various rankings of countries in terms of 'corporatism', see, for example, Schmitter (1981), Lehmbruch (1985) and, more recently, Crepaz and Lijphart (1995), as well as the country studies in Schmitter and Lehmbruch (1979), Lehmbruch and Schmitter (1982) and Kleinfeld and Luthardt (1993), all containing further references.

215; Lenschow 1999: 16; Schmidt 1999). The classification of the UK is contested: Cowles (2001: 165) speaks of pluralist government–business relations, while Schmidt (1999: 1) takes the UK as a statist example.

Confronted with this somewhat disparate state of affairs,[12] *we chose to develop our own typology.* This is even more important given the fact that we are focusing on one particular policy area, whereas the national patterns may differ from the archetypal national patterns assumed in the classic corporatism versus pluralism debate (which has not paid proper attention to meso-level variance). In an earlier publication, Falkner suggested placing more emphasis on the differences between policy areas when analysing public–private interactions (Falkner 2000c). We therefore built on, and extended, Falkner's original typology, which aimed at reconciling the two political science debates surrounding, first, corporatism versus pluralism and, second, policy networks. It incorporated a corporatist ideal type as well as a statist one into the well-known issue network/policy community dichotomy advanced by the British policy networks school.[13] Since our ongoing study focuses on a selected number of individual decision-making processes rather than following the development of a particular policy network over time, our typology can be even narrower. Only the dimension of interest group involvement will be taken into consideration (i.e. the process, not the structural dimension of corporatism). At the same time, further categories are introduced to account more specifically for the 'Nordic model' of autonomous social partner regulation that lacks any state involvement, and for the new EU-level model of 'complementary legislation', which mirrors the Belgian system of adopting binding legislation that turns the agreements concluded by the representatives of management and labour into binding law.[14]

Table 12.2 shows the categories of social partner involvement in policy formulation and implementation applied in this study.[15] While the role

---

[12] For a detailed analysis, see Falkner (2000c).

[13] On the basis of earlier work by authors such as Jordan and Richardson (1983), David Marsh and R. A. W. Rhodes elaborated the dominant typology (Marsh and Rhodes 1992; Rhodes and Marsh 1992) that distinguishes closed and stable policy communities from loose and open issue networks as the two polar ends of a multi-dimensional continuum (the term 'policy network' is thus a generic one, encompassing all types).

[14] During the negotiations for the Maastricht Social Agreement it was largely due to the initiative of the Belgian government that the system of complementary legislation was chosen as a template for the involvement of the EU-level social partners in the making of EU social policy. Belgium thus managed to 'export' its own model to the EU level. For details on the negotiation process, see Falkner (1998: 89–96).

[15] The same categories are also applied in order to be able to assess the social partners' role from the opposite perspective, i.e. as one of the independent variables that impinge on the timeliness and correctness of transposition (see Chapter 14). On the basis of our approximately 180 expert interviews we classified each of our 90 cases at two stages

Table 12.2 *Forms of interest group involvement in labour law decision-making*

Type	Social partner involvement
A. *No or negligible involvement*	If at all, only on the basis of personal contacts
B. *Consultation*	Only as lobbyists
C. *Concertation*	Joint process of decision-making between state and social partners
D. *Complementary legislation*	Social partners negotiate, and the state then gives *erga omnes* effect to their agreement
E. *Social partner autonomy*	Labour and industry both decide and implement on their own

of the social partners from type A to E is increasing, the role of the state is at the same time diminishing.[16]

(A) We speak of *no or negligible involvement* where the social partners do not participate at all or where the exchange of information with state actors is based on informal and strictly personal contacts.

(B) The notion of *consultation* is used when the social partners are able to give their opinion. This may either take place in hearings or on the basis of written statements. In this category the social partners may have a privileged position compared with other interest groups (say, if the latter are not involved at all), but they do not necessarily have to (say, if the hearing is open to everyone). The most important feature of this type of involvement is that the social partners have an opportunity to express their positions but there is no negotiation and no common decision-making process between the state and the two sides of industry.

(C) By *concertation* we mean a joint process of decision-making between the state and the social partners, where the latter possess a privileged position compared with other interest groups. This category is used, for instance, when negotiations take place in tripartite committees. It is not necessary for all three parties to sit at the same

with respect to social partner involvement: before a national government took part in a Directive's negotiation in the Council of Ministers (policy formulation stage) and when the Directive was transposed (policy implementation stage). Based on these classifications and on additional interview questions regarding the *general* social partner role in each member state, we then classified each country as a whole with respect to the *typical pattern of social partner involvement in the labour law field.*

[16] These categories describe *modes* of social partner involvement. They do not equate with the *actual influence* of management and labour, which is very hard to measure empirically.

table simultaneously. Concertation may also take place if draft legislation is exchanged several times between the government and the social partners, to be commented on before the government finally presents its proposal to parliament. It is also possible that a bipartite agreement between both sides of industry is reached as a first step and is then used by the government as a basis for its draft legislation (so-called 'negotiated legislation').

(D) Similar to 'negotiated legislation', *complementary legislation* is also based on a bipartite deal between management and labour. The crucial difference is that in this category the state only gives the social partner agreement an *erga omnes* effect.[17] This means that (unlike negotiated legislation, where the social partner agreement may be amended in the parliamentary procedure) it is not possible for state actors to change the results of the social partner negotiations. This is also the model practised in social policy by the 'corporatist policy community' at the EU level.

(E) Finally, the notion of *social partner autonomy* is used if matters of public interest are regulated without the state interfering in social partner affairs.

12.2   Effects of EU social policy on national public–private relations

We will begin by presenting an overview across all fifteen countries of the changes of national social partner involvement visible in terms of the categorisation presented above. At the same time, it should be pointed out that only quite dramatic change will be apparent against this background. Only in exceptional cases can a national system be expected to cross from one category to another. Further effects are relevant within the same ideal type of interest group involvement but do not actually transfer a country to another category. In addition, there may be situations where internal developments would have induced a move between types. In such instances, the Europeanisation effect could consist in actually *preventing* such a move (which would not be visible on the basis of the typology above). We will thus look at particularly interesting cases in order to demonstrate the Europeanisation effects occurring *within* the same ideal type of social partner involvement.

---

[17] In other words, the state guarantees that the social partner agreement is not only binding on the members of the contracting parties, but is generally valid for all employers and workers concerned. There are different legal procedures in the member states by which this can be achieved. However, such an instrument does not exist in all countries with regard to the area of labour law.

12.2.1   The upstream phase: social partner involvement and the national preparation of EU decision-making

Table 12.3 compares the way the national social partners are usually involved in 'purely national' labour law decision-making with their involvement in the national preparation of EU decisions in the same field. When EU Directives replace national regulatory instruments, the national social partners gain the opportunity to influence the policy formulation phase via the European peak organisations. If a 'normal' rather than a social partner Directive (negotiated via the procedure in Article 138 ECT) is at stake, involvement through ETUC, UNICE or CEEP is only a very indirect way of participating, however. It is therefore of interest to take a closer look at the *national* preparation of EU decisions as well, in order to find out just how far national social partners are permitted to present their positions before the national government decides on a Directive in Council.

As far as the social partner involvement in 'purely national' labour law decision-making is concerned, the fifteen member states can be divided into four groups according to our categorisation:[18] countries where social partner autonomy is the most typical pattern in the labour law field (Denmark); member states where complementary legislation is the most decisive feature (Belgium); 'concertation countries' (Austria, Finland, Sweden); and finally 'consultation countries' (Germany, Spain, France, Greece, Italy, Ireland, Luxembourg,[19] the Netherlands, Portugal and the

---

[18] These and the following classifications of the member states rely on our case studies, a comprehensive literature evaluation, and on our expert interviews. Some classifications may at first sight seem counterintuitive. Why, for example, are Austria, Sweden and Finland classed as 'concertation countries' while the Netherlands is not? In the framework of this book it is not possible to explain the classification of each individual country in detail. Therefore (in addition to the examples outlined in the text below), we would refer the reader to the three dissertations resulting from this research project. Each dissertation outlines at length, for the countries studied, the role of the social partners in labour law decision-making in general, as well as in the national preparation and implementation of EU social Directives (see Treib 2004 for Germany, the Netherlands, Ireland and the UK; Hartlapp 2005 for Belgium, France, Spain, Portugal and Greece; and Leiber 2005 for Denmark, Sweden, Finland, Austria, Italy and Luxembourg). Note, however, that most of the counterintuitive classifications (as with the example of the Netherlands) may be explained by the fact that we made a particular point of focusing on social partner involvement *in labour law matters*. While concertation is a common feature in the Netherlands in many areas of economic and social policy, we considered consultation to be the most typical pattern in the field of labour law. When it comes to the evaluation of our results, we are, of course, cognisant of the fact that concertation in a country like the Netherlands is not an unfamiliar way of public–private interaction. The table, however, strictly refers to labour law in order to provide an equal basis of comparison with the social policy Directives.

[19] As has already been noted above, this book establishes the most typical pattern of social partner involvement, focusing specifically on the field of labour law. In earlier publications

Table 12.3 *Impact of Europeanisation on domestic public–private interaction I: the upstream phase*

		Dominant form of social partner involvement in . . .	
	. . . national labour law regulation	. . . the national preparation of EU labour law decision-making (point in time t1)	. . . the national preparation of EU labour law decision-making (point in time t2)
DK	Social partner autonomy	Concertation	As t1
B	Complementary legislation	None or negligible	Consultation (since end 1990s)
A	Concertation	Concertation	As t1
FIN	Concertation	Concertation	As t1
S	Concertation	Concertation	As t1
D	Consultation	Consultation	As t1
E	Consultation	None or negligible	Consultation discussed (2001)
F	Consultation	None or negligible	As t1
GB	Consultation	Consultation	As t1
GR	Consultation	None or negligible	As t1
I	Consultation	None or negligible	Consultation (since end 1990s)
IRL	Consultation	Consultation	As t1
LUX	Consultation	None or negligible	Consultation discussed (2001)
NL	Consultation	Consultation	As t1
P	Consultation	Consultation	As t1

White cells: no significant change in social partner involvement between categories
Shaded cells: change in social partner involvement between categories (possibly compensated at point in time t2)
Period of reference: 1990–2002

UK). Given that we are examining labour law, an area highly relevant to both sides of industry, there are no member states in our research field where the most common interaction pattern consists of no or negligible social partner involvement.

The *white cells* of Table 12.3 indicate the countries where no change between the categories of social partner involvement was observed. This is particularly true for the entire group of 'concertation countries'. The involvement of the Swedish, Austrian and Finnish social partners in the national preparation of EU labour law decision-making is intense. This important role was granted to them by their governments during the accession negotiations, as a kind of compensation for the shift of competences towards the EU. This development was the clearest in Austria, where the participation of the social partners in the national preparation of EU decisions was even accorded as a statutory right (Karlhofer and Tálos 1996: 141–2). Usually, there is an exchange of information and of drafts between the administrative units in charge and the social partners, which takes several steps before a 'common position' (Interview A2: 1743–77; translation by the authors) is reached. In Sweden and Finland, the social partner involvement in this phase of the policy process is also well institutionalised. The peak organisations of management and labour (thus in a priority position compared with other interest groups) regularly take part in the meetings of the (inter-)ministerial committees or working groups preparing the national position on a draft Directive (Interviews S11: 212–54, S10: 488–500; FIN6: 761–5, FIN3: 550–631, 633–79). This does not mean that the participation of the social partners in the national preparation process of a Directive has to be considered *full* compensation for the shift of competences towards the EU. However, it is interesting to observe that in these countries, which have a tradition of strong social partnership, the shift was at least significantly counterbalanced.

Also for a significant number of the 'consultation countries' the manner of social partner involvement stayed the same. In Germany, the UK, Ireland, the Netherlands and Portugal, management and labour may regularly state their opinion on national labour law projects, and they are also consulted by the respective administrative units before EU Directives are negotiated in Council (Interviews D2: 999–1095; GB3: 602–23; IRL4: 1549–51; NL11: 59–67; P1: 343–9).

(see e.g. Falkner and Leiber 2004), we partly used a slightly different classification system: if different patterns co-existed in the wider social policy area, we assigned each member state to the form of social partner involvement that gives labour and industry the most far-reaching powers. This is why in some of our previous work, we attributed to Luxembourg the category of concertation rather than consultation.

The *shaded cells* of Table 12.3 show the member states where changes of categories became visible. As in Austria, Sweden and Finland, the Danish social partners are very intensely involved in the ministerial committee meetings preparing the Danish position on EU Directives (*concertation*).[20] However, the most common pattern of national social partner participation in the labour law field in Denmark is social partner autonomy. Historically rooted in the so-called 'September compromise' of 1899 between the two largest organisations of labour (*Landsorganisationen*, LO) and industry (*Dansk Arbejdsgiverforening*, DA), the Danish model of public–private relations has been based on a very high degree of self-regulation between management and labour. Unlike most of the other EU member states, state intervention in this field is not common in Denmark and most of the working conditions are regulated exclusively by collective agreements (see, for example, Petersen 1997; Jørgensen 1999; Scheuer 1999; Jensen 2002).[21] Thus, for Denmark, the extension of EU competences to this field means a qualitative change in the public–private relations, which may not simply be compensated for by intensive involvement in the preparation of EU Directives: where there was societal self-regulation before, now, inevitably, state actors have to be involved.

A certain shift towards a lesser degree of social partner involvement can also be observed in Belgium. The organisations of management and labour play an important role in Belgium in the field of labour law. The scope of collective agreements negotiated in the *Conseil National de Travail* (CNT) may be extended to all employers and employees in the private sector, making them a common regulatory instrument. Therefore, Belgium was assigned to the category of *complementary legislation*. But even where legislation is used, the social partners formally participate in the decision-making process via the CNT, which has to be consulted on all legislative projects in this policy area. As far as the national preparation of EU decisions is concerned, however, until the end of the 1990s the social partners were only involved informally. This was experienced as a real loss of influence on the social partners' side and gave rise to problems at the implementation stage. From the end of the 1990s onward, the government initiated regular formal consultations with the social partners in order to prepare the Belgian positions for the EU Council of Ministers. The government thus wanted to prevent a situation where both sides of industry, after not having been sufficiently involved in the formulation

---

[20] Interviews DK7: 659–89, DK3: 67–118. See also Laursen (2003: 105): 'The Special Committees have developed into real negotiating bodies where private and public interests are normatively merged'.

[21] An exception is the field of health and safety at the workplace, which is mainly regulated by legislation.

phase of a European Directive, would block the process in the transposition phase (Interviews B10: 334–46, B5: 517–48).[22] In terms of our categories, there was initially a shift from *complementary legislation* to *no or negligible involvement*, which was at least partly compensated for by the later change to *consultation* from the end of the 1990s onwards.

Although they have 'less to lose', the social partners' role in the preparation of EU Directives in five of the 'consultation countries' (France, Greece, Italy, Luxembourg and Spain) is also weaker than their participation in domestic labour law matters. While the organisations of management and labour in these countries are usually at least consulted on national legislative proposals, the most common pattern in the upstream phase of EU decisions is to ignore them (Interviews E1: 111; F12; GR9: 122–5; I8: 326–60; LUX1: 868–97). This observation is at any rate valid for the period up to the late 1990s (see the centre column of the table, denoting the point in time t1). In some of these member states, there were indications that this loss might be compensated for in the future. In Italy, similar to Belgium, the contacts between the administrative units preparing EU Directives and the National Economic and Labour Council (*Consiglio Nazionale dell' Economia e del Lavoro*, CNEL) were intensified at the end of the 1990s. However, our interview partners were not yet sure whether this new way of consultation would actually prove to be an effective tool (Interview I5: 102–20). In Spain and Luxembourg, a more systematic involvement of the social partners was discussed at the national level (Feyereisen 2001; Interview E2: 90–115), but at the time of writing, it has not yet been put into practice (see the right-hand column of Table 12.3, representing the status at point in time t2).

In sum, the most important changes took place at one end of the spectrum, where the role of the social partners at the national level was most intense and is now restricted by the EU Directives. This applies to a certain degree to Belgium, but most clearly to Denmark, where the shift to the EU level interferes with traditional social partner autonomy. In the middle ground covered by the 'concertation countries', there were no visible differences between social partner involvement in domestic policy-making and the national preparation of EU Directives – certainly, they did not amount to a shift from one of our categories to another. At the other end of the spectrum, finally, we observed a weakening of the social partners' role in some of the 'consultation countries'. However, this effect was partly offset by subsequent domestic reforms in certain countries. Moreover, it can be argued that the direct, and at times relatively

[22] This shows that there is an important link between the two perspectives on national public–private relations (as an independent variable influencing transposition outcomes and as the dependent variable being influenced by Europeanisation; see also Ch. 14).

far-reaching, EU-level involvement via the major European organisations is a comparatively more significant improvement for both sides of industry in these countries, offering additional compensation for the weakening effect brought about by Europeanisation.

12.2.2   The downstream phase: social partner involvement and the transposition of EU Directives

We will now take a look at the downstream phase and the involvement of the social partners in the transposition of EU Directives – in contrast to their usual involvement in 'purely national' labour law decision-making (see Table 12.4). In the course of doing so, we will examine if the 'soft incentives' towards a strengthening of national social partnership outlined above actually had an effect. We will distinguish between the social partners' participation in the transposition of *'normal' EU Directives* (negotiated by the Commission, the EU Council of Ministers and the European Parliament) and *EU social partner Directives* (negotiated between the EU-level social partners and then transformed into a generally binding Directive by the Council of Ministers). Two of the six Directives in our sample – Parental Leave and Part-time Work – are EU social partner Directives of this kind.

As in Table 12.3 above, the *white cells* in Table 12.4 indicate cases where no relevant change was observed. In some exceptional cases, a change of category is indicated in the table, but we know from our empirical studies that the respective changes were due to national reasons (or at least they were not caused by the European incentives we are investigating). These cases are marked with an asterisk. The *dark shaded cells* denote changes amounting to a shift between the categories. In contrast, the *light shaded cells* include cases in which we observed Europeanisation effects, but these were not far-reaching enough to reassign a country from one category to the other. In the following section, we will look at these developments country by country. We begin with the category-shifting Europeanisation effects, followed by the effects below the level of category changes.

12.2.2.1   The most visible cases: changing modes of public–private interaction   Table 12.4 indicates that, in the transposition of EU labour law Directives, three countries have moved away from their traditional ways of social partner involvement towards a qualitatively new mode of public–private interaction. Most importantly, Denmark has been forced to shift from its established model of social partner autonomy towards complementary legislation. In Ireland and Luxembourg, the observed changes have not been as far-reaching as in the Danish case. While in

Table 12.4 *Impact of Europeanisation on domestic public–private interaction II: the downstream phase*

	Dominant form of social partner involvement in . . .			
	. . . national labour law regulation	. . . the transposition of 'regular' labour law Directives	. . . the transposition of the Parental Leave Directive	. . . the transposition of the Part-time Work Directive
DK	Social partner autonomy	Complementary legislation	Complementary legislation probable	Complementary legislation
B	Complementary legislation	Complementary legislation	Complementary legislation	Partly complementary legislation, partly consultation
A	Concertation	Concertation	Concertation	Concertation
FIN	Concertation	Concertation	Concertation	Concertation
S	Concertation	Concertation	Concertation	Concertation
D	Consultation	Consultation	Consultation	Consultation
E	Consultation	Consultation	Consultation (concertation attempted)	Concertation (government and unions only)*
F	Consultation	Consultation	Consultation	Consultation
GB	Consultation	Consultation	Consultation	Consultation
GR	Consultation	Consultation	Consultation	Consultation
I	Consultation	Consultation	Consultation (concertation attempted)	Consultation (concertation attempted)
IRL	Consultation	Consultation	Consultation	Concertation
LUX	Consultation	Consultation	Concertation (complementary legislation attempted)	No transposition process
NL	Consultation	Consultation	Consultation	Consultation
P	Consultation	Concertation*	Concertation*	Concertation*

White cells: No significant EU-induced change in social partner involvement
Light shaded cells: EU-induced change in social partner involvement *below the level of the categories*
Dark shaded cells: EU-induced change in social partner involvement *between* categories
*: Change not EU-induced
Period of reference: 1990–2002

243

Denmark the changes have affected the transposition of EU labour law Directives *in general*, the developments in Ireland and Luxembourg have (so far) only concerned the transposition of *individual Directives*. Nevertheless they are of particular interest since they show that *the EU-level social partnership in the area of social policy actually trickled down into the domestic arena.*

Denmark: towards a new 'dual method' of implementation   As in the upstream phase, the most significant effect could be observed in Denmark. Danish public–private relations in the field of labour law are based on three main principles: a high degree of associational organisation, 'administrative corporatism' (Christiansen et al. 2001: 61) and collective agreements as a central instrument of regulation. As already explained, many of the working conditions in Denmark are a product of the autonomous negotiations between the social partners, which take place without any state intervention. The high degree of union organisation (with about 80 per cent of all workers being members of a trade union) is a prerequisite for this. In contrast to other countries where the social partners also play an important role, legislation that relates to employees who are not covered by collective agreements is unusual in most areas of labour law. In those fields that are traditionally covered by law, such as health and safety in the workplace, Europeanisation has not affected social partner participation. This is true for two of our six Directives, notably the Directives on Pregnant Workers and Young Workers, because in Denmark these only affected the area of occupational health and safety. Precisely those areas traditionally covered *solely* by collective agreements, however, pose a special problem. This was the case for the remaining four Directives.

The first Directive where this problem came up was the Employment Contract Information Directive. This area had hitherto been governed exclusively by collective agreements. Contrary to this tradition, the Directive was implemented by an Act of parliament. However, as the contents of the Directive were not regarded as substantial by the social partners, this loss of regulatory competences did not attract much attention and discussion.

It was the implementation of the Working Time Directive that for the first time concerned a topic which was of central importance to the social partners. The Danish transposition of the Directive thus gave rise to serious problems, not because of the substantive policy requirements involved, but rather because of the fact that it impinged on the specific Danish tradition of autonomous social partner regulation in the area of working conditions. This was particularly true for the Directive's provision on maximum weekly working time, which was the main standard that hitherto had not been covered by generally binding legislation, but solely by collective agreements. But the definition of maximum working hours was one of the core areas of the social partners' sphere of influence, which was the reason why the government and the major social partner organisations decided to make use of the EC Treaty's so-called 'Christoffersen clause' and implement the Directive solely on the basis of collective agreements (Interviews DK1: 153–307, DK3: 558–99).

Where necessary, therefore, the social partners incorporated the maximum weekly working time standard of forty-eight hours into their collective agreements during the 1995 bargaining round. After these negotiations, the Ministry of Labour considered the Directive implemented (Knudsen and Lind 1999: 148). However, the European Commission was critical of the fact that, even after the implementation via collective agreements, Denmark could not guarantee full coverage of the *total* workforce affected by the Directive (Madsen 2000). Danish collective agreements can basically provide coverage of about 80 per cent of all workers, but not complete workforce coverage, as the European Court of Justice demands in decisive case law.[23]

In response, the government and the large social partner organisations tried to defend their way of implementing, especially by way of a specific implementation agreement between the biggest trade union and employers' organisations, LO and DA, which was meant to increase the coverage of the collective agreement system (Madsen 2000). But the Commission upheld its criticism and sent a Reasoned Opinion to Denmark, threatening to bring the case to the ECJ. In taking this step, the Commission also reacted to protests against the mode of transposition from several smaller Danish trade union organisations, which were excluded from the established corporatist system. Two of these organisations, the independent union *Firma-Funktionærernes Fagforening* and the Christian union DKF, even filed an explicit complaint with the Commission (Petersen 1998). As a result of the increasing European pressure, the Danish government finally complied in early 2002. Even though neither the government nor the major social partner organisations found this solution to be satisfactory, they decided to deviate from the traditional 'Danish model'. Hence, complementary legislation was enacted which granted the minimum standards of the Directive to all employees not covered by collective agreements (EIRR 336: 5–6).

[23] See, for example, Judgment of the Court of 30 January 1985, case C-143/83, *Commission of the European Communities* v. *Kingdom of Denmark* [1985] ECR 427. For an overview of relevant case law regarding the implementation of EU Directives via collective agreements, see Adinolfi (1988).

A similar situation occurred when the Parental Leave Directive was implemented. This time, it was the need to adapt to the standard on *force majeure* leave that caused the difficulties. This area had traditionally been left to autonomous agreements between the social partners (Hall 1998). In the light of this tradition, the government and the social partners consented that the *force majeure* standard of the Directive should be implemented by the social partners themselves, which was indeed accomplished by several sectoral agreements and a national pact between the two major representatives of employees and workers, DA and LO (Clauwaert and Harger 2000: 25). As in the working time case, the Commission subsequently argued that collective agreements in Denmark were not able to guarantee coverage of all workers. At the time of writing, a Reasoned Opinion has been issued against Denmark (Interview DK1a), and it is very likely that Denmark will again enact complementary legislation to comply with the Directive fully.

The regulation of part-time workers' employment conditions in Denmark was also traditionally part of the autonomous competences of the social partners. When Denmark had to implement the Part-time Work Directive, some discrimination still existed. For example, the eligibility for particular employment-related benefits (such as the right to participate in occupational pension schemes) was often restricted to workers with a certain minimum weekly working time (Interview DK7: 323–85). Again, the government and the social partners agreed that the Directive should be transposed by the social partners autonomously, in accordance with the 'Danish model'. And, again, a combination of sectoral agreements and a LO-DA agreement at the national level was chosen to accomplish this task. However, the prospects that sufficient coverage could be achieved were even lower than in the working time case. In addition to the limited coverage of Danish collective agreements in general, a further problem resulted from the limited substantive scope of the LO-DA deal, which only covered non-discrimination regarding employment conditions set down in collective agreements, thereby excluding employment conditions agreed at company level or between the employer and individual workers (Interviews DK1: 638–700, DK4: 631–40).

When the end of the transposition period approached, the government, in concertation with the social partners, concluded that no sufficient (personal and substantive) coverage could be reached by collective agreements and that state intervention was necessary. Hence, complementary legislation guaranteeing non-discrimination against part-time workers was adopted in June 2001 (EIRR 330: 5; Jørgensen 2001). The relative ease and swiftness with which this decision to deviate from the traditional 'Danish model' was taken demonstrates that the Danish actors had already learned from the working time case that autonomous social partner implementation with insufficient coverage would be met with Commission intervention. In order to avoid this, they opted for compliance by legislation.

To sum up, the Danish attempts to transpose some of the Directives by means of autonomous social partner action proved incompatible with the European legal requirement of covering the whole workforce. Denmark was compelled to deviate from its traditional model of social partner autonomy and rely instead on complementary legislation. With regard to the 'Europeanised' parts of labour regulation, one can therefore speak of a change in category from *social partner autonomy* to *complementary legislation*. Against the background of the above-mentioned 'Christoffersen clause' this is a rather paradoxical outcome. Originally, the clause was intended to protect the Danish model. Whereas it might offer incentives for a strengthening of social partnership in other member states (in case these countries possess an *erga omnes* option to declare collective agreements generally binding), Denmark itself has been forced by ECJ case law to change its model in the opposite direction – towards less social partner autonomy.

Ireland: National social partners strengthened by EU social partner Directive   During the implementation of the Part-time Work Directive in Ireland, the fact that the Directive was based on a European social partner agreement induced the government department in charge of transposition to deviate from the usual procedure and set up a *tripartite working group*, which was meant to discuss how to incorporate the Directive into Irish law. The working group consisted of representatives from the employees' association ICTU, the employers' association IBEC, and a number of government departments. These types of tripartite talks between employers, unions and representatives of the state did not constitute something entirely new for Ireland; a whole series of tripartite national social pacts had been concluded since the 1980s (O'Donnell and Thomas 1998; Prondzynski 1999: 66–9; Dobbins 2000). However, it was the first time that such a tripartite working group had been set up in the context of preparing a piece of legislation *in the area of labour law*. Up to that point it was normal to consult the two social partners thoroughly, but separately. The officials in charge explicitly argued that the intensified involvement of both sides of industry in the transposition process was a reaction to the Directive in question being based on social partner negotiations at the European level (Interview IRL4: 436–43).

Luxembourg: EU social partner Directive induces experiment on a new national social partner model   When the Parental Leave Directive was implemented in Luxembourg, an interesting attempt was made to stray from the common procedure of interest involvement. In Luxembourg, the implementation of EU Directives in the field of labour law is usually effectuated by way of legislation. During the legislative process both sides of industry are formally involved in the preparation of an implementation law. Employers and employees in each sector of the economy are members of professional organisations which are legally entitled to submit an expert opinion on each piece of impending legislation.[24] Before the drafting of an implementation law, it is customary for the largest unions, OGB-L and LCGB, along with FEDIL on the employers' side, to be consulted as well (Interview LUX1: 939–60).

In the case of parental leave, an attempt was made to mirror the EU-level procedure of complementary legislation in the domestic process. Hence, the ministry in charge did not make any proposals of its own, but left it to the social partners to conclude an agreement (Interview LUX9: 573–625). This procedure (*complementary legislation*) can be considered a novelty in Luxembourg and the decision to pursue it was induced by the fact that the Parental Leave Directive itself had been negotiated between the EU-level social partners. However, the negotiations between unions and employers quickly faced constitutional problems. It had to be acknowledged that there was no legal base in Luxembourg for a procedure that would have allowed the government to render the social partners' agreement generally binding for all employees. Therefore, this attempt failed, the talks were broken off, and the Directive was later implemented via legislation (Interview LUX7: 204–58; Feyereisen 1998).

But even after this failure, the implementation process of the Parental Leave Directive displayed some notable characteristics with regard to the involvement of private interests. Now the implementation was combined with the negotiations over the National Action Plan for Employment 1998, so that the draft legislation was finally worked out in a tripartite co-ordination committee. As in Ireland, tripartite concertation in Luxembourg is common in certain areas of socio-economic interest, but rather less so in the labour law field. Whether this pattern will spread to other cases or will remain a singular phenomenon cannot ultimately be resolved on the basis of this study. As regards the implementation of the second social partner Directive (on part-time work), there has as yet been no

---

[24] Besides the organisation of management and labour under private law, there is a system of so-called professional chambers under public law with compulsory membership for the professional groups (Schroen 2001: 254–8).

implementation process in Luxembourg. The government considered the national rules to be already in line with the Directive. However, interview partners pointed out that the issue of 'social partner negotiations as a basis for the implementation of Directives' could come up at the next reform of the domestic legislation governing collective agreements (Interviews LUX7: 204–58, LUX1: 903–17). It remains to be seen if Luxembourg will then generally shift from the category of *consultation* or even *concertation* to *complementary legislation*.

12.2.2.2 Europeanisation effects below the level of category shifts
As already indicated above, the second major group of countries affected by Europeanisation comprises those cases where domestic changes could actually be discerned, but these were below the level of a shift from one category to another. They include Austria, Sweden, the UK, Spain, Italy and Greece. These examples underline that it is crucial for Europeanisation scholars not to focus exclusively on dramatic changes, but to take into account less momentous (but still significant) domestic effects as well.

Austria: Europeanisation stabilises corporatism in the social realm In Austria, both the structural and the procedural dimensions of corporatism (interest group organisation and involvement in policy-making respectively) are extremely well developed. There are a number of hierarchically organised 'chambers' (for business, labour, agriculture, etc.), i.e. interest associations with obligatory membership set up by Austrian law. The classic social partner organisations in Austria are thus the Chamber of Business (*Wirtschaftskammer Österreich*), the Chamber of Labour (*Bundesarbeiterkammer*), the Conference of Presidents of the Chambers of Agriculture (PRÄKO) and the highly representative Austrian trade union confederation (ÖGB). These pillars of social partnership co-operate both formally (in a plethora of working groups, for example) and informally with the other political institutions, on a daily basis. It is not uncommon for draft legislation to be negotiated between the social partners themselves or in conjunction with the relevant ministry before being rubber-stamped in parliament. Austria (at least until the end of the 1990s, before the centre-right government came to power) is therefore a classic case of our variant C of public–private interaction listed in Table 12.2, i.e. of concertation, with joint processes of decision-making encompassing both government/administration and a small group of privileged private actors.

A direct Europeanisation effect on Austrian corporatism stemming from legal misfit[25] has been neither expected nor experienced in Austria, for the Austrian model of tripartite concertation is not in conflict with EU law. But what has affected social partnership is the concertation-adverse centre-right government, in particular during its first term of office between 2000 and 2002 (Tálos and Kittel 2001). These domestic developments, however, occurred at a time when (at least in EU-level social policy) pro-corporatist stimuli emanated from the EU level. While in other areas the extensive consultations and tripartite negotiations known from the heyday of national corporatism were significantly cut back under the Austrian centre-right government, this was much less so in the field of social policy and labour law (Interview A4: 25–70). The implementation of EU Directives, in particular, has recently been the area where public–private co-operation has been the most intense compared with other areas of domestic policy-making (Interviews A1: 167–254, A2: 1743–77). The Europeanisation effect is therefore seen as a *conserving* one in this case. While the general thrust of the centre-right government's policy pointed towards less corporatism, the EU's pro-concertation impetus acted as a countervailing force. In sum, Austria witnessed a persistence of the traditional patterns of tripartite concertation in the area of labour law and social policy.

Sweden: punctual restriction of social partner autonomy and fear of recentralisation   In Sweden, unlike in Denmark, concertation rather than social partner autonomy is the most typical mode of social partner involvement regarding *the area of labour law*. Nevertheless, social partner autonomy is an important pattern practised in Sweden in this field as well – although not to the same extent as in Denmark. While Europeanisation did not trigger a change in the basic mode of public–private interaction, Swedish social partnership was not left untouched by the partial shift of decision-making towards the EU level.

When the Working Time Directive was implemented in Sweden, the challenge to social partner autonomy was not as fundamental as in Denmark. Still, the desire on the part of the Swedish government and the social partners to preserve social partner autonomy as much as possible led to an insufficient transposition of the Directive. The main problem posed by the Directive in Sweden was that the existing working time legislation, even though already in line for the most part with the European standards, allowed the social partners to agree on almost unlimited

---

[25] Where, for instance, ECJ conditions have been imposed to ensure proper implementation of EU Directives (as in the Danish case).

derogations from the statutory standards (Interview S7: 474–85). Primarily, the scope of these derogations had to be limited in order to bring the Swedish system into line with the Directive. In 1995, therefore, the government created a tripartite working group that had the task of discussing the question of general working time reductions, an issue which had been on the agenda as a possible solution to the problem of increasing unemployment since the beginning of the 1990s. The group was also meant to put forward proposals on how to implement the Working Time Directive (Interview S10: 175–87).

At the time, both sides of industry agreed that no fundamental overhaul of the legislation should be carried out because they feared that their autonomy might be severely curtailed in such a major working time reform. It was the employers who proposed to implement the Directive by creating a so-called 'fence system', which left as much flexibility for the social partners as possible. According to the 'fence system', a clause was added to the existing legislation which merely stipulated that derogations from the law could be made only in so far as they still guaranteed a level of protection consistent with the EU Working Time Directive (Interviews S7: 547–665, S12).[26] In essence, therefore, the Directive was not really *incorporated* into Swedish law, but was transposed by simple *reference* to the Directive.

Transposition by reference, however, does not meet the principles of *full effect* and *legal certainty* defined by the ECJ as preconditions for correct transposition.[27] Indeed, since the Directive is a very complex piece of legislation, there are many problems in the everyday operation of the 'fence system'. In essence, the EU Directive is mostly ignored by employers and worker representatives (see, for example, Interviews S5: 90–148, S10: 280–310; see also Chapter 6). The introduction of the 'fence system' thus represented merely a symbolic transposition of the Directive. In view of the huge difficulties faced with the existing transposition by reference, the trade unions changed their position and began to support the idea of implementation by revising the working time law (Interview S5: 90–148).

---

[26] The term 'fence system' was used by one of our interview partners. From this perspective, the way the Directive was transposed could be seen as a church (i.e. the existing legislation) surrounded by a fence (i.e. the Directive's standards). It is possible to leave the church (by way of collective agreements) but, in doing so, everybody has to stay within the fence (Interview S7: 449–545).

[27] The ECJ argued in several cases that the way a Directive is transposed must guarantee 'that, where the Directive is intended to create rights for individuals, [their] legal position . . . is sufficiently precise and clear and the persons concerned are made fully aware of their rights'. See Judgment of the Court of 23 May 1985, case C-29/84, *Commission of the European Communities* v. *Federal Republic of Germany* [1985] ECR 1661, para. 18. See also Prechal (1995: 89) with references to further ECJ case law.

Hence, in September 2000, the three largest Swedish trade union organisations issued a joint proposal providing for certain (cautious) measures to reduce working time and thereby fulfil the requirements of the Directive. At the time of writing, this project is still delayed, however, due to other domestic political reasons.[28] Nevertheless, sooner or later these reforms will (have to) be carried out, thus restricting the social partners' collective liberty.

The implementation of the Part-time Work Directive in Sweden for the first time created a situation comparable to Denmark, since the regulation of part-time work in terms of employment conditions *was part of the sphere of autonomous social partner agreements*. Therefore, the government called on the social partners to remove the existing discrimination in collective agreements (Interview S11: 142–75). These discriminatory clauses seem to have been quite frequent. Many collective agreements excluded part-time workers with a weekly working time of less than 40 per cent of the working hours of full-time workers from occupational pension schemes, supplementary sickness benefits or leave entitlements (Interview S3: 851–72, S7: 693–756). The plan to transpose the Directive by social partner agreements was supported by the trade unions. But the employers' representatives were sceptical for several reasons. First, they argued that the existing clauses treating part-time and full-time workers unequally were in line with the Directive's provision allowing unequal treatment on 'objective grounds' (Interview S3: 851–72, S12). Second, they felt that a general non-discrimination principle was alien to collective agreements, which usually regulate very specific issues rather than general principles (Interview S12).

Third, and most importantly, employers were very reluctant to conclude any agreements at the *central* level because they feared that this might lead to a recentralisation of collective bargaining in Sweden (Interview S12). A move towards decentralisation was notable in many European countries during the 1980s and 1990s, but was particularly strong in Sweden (Thörnqvist 1999: 71–2; Bruun 2002). In order to reach sufficient workforce coverage, the transposition of the Directive would have

---

[28] It was expected that the government would subsequently table a legislative proposal translating the unions' agreement into a legal text. But this plan was thwarted by one of the two parties that lent support to the social democratic minority government under Göran Persson. While the former communist Left Party signalled its acquiescence, the Greens insisted on a more radical working time reduction, ultimately leading to a thirty-hour week. As a result of this veto, the trade unions' proposal was dropped, and a new tripartite commission was created with a view to discussing the issue further (Interviews S7: 571–87, S10: 175–217; Berg 2000, 2001b, 2002a). Since then, the external pressure has increased with the Commission issuing a Letter of Formal Notice (20 March 2002) due to the incorrect transposition of the Directive (Interview S12). So far, however, the debates are still continuing and the insufficient 'fence system' is still operational.

called not only for sectoral or company-level agreements but also, most likely, for a cross-sectoral agreement at the national level. As a result of the employers' reluctance, the debates between the social partners could not be concluded successfully, even after lengthy negotiations. Therefore, the government finally used the instrument of law to end this situation (Interview S11: 142–75; Berg 2001a, 2002b).

In sum, it is less likely that a European Directive will encroach on social partner autonomy in Sweden than it will in Denmark, but it is not impossible. So far, there has only been one case where transposition by collective agreements has been seriously considered. In this case, the relevant question in terms of EU law did not even come to bear, namely whether implementation via collective agreement could actually provide sufficient coverage. The employers' opposition prevented this. But if the employers had co-operated and the Directive had been transposed via agreements only, the most likely reaction of the Commission would have been the same as in the Danish cases.[29] There might, however, be European Directives to come which will again interfere with Swedish social partner autonomy. One example is already being discussed in Sweden, the potential Directive on Temporary Agency Work currently being negotiated at the European level. In addition, another *potential* Europeanisation effect was illustrated here (even if in this case it has not yet transpired). If social partners are to be involved in the implementation of European Directives, this requires collective agreements or at least co-ordination between the central level organisations for practical and coverage purposes. These requirements are therefore in contrast to possible decentralisation trends in the domestic collective bargaining system.

The UK: insider knowledge through EU social partner negotiations improves national social partners' position The examples of the implementation in the UK of the Directives on Parental Leave and Part-time Work bring us back to the supportive effects of the EU social dialogue Directives on social partner participation in domestic decision-making. The trade unions in particular feel that European integration and especially the emergence of collective negotiations on social and employment issues at the EU level have improved their position. Under the Conservative governments of Margaret Thatcher and John Major, the unions

---

[29] It should be mentioned that during the accession negotiations, Sweden secured the inclusion of a clause into the Accession Treaty, which was intended to guarantee the maintenance of the autonomous Swedish model. A closer analysis of the commitments to Sweden in the Accession Treaty and the associated exchange of letters with the European Commission, however, leads to the conclusion that implementation by collective agreements would not have been accepted on this basis (for details see Leiber 2005).

were consulted in a way that they considered to be merely 'pro forma' (Interview GB2: 96–100, 497–8). 'We have had 14 years of basically being ignored by our national government, and the European level gave us huge power. I mean we were increasingly having a voice in Europe and becoming influential as a social partner in a way that we just didn't have in our own country' (Interview GB6: 122–4). Clearly, the unions have regained some influence in the domestic arena since Labour has been in office. Nevertheless, the influence they may exert via the European social dialogue would still be there even after another change of government.

But participation in EU-level social partner negotiations does not just give domestic interest groups like the British unions an important say in EU decision-making; it may also improve their standing in the subsequent 'downloading' process at the national level. When the Parental Leave and Part-time Work Directives were transposed in the UK, both sides of industry were consulted much more intensely than before. Union representatives attributed this to the specialist insider knowledge gained by the interest groups in the EU-level negotiations. The government wanted to profit from this insider knowledge at the implementation stage and thus had an interest in holding intense discussions with those who had been sitting at the negotiation table in Brussels (Interview GB2: 358–66). The fact that domestic interest groups could exploit this privileged position by actually exerting more influence in the implementation process is best illustrated by the part-time work case. With the help of internal negotiation documents, the unions were able to convince the government that the basic principle of non-discrimination should be applied to 'workers' (Interview GB6: 598–619; TUC 2000: 2–3; *Financial Times*, 4 May 2000, p. 6), whereas at first the government had wanted to limit the scope to 'employees', as had traditionally been the case in the area of labour law (Interview GB10: 177–203; see also Chapter 9).

Spain: complementary legislation to transpose EU social partner Directives fails due to lack of social partner interest   We have already described some cases above where the EU social partner Directives induced a slight strengthening of the social partners' role in the domestic arena. In Spain, we found an example where the incentive to base the transposition on a social partner agreement was taken up by the government, but then failed due to a lack of interest by the social partners.

The existing Spanish parental leave regulations already encompassed a high level of protection so that the need for adjustment was rather small. Arguing that it would mainly affect the negotiation of non-binding standards, the government made a proposal to both sides of industry to negotiate autonomously the transposition of the Directive into national law (Interview E4: 607–21). The legal prerequisites for such a move are fulfilled in Spain, as Article 83/3 of the *Estatuto de los Trabajadores* guarantees the *erga omnes* effect of collective agreements. Previously, however, no EU Directive had been implemented solely through social partner agreements. Given that an autonomous implementation of the Directive would have strengthened the position of the social partners with regard to EU affairs, the ministry officials were astonished about the lack of interest that the social partners exhibited for autonomous collective negotiations (Interview E4: 618–23). But obviously neither side estimated the possible gains for their clients or the advantages for strengthening the social partners' national position as being any greater than the potential costs of the conflicts they expected to occur over how to implement the soft-law provisions of the Directive. After a period of inertia, the Directive was finally implemented by a piece of legislation. The social partners were consulted, but did not directly involve themselves in the drafting of the law. They were even consulted fairly late on this issue compared with other reform processes in the same area (Interview E4: 842–52 and 1674–88; Secretaria Confederal de la Mujer CCOO 1999).

Italy: attempts at autonomous social partner implementation   In the Italian transposition of the Parental Leave Directive, the social partners, encouraged by the fact that the Directive stemmed from successful social partner negotiations at the European level, intended to negotiate a national agreement on the implementation of the Directive, which then should have been given legal effect by the government. But this procedure failed because the social partners could not agree on a common solution because of fierce employer opposition to the extension of the existing parental leave provisions (Interviews I6: 294–327, I9: 114–34). When the end of the transposition period approached, the government decided to bring in its own legislative proposal, which finally formed the Italian transposition of the Directive. Furthermore, in the case of the Part-time Work Directive, the intention was to use an agreement between the social partners as the basis for the transposition law ('negotiated legislation'). Owing to an unforeseeable event, however, the letter in which the social partners asked the government to grant them a certain period of time for the negotiations never reached its destination.[30] When the government was finally informed about the social partners' willingness to negotiate,

[30] The letter should have been delivered by Massimo D'Antona, an advisor to the Italian Labour Minister. But before D'Antona could hand over the letter to the Minister, he was assassinated by terrorists from the Italian Red Brigades in May 1999 (Interview I5: 138–97; see also *Süddeutsche Zeitung*, 21 May 1999, p. 8).

the expiration of the transposition deadline was already imminent, with the result that the government only granted the social partners a two-month period of grace, which was much too short for them to reach an agreement. Therefore, the government again proceeded with its own legislative plans and quickly adopted a legislative decree which transposed the Directive into Italian law (Interview I5: 138–97). Both implementation processes are examples of where the EU-level concertation lent additional support to the attempts to create a stable basis for *concertazione*, which have taken place in Italy in particular since the beginning of the 1990s (see, for example, Regalia and Regini 1999). Mainly as a result of the conflicts between the social partners themselves, however, an agreement between both sides of industry could not be reached and thus concertation failed.

It should be mentioned, however, that in Italy there was also an attempt to transpose a European Directive against the national tradition by means of *autonomous* action on the part of the social partners. This did not concern a 'social partner Directive', though, but an earlier Directive, the Directive on European Works Councils, which is not part of our sample. This Directive was implemented in Italy by way of an agreement signed by the General Confederation of Italian Industry (*Confindustria*), the employers in the banking sector (*Assicredito*), as well as the unions CGIL (*Confederazione Generale Italiana del Lavoro*), CISL (*Confederazione Italiana Sindacati Lavoratori*) and UIL (*Unione Italiana del Lavoro*) on 6 November 1996. When the European Commission was notified of the agreement as the Italian implementation Act for the Directive, the Commission argued that the agreement only covered a number of sectors and would thus have to be declared generally binding by law (COM [2000] 188; Hall 2000). The Italian constitution actually provides for such a procedure, but so far it has not been possible to put it into practice, mainly because of opposition from the Italian unions (Biagi 1998: 103), which fear that they would lose intra-organisational autonomy (Interview I8: 102–70). The solution expected now is a governmental statute incorporating the social partner agreement, hence a form of 'bargained legislation' (Biagi 1998: 103).

Greece: general backing of national social dialogue by normative role model of the EU   In Greece we also found no effects of EU social policy on the national social partner relations at the level of category shifts. However, in accordance with recent literature on developments in the Greek social dialogue, our expert interviews confirmed that, in a country without a tradition of social dialogue in public policy-making, the political actors feel that the idea of social dialogue as a form of 'good

governance' has spread and that the EU is pressing Greece to inten-
sify its social dialogue (Interview GR5: 378–90, GR11: 488–90). During
the 1990s, Greece saw the creation of a number of bipartite and tripartite consultation committees, among them the National Labour Institute
(EIE), the Office for Mediation and Conflict Resolution (OMED), the
Economic and Social Council (OKE), the National Centre of Occupational Education (EEKEP) and the Hellenic Institute for Occupational
Health and Safety (ELINYAE), the first bipartite body established in
Greece (EIRR 295: 28–32; Yannakourou 2003). According to Ioannou
(2000: 221), the 'founding of new bipartite and tripartite institutions can
be perceived as the outcome of this emerging social dialogue rhetoric
and/or approach that was heavily influenced by the Delors presidency of
the EU Commission'. In April 2003, moreover, the Greek parliament
adopted a piece of legislation devoted to improving the Greek social dialogue. This law established two new arenas for public–private debates:
the National Employment Council and the National Social Protection
Council, where issues such as parental leave or shorter working hours for
pregnant women are to be discussed (EIRR 352: 8).

12.3   Conclusions: moderate convergence of national social partnership

The observed changes in the fifteen member states add up to a *slightly
convergent development*, leading to a moderate social partnership model
of involving private interests in the making of social policy. It should be
noted that the outcome in terms of public–private interaction patterns
at the domestic level is not homogeneous, nor are the member states all
developing in this direction. As far as tendencies or attempts at change
in the individual countries are discernible, they point (at least in sum)
towards a form of *erga omnes* legislation as has been practised in EU level
social policy since Maastricht. This means that labour law standards are
negotiated by the social partners and are then declared generally binding
by the state (or by the EU Council of Ministers in case of the EU) without
any change in the substance.

Hence, countries with an extremely strong corporatism (Denmark) are
showing a tendency to move away from autonomously negotiated and
implemented collective agreements on labour law issues and are moving in the direction of a more moderate corporatist mode. In this mode
of 'complementary legislation', the social partners pre-negotiate agreements, which are then moulded into law or are made generally binding
by way of an *erga omnes* declaration. Alternatively, the social partners will
work directly together, in a tripartite mode with public actors, on the

drafting of laws. However, they are no longer able to determine social policy regulations completely without the intervention of the state. On the other side of the continuum, some countries without a corporatist tradition (such as Greece or the UK) have started to move slightly in this direction, or at least (this is the softest type of noticeable effect emanating from the EU-level stimuli) have felt pressure to do so. In between, in the central part of the continuum, we have witnessed efforts to move from social partner involvement via hearings, or at best 'bargained legislation', to a kind of *erga omnes* legislation (Italy and Luxembourg). In overall terms, a trend towards 'convergence towards moderate diversity' can be discerned.[31]

In terms of an overall evaluation of the tendencies of change that were found in the individual countries, it first has to be said that *no revolutionary transformation* of national interest intermediation systems has taken place. Neither has a change from a corporatist to a pluralistic model (or vice versa) taken place in a member state, nor a true convergence of national patterns in the sense of the same model being reproduced in all countries. These findings fit the common and theoretically well-founded expectation that national institutions are usually very powerful resisting forces (see, for example, Thelen and Steinmo 1992; Immergut 1998; Thelen 1999; Pierson 2000) and that the individual states sometimes even defend their own arrangements against supranational influence (Duina 1997; Knill and Lenschow 1998; Duina 1999; Duina and Blithe 1999; Börzel 2000; Knill and Lenschow 2000a; Knill 2001; Knill and Lenschow 2001).

Certainly, change below the level of profound systemic transformation (for critical junctures versus incremental processes of institutional change, see *inter alios* Pierson 2000; Thelen 2003) is of interest as well, and in this category we found some interesting developments. As described above, these are moving towards a moderate model of corporatism in public policy-making. From an optimistic viewpoint, this can be said to optimise the potential of private interest involvement in public policy-making: the interest groups unburden the state and add their specialist knowledge to agreed standards, while at the same time allowing all members of the political system (even those who are not members of the relevant associations) to profit from the protection offered by such collective deals. From a more critical perspective, however, the developments in Denmark in particular, and to a certain extent those in Sweden, can be seen as an unnecessary and illegitimate intrusion of European law into the member states. Even worse, they appear to be an intrusion on the

---

[31] See Falkner (2000c) on an abstract argument to this end.

grounds of rather legalistic arguments, for the old system of autonomous labour law-making by the Danish and Swedish social partners seems to have worked quite well and, most importantly, without any significant number of complaints from citizens outside the agreements' (theoretical or practical) reach.

The degree of change is significant in some countries but nevertheless strictly limited in overall terms. The trend towards light convergence at present only refers to the area of 'Europeanised national social policy' where individual member states act as one among many participants in the EU-level decision-making process and subsequently have to implement the resulting Directives. The fact that this trend (*ceteris paribus*) could spread to the other area of member states' social policy, which continues to be an exclusively national matter, cannot be ruled out, however. Any potential broadening of the trend described strongly depends on the status of EU social policy in the years to come. At least, to date, the legislative activity in the field has not declined to any significant extent (see Chapter 3).

In terms of different transmission mechanisms of Europeanisation we clearly observed that the 'hard' incentives, which were based on the binding force of EU (case) law, had the most far-reaching effects, whereas the 'soft incentives' were only taken up occasionally. From an overall perspective, this has led to the somewhat paradoxical situation whereby, despite significant progress of EU level social partnership in the field, EU social policy not only promotes the involvement of both sides of industry in domestic policy-making, but also contributes to a weakening of (a certain type of) national social partnership.

13 Implementation across countries and Directives

In the previous chapters, we have analysed the domestic impact of our six Directives in detail and we have provided an overview of a number of other aspects of the implementation process, notably the voluntary reforms that were prompted by the Directives, the EU Commission's policy against non-compliant member states, and the effect of the Directives on domestic patterns of state–society relations. In this chapter, we will provide a cross-country, cross-Directive summary of the adaptation requirements that had to be overcome and of the implementation outcomes finally reached.

13.1 Costs and overall misfit in comparative perspective

The system of categorising costs outlined in Chapter 2 is indicative of the maximum potential costs for our six Directives outlined in Table 13.1 (with the numbers referring to the cost categories listed in Chapter 2).

The only Directive in our sample that is marked by a potential for comparatively much higher long-term costs is the Parental Leave Directive since more men might take up their right in the future. We did not take this into account in our analysis of factors that potentially affect the transposition performance, since the interviews revealed that politicians and experts either did not regard the longer-term perspective as likely to diverge significantly from the present or did not include this in their short-term evaluation.

What were the costs that our six Directives actually created in the fifteen EU member states? Table 13.2 lists the four potential levels of costs and the number of cases found in each. These results indicate that our operationalisation of costs did not over-estimate the effect created by European social policy Directives: in 84 per cent of our cases, the costs are at best 'low'. This seems a valid result if we take into consideration that social policy is a field where the member states have old and well-established domestic models. More specifically, each and every member state already had an elaborate system of labour

Table 13.1 *Categories of potential costs arising from six labour law Directives*

	Cost category potentially arising from particular Directive	Sectors and groups of workers affected	Maximum short-term cost potential	Higher long-term cost potential
Employment Contract Directive	(6) administrative burden to issue written information	all	low	–
Pregnant Workers Directive	(1) pay or allowance during leave (if social insurance pays) (3) costs of replacement, leave, transfer or suspension (4) risk assessment costs (6) administrative burden of providing information	only particular and small group of workforce included	medium	–
Working Time Directive	(2) fewer hours per worker make effective labour costs rise (additional workers needed or extra pay for overtime) (4) costs of improved health protection (e.g. checks for night workers) (5) change in shift schedules etc. (6) administrative burdens (record keeping, notification of night work, etc.)	cuts across categories and sectors	high	–
Young Workers Directive	(2) working time reductions (costs of additional workers or more expensive adult workers) (4) costs of improved health protection (5) change of work schedules etc.	applies to small group of workers only	medium	–
Parental Leave Directive	(3) replacement costs (selection procedure, training) (6) some administrative burden if parental leave is new or if new system is more flexible	applies to group of workers only (parents)	low	yes (if more fathers take up their right)
Part-time Work Directive	(2) higher costs via non-discrimination in wages and working conditions (5) change in work schedules	applies to group of workers only (part-timers)	medium	–

The numbers refer to the cost categories listed in Chapter 2 at 2.4.

Table 13.2 *Overall costs triggered by six Directives in fifteen member states*

	None	Low	Medium	High
Employment Contract	–	15	–	–
Pregnant Workers	–	12	3	–
Young Workers	–	15[a]	–	–
Working Time	–	8	5	2
Parental Leave	–	15	–	–
Part-time Work	1	9	5	–
Total (90 cases)	1	74	13	2
% of total cases	1%	83%	14%	2%

[a] The UK is a special case with regard to this Directive for there were two phases of implementation with rather different reform implications. Since our interest here lies in the overall effect of the Directives, we have summarised all reform requirements of both phases in this table, resulting in low overall costs for the UK (see also Chapter 7 above)

law legislation even before entering the EU. The Directives therefore rather refined what was already there and added costs that seem minor if compared with, for example, the costs created when the first national laws in the field were adopted. Additionally, it is crucial to note that minimum standards in labour law are emphatically *not* the most expensive part of the EU's social policy efforts. Much higher costs arise from the social security Regulations that secure equal treatment for workers from other EU member states and the cross-national addition of social security claims (see, for example, Falkner 2003b). So the scale of costs is realistic in the frame of intra-policy comparison. On the level of inter-policy analysis, too, the rather small amount of costs created by our six Directives seems adequate. As already mentioned for environmental policy, other fields show a much more far-reaching effect of EU activity.

This does not indicate that the innovation introduced by our six Directives is negligible. As discussed in Chapter 2, costs are but one dimension of misfit. Looking at the other elements of *total misfit*, we find more of a departure from the domestic status quo ante in the fifteen member states (see Table 13.3). Still, only a small number of all cases show high degrees of misfit (ten cases), while almost exactly 50 per cent show small-scale misfit. Again, this seems realistic if one wants to be able to use the operationalisation for intra-policy and/or inter-policy comparison.

We can also use our operationalisation to compare the overall adaptational pressure for the different member states and the different Directives.

Table 13.3 *Total misfit created by six Directives in fifteen member states*

Degree of Misfit	Directives							
	EC	PW	WT	YW	PL	PTW	total	%
None	0	0	0	0	0	1	1	1%
Low	12	6	6	9	6	7	46	51%
Medium	3	8	6	6[a]	5	5	33	37%
High	0	1	3	0	4	2	10	11%
Total	15	15	15	15	15	15	90	100%

EC   Employment Contract   YW   Young Workers
PW   Pregnant Workers   PL   Parental Leave
WT   Working Time   PTW Part-time Work

[a] The UK is a special case with regard to this Directive for there were two phases of implementation with rather different reform implications. Since our interest here lies in the overall effect of the Directives, we have summarised all reform requirements of both phases in this table, resulting in medium-scale misfit for the UK (see also Chapter 7).

The country ranking (see Table 13.4) makes it evident that the greatest amount of misfit for our six labour law Directives was created in the UK (for details, see Oliver Treib's dissertation 2004). This is hardly surprising, considering that this country has the most non-interventionist labour law tradition in the EU. It is well known that the UK even enjoyed an opt-out from EU social policy harmonisation under the Maastricht Treaty, which ended only when the Labour government came into office and accepted the social Directives adopted by the other member states (see, for example, Falkner 2002). The Irish situation is somewhat similar, but there is a different economic background to the comparatively low protection standards preceding the EU regulation. Against this background, it was even more impressive that the Irish government did not oppose minimum harmonisation in the social realm as ruthlessly as the UK and accepted the Maastricht Social Agreement (Falkner 1998: 87). Denmark, too, is one of the rather reluctant countries when it comes to EU social regulation. However, this is not due to Danish actors expecting the EU's social policy Directives to imply high degrees of policy misfit for Denmark, but rather to a general effort to protect national autonomy. In the light of this, the comparatively high degree of overall misfit actually created by our six Directives is surprising. A closer look at our elaborate operationalisation helps to clarify matters: the wide-ranging impact of our Directives in the *politics dimension* explains the rather high degree of misfit overall. In fact, the Danish system of social partner autonomy in the regulation of working conditions was rather strongly affected by

Table 13.4 *Different degrees of overall misfit arising in the fifteen member states*

MS	Degree of overall misfit	Number of cases	Average misfit scores	MS	Degree of overall misfit	Number of cases	Average misfit scores
GB	low	1	2.3	GR	low	3	1.5
	medium	2[a]			medium	3	
	high	3			high	0	
DK	low	2	2.2	LUX	low	4	1.5
	medium	1			medium	1	
	high	3			high	1	
IRL	low	1	2.2	FIN	low	4	1.3
	medium	3			medium	2	
	high	2			high	0	
A	low	1	1.8	D	low	5	1.2
	medium	5			medium	1	
	high	0			high	0	
P	low	1	1.8	E	low	6	1.0
	medium	5			medium	0	
	high	0			high	0	
I	low	2	1.7	F	low	6	1.0
	medium	4			medium	0	
	high	0			high	0	
S	low	3	1.7	NL	low	4	1.0
	medium	2			medium	1	
	high	1			high	0	
B	low	3	1.5				
	medium	3					
	high	0					

Scores for different degrees of misfit:
none = 0 (not indicated in the table), low = 1, medium = 2, high = 3
[a] GB is a special case with regard to this Directive for there were two phases of implementation with rather different reform implications. Since our interest here lies in the overall effect of the Directives, we have summarised all reform requirements of both phases in this table, resulting in medium-scale misfit for GB (see also Chapter 7).

EU social policy and had to be changed in the direction of greater state intervention (Leiber 2005).

At the other end of the continuum are France, the Netherlands and Spain. The latter may come as a surprise to those who assume that the southern members are generally laggards in social policy. This assumption is certainly not true in labour law and our operationalisation produces a result that squares with the expectation of the more initiated.

Table 13.5 *Different degrees of overall misfit created by six labour law Directives*

Directive	Degree of overall misfit	Number of cases	Average misfit scores
Parental Leave	low	6	1.9
	medium	5	
	high	4	
Working Time	low	6	1.8
	medium	6	
	high	3	
Pregnant Workers	low	6	1.7
	medium	8	
	high	1	
Part-time Work	low	8	1.6
	medium	5	
	high	2	
Young Workers	low	10	1.3
	medium	5[a]	
	high	0	
Employment Contract Information	low	12	1.2
	medium	3	
	high	0	

Scores for different degrees of misfit:
none = 0 (not indicated in the table), low = 1, medium = 2, high = 3
[a] The UK is a special case with regard to this Directive for there were two phases of implementation with rather different reform implications. Since our interest here lies in the overall effect of the Directives, we have summarised all reform requirements of both phases in this table, resulting in medium-scale misfit for the UK (see also Chapter 7).

The reason is that Spain, Portugal and Greece, by the time of their EU entrance, started from a legacy of extremely rigid regulation. This had originated in prior authoritarian regimes and was only slowly transformed in domestic reforms subsequently. This made EU labour law look rather minimalist in its re-regulative elements, and the liberalising elements were at times those that accounted for misfit (for further details on the southern member states, see Hartlapp 2005). In general, it should be stressed that there is no clear and consistent north–south divide in the regulative level of labour law.[1] This is underlined by our findings that Spain is among the member states at the bottom of the ranking when it comes to overall misfit, Greece is somewhere in the centre (on a par with Belgium

---

[1] This is confirmed by Italy, where the working conditions also tend to be highly regulated.

and Luxembourg), and Portugal is among the countries in the top half of the table, but ranking still behind the UK, Denmark and Ireland. At the same time, Sweden and Austria show much greater misfit than the protagonists of a north–south split would have us believe. This substantiates our findings from the 90 in-depth studies and the approximately 180 expert interviews (which give a more general overview on the broader field of EU social policy), namely that, even in member states with very advanced welfare and labour law systems, the EU's social Directives do at times create significant misfit (see chapters on individual Directives).

If we look at the overall misfit created by the different Directives, a rather surprising picture emerges (see Table 13.5). The Parental Leave Directive, which was one of the policy measures in our sample that only implied minor costs in all countries (see Table 13.2), turns out to be the Directive that caused the greatest amount of overall misfit in all fifteen member states. This large overall impact is due to the fact that four countries had to introduce a statutory parental leave scheme for the very first time, and that many member states were forced to transform their gender-specific regulations qualitatively into schemes for both mothers and fathers (see Chapter 8). At the other end of the spectrum, the Employment Contract Directive involved the lowest number of reforms. Although there was surprisingly little legislation in this area, many workers already had the right to a written employment contract on the basis of collective agreements.

13.2   Timing and correctness of transposition

Turning to implementation outcomes, a number of striking results in terms of transposition timing and substantive correctness arise from our analysis.

The discipline of the member states in implementing the labour law Directives is very weak. In *more than two-thirds of all cases*, the adaptation requirements experienced a *delay of two years or more before they were fully met*. In other words, in 69 per cent of all cases (sixty-three out of ninety-one), complete correctness of implementation was only achieved after a minimum of two years from the legal deadline (and often much later).[2]

By contrast, *only ten out of ninety-one* transposition cases were *both on time and fully correct* (approximately 11 per cent), while only seventeen

---

[2] Since we are interested in the member states' implementation performance, the total number of cases here is ninety-one. The UK's implementation of the Young Workers Directive is therefore counted as two cases. There were two implementation phases with two different deadlines, giving the UK government two separate opportunities to obey or disobey the EU rules.

were either on time or not more than six months delayed (19 per cent). If we relax the correctness criterion by accepting essentially correct transposition, i.e. non-compliance where only a few minor aspects are disregarded (see below for more details on this category), then sixteen cases were fully on time and a further twelve cases were no more than six months delayed.[3] In other words, *not even one-third of all cases was transposed 'almost on time' and 'essentially correctly'* (twenty-eight out of ninety-one cases or 31 per cent).[4]

Do we observe *permanent non-compliance*? It is true that, in the long run, all member states seem to comply with those implementation requirements that are enforced by the Commission. The threat of steep fines has made all those countries facing a second ECJ judgment on the same case align themselves rather promptly. However, this argument cannot be generalised to all cases of non-compliance in the member states. This is because the European Commission is not aware of some cases of non-compliance, and it does not enforce many of the others it does know about. The lack of enforcement on the supranational level concerns, in particular, cases of insufficient or incorrect transposition of a Directive and cases of deficient application (see Chapter 11 for more details).

13.2.1 Correctness of transposition

Clearly, it is useful to compare the adaptation outcome with the misfit created by any EU law. Our study has revealed, however, that one needs intermediary categories in a number of cases where the categories applied to misfit are too crude to capture all the aspects of the practical outcome. The complexity of this issue becomes clear if we take into consideration that a full adaptation in the sense of 100 per cent will often be difficult to reach in practice, even in the transposition stage of a Directive's life cycle (and even more so during application). A further complication is that EC law evolves over time, for example via judgments of the ECJ. Since the boundaries between the specification of known provisions and the full-blown reinterpretation of what previously was taken to be the law are blurred, one cannot but try to work on the basis of what appears to be the majority consensus of interpretation at the time of adoption.[5]

---

[3] Note that among the sixteen cases that fulfilled the EU standards essentially correctly within the given deadline, there are four cases where this stage had already been reached from the outset.

[4] Again, these calculations are based on a total number of ninety-one cases, with the implementation of the Young Workers Directive in the UK being counted as two separate cases.

[5] If, for example, one member state interprets one provision differently (which typically results in not having to change domestic laws) but all or most of the others, possibly

Often, many different sectors of the economy and, in addition, many different categories of workers are treated individually by different national laws. Consider, for example, the Working Time Directive: in many countries there are specific laws for certain sectors (such as mining) and for specific groups of workers (e.g. shift workers). Taking into account that in a number of EU member states, even subnational regional units will come into play in the field of regulation (say, by adopting laws for *Länder* employees who will be exempted from federal laws on the same issue), a hugely complex matrix results in any study aiming to establish the actual adaptation to a particular EU Directive. The multitude of domestic laws and arenas affected makes transposition a rather protracted and incremental process in which the required adaptations are usually not accomplished at one fell swoop, but by a whole series of individual reforms. Against this background, should any remaining minimal misfit on any dimension lead to a country's scoring as a non-complier? For example, if a minimal point of one standard is not granted to a small group of public sector workers in one region, but is implemented in the rest of the country?

Such a strict view can make sense if the issue is approached from certain perspectives (for example, if the focus lies on the members of the excluded groups). However, if we want to establish the policy effects of EU laws or to analyse systematically the reasons for (non-)compliance across many cases, it may make sense to concentrate on the relevant part of the adaptation process. In the end, it may be an irrelevant minor reason that differs from the main national transposition process if, in one out of the sixteen *Länder* in Germany, a small part of the adaptation requirements has not been fulfilled correctly. It seems fair to mention that federalism is indeed a stumbling block for perfect transposition in a number of cases. To stress unilaterally in each case study any remaining trace of misfit would, however, distort the overall picture greatly. It would, first, hide even major adaptation accomplishments and, secondly, emphasise to an undue extent the reasons that account for the last remaining bit of non-adaptation, to the detriment of those reasons that account for compliance with larger parts of the misfit in earlier stages.

For all these reasons, we decided to differentiate between the date when '*essentially correct' transposition* is accomplished (and, similarly at a later stage, essentially correct application; for the moment, we shall focus on transposition), and the date of full legal adaptation without any remaining misfit. Wherever possible we established both essentially

including the Commission, rely on another understanding of the rule, we coded this as insufficient implementation in the one deviating country.

and completely correct transposition.[6] 'Completely correct transposition' denotes full compliance with all adaptation requirements in the transposition stage and notification of the relevant laws to the European Commission. 'Essentially correct transposition', by contrast, refers to an essentially successful fulfilment of most requirements (this contains a *qualitative* consideration of how good adaptation was and whether it captured the essential parts of the Directive) and, simultaneously, of the most central requirements[7] of any Directive (this contains two *quantitative* considerations: how many requirements are fulfilled and how many of these are crucial in terms of the Directive's aim). In other words, if a Directive is transposed in an essentially correct manner, only a few elements required for full adaptation may be unresolved, and these cannot be essential in terms of the general goals of the Directive. If, as a fictitious example, a Directive on doctors' working time were to be implemented in such a way as to allow doctors in one entire region in a federal state to work double overtime, this would not be essentially correct transposition. If, by contrast, a cross-sectoral Directive on working time (like the one we studied) affects a very large number of groups of workers, and if one group in one of several regions in a federal state is not yet covered by the transposition laws, this may still be essentially correct (given that no other mistakes or shortcomings exist which add to the extent of non-compliance).[8] When we discuss the main reasons for non-compliance (see Chapter 14) we focus on the reasons for and the timing of 'essential' correctness in the transposition phase.

What are our findings? Seventeen out of ninety-one cases (i.e. 19 per cent) were still not essentially correct by the end of April 2003 (note that the transposition deadlines for our six Directives ranged from 30 June 1993 to 20 January 2000).[9] Full correctness had not been reached in

---

[6] Note that the regional implementation laws add a large number of 'cases' to the ninety-one already studied. For practical reasons, we had to rely on the information on the regional state of implementation given by federal experts from the relevant country. We could not carry out a case study for each region with a separate implementation law for any group of workers.

[7] If a Directive has two equally important aims, e.g. protecting pregnant workers and allowing for their employability, both must be realised in an at least essentially correct manner.

[8] Should there be any developments that move counter to the goals of the Directive, this must be taken into consideration and deducted from the degree of adaptation accomplished.

[9] Special deadlines, such as those granted to the UK in the case of those Directives adopted under the original opt-out, are deducted in our calculation of months of delay. So are special extensions of deadlines granted by the European Commission for intense social partner involvement in domestic decision-making on the implementation.

almost half of our cases, i.e. forty out of ninety-one cases.[10] It is interesting to note that the Directive with the latest transposition deadline (the one on part-time work) does not show more cases lacking full correctness (in fact only six) compared with earlier Directives. The highest number is with the Working Time Directive (ten cases), where the deadline was 23 November 1996. The lowest number is with the Directive involving the lowest amount of overall misfit, i.e. the Employment Contract Information Directive (three cases). The number of cases still not essentially correct is not only smaller but also more equal across Directives (with a scale from one case to six cases) and across countries (between two cases and none at all).

13.2.2   Who is misbehaving?

Our empirical analysis shows that all member states misbehave to some extent, but some do so less frequently and less persistently than others (see Table 13.6; for a more in-depth discussion of cross-country patterns beyond the level of merely looking at the delays encountered in our six sample Directives, see Chapter 15).

The table considers the point in time at which the countries had reached essentially correct transposition. It sums up for each country the total delay (in months after the respective deadline) until this status was achieved. It reveals that each and every single member state has at least one case where essential correctness took at least two years of delay to realise. If we focus on delays exceeding four years, all member states but Ireland have at least one case.

According to this benchmark, the Netherlands score best, followed by Ireland, Denmark, the UK and Sweden. The good record of Ireland and the UK is especially remarkable since these two countries were among those that were confronted with the highest degree of overall misfit. At the lower end of the spectrum, France performed worst, with Portugal, Italy, Greece, Belgium, Luxembourg and Germany also evincing a rather bad compliance record. This outcome does not go well with a misfit-centred view on compliance either, since France was among the countries that were confronted with the lowest overall misfit among all member states, and Germany also had to cope with rather low degrees of adaptational pressure (see Table 13.4 above). In Chapter 15, we will provide an explanation for these national patterns, and we will put these figures in perspective where the outcome-oriented ranking represents a misleading picture of the underlying causal mechanisms.

---

[10] The transposition of the Young Workers Directive in the UK was, again, counted as two separate cases.

Table 13.6 *Total delays until essentially correct transposition: country ranking (in months after deadline)*

	EC	PW	WT	YW	PL	PTW	Average
NL	6.0	0.0	1.0	82.5	0.0	(0.0)	14.9
IRL	11.5	3.5	26.0	30.0	25.5	11.0	17.9
DK	0.0	0.0	65.0	0.0	45.0	4.5	19.1
GB	5.0	1.5	59.0	31.0[a]	25.0	3.0	20.8
S	0.0	69.5	78.0	4.5	0.0	17.5	28.3
E	62.0	102.5	0.0	0.0	17.0	14.0	32.6
FIN	0.0	102.5	1.0	82.5	0.0	16.0	33.7
A	0.0	102.5	68.0	30.5	7.0	(0.0)	34.7
D	25.0	102.5	78.0	8.5	31.0	0.0	40.8
LUX	23.0	82.5	27.0	57.0	57.0	(0.0)	41.1
B	114.0	7.0	78.0	35.5	0.0	14.0	41.4
GR	12.0	100.0	77.0	21.0	57.0	0.0	44.5
I	47.0	102.5	77.0	37.5	26.0	2.5	48.8
P	6.0	102.5	78.0	57.5	18.0	39.5	50.3
F	118.0	90.5	53.5	56.0	(0.0)	0.5	53.1

[a] The figure given for the British young workers case represents the average delay encountered in the two implementation phases.

Brackets denote cases where essential correctness was present from the outset.

Shaded cells refer to cases in which essentially correct transposition still had not been reached (as of 30 April 2003), i.e. where the delay will probably increase even further.

Cases where transposition had been completed before the end of the deadline have been counted as involving a delay of 0 months (no negative values).

EC   Employment Contract   YW   Young Workers
PW   Pregnant Workers   PL   Parental Leave
WT   Working Time   PTW   Part-time Work

13.3   The importance of monitoring and enforcement

For the implementation of Directives in the EU multi-level system, monitoring and enforcement are important on two levels: the supranational level and the national level. At the supranational level, the EU Commission influences member state compliance with EU standards via

Table 13.7 *Effectiveness of national enforcement systems (1990s and early 2000s)*[12]

		Criteria Pressure capacity		
Shortcomings	Co-ordination and steering capacity	Resources	Availability of sanctions	Availability of information
None or minor	A, D, F, GB, S	B, D, DK, FIN, I	B, D, E, GR, P	A, B, D, DK, FIN, GB, S
Some	B	A, E, F, GB, LUX, NL	DK, GB, LUX, NL, S	E, GB, P
Significant	E, GR, I	GR, IRL, P	F	GR

infringement procedures that can lead to severe financial sanctions. When and how these infringement proceedings took place and what effect they had on the national implementation processes of the Directives studied here has been analysed in detail in Chapter 11. At this juncture, therefore, we will sum up our most important findings with respect to monitoring and enforcement at the domestic level.

In Chapter 2 we argued that an effective enforcement policy is one (of several)[11] determinants of good compliance with EU law. We set up an analytical framework specifying that national enforcement systems have to meet three criteria to make good application possible: they have to possess adequate *co-ordination and steering capacities*, they must be able to exert sufficient *pressure* on non-compliant individuals, and they have to provide enough *information* to target actors. Table 13.7 gives an overview of the relative performance of different national enforcement systems with regard to these criteria (where the pressure capacity has been further differentiated into resources for inspections and availability of sanctions, to give an even more differentiated picture). The shortcomings of member states are classified according to the categories none or minor, some, or significant. In some cases it just was not possible to assess the information on a country's performance regarding a particular criterion to any definite extent, despite in-depth research. Due to lack of information, therefore, we had to exclude some individual cases from our analysis. If there are significant shortcomings for one or more of our criteria, effective

---

[11] Note that successful application can also be obstructed by other factors such as unclear transposition legislation. Thus, an enforcement system with no or only minor shortcomings is a necessary, but not sufficient, condition for correct application.

[12] Countries or cases that do not show up in the table had to be left out due to lack of information.

enforcement by the member states is not possible and thus we expect application problems. If there are inefficiencies for more than one criterion, enforcement is seriously hampered and application problems become even more likely – at least for specific standards (see also Table 2.3 in Chapter 2).

We cannot provide a summary ranking of effectiveness for two reasons. An overall assessment is difficult because of the varying amounts of information available from the different the countries. Furthermore, it has been argued in Chapter 2 that an enforcement system might perform well for one standard while correct application for another standard is not properly assured. In the remainder of this section, however, we will explain where and why some of the member states have significant enforcement problems and, in doing so, highlight typical deficiencies of national enforcement systems.

Significant shortcomings with regard to the *co-ordination and steering capacity* were observed in Spain, Greece and Italy. In Spain, uneven and overlapping competences of central enforcement authorities and the labour inspectorates in the Autonomous Regions, often working against each other, impede an optimal use of the limited resources (EASHW 1998: 53; Interviews E3: 1257–61, E5: 395–8). However, federal structures do not have to lead to reduced steering capacity on the part of the enforcement system, as the successful work of a specialised co-ordination committee in Germany (*'Länderausschuss für Arbeitsschutz und Sicherheitstechnik'* LASI) shows. In Greece, for most of the 1990s, the decentralised labour inspectorates were attached to the local prefectures. Common data collection or evaluation of problems was lacking. The system as a whole was neither co-ordinated, nor could it react adequately to the most common compliance problems (Interview GR8: 30–5).[13] In Italy, the existence of a whole range of actors (the National Institute of Occupational Safety and Prevention, the Italian Workers' Compensation Authority, the ministerial health service, as well as a number of regional and local bodies) means that the co-ordination efforts of the inspection activities are cumbersome. Against this background, quick interventions geared towards specific situations are impossible, and diverging institutional interests and methodological approaches further paralyse the enforcement system (Interview I11: 65–189).

With regard to the *resources* of national enforcement systems, our analysis reveals that in Austria, France, Germany, Ireland, Luxembourg, the

---

[13] Note that in 1999 the Greek system of labour inspection was recentralised. Although the system has still many shortcomings, its co-ordination and steering capacities have improved since then.

Netherlands, Portugal, Sweden and the UK, the number of inspectors calculated as a ratio for 100,000 dependent workers is below the EU average of 12.56 (albeit in some cases only slightly below). France, Ireland, Luxembourg, Portugal and Sweden have the lowest numbers. In Ireland '[t]he lack of staff [in the central labour inspectorate] has led to a situation where inspections focus heavily on the Dublin area, leaving the rest of the country almost unmonitored' (*Irish Times*, 25 July 2001, p. 7, see also 13 August 2001, p. 16). In three of the remaining countries (France, Sweden and, to a lesser degree, Luxembourg), functional equivalents (occupational physicians, actively monitoring insurance companies and social partners) counterbalance the lack of public inspections.[14] On the other hand, even a high number of inspectors does not guarantee that resources are used efficiently. Even though, in 2000, Greece shared with Denmark the highest ratio of labour inspectors of all fifteen member states, many of the inspectors had not been properly trained by that date (Koniaris 2002: 68; EIRR 302: 25–6). Moreover, inspectors usually spend a rather small amount of their time in the field. Thus the resources actually used for inspections are insufficient.

We would also like to draw attention to a factor that is not linked directly to either the overall number of inspectors or the type of inspections, but that is nevertheless of the utmost importance for explaining application problems of the Directives studied here: the lack of health and safety experts adequately trained to carry out workplace assessments. Such individual workplace assessments were, in many countries, introduced for the first time with the transposition of the Health and Safety Framework Directive of 1989. However, during our research (carried out more than ten years after the adoption of this Directive), we found that in some countries there were still far too few persons able to carry out these assessments. Often, training courses did not start to run until the late 1990s. The effect was that there were no functioning structures on which to build the application of many of the standards contained in the Pregnant Workers and Young Workers Directives and in the Working Time Directive. These shortcomings were most severe in Greece and Portugal (Vogel 1994: 223 and 303).

In France, Sweden, Ireland, the UK, the Netherlands (until 1999) and Denmark (until 2002), no *administrative sanctions* exist. Two points are worth mentioning in this context. First, the introduction of admin-

---

[14] To give just one example: if occupational physicians and actively monitoring insurance companies were added to the number of state inspectors, France would almost double the highest ratio in the fifteen countries included in our study (27.3 in Denmark). However, these actors only dedicate part of their time to workplace inspections and thus a realistic ratio should be situated somewhere in between.

istrative sanctions in two of the six countries that had not known such sanctions before shows an (albeit weak) tendency to convergence. Second, in most of the cases where administrative sanctions are absent, this is tied in with well-functioning arbitration and conciliation institutions (e.g. the Advisory, Conciliation and Arbitration Service (ACAS) for general labour law questions in the UK or the *Commissie Gelijke Behandeling* for discrimination issues in the Netherlands) or with a co-operative management approach that is geared towards the prevention of non-compliance problems from the outset (Sweden). A clear example where the lack of administrative sanctions significantly decreases the pressure capacity of the enforcement system is France. Here, the congestion of the court system delays decisions for years and de facto prevents pressure via legal channels, leaving inspectors with no adequate means to make unwilling addressees comply with EU labour law standards within an acceptable time span. This problem is most acute in the Paris region, while it is likely that resources in the other regions are more apt to provide the necessary enforcement (Interview F10: 424–34). It should be noted that, within the French enforcement system, pressure might also be successfully exercised through other actors such as insurance companies (see above, note 14).

The classification of member states with respect to the *availability of information* has to be treated even more carefully than for the other criteria, since in general the degree of information received or provided is difficult to assess. Moreover, many different actors come into play and thus the effectiveness of an enforcement system varies with respect to the standard and group of workers under scrutiny. A good example is Greece, where the overall availability of information is clearly insufficient, due to a mainly reactive public enforcement policy and the fact that trade unions are comparatively uninterested in the standards studied here, while at the same time, some newly established institutions for specific aspects, such as the Hellenic Institute for Occupational Health and Safety (ELINYAE) or the Administrative Research Council for Equal Opportunities (KETHI), counterbalance the deficit to some extent.

A look at the three criteria for the potential ineffectiveness of domestic enforcement systems results in six EU member states having *significant problems* in one or several of our categories (see Table 13.7). In two of these countries (France and Spain), the shortcomings appear to be less grave than the ones in the remaining four member states. The enforcement and application problems observed in Greece, Ireland, Italy, and Portugal, however, are so significant in overall terms that we regard these countries as *neglecting their duty to ensure* not only legal transposition, but also *a reasonable level of practical compliance*. The enforcement system in

Greece has considerable problems in all three main categories, which seriously hampers its performance. In Ireland and Portugal, the number of inspectors is much too small to guarantee that violations of the legal rules may actually be discovered and prosecuted. In Italy, finally, the poor co-ordination among the multitude of different monitoring actors is a serious obstacle to proper enforcement.

It is also important to emphasise that, even though the quality of domestic enforcement systems does have an important influence on application success or failure, no single government can completely ignore EU standards by simply omitting effective enforcement. Complete implementation of EU Directives even in the absence of active state efforts can be induced by individual complaints in national courts and by active interest groups (depending on their *locus standi* in the member state). Moreover, the direct effect doctrine of the European Court of Justice even means that employees in the public sector, where the state acts as an employer, may directly invoke the rights arising from EU Directives, irrespective of whether or not they have been implemented properly by the domestic government.

In sum, our study clearly indicates that there is a non-compliance problem in the European Union. This has been contested at times in the literature on the basis of available statistical data. For example, Tanja Börzel has argued that 'we have simply no evidence that the European Union suffers from a serious compliance deficit which is claimed by the European Commission and academics alike' (Börzel 2001: abstract). We can now offer data that actually do measure the actual level of non-compliance in the EU member states. In our field of empirical analysis, one must no longer rely on data that represent but 'the tip of the iceberg' and furthermore distort the representation of compliance (see also Chapter 16).

14   Why do member states fail to comply?
Testing the hypotheses suggested
in the literature

This chapter discusses in detail the hypotheses on the reasons for implementation success or failure which we derived from the existing literature as well as a number of new ones which we formulated on the basis of our own theoretical considerations (see Chapter 2). We argue that the 'upstream phase' (i.e. features of the decision-making process which leads to the adoption of a Directive) has only a limited impact on the 'downstream phase' of adaptation at the national level. Furthermore, we highlight the differential impact of domestic factors in EU policy implementation. The analysis reveals that no single overriding variable may account for the transposition performance of member states, but that we need to look at the interaction of several factors. As the next chapter will show in more detail, the relevant combinations of factors and the logic of their interplay vary fundamentally in different country clusters.

14.1   Implementation problems as a result of 'opposition through the backdoor'?

According to an intergovernmentalist view of European policy-making,[1] the preference formation processes of the lower-level polity and the higher-level polity are clearly distinct. This implies that in cases where a national government is unsuccessful in 'uploading' its own preferences at the EU level as the template for the joint measure or standard, it will try to resist during the 'downloading' process, i.e. later at the implementation stage.[2] Hence, in those cases where there is no national objection to a specific measure during decision-making at EU level, implementation should be unproblematic. Non-transposition or incorrect implementation could thus be considered as a way of protesting against defeat in the EU decision-making process, i.e. as 'opposition through the backdoor'.

---

[1] For intergovernmentalism in European integration research, see most importantly Moravcsik (1993).

[2] For the uploading versus downloading terminology, see Börzel (2002a).

Although our cases revealed some instances of this pattern, the pattern clearly could not account for a major part of all the transposition problems observed. It has to be noted, however, that establishing which governments actually resisted individual provisions of a draft Directive at some point in the negotiations is not an easy task. The final voting behaviour is not a very good indicator of support or opposition. Especially under the qualified majority rule, which forms the basis of most of our Directives, governments may preventively discard certain policy options which they might have pursued under unanimity. Hence, there may very well be a certain amount of concealed opposition during the EU-level negotiations. On the other hand, it is by no means necessary that a government should resist the transposition of a provision whose adoption it regards with a certain scepticism.

At any rate, our empirical analysis revealed only three out of ninety-one cases where opposition at the beginning of the EU decision-making process was followed by opposition at the implementation stage or, in other words, where opposition through the back door was the main reason for late or incorrect adaptation (Falkner et al. 2004). Hence, the Conservative UK government resisted transposing the Working Time and Young Workers Directives because the Commission's 'treaty-base game' (Rhodes 1995: 99) made it impossible for the UK to veto these proposals in Brussels. Similarly, the German government refused to transpose the Working Time Directive correctly because it had failed in its attempts in Brussels to ensure that the Directive did not interfere with central elements of its own deregulation plans (see Chapters 6 and 7).

Among the three countries which joined the EU in 1995 (Austria, Sweden and Finland), there might be further cases where transposition problems could possibly have been avoided if the respective governments had taken part in the negotiations at the EU level. Hence, Austria had no chance of protesting against being compelled to lift its general night work ban for pregnant women since it had not been a member of the EU when the Directive was adopted. The same is true for Sweden with regard to the need to introduce a compulsory maternity leave of two weeks (see Chapter 5). It could also be speculated that Austria might have pressed for a softening of the Working Time Directive's effects on the Austrian hospitals sector, had it been able to do so when the Directive was agreed in Brussels. Maybe the Swedish government also would have attempted to ensure more flexibility in the Working Time Directive in order to preserve social partner autonomy at the domestic level (see Chapter 12).

Given the relatively small share of transposition problems caused by explicit opposition through the backdoor, we can nevertheless conclude that the intergovernmentalist view is clearly insufficient for explaining the complex reality of non-compliance with EU Directives. To be more precise, while one part of the argument is at least not completely flawed, the other is almost totally disproved by our empirical cases. As to the former part, it is indeed not unlikely that governments use the transposition phase as 'a continuation of policy-making by other means'. Hence, if governments actually voiced fierce opposition during the negotiation process, there were a number of examples among our cases in which they actually chose to refuse proper implementation afterwards.[3] Since these three cases all belong to the group of Directives adopted on the basis of qualified majority voting, we can conclude that this decision mode increases the likelihood of domestic opposition as a reaction to defeat during the EU-level negotiations. Hence, we should expect that this particular problem of opposition through the back door should increase somewhat with the proliferation of qualified majority voting in Council (and with increasing powers of the European Parliament to push through decisions which might contradict the interests of certain governments). However, as we will demonstrate in Chapter 15, cultural factors make it unlikely that opposition by a government in the decision-making process is met with resistance by the same government at the implementation stage. In other words, the intergovernmentalist assumptions, in so far as they draw an accurate picture of empirical reality at all, do not hold for all countries alike.

The inverse argument, notably that we should expect *no* transposition problems if governments agreed to a particular Directive, has to be clearly refuted on the basis of our empirical material. There are indeed many other causes for domestic non-compliance which are totally unrelated to the features of the prior decision-making process at the European level. In the light of this finding, therefore, the potential negative effect of qualified majority voting in terms of transposition effectiveness has to be narrowed considerably. In our cases, most compliance problems were unrelated to how decisions were taken at EU level.

---

[3] Note that this is only true for opposition to too far-reaching provisions of the Directives. Since we are talking about minimum standards which do not force member states with higher standards to lower their levels of protection, this does not make sense if governments are concerned about the Directives being too modest, as was the case with Italy's and Spain's objections to the huge amount of exemptions granted to the UK by the Young Workers Directive, or with Italy's protest against the low level of maternity pay granted by the Pregnant Workers Directive (see Chapters 5 and 7). By implication, this argument can also be extended to the social dialogue Directives. In the part-time case, German and French unions criticised the low level of ambition of the agreement and refused to approve of it within the ETUC (see Chapter 9). However, these unions had no reason to exert opposition during the transposition process, since the relatively low level of the agreed standards, if compared with the existing rules, did not mean that the domestic regulations had to be lowered.

Finally, the 'uploading' and 'downloading' metaphor seems to be flawed in yet another respect. It rests on the assumption that governments are for the most part struggling to export their national regulatory models to Europe in order to minimise adaptation costs. However, our empirical analysis has revealed quite a number of cases where governments openly accepted EU Directives even though they required far-reaching changes at the domestic level. In November 1993, for example, the Working Time Directive was passed with the favourable votes of the Irish centre-left government, although the Directive meant a fundamental (and costly) tightening of the loose statutory working time regime in place in Ireland (see Chapter 6). In October 1993 and in November 1994, the same Irish government also supported the draft Parental Leave Directive when it was still being debated in the Council of Ministers, despite the fact that the Directive obliged Ireland to introduce a completely new parental leave scheme. This is all the more remarkable since Irish employers' organisations fiercely lobbied the government to vote against the proposal (*Irish Times*, 18 November 1993, p. 8, 23 September 1994, p. 2). The same applies to Luxembourg, where the government accepted the Parental Leave Directive although it also implied the introduction of a completely new parental leave system (Interview LUX11: 77–102, 774–830). There are even strong indications that the government welcomed the Directive as an opportunity to overcome national employers' opposition to such a project. Similarly, the social democratic Danish government voted in favour of the Young Workers Directive in the Council of Ministers even though it entailed considerable restriction of the comparatively liberal Danish child labour system.

It is quite obvious that, in all of these cases, the domestic governments were not motivated by the will to defend their own regulatory models against interference from Brussels. Quite the contrary, they supported the measures debated in Council for political reasons, specifically because they corresponded to their own reform agendas. In the cases just mentioned, it is obvious that party politics or ideologies played a major role in bringing about support for the seemingly 'inconvenient' labour law reforms. In other words, the parties in government were ideologically inclined to accept the 'costs' resulting from the proposed Directives. The 'two-level game' (Putnam 1993) helped overcome domestic opposition.

14.2   Domestic 'agency loss' and unintended consequences as a cause for transposition difficulties?

According to historical institutionalist or constructivist approaches, the EU policy-making process entails many more possibilities for decisions being made that do not represent the preferences of domestic governments. First, such decisions could result from 'agency loss' (Kiewit and McCubbins 1991: 5), i.e. processes of learning or socialisation on the part of domestic negotiators taking part in COREPER and the Council working groups (Hayes-Renshaw and Wallace 1997; Joerges and Neyer 1997; Jørgensen 1997; Lewis 1998; Christiansen et al. 1999; Joerges and Vos 1999; Lewis 2000). Secondly, the complex character of the issues in question and the large number of individual items on the agenda may confront negotiators with serious *information problems* so that they might not be able to assess the consequences of the options on the table properly (Eichener 1996: 276–7; Pierson 1996: 136–9; Eichener 2000: 309–14; for an early version of this argument, see also Weiler 1988: 352).

While we have not detected any significant cases of agency loss in the sense of domestic negotiators agreeing to issues which ran counter to the instructions they received from their capitals,[4] our empirical analysis did reveal several instances where negotiators were not fully aware of the true consequences of the Directives on the negotiation table. This was mainly the case when the Commission or the ECJ reinterpreted the meaning of certain provisions long after the adoption of the underlying Directives. The most prominent example is the ECJ's *SIMAP* ruling, in which the judges considered on-call duties to be an integral part of working time while most countries hitherto had treated such duties (partly) as rest periods (see Chapter 6). Unless the ongoing negotiations on revising the Directive will modify this provision, many countries may have to bear considerable costs resulting from a change to the shift systems especially in hospitals. It is obvious that national governments were not aware of this effect when they agreed on the text of the Working Time Directive in 1993.

Similarly, the Danish government was, most definitely, originally unaware of the fact that it was actually impossible, under Danish conditions, to make use of the Maastricht Treaty's 'Christoffersen clause', which explicitly allowed member states to endow the social partners with the task of implementing EU Directives. When the Danes first tried to take advantage of this clause in the case of the Working Time Directive,

---

[4] Note that here we are talking about *significant* cases of agency loss. We cannot rule out the possibility that minor instances of agency loss also occurred in our cases. However, we did not find any major cases where negotiators ignored significant parts of their negotiation mandates. It has to be noted, nevertheless, that the main focus of our research design lay on analysing transposition processes rather than EU-level negotiations. Hence, we did not (and, for reasons of time and resources, *could* not) explicitly concentrate on discovering instances of domestic agency loss during the negotiations. Thus, the fact that we did not find such phenomena does not necessarily mean that no instances exist.

it took a painful learning process before they realised that the ECJ's criterion with regard to full coverage of the relevant workforce was too high a benchmark for the Danish system of autonomous collective bargaining to attain (see Chapter 12).

Likewise, when member state governments agreed on the Pregnant Workers Directive, it was not clear to all of them that the Directive would subsequently be interpreted by the Commission in such a way as to challenge the general night work bans on pregnant workers operational in many member states. In particular, the Commission told German officials during the EU-level negotiations that the Directive would allow Germany to sustain its ban on night work, which formed the basis of Germany endorsing the Directive. Subsequently, though, the Commission changed its mind and began to use its powers as a 'guardian of the Treaties' in order to attack the general night work ban in Germany and a number of other countries. Hence, the Commission employed a 'Trojan horse strategy' by consciously exploiting the interpretative leeway the Directive offered for pushing through policy goals of which member state governments were originally not aware.

However, the extent to which these problems of agency loss and incomplete information actually occurred did not vary systematically between different member states. From the literature on the various institutional models for organising the EU-related decision-making process prevalent in the different member states, we could have expected cross-country variance, with tightly co-ordinated and effectively monitored systems being better in avoiding these problems than loosely co-ordinated and poorly monitored systems driven by departmental autonomy and immense leeway for negotiators in Brussels (Kassim et al. 2001a, 2001b; Wessels et al. 2003). And yet this expectation does not hold true if we look at our empirical studies. First of all, agency loss does not seem to have been a major problem in our cases. Hence, both centralised systems with effective horizontal and vertical co-ordination mechanisms, like the French, Danish or British ones, and loosely co-ordinated systems, like the German or even the Greek ones, were able to prevent the civil servants negotiating in Brussels from agreeing on points which were significantly at odds with the policy positions of their respective governments back home.

Second, the observed problems resulting from incomplete information about the consequences of legal texts agreed in Brussels were such that they could not be avoided by organisational factors. Even a negotiator with perfect information about the possible consequences of a particular Directive could not have foreseen the Court's reinterpretation of the Working Time Directive in the *SIMAP* case or the Commission's change of strategy with regard to the issue of general night work bans for pregnant women. Hence, we can conclude that, regardless of their specific administrative institutions, member states were able (or unable, as the case may be) to assess the consequences of the policy decisions taken in Brussels. But none of them could avoid being affected by the considerable leeway granted to the ECJ and the Commission in interpreting these decisions.

14.3 Facilitating smooth adaptation through effective and widespread consultation in the upstream phase?

One of the main conclusions of early research into the implementation of EU Directives was that implementation problems could be remedied if the government consulted all the relevant domestic actors (especially parliaments and important interest groups) during the EU-level negotiations. Otherwise, the actors who had been ignored in the upstream phase might obstruct implementation during the downstream phase.[5]

In our cases this factor played a certain but by no means decisive role. While significant consultation deficits in the upstream phase might have been a serious problem at the end of the 1980s and the beginning of the 1990s, the situation seems to have improved in the course of the 1990s. In the meantime, all member states have established some sort of procedure to keep their parliaments up to date on EU policy-making. While there are great differences in the actual powers of the domestic parliaments within these procedures (Maurer and Wessels 2001), only the Austrian and Danish parliaments have the power to issue negotiation mandates that are compulsory for the government.

Hence, all *domestic parliaments* are in some way involved in everyday EU affairs, but they usually have no decisive say in determining the stance their government should take in Council.[6] But parliaments are no veto players in the transposition process, either. All fifteen member states now have a parliamentary system of government in which governments are usually supported by a majority in parliament. Hence, both governments and their parliamentary majorities are not usually opposed to each other, but co-operate, since they are both tied together by party cohesion.[7] At

---

[5] See, for instance, Ciavarini Azzi (1988: 196–8); Kooiman, Yntema and Lintsen (1988: 601–2); Pag and Wessels (1988: 172–3); Rasmussen (1988: 111–13); Weiler (1988: 349–50); Schwarze, Becker and Pollack (1993b: 82–3); Van den Bossche (1996: 377–8); and Ciavarini Azzi (2000: 59–60).

[6] Even where parliaments *formally* enjoy far-reaching rights, as in Austria and Denmark, *in practice* the workload is often very high, which makes it difficult for the parliamentary committees concerned to make use of their rights effectively (see, for example, Falkner et al. 1999; Müller 2000; Pedersen 2000).

[7] The situation is different in countries such as Denmark and Sweden (and to some extent Portugal and Spain), where minority governments are a frequent phenomenon.

any rate, we have not found a single case where a parliament blocked the transposition of a Directive simply because it had not been properly consulted before the decision was taken at the EU level.

When it comes to the *role of important interest groups* such as the social partners, at least some of our cases stress the importance of involving these actors in the upstream phase. Social partner organisations, like national parliaments, do not enjoy *formal* veto power in the transposition process. Nevertheless, they may be 'powerful players' (Strøm 2003: 32) in the sense that they can exert influence on actors with veto power and therefore might be able to delay or even block the transposition process. In the light of the above-mentioned literature, problems are most likely to occur in cases where social partner involvement is particularly weak in the upstream phase, but strong as regards the implementation of Directives. In order to assess this assumption empirically, we classified our cases according to a taxonomy of social partner involvement that includes the categories of *no or negligible involvement, consultation, concertation, complementary legislation* and *social partner autonomy*. These categories were applied to both the upstream and the downstream phase.[8]

One of the results of this analysis was that an unbalanced social partner involvement between the negotiation and the implementation phase was proven to be quite rare. In many countries where the social partners are strongly involved in the national transposition process (either in the form of concertation, supplementary legislation or even autonomous transposition by way of collective agreements), they are also regularly involved before a national government decides upon a draft Directive in the Council.[9] This is, for example, the case in Denmark, Finland, Sweden and Austria, where there are formalised procedures granting the social partners participation in the upstream phase.[10]

An important example of differential social partner involvement, however, is Belgium. In Belgium the social partners play a very important role in the field of social policy and labour law. A collective agreement

Particularly if the supporting parties of the minority government vary from one legislative project to the next, party cohesion will only work as a loose bond. A consensual relationship between government and parliament prior to EU decisions is therefore more important. The case of the Young Workers Directive in Denmark (see Chapter 7), however, underlines that even a strong parliamentary involvement at this stage is no guarantee for smooth implementation if a change of government occurs between the EU level negotiation and the implementation process.

[8] For the operationalisation of these categories, see Chapter 12.

[9] On the other hand, where the social partners only play a minor role during the transposition process, their role during the upstream phase is often relatively weak as well. This is true for countries such as France, the UK or Greece.

[10] The cases in which the Directives were negotiated at EU level before Sweden, Finland and Austria joined the EU were, of course, exceptional in our sample.

(*convention collective de travail*, CCT) concluded by the main social partner organisations is a common legal instrument in the area of labour law. Once the social partners have reached agreement, as occurs in the sectoral joint committees or the National Labour Council (*Conseil National du Travail*), it is possible to give their agreements *erga omnes* effect for the entire workforce in the private sector (Engels and Vanachter 1998: 35; Interview B5: 72–90). This procedure can also be applied to the transposition of Directives, which allocates the social partners an important role in this phase. During the negotiations of Directives at EU level, in contrast, Belgian administrative routines failed for a long time to provide a formal means of social partner involvement. It is only since 1999 that the social partners have been officially consulted by the Ministry of Labour in the run-up to each Council meeting concerned with labour and social affairs. Interviews revealed that the ministry wanted to prevent frequently occurring conflicts between the government and the social partners during the transposition phase (Interviews B10: 334–46, B5: 517–48). The perception among ministry officials was that existing informal contacts at the preparatory stage of Directives were not sufficient to avoid transposition problems. Indeed, at least one of our Belgian case studies corroborates this picture (Working Time Directive). In this case, conflicts between the government and the social partners significantly contributed to the transposition process being seriously delayed.

In Austria, there was also one case where the exclusion of an important social partner organisation from the EU negotiations contributed to implementation problems. When the EU-level social partners held their talks on the parental leave issue, the Austrian Federal Economic Chamber (*Wirtschaftskammer Österreichs*, WKÖ) was excluded from these negotiations. As an organisation with compulsory membership, it is not allowed to become a member of UNICE and so it could not take part in the negotiations between the European social partners.[11] When the Directive was implemented, the WKÖ fiercely opposed the introduction of the individual right to parental leave, trying to argue that the Directive's wording was ambiguous (Interviews A1: 885–97, A8: 506–49). Since the Austrian grand coalition government at that time aimed at a compromise solution between the social partners, the transposition process was delayed. In

[11] This problem has since been resolved. The WKÖ is a member of UEAPME, the major European organisation for small and medium-sized enterprises. After the adoption of the Parental Leave Directive, UEAPME instigated an ECJ procedure in order to lodge a complaint about its exclusion from the negotiations and have the Directive nullified. The case was rejected by the ECJ but nevertheless, in 1998, UNICE and UEAPME agreed that in future EU social partner negotiations UEAPME would be represented in the UNICE negotiation team, thus enabling the WKÖ to be involved as well.

addition, the compromise solution was not fully in line with the Directive (see Chapter 8).

Despite these singular examples, the overall picture we gained from our cases was that a lack of social partner involvement in the upstream phase was not a very significant problem. In many cases where discussions with the social partners caused implementation problems (see also section 14.12 below), this was not directly linked to opposition against the standards of the Directive, but rather concerned other issues linked to the transposition process. It seems that the two phases are ultimately not as closely connected as one might have expected. There are many examples where the national transposition process gained a dynamic of its own, especially if the incorporation of the EU standards into national law became linked domestically to other controversial issues on the agenda. These additional, domestically created conflicts could not be foreseen when the Directive was negotiated. Hence, they could not have been avoided even if the social partners or other important actors had been intensively involved in the upstream phase.

14.4 Improving compliance by drafting clearer Directives?

Contrary to the limited explanatory power of the factors discussed so far, we have found some empirical support for the argument that proper adaptation becomes difficult if the text of the Directive to be transposed is worded vaguely and lacks clarity and consistency.[12] The rationale underlying this argument is based on the reasoning of principal-agent theory and contract theory (Williamson 1985; Hart and Homström 1987; Kiewit and McCubbins 1991). From this perspective, an EU Directive (or any other piece of legislation) may be understood as a contract between legislators (the principals) and implementing actors (the agents). Ambiguous wording of the legislative measure means that the contract is 'incomplete'. This leaves ample room for 'agency loss', which then gives rise to deficient implementation outcomes. Indeed, our empirical results show that a lack of legal quality with particular provisions gave rise to serious interpretation problems at the transposition stage in quite a number of cases. As a result, either transposition was delayed due to long debates about the proper interpretation or individual provisions were transposed incorrectly because governments decided to follow an erroneous interpretation.

---

[12] See, for example, Weiler (1988: 354–5); Schwarze, Becker and Pollack (1993b: 94); Van den Bossche (1996: 383); Demmke (1998: 94); Ciavarini Azzi (2000: 52).

In fifteen out of our ninety-one cases, at least some implementation problems were caused by a lack of clarity and consistency with regard to the underlying Directives.[13] The clearest example of this pattern is the Pregnant Workers Directive, which created a number of implementation problems due to the ambiguity of its general policy goals and its wording. The negotiations on the Directive were characterised by a clash between those who favoured a prohibitive approach to protecting pregnant women from harmful working conditions by means of general employment prohibitions and those who wanted to avoid as much as possible the creation of unnecessary obstacles to women participating in the labour market. Since this clash of regulatory philosophies was never resolved, the resulting Directive was 'Janus-faced' in that it contained elements of both approaches.[14]

This caused confusion in Luxembourg, where the government, encouraged by a misleading provision in the Directive, initially enacted a reform which was very prohibitive and clearly violated the individual risk assessment approach of the Directive. As already mentioned above, the German government, encouraged by an informal statement from the Commission, interpreted the Directive in a way which meant that the general ban on night work for pregnant women in Germany could be upheld. But then the Commission changed its mind, with the result that Germany (at the time of writing) faces the threat of legal action if it does not lift its ban. A slightly different problem occurred in Spain. Here, the fact that the Directive envisaged the drawing up of guidelines

---

[13] The following cases were counted: Pregnant Workers Directive in Germany (general night work ban on pregnant women), and in Luxembourg and Spain (risk assessment); Working Time Directive in Belgium, Greece and the UK (qualifying periods for annual leave entitlements); Young Workers Directive in Austria and Finland (weekly rest period); Parental Leave Directive in Ireland, Luxembourg and the UK (cut-off date), and in Greece and Spain (definition of *'force majeure* leave'); Part-time Work Directive in Belgium (scope of exemption for 'work on a casual basis' and meaning of 'objective reasons' legitimising unequal treatment) and in Ireland (meaning of the term 'employment conditions'). In principle, this list would have to be extended to include countries like Austria, Germany, Ireland, the Netherlands or Spain, where the *SIMAP* ruling of the ECJ arguing that on-call duties have to be fully counted as working time requires significant adaptations in hospitals and other areas where on-call work is a widespread phenomenon. But since we did not count adaptational pressure arising from this complete and largely unforeseeable reinterpretation of the Working Time Directive as a violation of the Directive itself, we did not include these cases in the calculation here.

[14] To a lesser degree, this is also true of the Part-time Work Directive. Here, the tension is between the binding part of the Directive, which focuses on the protection of part-time workers, and the soft-law provisions, which contain further elements of protection as well as a number of recommendations aiming to facilitate the access to part-time work and to remove obstacles to this type of work. Since the ambiguity of this Directive is only contained in the non-binding parts, it posed less of a problem in terms of compliance.

for the implementation of the annexes, which were only published eight years after the adoption of the Directive, provided an elegant pretext for the Spanish government to postpone (and in essence to abandon) transposition of the annexes of the Directive (see Chapter 5).

It is noteworthy that most of the interpretation problems were accompanied by political resistance from governments or important interest groups towards the provisions in question. In other words, most interpretation problems only occurred when a particular provision was contested by domestic actors. In such a situation, however, vaguely worded provisions often encouraged national governments to explore the limits of what might or might not be allowed by simply transposing the provisions in question according to an interpretation which caused the least controversy domestically. It also seems that sometimes they even anticipated a negative ruling by the ECJ, but took this into account because it was politically less costly for them to discount strong interest group pressure if they could point to an authoritative judgment by the ECJ.

In Ireland and the UK, for example, the introduction of a cut-off date excluding certain parents from the right to take parental leave was caused by fierce lobbying by employers in order to avoid 'unnecessary' costs. The introduction of such a cut-off date was neither unequivocally allowed nor explicitly prohibited by the Directive. Therefore, the two governments gave in to employer pressure and waited for the Commission or the European Court of Justice to issue an authoritative interpretation which finally disallowed the cut-off date (see Chapter 8). The same was true of the introduction in the UK of a qualifying period of thirteen weeks before workers could be eligible for annual leave. Employers' organisations had pressed hard to reduce the costs of implementing the Working Time Directive. Hence, the UK government introduced a qualifying period excluding workers on short-term contracts from the right to annual leave. But since the Directive was far from clear on this point, it took an ECJ ruling to clarify that the operation of such a qualifying period was not in line with the Directive (see Chapter 6).

At least some of these problems could have been avoided if the Directives had been worded less loosely. But ambiguous wording is often an inbuilt consequence of the negotiation dynamics prevailing at the European level. In other words, unclear wording sometimes serves as an instrument to make proposals agreeable in the Council of Ministers, as was obviously the case when the Pregnant Workers Directive was negotiated (Schuster 2000). Hence, the conclusion that implementation could be improved by drafting clearer Directives is perhaps of little assistance under real-world conditions. The Commission could alternatively try to improve its contacts with national officials in order to clarify interpretation problems before they lead to implementation flaws.

Our empirical analysis has revealed that the amount of informal communication between the Commission and national capitals during the transposition phase is surprisingly small, at least in the area of labour law, and could certainly be intensified. For example, the practice of creating specific working groups bringing together Commission officials and national civil servants in charge of transposing a particular Directive could be extended beyond the present level. At any rate, no such working group was set up with a view to implementing our six Directives. According to our information, from the labour law Directives enacted in the 1990s, only the transposition of the Directive in European Works Councils was accompanied by such a working group – apparently with rather positive results (see, for example, Weber 1997).[15]

14.5   The failure of the misfit hypothesis

One of our main results is that the misfit hypothesis, which has characterised much of the recent literature on the implementation of EU policies, cannot adequately explain our ninety-one cases of labour law (non-) transposition. Francesco Duina and Frank Blithe (1999) offer probably the clearest formulation of the misfit hypothesis (see also Duina 1997, 1999):[16]

'[W]e hypothesize that implementation of common market rules depends primarily on the fit between rules and the policy legacy and the organization of interest groups in member states. Rules that challenge national policy legacies and the organization of interest groups are not implemented fully and on time; they are normally rejected, typically reaching domestic systems only partially and long after the official deadlines. ... When, on the other hand, rules propose principles consistent with those found in national institutions, implementation is a smooth affair and the common market reaches smoothly and deeply into the nation-state.'

In other words, if the degree of misfit is high, transposition should be seriously hampered, whereas we should expect smooth adaptation if the amount of changes required by a Directive is small.

---

[15] As some of the Directives impinge on the area of occupational health and safety, they might have been debated in the Advisory Committee on Safety, Hygiene and Health Protection at Work in Luxembourg. However, this is not the same as the specialised implementation working groups to which we refer in this paragraph.

[16] Similar arguments have been presented by Knill and Lenschow (1998, 1999, 2000a) and, in a slightly less deterministic way, by Börzel (2000). For a critical view of the misfit hypothesis, see Héritier and Knill (2001).

Table 14.1 *Degrees of misfit and transposition performance*

	Degree of misfit		
Timing (Months after deadline)	low	medium	high
(almost) on time (0–6)	11	9	2
significantly delayed (>6)	33	24	8

Benchmark: essentially correct transposition
Dark shaded cells represent cases which are inconsistent with the misfit hypothesis.
White cells refer to cases for which no clear expectations may be derived from the hypothesis.
Light shaded cells denote cases which are in principle consistent with the misfit hypothesis.
Four cases have been omitted since essential correctness existed from the outset.

As Table 14.1 shows, only 22 per cent of all cases are completely in line with the expectations of the hypothesis (light shaded cells), either because small adaptation requirements were indeed followed by smooth transposition or because large-scale misfit accompanied significantly delayed adaptation. However, 40 per cent of all cases are at odds with the misfit hypothesis (dark shaded cells). A further 38 per cent of our cases are located in the area of medium adaptational pressure, for which no clear expectations may be derived from the hypothesis. In order to explain these cases, Knill and Lenschow (2001: 124–6) point to the presence or absence of a 'supportive actor constellation' without, however, specifying what such a constellation should look like. The theoretical models of scholars like Börzel (2000) or Duina (1997, 1999) do not cover these cases at all, although they are far from being negligible empirically.

In order to avoid the 'black box' of medium-scale adaptational pressure, we could treat 'misfit' also as a continuous variable. The misfit hypothesis would then postulate that implementation problems should increase with rising degrees of misfit. Even under these modified assumptions, however, our data are far from corroborating the argument (see Figure 14.1).

The figure shows the relationship between the average degree of misfit with which the fifteen member states had to cope when transposing our six Directives and their actual performance measured in terms of average transposition delays. Clearly, the data does not square with the expectations of the hypothesis. Rather than the expected correlation, the figure, surprisingly, reveals an inverse relationship: the higher the degree of misfit, our data suggests, the better the member states' transposition performance. In other words, countries that on average had to overcome only

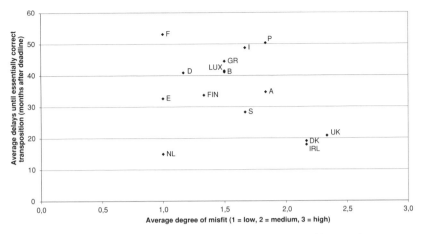

Figure 14.1 Average degrees of misfit and transposition performance

minor misfit, such as Germany or France, showed a rather bad compliance record, whereas countries that were confronted with relatively high degrees of adaptational pressure, such as Denmark, Ireland or the UK, tended to be among the member states with the best transposition performance.

These results clearly disprove the misfit hypothesis. But what about the inverse relationship between misfit and transposition outcomes suggested by Figure 14.1? Does transposition really become easier with rising adaptational pressure? The discussion in the next chapter will demonstrate that this counterintuitive logic does actually exist, but that it applies only to a specific group of cases. With regard to the remaining cases, it will actually prove to be a spurious correlation. In fact, the largest part of the observed transposition performance of member states may be explained by other factors. We can thus conclude that if there is any direct causal impact of the degree of misfit on member state compliance, the effect is undoubtedly much weaker than many scholars would expect, and the direction of this effect is sometimes even inverse to what has been suggested in the literature.

14.6 Qualitative mismatches as a partial explanation for implementation problems

The explanatory power of the misfit argument increases somewhat if we specifically focus on cases in which regulatory philosophies or deeply entrenched national models were challenged. In these cases of qualitative misfit, domestic governments frequently did react as expected by a misfit-centred view, i.e. they 'acted as guardians of the status quo, as the shield protecting national legal-administrative traditions' (Duina 1997: 157). However, the occurrence of such qualitative misfit does not *necessarily* lead to domestic resistance, as is implied by the misfit hypothesis. While governments in some cases actually reacted with opposition, they readily gave up their regulatory traditions and transformed their existing systems in others.

For example, the Swedish government initially refused to comply with a clause enshrined in the Pregnant Workers Directive which required it to introduce a period of two weeks' *compulsory* maternity leave. This resistance was based on the argument that such a step would run counter to the employability-centred character of the existing Swedish regulations, which offered pregnant women the choice of whether or not they wanted to go to work (Interview S12). The Swedish opposition could only be overcome after the Commission had initiated an infringement procedure.

In a similar way, but against a totally different background, the governments of Austria and Italy have so far resisted the employability pressure that the same Directive exerted on their prohibitive systems. Both have so far refused to lift their general bans on night work for pregnant women since they considered their existing schemes superior to the Directive's system based on individual medical certificates. The same was initially true for Luxembourg, which only lifted its ban after the Commission had taken legal steps. Similarly, the Portuguese government only partly lifted its ban, but continued to prohibit night work by pregnant women for three months around the date of birth. Germany has hitherto also refused to lift its general ban on night work for pregnant women. However, recent debates within the left-wing government parties indicate that a process of incremental change has taken place, supported by corresponding party-political agendas, which might ultimately lead to a fundamental overhaul of the prohibitive approach of the German pregnant workers legislation (see above, Chapter 5).

A similar case is the defence by the Danish and Swedish governments of their traditions of autonomous social partnership. In the working time case, both governments tried to preserve these traditions, Denmark by delegating transposition to the social partners, Sweden by enacting a fence system which interfered as little as possible with the autonomy of the social partners. However, both measures were insufficient to meet the requirements of the Directive and more intrusive state intervention was necessary. Denmark finally gave in to Commission pressure and passed legislation to comply with the Directive, while Sweden is still struggling to create an adequate replacement for its more or less symbolic transposition (see Chapter 12).

However, the Danish case reveals that resistance may gradually be overcome as actors learn to cope with new circumstances. Autonomous social partner implementation was once more attempted in the case of parental leave, but again this measure was criticised by the European Commission as not being able to guarantee full coverage for all employees. Therefore, Denmark refrained from this sort of implementation when the Part-time Work Directive had to be transposed. Although this Directive also touched on an area which had traditionally been left to autonomous social partner regulation, the Danish government and the social partners agreed not to insist on defending the 'Danish model'. Instead, the Directive was implemented by way of a new system of 'negotiated legislation' in which the social partners determine the substance of an agreement, which is then made generally binding by supplementary legislation (see Chapter 12). Hence, these examples also underline the fact that an exclusively misfit-oriented perspective is not able to grasp this kind of adjustment of national actors to new circumstances. This is only possible if time sequences are taken into consideration as well.

A further example of domestic resistance to qualitatively mismatching provisions enshrined in EU Directives is the (initial) reaction of the Austrian and German governments to the Parental Leave Directive. In both countries, the Directive's gender equality thrust qualitatively challenged the existing schemes, which excluded single-income families (and thus the typical male-breadwinner couples) from the right to take parental leave. Moreover, the Austrian scheme in general was primarily focused on mothers, while fathers only had the opportunity to take leave if the mother refrained from her right. The Austrian government was bent on defending its existing system. As a result, the Austrian parental leave scheme is still not fully in line with the Directive's individual rights provision, but continues to provide mothers with an (albeit very small) advantage over fathers.

In Germany, the government initially refused to take any steps to implement the Directive. Hence, it rejected extending the right to parental leave to single-income couples. However, this attitude was dropped once the conservative-liberal government coalition had been replaced by a centre-left government. Rather than refusing to adapt, the gender equality thrust of the Directive was suddenly supported by the new government. As a consequence, the right to parental leave was extended to single-income couples and the government, moreover, took on board some of the soft-law provisions of the Directive, thereby improving the incentives for fathers to take parental leave.

It seems, therefore, that qualitative mismatches do not necessarily lead to domestic resistance. Rather, it depends on the political constellation at the national level whether such innovations are opposed or might even be supported. The latter was the case when Italy implemented the Parental Leave Directive. As in Austria, the Directive challenged the existing system, which was predominantly focused on mothers. But instead of defending this system, the centre-left government unequivocally embraced the new equality-based policy model. In this context, the Italian government even went beyond the compulsory minimum requirements of the Directive: by providing fathers with an extra month (if they were to go on leave for at least three months).

A similar pattern of acceptance despite qualitative misfit could be observed in the case of the Young Workers Directive in Denmark, where the left-wing government explicitly supported the considerable raising of the age limit imposed on children undertaking light work, although many conservative or liberal politicians argued that this undermined one of the core principles of the existing system and therefore wanted to preserve the scheme in place. Portugal and Italy also used the opportunity offered by the Part-time Work Directive to overhaul their part-time work regulations fundamentally. Even though one of the major goals of the Directive, which was to increase the opportunities for part-time work, contradicted the traditionally rather restrictive regulatory approach in both countries, the centre-left governments in both countries wanted to increase labour market flexibility, and thus fundamentally transformed their rules so as to boost part-time work. (For more details on the role of party politics on transposition outcomes, see section 14.13 below.)

In conclusion, our analysis suggests that while domestic governments may indeed resist adaptation if deeply entrenched traditions or regulatory philosophies are at stake, such a reaction is far from being necessary. Rather, domestic politics may very well lead to the opposite outcome.

14.7   Planting new trees versus rearranging old forests

Kenneth Hanf (1991: 8) has presented a further argument related to the amount and types of changes required by EU policies. Despite also building on historical institutionalist thinking, the thrust of his argument runs counter to the misfit hypothesis: he argues that it should be easier to implement a particular Directive in cases where no prior statutory rules are in place than in the presence of an established legislative system. In the former case, implementation should be facilitated by the fact that governments can begin from scratch while, in the latter case, governments should have more trouble in reorganising their established systems so as to bring them in line with EU requirements. In other words, planting new trees should be easier than rearranging old forests.[17]

Our case studies do not lend support to this view. From this perspective, it should have been easier for the UK government to meet the massive policy demands of the Working Time Directive or to overcome the still significant reform requirements created by the Directives on Parental Leave and Part-time Work (all three cases involving the creation of completely new legislation) than to adapt the existing rules and regulations in order to meet the standards of the remaining Directives. Empirically, this was certainly not the case. Transposing the Working Time Directive in the UK was one of the most contentious processes in our sample and involved serious delays (see Chapter 6). The implementation of the Parental Leave Directive was also highly contested and could only be accomplished correctly after intervention by the Commission and the ECJ (see Chapter 8). On the other hand, implementing the Employment Contract Information Directive and the Pregnant Workers Directive (both cases where domestic legislation already existed) could be completed on time or almost on time (see Chapters 4 and 5).

We could add many more empirical examples to demonstrate that this argument does not hold. But there are also theoretical arguments for this finding. First of all, the view seems to rests on a rather state-centric conception of policy-making. The focus lies on the ease or arduousness with which politicians and bureaucrats might be able to meet certain policy requirements. From this perspective, it should indeed be easier to create a new law from scratch than be forced to revise a raft of existing rules and regulations. But what if we also take the addressees of the legal rules into account? From the viewpoint of employers, a newly created law demanding a fundamental restructuring of working practices is by no means easier to digest than a reform which involves the revision of an existing legal framework but has the same effect. What counts for them is the actual costs of such a reform rather than the legal complexity of bringing it about. Hence, they will be as fiercely opposed to the former as to the latter reform, which means that if the costs of a reform are significant it should per se not be easy to enact such a reform because of employers' resistance. A focus on societal actors rather than state bureaucrats also helps to make clear that, for companies, a lack of statutory regulation does not mean that there are no entrenched rules and practices which might have to be changed if a legal reform is enacted. This is particularly true for the area of labour law, where the relationship between employers and employees is usually regulated by a dense web of collective agreements.

---

[17] We are indebted to Fritz Scharpf for this metaphor.

In sum, researchers interested in the relative reform requirements of a particular Directive in different countries should focus on the difference between the European standards and existing domestic policies (including the actual costs for societal addressees), rather than look at the legal arduousness of implementation for state actors. This is exactly the approach we followed in our empirical studies. Moreover, our research has shown that, even if the actual reform requirements have been established, we still know little about the likely outcome of domestic adaptation since there are several other important factors determining whether or not a Directive is transposed correctly and on time.

14.8   The failure of the veto player argument

Another popular argument in the literature starts from the assumption that the political systems of the member states differ in their capacity to enact reforms that would change the status quo. According to the famous veto player theory developed by George Tsebelis (1995), the reform capacity of a political system decreases as the number of distinct actors whose agreement is required to pass such a reform increases. Hence, countries with higher numbers of veto players should be plagued much more frequently by reform impasses than systems with low numbers of veto players.

Since the transposition of EU Directives also requires the enactment of legislative reforms at the domestic level, this argument, which was originally developed in the general context of comparative politics, could also be applied to the more specific area of EU implementation research. In fact, this was done by Markus Haverland, who criticised the misfit approach by arguing that, in his case studies on the implementation of the Packaging Waste Directive in three countries, 'veto points tend to shape the timing and quality of implementation regardless of differential gaps in the goodness of fit between European requirements and national traditions' (Haverland 2000: 100).

As it turns out, however, Haverland's argument, which certainly tied in with his three cases, does not fare better than the misfit hypothesis if applied to our ninety-one cases (see Figure 14.2).[18]

---

[18] It should be noted that we use the original version of the veto player theory here (Tsebelis 1995) since this is also the version that was introduced to EU implementation research by Markus Haverland. Therefore, our analysis does not cover the recent modification by George Tsebelis (2002) which argues that policy outcomes do not only depend on the number of veto players, but also on the ideological distances between these veto players.

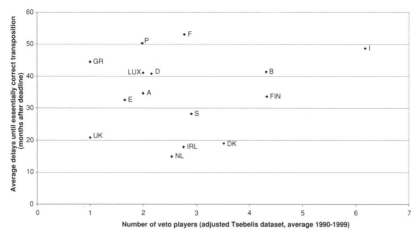

Figure 14.2 Veto players and transposition performance[19]

The figure suggests that the number of veto players does not have a decisive impact on member state implementation performance. To be sure, some countries apparently do seem to correspond to the expectations of the veto player theory, like the UK and Italy. But many of the other countries do not fit in nicely. Hence, Greece has as few veto players as the UK, but nevertheless emerges much worse than the latter. Luxembourg, Germany, Portugal, and France are also examples of countries whose performance is far poorer than one would have expected on the basis of their moderate numbers of veto players. Denmark, on the other hand, is clearly better than its institutional reform capacity would suggest. Altogether, therefore, the world seems to be more complicated than implied by such parsimonious hypotheses.

---

[19] This Figure is based on an adjusted version of the veto player data set provided by George Tsebelis (http://www.sscnet.ucla.edu/polisci/faculty/tsebelis). First, missing data for Italy (1996–1999) and Greece (whole period of analysis) were added using information reported in Ismayr (2002). Second, we did not count the German *Bundesrat* as a veto player even for periods where the government parties did not hold a majority in the second chamber of the German legislature since the transposition of the largest part of our six sample Directives did not require the approval of the *Bundesrat*. Third, following the argument by Steffen Ganghof (2003; see also Ganghof and Bräuninger 2003), we adjusted the data in order to account for the specific situation of minority governments, which is not properly reflected in the Tsebelis data set. Since a minority government needs the support of the parliamentary opposition to get legislation enacted, we calculated one more veto player for periods of minority government.

14.9   The limited explanatory power of effective administrative co-ordination and efficient regulatory procedures

In the context of early studies on the implementation of European Directives, it has been argued that many transposition problems were caused by administrative co-ordination problems, such as a lack of co-operation between different ministries in charge of preparing parts of the transposition legislation, and by long-drawn-out legislative procedures (Mény 1988: 297; Schwarze et al. 1993b: 71–2, 94; Van den Bossche 1996: 380–2; Ciavarini Azzi 2000: 57–9).

In terms of implementation problems caused by *administrative co-ordination problems*, our case studies have revealed some instances of this pattern. Responsibility for transposition was indeed frequently divided between different administrative units, especially in the case of the Working Time, Young Workers and Pregnant Workers Directives which encompass both general employment rights as well as health and safety provisions. However, such a separation of responsibilities did not necessarily mean that transposition was late because of co-ordination problems. It is true that in these cases the likelihood of delays due to administrative overload increases (see section 14.11 below) since multiple administrative units come into play. But genuine co-ordination problems occurred only very infrequently.

We have registered seven cases in which administrative co-ordination problems caused some delays. In some of these cases, however, other factors accounted for the greater part of the delays. In Italy, the Employment Contract Information and Pregnant Workers Directives were clear examples of delayed transposition due to administrative failure. Although the required adaptations did not provoke great interest or conflicts among political actors, it took more than two years in the case of the Pregnant Workers Directive and almost four years with the Employment Contract Directive until the first transposition decrees were adopted.[20] Implementation of the Employment Contract Information Directive in Belgium

---

[20] For the implementation of the Working Time and Parental Leave Directives in Italy, the possibility cannot be ruled out that administrative problems also contributed to the delayed transposition there. However, the main reason was the conflict between the political parties and the social partners against the backdrop of an unstable political situation. In contrast, the case of the Part-time Work Directive shows that timely implementation is possible in Italy, which goes against the grain of arguments that assume a general inability on the part of the Italian administration to cope with European challenges. As the Part-time Work case is the most recent Directive in our sample, this may be interpreted as a sign that the various administrative reforms carried out in Italy during the 1990s have had some effect. However, it is still too early to draw valid conclusions about this issue.

was stalled for several months because no agreement could be reached within an interministerial working group that had been set up in order to present a transposition proposal. But the greater part of the delays was caused by the fact that Belgian officials, after having been warned by the Commission, gave notification of a draft law which, however, never made its way onto the statute books nor was replaced by another piece of legislation subsequently – a fact that seems to have been overlooked for several years (see Chapter 4).

A small part of the still incorrect transposition of the Pregnant Workers Directive in Greece was also due to conflicts between the Ministry for Social Affairs and the Ministry of Defence. In Belgium, the co-ordination between the units for general labour law, health and safety aspects and gender equality was cumbersome and thus contributed to the (albeit not very significant) delay in transposing the same Directive. Similarly, the significantly late transposition of the Young Workers Directive in Greece was caused in part by the need to co-ordinate the positions of two separate administrative units. However, this only added a few months to the delays already caused by the indifference of both government and administrative actors, which had led to a long phase of inactivity at the beginning of the transposition period. In Luxembourg, implementation of the same Directive was delayed somewhat by the complicated debates in an interministerial working group. But by far the greater part of the considerable time lag was caused by permanent administrative overload preventing an early initiation of the whole reform process (see Chapter 7).

Timely transposition of the Employment Contract Information Directive in Germany was seriously hampered by a conflict between the Department of Labour and Social Affairs and the Department of Economic Affairs over the question of whether or not to use an exemption option offered by the Directive. But as has been argued in Chapter 4, the tediousness of this conflict stemmed from the fact that the two ministries were headed by ministers from different coalition parties. Hence, it was an inter-party rather than an inter-ministerial conflict, and that is why it took so long to resolve the controversy. This becomes even clearer if we compare this case with the transposition of the Part-time Work Directive in Germany, where the Department of Economic Affairs again had serious objections to the proposal issued by the Department of Labour and Social Affairs. But since the former was headed by a minister without party affiliation, this conflict could be resolved much faster and hence transposition was not delayed.

With regard to the role of different *types of regulatory procedure* as a source of delayed adaptation, our empirical results also lend little support to the expectation that long parliamentary procedures as such are a major impediment to timely implementation. In our sample, there are many cases in which transposition was accomplished swiftly despite the fact that the required changes had to be enacted on the basis of the regular legislative procedure which entailed extensive parliamentary involvement.[21] At the same time, we observed a considerable number of cases where the incorporation phase was concluded with serious delays, even though transposition was carried out by fast-track delegated legislation without, or with only limited, parliamentary involvement.[22]

Hence, we can conclude that the type of regulatory procedure as such does not have a decisive impact on the timeliness of transposition. Obviously, domestic parliamentary procedures are not so protracted as to make it impossible for countries to fulfil their duties within the already rather generous time limits of two or three years. And if governments or administrations simply remain inactive for several years before they actually begin transposing a Directive, as was often the case in Greece or France, the potential advantages of fast-track decrees are more than offset by such inertia. Moreover, if the government does not possess the wide-ranging competences to enact implementing legislation from the outset (as is the case in Greece), but delegation from parliament to government has to be carried out for each Directive, this can cause serious delays as well. Several Italian cases illustrate this point. Some observers had expected that Italy's serious transposition problems would be solved by the introduction of the *legge comunitaria* in the early 1990s, an annual law which was intended to transpose all EU Directives still to be implemented once a year or to enable the government to do so in the form of fast-track delegated legislation (see, for example, Ciavarini Azzi 2000). Despite certain improvements since the early 1990s (see Fabbrini and Donà 2003), it transpired that several of these summary laws could not

---

[21] These cases include the transposition of the Employment Contract Information Directive in Austria, Denmark, Finland, the Netherlands, Sweden and the UK, the Pregnant Workers Directive in Denmark, the Working Time Directive in Finland, the Netherlands and Spain, the Young Workers Directive in Denmark and Spain, the Parental Leave Directive in Finland, the Netherlands and Sweden, and the Part-time Work Directive in Denmark, France, Germany and Greece. Note that Directives are often transposed through a mixture of Acts of parliament and fast-track delegated legislation. For example, decrees are often used if an infringement procedure by the EU Commission requires fast adjustments to the existing law. Hence, the cases listed here are only those where the whole transposition was accomplished exclusively by one of the two legal instruments.

[22] The following cases were achieved by delegated legislation, but nevertheless involved delays of more than two years until the EU standards had been fulfilled essentially correctly: the implementation of the Employment Contract Information Directive in France and Italy, the Pregnant Workers Directive in Greece and Italy, the Working Time Directive in Greece and the UK, the Young Workers Directive in France, Italy and the UK, and the Parental Leave Directive in the UK.

be passed by parliament because of the general political instability involving coalition crises and frequent changes of government, or because of actual conflicts over the exact scope of delegation and the content of the specifications to be given to the government along with the competency to enact implementing decrees. In sum, our analysis reveals that the type of regulatory procedure was much less important in determining transposition outcomes than factors such as political conflicts, administrative overload, or the general attitude towards complying with EU law prevalent among political elites.

14.10 The irrelevance of administrative watchdog mechanisms

Some authors have argued that the transposition performance of member states could be improved by the creation of effective administrative watchdog units, which would ensure that the individual ministries fulfil their duties arising from EU Directives (Szukala 2002). Based on institutional parameters such as the number of personnel working for these units and their hierarchical position within the administration, one could expect member states with large and resourceful supervisory bodies that are directly subordinate to the head of government to perform best, while countries without such structures, or with only weak ones, would fare worst.

If we look at our empirical results, there is little evidence that would support this expectation. Among the worst performers in terms of timely and correct transposition are France and Italy (see Table 13.6 above), both of which have relatively powerful watchdog units with ample resources and with direct access to the hierarchical powers of the head of government.[23] On the other hand, the comparatively good performance of the UK would seem to square with this view, since the UK also has a very strong co-ordination unit in charge of ensuring compliance with EU law, the European Secretariat of the Cabinet Office (see, for example, Kassim 2000: 35; Armstrong and Bulmer 2003: 11). Nevertheless, our case studies indicate that non-compliance, especially for political reasons, is a frequent phenomenon in the UK despite the relative strength of the European Secretariat.

To put it more generally, administrative watchdog units might be able to reduce administrative problems arising from insufficient co-ordination or the like. But if, as in our cases, a large part of the implementation deficit

---

[23] The units are the *Secrétariat général du comité interministériel* (SGCI) in France and the *Dipartimento per il coordinamento delle politiche comunitarie* in Italy (Belloubet-Frier 1995; Sepe 1995; Secrétariat Général 2001: 180–3; Gallo and Hanny 2003; Szukala 2003).

has totally different sources, *administrative* supervision mechanisms are inadequate to improve compliance. As will become clear in section 14.13 below, effective administrative watchdogs are generally useful, but they cannot ensure that political actors are willing to comply. In other words, if resistance or negligence by political actors is one of the main problems, we do not only (or even primarily) need administrative monitoring mechanisms, but also measures to raise awareness of the importance of fulfilling EU demands among political actors.

14.11   The partial significance of insufficient administrative resources

Apart from administrative co-ordination problems and a lack of effective watchdog mechanisms to avoid such problems, it has also been argued in the literature that transposition may be delayed because the administrative units responsible for drawing up draft transposition laws either lack adequate resources or are temporarily overloaded with the result that the necessary work cannot be done in time. Indeed, our case studies have revealed that a shortage of administrative resources does play a certain role in delaying transposition.

In twenty-one out of ninety-one cases, permanent or temporary administrative overload or general administrative inefficiency actually played a role in causing transposition delays.[24] This was particularly severe in Luxembourg, where the Ministry of Labour and Social Affairs clearly lacks adequate resources to cope with all the Directives it has to transpose. Under these conditions, long delays are the rule rather than the exception, especially if the Directives to be tackled entail only limited adaptational pressure and thus appear to be of little importance. A structural deficit of resources could also be observed in the Irish Health and Safety Authority, which is responsible for drawing up draft laws in the area of occupational health and safety. Hence, every time a Directive involved aspects of health and safety, transposition was delayed. The same is true for the Greek ministry unit responsible for health and safety at work.

But apart from these cases of structural administrative shortcomings, problems could also be observed if administrative units which could generally be said to have enough resources were confronted with a sudden

---

[24] The cases comprise: the implementation of the Employment Contract Information Directive in Greece, Ireland and Luxembourg, the Pregnant Workers Directive in Austria, Greece, Ireland and Luxembourg, the Working Time Directive in Greece, Ireland, Luxembourg, Portugal and the UK, the Young Workers Directive in Belgium, Greece, Ireland, Luxembourg and the UK (in both phases), and the Part-time Work Directive in Belgium, Ireland and the UK.

surge of work leading to temporary overload. This could be observed in the UK after the Labour government had assumed power in 1997. The administrative actors responsible for employment rights legislation then had to cope not only with a certain backlog of EU Directives which the Tory government had refused to transpose, but also with a number of new reform proposals, such as the national minimum wage legislation, which the Labour Party had promised to enact if it won the elections. Since these genuinely national projects were treated with high priority, a number of EU Directives only received secondary attention. Hence, their transposition was delayed.

In sum, we can conclude that compliance could indeed be improved considerably in some countries if administrative bottlenecks due to insufficient resources were avoided. At the same time, we should not forget that a reference to inadequate administrative resources may always be treated as a façade to conceal a political decision not to comply.

14.12 The impact of social partner involvement

Interest groups – even in countries with very strong corporatist traditions such as Austria or the Nordic member states – do not possess *formal* veto power in the transposition process. Nevertheless, they can be 'powerful players' (Strøm 2003) which may exert influence in political decision processes.[25] As yet not much attention has been paid to the role of interest groups in the transposition of EU Directives. In particular, no real knowledge has been acquired of the *direction* of the effects exerted by interest group involvement. Some authors argue that interest groups and other societal organisations might serve as a 'pull' factor by exerting pressure on reluctant public administrations to fulfil EU requirements (Börzel 2003a: 36). Others stress their potential blocking power, which may, however, be overcome by 'a decisional tradition capable of surmounting formal and factual veto points by way of consensual tripartite decision-making' (Héritier 2001a: 44; similarly Lampinen and Uusikylä 1998).

[25] Some authors talk about *factual* veto power (Héritier 2001a, 2001b); others only apply the term 'veto player' to actors with *formal* veto rights such as government parties or certain second chambers (see, for example, Tsebelis 1995). Against this background, we follow Kaare Strøm's (2003: 21) precise conceptual distinction: 'We call a player whose consent is both necessary and sufficient a *dictator*, one whose support is only necessary a *veto player*, and one whose consent is only sufficient a *decisive* player. Even players whose agreement is neither necessary nor sufficient are not necessarily irrelevant, however. If A can credibly threaten to take action that will affect the payoffs of a dictator, veto player, or decisive player, then A is a *powerful player*' (emphasis in original).

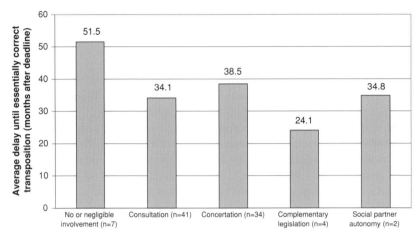

Figure 14.3 Type of social partner involvement and transposition performance

In view of these diverging interpretations in the literature, our empirical material is able to shed new light on the role of organised interests in the implementation of EU Directives. The field of labour law is a particularly good area for such a study since trade unions and employers' organisations (the social partners) play an important role in many countries, even though, at the same time, there are important differences in the way these interest groups are involved in the policy-making process. We thus can answer the question of whether *the type of social partner involvement* in the transposition of our Directives makes a difference and, if so, in what way. To this end, we distinguish between no or negligible involvement, consultation, concertation, complementary legislation, and social partner autonomy (for an operationalisation of these categories, see Chapter 12).

Our empirical results indicate that there is no systematic relationship between a certain category of social partner involvement and a particularly good or bad transposition record. Figure 14.3 shows the average time taken until the status of essentially correct transposition was reached for each of the above-mentioned categories of social partner involvement, which vary from weak (no or negligible involvement) to strong (social partner autonomy). Two extreme assumptions can clearly be rejected by means of these data: stronger social partner involvement does *not* systematically cause more transposition problems (for example, as a result of lengthy discussions between the government and the social partners). Nor does the opposite hypothesis hold for our cases, either: a strong role of

time, in most cases, even if there were strong conflicts between the social partners, other countries[31] did not (no matter whether the social partners were only consulted or involved more intensely). This leaves us with the conclusion that (strong) social partner involvement does not necessarily harm transposition processes. Rather, it very much depends on the governments' will and priorities for compliance with EU law. This topic will be developed further in the next chapter.

14.13 Ideology versus misfit: parties sometimes do matter too

While the misfit-oriented view of implementation within the EU starts from the assumption that governments are motivated exclusively by the will to protect their domestic policies and practices from being fundamentally overhauled by EU policies, our empirical case studies provide ample evidence suggesting that governments may also act according to a more political logic.

Indeed, we have found clear party effects in altogether sixteen out of our ninety-one cases.[32] For methodological reasons, this figure might even under-estimate rather than over-estimate the frequency of party political effects, since these tend to become clear only if there is a major change of government. Hence, we have found that party politics was a central factor in many cases in the UK and in Germany. In these two countries, a fundamental change of government from a conservative to a centre-left government occurred in 1997 and 1998 respectively. In other member states, such as Austria, Belgium, Luxembourg and the Netherlands, such decisive changes of government did not take place during the 1990s.[33] Hence, potential party effects might have been concealed in these countries because it failed to emerge how a government with a different party political profile might have acted. However, we will argue in Chapter 15

---

[31] Including, even, other corporatist countries like Austria.

[32] We include the following cases: the implementation of the Employment Contract Information Directive in the UK, the Working Time Directive in Ireland, Italy, Sweden and the UK, the Young Workers Directive in Denmark, the Netherlands and the UK (both phases), the Part-time Work Directive in Spain, and the implementation of all six Directives in Germany.

[33] In all of these countries, changes of government took place. But ideologically they were not as far-reaching as the ones in Germany and the UK since they involved changes from a grand coalition to either centre-left or centre-right governments or vice versa, but not a clear-cut left-right alteration. Hence, in Belgium and the Netherlands, governments changed from a grand coalition to a centre-left government, and, in Austria and Luxembourg, grand coalitions were followed by centre-right governments. Moreover, most of these changes of government did not occur until rather late, in 1999 or 2000, so that many of our cases could no longer be affected.

that there are also other reasons why party politics frequently played a role in some countries, while it did not in others.

At any rate, the sixteen cases make it clear that there may be a party political logic to domestic adaptation in addition to, and sometimes even instead of, the misfit logic. Rather than acting as guardians of the domestic status quo, governments also assess the usefulness of European policies on the basis of their party political preferences. Thus, even far-reaching reform requirements may be satisfied without major problems if they correspond to the party political goals of the respective government. Conversely, even the realisation of minor adaptations is bound to fail if these modifications are rejected on party political grounds.

These patterns could be observed in the three cases of 'opposition through the backdoor' already mentioned above (the Working Time and Young Workers Directives in the UK, the Working Time Directive in Germany). But party politics may also give rise to opposition at the end of the EU policy process without prior opposition at the beginning. Hence, the German centre-right government agreed to the social partners' parental leave agreement in the Council of Ministers, but afterwards refused to comply with the (altogether quite minor) reform requirements arising from the Directive. Only the incoming centre-left government under Gerhard Schröder brought German law fully in line with the Directive and even followed many of its non-compulsory recommendations.

On the other hand, party political support may even lead to acceptance of measures with significant adaptational pressure. The Working Time Directive confronted Ireland with roughly the same amount of misfit as the UK. However, unlike the UK Conservatives, the Irish centre-left government not only voted in favour of the Working Time Directive in the Council of Ministers but also readily implemented (and even considerably over-implemented) it afterwards. Likewise, the Danish centre-left government supported the controversial raising of the age limit required by the Young Workers Directive and subsequently even defended its transposition resolutely against pressure from opposition parties (see Chapter 7).

The latter case demonstrates that the veto player argument, while apparently of little assistance as a single factor in determining implementation outcomes, is nonetheless highly valuable if used as a tool for analysing interactions between political parties that try to influence the outcome of transposition processes. Hence, the Danish liberals, who were opposed to raising the minimum working age of children, as required by the Directive, exercised considerable influence on the transposition process when the centre-left government lost its parliamentary majority in the aftermath of the 1994 elections and consequently had to seek support among the opposition parties. In this critical situation, timely transposition could only be secured by offering the liberals some concessions in other areas (see Chapter 7). In a similar vein, the attempt of the Swedish social democratic minority government to enact a comprehensive reform that would have brought Swedish law fully in line with the Working Time Directive foundered on the more far-reaching ambitions of the left-wing opposition parties. Likewise, the move of the Italian minority government in 1996 to give legal effect to an agreement of the social partners that would have transposed the Working Time Directive also failed because the Communist Party, which lent parliamentary support to the government, struggled for a more comprehensive reform than the one envisaged by the social partners (see Chapter 6).

But controversies may also arise between coalition partners with different political goals. Hence, transposition of the Employment Contract Information Directive in Germany was held up considerably by a conflict between the liberal Minister for Economic Affairs and the christian democratic Minister for Labour and Social Affairs over the question of whether or not a particular exemption clause should be used (see Chapter 4).

Taken together, these findings correspond in principle to what has been widely debated among scholars of comparative politics as the 'parties-do-matter' hypothesis (see, for example, Castles 1982; M. G. Schmidt 1996a, 1996b, 2000: 378–89). The hypothesis proceeds from the assumption that christian democratic, liberal, or social democratic parties have clearly distinguishable policy programmes since they represent the interests of different constituencies, and that these programmatic differences also result in different policy choices made in the course of the everyday operation of these governments. Especially in a traditional area of party conflict like economic and social policy, therefore, we should expect governments with different ideological profiles to react differently to EU Directives that usually involve an expansion of workers' rights.

Seen against the background of our empirical results, however, this simple view has to be modified somewhat. First of all, a differentiated approach is needed if we are to assign individual parties to different party families. On the basis of observations about the behaviour of the government parties in our case studies, it is possible to distinguish between four different party families with different basic policy positions on employment rights regulation.

Parties with a clear *neo-liberal* profile like the liberal parties in Belgium (VLD/PRL), Germany (FDP), Ireland (PD), and the Netherlands (VVD) or the British Conservative Party are deeply sceptical about the regulation of the labour market. In contrast, we may expect *traditional social democratic parties* like the socialists in Belgium (PS/SP), France (PS),

Portugal (PS) and Spain (PSOE), the Irish Labour Party or the social democratic parties in Austria (SPÖ) and Germany (SPD)[34] to be generally in favour of regulations aimed at improving the protection of workers' rights. Situated between these two poles are *conservative and christian democratic parties* such as the Austrian ÖVP, the Belgian CVP/PSC, the Dutch CDA, the German CDU, the Luxembourg CSV, the Portuguese PSD and the two Irish 'catch-all' parties *Fianna Fáil* and *Fine Gael*. These parties are in general not hostile to the creation and improvement of statutory employment rights, but place much more emphasis on market principles and on the needs and demands of business and employers' organisations than traditional social democrats do.

It is important to note that *'modern' social democratic parties* like, in particular, the British Labour Party under Tony Blair or the Dutch PvdA, have similar positions. Within these parties, general worker friendliness is also moderated to a considerable extent by the aim of keeping financial burdens on business as minimal as possible (see also Seeleib-Kaiser 2002). Hence, it is very possible that governments led by such 'new' social democratic parties also pursue policies of deregulation, which may bring them in opposition to EU employment rights standards, as was the case with the transposition of the Young Workers Directive in the Netherlands (see Chapter 7).

While the actual position of christian democratic and 'modern' social democratic parties vis-à-vis individual labour market regulations is determined by several factors such as the relative strength of different party factions or the economic costs of the issues at hand, there is an unequivocal difference between these two families with regard to *family policy and gender issues*. Christian democratic and conservative parties are usually inclined to a traditional conception of the familial and professional roles that men and women should play in life. As a consequence, they are normally not very enthusiastic about political measures aiming to improve gender equality. In marked contrast, the secular origins of both 'traditional' and 'modern' social democratic parties makes them much more open to accept and support such initiatives.

The second modification concerns the question of when we should expect support for, or opposition to, employment rights Directives. On the one hand, the working time cases in Sweden and Italy have demonstrated that left-wing parties do not automatically have to be in favour of

---

[34] The classification of the SPD as a 'traditional' social democratic party refers to the situation in the 1990s, when the largest part of our Directives were implemented. The recent debates surrounding the 'Agenda 2010' reform package indicate that the SPD may currently be in the process of transforming itself into a 'modern' social democratic party.

the transposition of Directives that improve worker rights. In particular, they may oppose such reforms because they favour more far-reaching action. Moreover, the thrust of some of our Directives, at least in some countries, proved to be more compatible with conservative objectives than with traditional left-wing aspirations. This was especially true for the Part-time Work Directive with its aim of boosting part-time work. In the Southern European countries, this kind of work had traditionally been considered second-class by trade unions and left-wing parties, and thus had been treated rather restrictively. Therefore, the Spanish conservative government had no problem with the Directive, but welcomed it as an opportunity to make the Spanish labour market more flexible (see Chapter 9).

In sum, we can conclude that party politics indeed sometimes do matter. In order to identify the direction of these party effects, however, we have to be careful to understand the individual context conditions correctly and the specific ideological thrust of a particular Directive.

14.14 Domestic issue linkage as an obstructing and facilitating factor

Our empirical case studies have uncovered one factor which so far has been totally neglected in EU implementation research: while previous research has hitherto tended to treat the implementation of each EU Directive as an isolated process, we have found that national adaptation is frequently linked to other political processes at the domestic level (see also Falkner et al. 2004). The sheer number of cases in which issue linkage has played a role indicates that this is far from being a negligible phenomenon. On the contrary, it needs to be systematically included in a proper analysis of implementation processes. In almost half of all our cases (forty-one out of ninety-one) transposition was linked to some other domestic reform. And in many of these cases, this linkage had a crucial impact on the final outcome.

We can distinguish between linkage resulting from *deliberate decisions by national governments* and linkage stemming from *material interdependencies* that make it very hard to tackle the different issues separately. The greater part of our cases belongs to the first category. It is quite obvious that domestic governments, rather than being mere implementation machines, often exhibit considerable 'creativity' when transposing EU Directives. They are not only there to fulfil European policy requirements, but frequently pursue their own policy goals in addition to (and from time to time even instead of) the demands emanating from Brussels. On the other hand, close material interdependencies between the implementation of a Directive and other domestic reforms may be so strong that it is only natural for national actors to treat these two issues jointly. Under these conditions, breaking up the linkage and treating both subjects separately would be very hard to accomplish.

Thus, one fundamental lesson to be drawn from our research is that we should always be aware of the possibility that the 'downloading' process of EU policies may become intertwined with the idiosyncratic logics of domestic policy-making. This intermingling, however, may have detrimental as well as beneficial effects. In our cases, the most frequent consequence of issue linkage was belated transposition. In twenty-three out of our forty-one cases of issue linkage, the *effect was one of delay*. Usually, this was caused by *additional conflict dimensions* 'imported' from the linked issues. For example, the German government added two very controversial issues to the transposition of the Pregnant Workers Directive. The additional debates surrounding these issues went on to cause considerable delay in adopting the altogether rather uncontroversial provisions stemming directly from the Directive (see Chapter 5). In several countries, transposition of the Working Time Directive was severely hampered because it was coupled with highly contested issues, such as the significant reduction of statutory weekly working hours to thirty-five (in France and Italy; see Chapter 6) or even thirty hours (in Sweden; see Chapter 12). In France and Italy, this process was further obstructed because it was materially linked to the contentious issue of lifting the general ban on night work for female blue-collar workers (see Chapter 6). The same is true for French adaptation to the Pregnant Workers Directive (see Chapter 5).

A parallel effect of (potential) delay due to additional conflict can be brought about if the government decides to over-implement significantly a particular Directive – as witnessed, for example, in the context of Ireland's transposition of the Working Time Directive (see Chapter 10 for more details on over-implementation). Although they are structurally similar, however, we have not subsumed such cases under the heading of 'issue linkage' since the additional controversies were directly associated with particular standards or recommendations of the Directives in question.

Delays due to issue linkage might also be brought about by the fact that the linked processes simply follow a *different timetable*. In the Netherlands, for example, transposition of some parts of the Young Workers Directive could only be accomplished belatedly because the law that had to be revised was part of a larger, and thus rather complex and time-consuming, process of legal consolidation and simplification (see Chapter 7).

But issue linkage does not always have to entail negative consequences. If the linked processes are uncontroversial and fit in with the time constraints imposed by the implementation deadlines, the effect of issue linkage could very well be *neutral*. This was true in six of our cases. For example, Spain coupled the transposition of the Young Workers Directive with the incorporation of the Health and Safety Framework Directive, the Swedish government decided to implement the Part-time Work Directive together with the Fixed-Term Work Directive and Austria transposed the Employment Contract Information Directive in conjunction with the Directive on Transfers of Undertakings. In all three cases, this coupling involved no large-scale conflicts and thus had no visible negative consequences.

Further to these neutral cases, issue linkage could also have an *accelerating or facilitating effect*. This could be observed in twelve of our cases, mostly because the transposition of a Directive could be easily *fed into an ongoing reform process*. For example, the Dutch and Spanish transposition of the Working Time Directive could be brought to fruition relatively easily because it was carried out in conjunction with a larger reform of the existing working time legislation already initiated earlier (see Chapter 6). A similar pattern could be observed in the context of implementing the Young Workers Directive in Belgium and Spain.

Another facilitating consequence of issue linkage comes in the form of *package deals* in which negative transposition consequences for certain actors are traded against concessions in other areas. In our cases we have discovered only a limited number of such package deals. But if such deals were struck, this was typically a reaction to resistance provoked by over-implementation. Hence, the German government ensured timely adoption of its considerably over-implemented version of the Part-time Work Directive by coupling this process with the transposition of the Fixed-Term Work Directive (see Chapter 9). Likewise, the Luxembourg government coupled the transposition of the Parental Leave Directive, whose significant 'gold plating' was heavily criticised by employers' organisations, with a number of other employment issues, including measures to increase working time flexibility (Interviews LUX6: 575–92, LUX10: 833–58; see also Chapter 8).

In countries that frequently neglect their obligations arising from EU law and thus react to imminent implementation duties with inertia rather than active transposition efforts (see Chapter 15 for more details on this group of countries), issue linkage may have yet another beneficial effect. Under these circumstances, transposition may be delayed due to additional controversies arising from the linked issues, but at least such linkage with other domestic reforms induces governments and administrations to act at all. In this sense, *activation due to issue linkage* followed by a certain amount of delay due to imported controversies is the 'lesser evil' compared with the standard outcome of years of inertia. This could be witnessed in a particularly obvious fashion in Greece. Here, transposition obligations are typically neglected and the process usually only starts after the Commission has initiated infringement proceedings. In the case of the Parental Leave and Part-time Work Directives, however, transposition was attached to other domestic reform processes which were debated at the time. Hence, adaptation to the Part-time Work Directive could be accomplished on time. And as far as the Parental Leave Directive is concerned, the transposition law could at least be adopted comparatively quickly, although transposition to date is still not correct because of material shortcomings in this law.

Finally, it has to be noted that issue linkage is not usually unavoidable. Even though material interdependencies may sometimes be so strong that it would be hard to uncouple the issues at hand, it still remains a *political decision by domestic governments* whether or not to treat similar issues in conjunction. A government like the French one, which has to perform the (highly controversial) task of lifting a long-established general ban on night work for all women in industry and at the same time pull off the (less controversial) job of lifting a general ban on night work for pregnant women, is certainly inclined to treat these materially interdependent issues as one. But such a linkage is by no means necessary. If the fulfilment of EU-related requirements were a highly valued goal, the government could also decide to uncouple both issues in order to satisfy EU demands. Unlike its French colleagues, the Finnish government took such a decision when implementing the Parental Leave Directive. Originally, the Directive had been attached to a wider revision of the main piece of Finnish labour law. However, as the implementation deadline approached, the adaptation to the Directive was taken out of this package and enacted separately in order to ensure timely transposition (Interview FIN3: 361–489).

In terms of different Directives, our cases show that the Working Time Directive clearly produced the most cases of domestic issue linkage (eleven cases), followed by the Pregnant Workers Directive and Young Workers Directive (seven cases each), the Parental Leave Directive (six cases), and the Directives on Part-time Work and Employment Contract Information (five cases each). Hence, it seems that the transposition of Directives with a broad policy scope is more likely to be linked to other domestic reforms. Moreover, the likeliness of issue linkage seems to depend on the specific policy area and the particular historical context at hand. In our cases, the regulation of working time issues was an area in which domestic reforms were particularly frequent, at least during the 1990s. Therefore, issue linkage was a recurrent phenomenon with regard to this Directive.

15　Three worlds of compliance: a typology

> A well-constructed typology can work miracles in bringing order out of chaos (Bailey 1992: 2193).

15.1　Constructing a typology: methodological and practical background

It has been mentioned in the previous chapters that the considerations of domestic politics have been underrated in recent writing on compliance with EU law. The great importance of national preferences and ideology for the implementation performance of many countries is one major finding of this study. However, this is not a single overriding factor which determines the compliance performance of member states and could thus serve as a safe anchor for predicting the success or failure of future implementation cases in all of our fifteen countries. Therefore, it should not be read as a new over-generalised theory for explaining the implementation of EU law. In fact, an untidy overall picture emerges once the manifold hypotheses we derived from the different literatures have been discussed: no causal condition pre-supposed by existing theories is able to explain our empirical observations. This suggests, once again, that the search for law-like generalisations and for simple isolated causes that could explain complex empirical phenomena is futile (see, for example, Scharpf 2002b).

Classic factors from the comparative welfare state literature do not help either. Most importantly, there is no direct correlation between social expenses and compliance records. For example, the UK ranks fourth when it comes to delays in transposing our six Directives, but is on the lower end of the scale of social expenses in Europe. Although compliance in the Nordic countries is comparatively better, there is no general north–south

Many thanks to Adrienne Héritier for helpful and thorough comments on this chapter and, in particular, for the 'culture versus self-interest' argument. We are also grateful for constructive feedback by Kees van Kersbergen, Frans van Waarden and Ulf Sverdrup during a workshop on EU implementation issues at Leiden University.

division and there is also no plausible hypothesis on why geography should in fact matter. Finally, as already mentioned in Chapter 13, labour law does not fit the classic typologies of 'worlds of welfare capitalism' (Esping-Andersen 1990; Rhodes 1997; Ferrera 1998). An example of where the actual findings do not match either, is the fact that among the conservative welfare states we found that Austria is in the middle-rank but France is at the lowest end of the scale in terms of delays in transposition.

Instead of giving in to the apparent complexity of the empirical observations we had gathered, we still wanted to bring order to chaos. At that point in our project, we decided to follow the *methodological recommendations of the 'grounded theory' school* in social sciences (Glaser and Strauss 1967; Strauss and Corbin 1990, 1997; see also Lichbach 2003: 190), notably to work on the theoretical and empirical levels repeatedly and in turn in order to allow fresh insights from each field to improve our work in the other. On our search for compliance patterns across our fifteen EU member states, we thus went back to the insights on each country that we had derived from our interviews. Through a systematic comparison of what the researchers responsible for each member state had concluded after all the lengthy interviews, we finally discovered three clusters of countries, each showing a specific typical pattern of reacting to EU-induced reform requirements. Since the constitutive factor that separates these three clusters of countries (i.e. different modes of adaptation) had not been recognised in the literature before, the specific pattern did not come to the fore when we simply tested the prevailing hypotheses against our cases. It could only be detected with a broader knowledge about the countries and a reinterpretation of the outcomes on this basis.

Beyond the knowledge about our ninety cases, we have, during our interviews, come to know the fifteen national systems well enough to capture their essential features on a more general level. This played a crucial role in generating the results to be presented below: although ninety cases seem a lot compared with the typical EU implementation studies, six cases per member state still offer quite limited information to the researcher. However, our expert interviews in each member state revealed much more information than we would have needed just to measure compliance in six specific cases per country. Thus, information on the background of domestic (non-)compliance and on other cases outside our sample did not escape our notice. The method of in-depth expert interviews conducted on the basis of semi-structured questionnaires yielded much more than an understanding of specific implementation processes. This is because we asked questions on the specific as much as on the typical implementation processes, and because experts usually added what they considered to be relevant additional information to their answers. When we finally departed from our original method of uniformly applying the hypotheses taken from the existing literature to all member states alike, the pieces of our jigsaw slowly fell into place and revealed a new and meaningful pattern.

In fact, some EU member states displayed quite a regular pattern of compliance or non-compliance, regardless of how the specific provisions actually fitted with the relevant national policy legacy and governmental ideology. This indicates that a grouping of countries may be useful, such as that found in the 'worlds of welfare capitalism' (Esping-Andersen 1990) and 'families of nations' (Castles 1993) literature. According to our findings, the relatively best point of reference for predicting the fate of any forthcoming case of policy implementation is in fact the specific *national culture of digesting adaptation requirements*. This suggests that there is a factor at work that is worth considering but has not yet been elaborated in depth[1] in the European implementation literature: domestic compliance cultures in the field of EU law. 'Culture' has been defined as a 'general set of cognitive rules and recipes in terms of which agents, institutions, and structures are constituted' (Berger and Luckmann 1967 quoted in Swidler 2001: 3064) or as a 'shared interpretive scheme' (Douglas 2001: 3149). Since cultural norms typically change slowly and reflect enduring patterns of political action, political culture is a critical element in understanding politics across countries (Almond et al. 2000: 49f.).

While our study indicates that attitudinal factors should play a central role in the study of EU-triggered implementation processes, only a few studies have already taken this into consideration. Outside the area of EU implementation research, a similar approach to ours was followed by Jeremy Richardson and his collaborators, who argued that Western European countries are characterised by certain 'policy styles' (Richardson 1982b). By policy styles, they meant 'the *main* characteristics of the ways in which a given society formulates and implements its public policies' (Richardson et al. 1982: 3, emphasis in original). However, there are two important differences between our approach and that of the policy styles literature. First, while the policy styles literature focused on specific national approaches to policy-making and implementation *at the domestic level*, we sought to establish regularities in how European countries react to policy demands *stemming from the European Union*. Second and more importantly, the 1982 volume identified a convergence of policy styles among European countries (Richardson 1982a: especially 197–8), whereas we discern clusters of countries, each showing different patterns

---

[1] But see the more general (but rather atheoretical) legal discussion on 'legal cultures' mentioned in Ch. 2.

of response to EU-induced adaptation requirements. In this sense, our findings are also in stark contrast to the analysis of Dimitrakopoulos (2001: 453ff.), who extends the logic underlying the policy styles literature to EU implementation research and identifies one 'European style of transposition'.

More in line with our results is the recent work by Ulf Sverdrup on the way the Nordic countries comply with EU law. In this context, Sverdrup has pointed at a 'Nordic model' of good compliance. He argues that a culture of compliance and of compromise, together with transparency and organisation of the administration, is a crucial factor for a country's implementation performance (Sverdrup 2002a). All these factors are considered to be superior in the Nordic countries. Sverdrup contrasts the 'Nordic model' with the big Continental member states which are found to react more slowly and less readily in compliance conflicts (Sverdrup 2002b). The author concludes that the Nordic model is relatively 'less important in relation to the earlier stages of the infringement proceedings, but it is more important when accounting for variation regarding reasoned opinions and court rulings' (2003: 20f.). Unlike our research design, Sverdrup's studies start from Commission data on infringement proceedings (thus looking at the tip of the iceberg only, see Chapter 11) and derive their conclusions from statistical correlations. By contrast, our 'ideal types' (Weber 1947, cited in Bailey 1992: 2188) are more inclined to be 'real types' (Hartfiel 1982: 656) in the sense that they are derived from empirical information about the logic of reacting to EU-induced adjustment requirements in the fifteen national systems.

On a much more general level than Sverdrup's studies of infringement proceedings, an interesting paper by Klaus Goetz (2002) identifies 'Four Worlds of Europeanization'. It refers to a Nordic world, a North-Western world, a Mediterranean world, and a Central and Eastern European world. It focuses on when individual member states accept EU-related duties (for example, does a country have founding member status?) and combines this with very broad patterns of domestic effects (for example, are there particular effects of social division triggered by European integration?). Our approach is, again, very different. Our typology has a much more limited scope since it targets only policy implementation and, in contrast to both Goetz and Sverdrup, we proceed along analytical categories rather than geographical lines. Additionally, we offer a theory on why a 'world' with comparatively better compliance is possible.

Since we discerned three different ideal-typical patterns of how member states handle the duty of complying with EU law (with differing weights of cultural, political and administrative factors in the implementation process) a typology seemed the natural solution to going beyond casual empiricism (Castles 2001: 141). Our intellectual map now builds on three different *worlds of compliance* within the fifteen EU member states covered by our study: a *world of law observance*, a *world of domestic politics*, and a *world of neglect*. This should not be confused with worlds of good, mediocre, or bad compliance in terms of outcomes. We refer to the typical patterns of *how a duty to implement* a piece of EU law in the national context *is tackled procedurally*. This does not necessarily equate with the outcome of these processes.

The implementation performance in a sample of cases may be as mediocre (or bad) in a country belonging to the world of domestic politics as in a country in the world of neglect, or it may turn out to be as good (or mediocre) as in a country from the world of law observance.[2] The three worlds do not indicate outcomes, but typical modes of treating implementation duties. The specific results of particular examples of compliance tend to *depend on different factors* within each of the various worlds: the compliance culture in the field can explain most cases in the *world of law observance*, while in the *world of domestic politics* the specific fit with political preferences in each case plays a much larger role, and in the *world of neglect* this is true for administrative non-action.

It should be stressed that these patterns seem to be *rather stable over time*, and that they outlive governments of opposing ideological orientation. For example, the pattern we found in the UK during the Major government did not change as such once the Labour Party was in office. Although the Labour government immediately decided to transpose two of the Directives that had been left unimplemented by its predecessors, the procedural pattern was still one based on domestic political considerations (rather than on a culture of dutifulness vis-à-vis EU law, such as in other countries). In fact, our findings indicate that each of the fifteen member states belongs to one characteristic 'family' out of three.

15.2   Three worlds of compliance: typical modes of reacting to adaptation requirements

In what we term a *world of law observance*, the compliance goal typically overrides domestic concerns because it ranks so high (see Table 15.1). Even if there are conflicting national policy styles, interests or ideologies, transposition of EU Directives is usually both in time and correct. Application of the national implementation laws is characteristically successful, too, for the transposition laws tend to be well considered and well adapted to the specific circumstances. Additionally, citizens are used to

[2] We certainly cannot predict outcomes at the level of individual cases.

Table 15.1 *Three worlds of compliance*

	World of law observance	World of domestic politics	World of neglect
Political importance of compliance with EU law	Highly valued, typically overrides domestic concerns.	One ambition among many, domestic concerns frequently prevail.	Not an aspiration per se.
Transposition is typically ...	... on time and correct (even where conflicting domestic interests exist).	... on time and correct only if there is no conflict with domestic concerns.	... late and/or 'pro forma'.
Factors facilitating compliance	Culture of good compliance as a self-reinforcing social mechanism.	Fit with preferences of government and major interest groups.	Accelerating issue linkage with domestic reforms, high profile of particular cases.
Conditions of non-compliance	Unawareness; otherwise non-compliance occurs rarely and briefly.	Political failure (lack of compromise among conflicting interests or compromise against the terms of EU law). If non-compliance occurs, it tends to be rather long-term.	Bureaucratic failure (inefficiency, overload, non-attention). Non-compliance is the rule rather than the exception.
Predominant logic	Cultural.	Pursuit of political interests.	Pursuit of interests within the administration.
Typical process	Dutiful adaptation.	Conflict / compromise.	Inertia.

complying. This (at least from the EU's top-down perspective, clearly most successful) pattern is supported by a national 'compliance culture' (about this self-reinforcing socio-political mechanism, see section 15.4 below). Non-compliance, by contrast, typically occurs only rarely and (at least willingly) not without fundamental domestic traditions or basic regulatory philosophies being at stake. In addition, the tendency is for instances of non-compliance to be ended quickly. Probably as a result of the preoccupation with fulfilling the compulsory requirements, voluntary adaptations (for example, incorporating EU soft law) hardly ever occur in this group of countries.

In the *world of domestic politics*, by contrast, obeying EU rules is at best one goal among many. Domestic concerns frequently prevail if there is a conflict of interests, and each single act of transposing an EU Directive tends to happen on the basis of a fresh cost–benefit analysis. Transposition is likely to be timely and correct where no domestic concerns dominate over the fragile aspiration to comply. In cases of a manifest clash between EU requirements and domestic interest politics, non-compliance is the likely outcome (at least for a rather long time). While in the countries belonging to the world of law observance, breaking EU law would not be a socially acceptable state of affairs, it is much less of a problem in one of the countries in this second category. At times, their politicians or major interest groups even openly call for disobedience with European duties – an appeal which in these countries is not seriously denounced socially. In many cases, European soft law is treated in a comparable manner as binding EU law in these countries. The fate of such non-binding recommendations typically depends on the preferences of government parties or important interest groups. EU recommendations are incorporated into domestic law if they fit in with the agendas of important political actors at the domestic level. In our cases, this happened rather frequently, and it is for this reason that most of the voluntary adaptations we observed occurred in countries that belong to the world of domestic politics.

In the countries forming the *world of neglect*, compliance with EU law is no goal in itself. Those domestic actors that are calling for more obedience thus have even less of a sound cultural basis for doing so than in the world of domestic politics. At least as long as there is no powerful action by supranational actors (like an infringement procedure triggered by the European Commission), compliance obligations are often not recognised at all in these 'neglecting' countries. A posture of 'national arrogance' (in the sense that indigenous standards are typically expected to be superior) may support this, as may administrative overload or inefficiency. In fact, Figure 2.3 in Chapter 2 included a 'road' to transposition failure called 'inertia'. This is what we actually found as the most frequent pattern in our countries of neglect: the typical initial reaction to an EU-related implementation duty is inactivity. This pattern of initial inertia was usually caused by governments and administrations remaining passive while, at the same time, there were no interested societal groups acting as successful 'policy entrepreneurs'.

After an intervention by the European Commission, the transposition process may be initiated and may even proceed rather swiftly. The result, however, is not infrequently correct only at the surface. This tends to be the case where ministerial decrees are used (instead of laws) and where literal translation of EU Directives takes place (instead of a proper detailed translation that fits not only the words, but also the spirit of the EU rule, which typically needs specification and embedding in the specific context of the existing domestic rules). EU soft law often shares the fate of being neglected in these countries. However, if inertia is eventually overcome and if a political process of transposition is initiated, over-implementation does also occur in this group. Under these special conditions, much the same logic prevails as in the world of domestic politics.

Approaching an explanation of these patterns, it seems useful to distinguish, in an ideal-typical fashion, between the *administrative* and the *political phases of the transposition process*.[3] It is the task of the administrative systems in the member states – usually the ministries in charge of the specific dossiers – to identify reform requirements implied by EU law and to initiate a process leading towards adaptation. The second phase then typically involves more than administrators only. In a political process, politicians, interest groups and potential further actors in a country's political system interact in order to reach decisions on domestic transposition and implementation. We found that in each world a characteristic pattern of (more or less) dutiful action dominates in each phase. In the world of law observance, abiding by EU rules is usually the dominant goal in both the administrative and the political systems. The same is only true for the administrative system when it comes to the world of domestic politics. There, the process can easily be blocked or diverted (towards incomplete or even flawed adaptation) during the phase of political contestation. In the world of neglect, by contrast, not even the administration acts in a dutiful way when it comes to the implementation of EU Directives. Therefore, the political process is typically not even started when it should be. It needs to be mentioned, however, that politicians in the world of neglect also do not tend to take compliance with EU law very seriously, otherwise the bureaucrats could not get away with such behaviour, at least in the longer run. Table 15.2 outlines these patterns for all three worlds.

To be sure, there are some country-specific patterns even below this level of analysis. In some cases, it seems useful to differentiate between

---

[3] As a matter of course, it is difficult in practice to draw a sharp line between the political and the administrative systems. Since we are interested in the (ideal-)typical characteristics of different worlds of compliance, however, we would still maintain that trying to do so is worthwhile in order to find out more about the way different member states typically react to reform requirements arising from EU law.

Table 15.2 *Law-abidingness of administrative and political systems in the three worlds of compliance*

EU law-abidingness dominant in ...	World of law observance	World of domestic politics	World of neglect
... administrative system	+	+	−
... political system	+	−	−

willingness, on the one hand, and *capacity*, on the other hand, for both the political and the administrative levels. With regard to the administrative system, this may best be illustrated by two countries that belong to the world of neglect. In Luxembourg it seems that there is indeed a shortage of administrative capacity, while the bureaucrats in the small administration seem to realise quite well what the needs would be, in principle. They just decide to pursue other administrative interests and not to initiate the transposition of EU Directives, at least in the short and medium run. In the French administrative system, by contrast, lack of capacity is not a major problem. What often seems to be lacking, however, is the insight that adaptation is actually needed. The administration does not appear to have an interest in even looking closely at new social policy Directives. With regard to political systems, it is also useful to distinguish between willingness and capacity. While political willingness primarily depends on the presence of a culture of good compliance or the ideological fit with government preferences, even willing government parties are confronted with differing capacities to enact the necessary reforms. In the British 'Westminster' system, for instance, which is characterised by very few veto players, there are virtually no obstacles for successful reforms if the single party in government supports the goals of the Directive to be transposed. In the Italian system of multiple veto players, in contrast, the largest party in government, even if it is willing to transpose a Directive, is still confronted with potential resistance by one of its numerous coalition partners.

Going beyond analytical description, political science theory suggests looking at the relative weight of *culture versus interests* in the implementation process. In fact, the attitudinal factor dominates quite regularly in the world of law abidance, which typically leads to dutiful adaptation. Culture, however, impacts much less strongly on compliance issues in the two other worlds. By contrast, interests predominate. These are typically political interests in the world of domestic politics, and interests within the administrative system (or rather: non-interest by the administration) in the world of neglect.[4] While the balance between culture and self-interest obviously diverges between our worlds, it is still crucial to note that we do not see any worlds of 'consequentiality' or worlds of 'appropriateness' (March and Olsen 1989). Considerations of appropriateness and of consequentiality are typically present at the same time, everywhere. They just often relate to different levels (for example, bureaucrats disregarding EU laws can at the same time be quite dedicated rule-followers with respect to a given domestic administrative culture), and they may receive different weight in the overall process. In addition, it seems that actors in the world of law observance adhere to a conception of self-interest that is more oriented towards a long-term and communitarian rationale[5] while in the other two worlds, administrators and politicians strive rather for a shorter-term specific interest that can easily impede dutiful compliance.

15.3   Transposition versus enforcement and application

When applying our typology of three worlds of compliance, it is crucial to differentiate properly between stages of the implementation process (see Chapter 1) when sorting countries into the different categories. This is because neglectful enforcement of a Directive's standards, giving rise to application problems, may counterbalance dutiful performance during the transposition stage. In fact, this may even be an explicit (though not publicly disclosed) strategy of countries that might want to appear as 'good guys' while actually free riding. Hence, a typology for the transposition stage may be helpful,[6] but can only be a first step towards an understanding of compliance at large. Therefore, we suggest looking at

---

[4] As an example, consider an administrative unit that is confronted with the transposition of six Directives to be processed within the following year but could cope with only five of them on the basis of its standard operating procedures. This unit has two options. First, it could try to fulfil its duties, even if this would involve 'costs' in terms of either doing overtime, lobbying for more resources within the wider organisation, or carrying out organisational reforms that would raise its productivity. Second, it could try to avoid these extra costs by sticking to its standard operating procedures, which means that some tasks would have to be prioritised over others, and some of the duties under EU law would have to be ignored, at least temporarily. The second option represents one version of what we call the pursuit of interests within the administrative system, notably the interest in avoiding inconveniences that would arise from acting dutifully.

[5] The following quotation from one of our Danish interviews corroborates this argument: 'If you have agreed to something, you stick to that agreement. And if the Danish government says yes [to a Directive], they are bound by that promise. But besides that it is also in the Danish interest. Because ... Denmark wants other member states also to respect Community legislation. And if we don't do it ourselves, we can't point fingers at other member states (Interview DK3: 950–71).

[6] This is especially true if we bear in mind that the largest part of all studies so far did not go beyond the transposition of EU Directives.

both the stage of transposition and the subsequent stage of enforcement and application when assigning countries to the different worlds of compliance. Since membership in different worlds is possible for different phases, our typology may also be used for studies that focus on the transposition process only.[7]

As outlined elsewhere in this book, we could not conduct an in-depth study of application and enforcement since a grass-roots enquiry was beyond our means. However, we did collect information on specifically serious instances of non-application and on systematic flaws in enforcement (see Chapter 13). To account more realistically for the likely outcome of implementation processes in the three different worlds, we decided to differentiate between the transposition stage of an EU Directive (where we have detailed results for all cases) and the enforcement and application stage. As our information on the latter stage is less comprehensive, we cannot directly qualify in overall terms each domestic system. Hence, we opted for giving 'discounts' where we found good arguments – in our interviews, in the literature and in the transposition laws – that compliance in overall terms should be significantly worse than transposition performance due to a neglect of the duty to bring the legal rules into practice.

In those cases where we actually identified shortcomings in the enforcement systems that were, in overall terms, both serious and systematic, we moved the countries in question from one of the other categories to the world of neglect. In both empirical cases where we proceeded along these lines (see below), we consider our findings to be both fairly reliable and significant in overall terms. For all other countries that are outside the world of neglect, neither our own empirical information nor the available literature point to serious and systematic problems in the respective enforcement systems.

By contrast, countries characterised by neglect at the transposition stage do not move into one of the other categories if they have organised their enforcement systems in an effective manner. This is because dutiful enforcement and application are inherently impossible where transposition of an EU Directive in domestic law is not properly realised. Hence, neglectful transposition cannot be outweighed by good enforcement. It is true that complaints by the European Commission frequently trigger legal

---

[7] It should be noted that the grouping of countries presented below is based on the implementation process as a whole. Therefore, two countries that follow a logic of domestic politics when it comes to transposition but neglect their duties to ensure proper enforcement were included in the world of neglect. If the focus is on transposition only, these two countries (Ireland and Italy) will have to be treated as belonging to the world of domestic politics.

compliance that had originally been neglected or rejected because of domestic policy choices. However, since our findings reveal that the Commission enforces only a part of all non-compliance cases (see Chapter 11), one cannot trust this to make up for transposition failures.

15.4   The scope of our typology

We developed the typology with the implementation of EU labour law in mind, more specifically the implementation of EU labour law Directives. We expect, however, that the scope of our findings will be broader. Compliance with other forms of EU law could follow similar patterns (for example, the application of Regulations).[8] With regard to policies, we expect that the leeway of any administration to disregard EU implementation duties will not fundamentally differ between issue areas. Additionally, the specific cultures can reasonably be expected to cover not only the labour law and even the social policy arena, but all or many EU-related policies. Finally, the compliance culture relating to EU law will often, but not always, go hand in hand with the compliance culture relating to domestic law. Empirically, this is clearly shown in the Danish case, for this country is the most Euro-sceptic member but nevertheless its good compliance culture applies to EU law as well as national law. This differs from other cases such as France, where neglect predominantly applies to rules stemming from the EU, while domestic law is generally respected. There are, however, good reasons why any other law originating from outside the country should be treated in a similar way to EU law in France. Since further research is needed on all these issues, however, we do not, at this point, stretch the lines of our typology beyond the field we studied, i.e. the implementation of the EU labour law Directives.

The stability over time of the seemingly more endangered world(s) and the prospects of switching to a different world are crucial issues in this context. By contrast, it is beyond our reach here to speculate about the historical development of the different worlds. At least, we can explain in abstract terms both transitions between worlds, on the one hand (item (b) below), and the non-transition of countries in the most dutiful of our worlds (item (a) below).

(a) *How can a world of law observance persist* next to other worlds that do not take their EU-related duties as seriously? Our research revealed

---

[8] However, more research is needed in respect of countries like France and Luxembourg, which belong to the world of neglect in the transposition phase, but possess proper enforcement systems and are thus not plagued by significant application problems. In these countries, we could expect a much better overall compliance performance in the case of directly applicable EU law.

| t 1: good compliance culture | ⇒ | Society expects compliance, elites feel pressure to comply (and typically do so, as well as providing for the necessary administration). | ⇒ | Government can impose compliant behaviour on adversely affected interests who are generally used to complying, too. | ⇓ |
| t 2: good compliance culture reinforced | ⇐ | Expectations raised that next time good compliance will prevail again (and other actors may profit in turn). | ⇐ | Public discourse stresses long-term gain for all of respected rule of law (rather than short-term advantages of non-compliance). | ⇐ |

Figure 15.1 A socio-political mechanism reinforcing good compliance

a number of elements that can be combined to form a larger picture suggesting a *socio-political mechanism* that reinforces tendencies to take compliance seriously (see Figure 15.1).

This mechanism interrelates cultural and actor-related aspects in stressing that institutionalised patterns create expectations and cost–benefit calculations that induce actors (here governments) to behave in a certain way. Although this is a probabilistic mechanism rather than an automatism – governments may at times act against a national culture of good compliance – our cases indicate every bit as much as aggregate statistics (see, for example, Sverdrup 2002b, 2003: 20f.) that this 'good compliance mechanism' produces rather regular effects in some member states. This mechanism meets two of the main criteria for any cultural explanation as suggested by Mark Lichbach (2003: 94–5). First, it illustrates how 'norms become internalized in individuals', thereby explaining how a culture of good compliance may become the dominant action orientation of political elites. Second, the probabilistic nature of the mechanism underlines that the impact of the cultural factor in our explanation is not a deterministic one, but that other courses of action, which go against the cultural logic, are possible in individual cases.

(b) *Stability over time* is a second crucial issue in this context. In our study, all fifteen countries exhibited a rather stable pattern so that we could unequivocally categorise them. In principle, however, it should be possible that countries move from one world to another. More research is needed here, but only longitudinal studies with a quite specific research design should be able to track such shifts should they happen.

Table 15.1 above suggests a number of hypotheses regarding potential changes from one world to another. The change from the world of neglect to the world of domestic politics seems to be comparatively the easiest. If a government decides to make compliance a priority, and effectively imposes this on its administrative system, the administrative kick-off phases should be allowed to function much more regularly soon thereafter. However, this will not always be easy to put into practice, as it will require an increase in administrative resources, a more effective organisation of the administrative system or even efforts to raise awareness of compliance issues among bureaucrats.

In contrast, it will be much harder for a government to move its country into the world of law observance, at least in the short run. A culture of good compliance needs time to mature, and many small-scale struggles will have to be won against those who advocate departures from the path of virtue in individual cases. Over a longer period, however, incremental but constant trials and a slowly increasing number of victories in individual cases of implementation may reinforce each other and may finally add up to a slow process towards increasingly better compliance.

Concerning the trigger of changes between worlds, both the 'logic of appropriateness' and the 'logic of consequentiality' may prevail. For example, the constant 'naming and shaming' of bad compliers can have an impact. At the same time, the costs of frequent infringement proceedings and potentially even costly fines imposed by the ECJ may bring about change, as may the reasoning that a bad reputation may impinge on the negotiation leverage of a certain government in the Council of Ministers. Note, however, that the logic of consequentiality does not necessarily have to foster compliance. On the contrary, considerations of domestic self-interest (at least those that are of a short-term nature) point often enough towards non-compliance as the favourite option. In the European multi-level system, therefore, it seems that member states are permanently struggling with the choice between pursuing their (long-term) interests in being a 'good guy' and following their (typically more short-term) domestic interests, even if this results in non-compliance with EU law.

15.5   Fifteen countries in the three worlds of compliance

In principle, no empirical case can be expected to fit any ideal type perfectly. The country-by-country perspective is nevertheless instructive in highlighting that our typology has an empirical basis. It goes without saying that looking at six cases per country may sometimes yield a somewhat distorted picture (for example, the Nordic countries experienced implementation problems of untypical magnitude in our cases). As has already been pointed out, however, our interviews allowed us to gain much broader insights about the specific cultures prevalent in the different member states. With the benefit of this knowledge, we were able to identify the typical compliance pattern for each country, thereby supplementing the impression gained from investigating into our six specific sample Directives.

15.5.1   The world of law observance

Our cases confirm that Denmark has a very good compliance record. Four out of six Directives were transposed in a fully correct manner, and only one of them experienced a short delay of less than six months. These four Directives even include one with a high degree of misfit (Part-time Work) and one with medium-scale misfit (Young Workers). Where transposition problems occurred (i.e. in the Working Time and Parental Leave cases), they were due to an uncertain legal situation.[9] Once the legal situation was clarified, Denmark complied rather speedily in one case (Working Time) and announced that it would fulfil the EU requirements in the other (Parental Leave). When the same issue arose again in relation to the Part-time Work Directive, Denmark avoided breaching European law from the outset. Our interviews with various Danish actors highlight that implementing on time and avoiding infringements are taken very seriously by the Danish government (Interviews DK7: 719–28, DK4: 456–79, DK3: 950–71). In the Part-time and Working Time cases, the government complied with the EU's demands even in the face of strong domestic opposition from the large social partner organisations (see Chapter 12). And in the Young Workers case, the Danish minority government was confronted with fierce resistance from opposition parties on the issue of raising the age limit for light child labour. Still, it worked very hard to convince the opposition parties to support the transposition law in order to fulfil the European demands correctly and within the given time. On the basis of a package deal thrashed out by the Minister of Labour, these efforts finally succeeded (see Chapter 7).

Sweden also has a good implementation record with comparatively few delays. Clear examples are the Directives on Parental Leave and Part-time Work, where the government, in order to be on the safe side in terms of compliance with EU law, decided to enact legislation even before it was clear that its originally preferred option of implementation by collective agreement would be insufficient (see Chapter 12 and Leiber 2005). In general, fulfilling European obligations is taken very seriously by the Swedish government. Exceptions to the good Swedish compliance record among our Directives are the Working Time and Pregnant Workers cases. When the Working Time Directive was implemented, Sweden used the so-called 'fence rule' and simply included a reference to the Directive in its existing working time law. This step, however, was not intended to undermine the Directive's standards, but to protect the freedom of the

---

[9] As outlined in Chapter 12, it was initially not clear (even to the Commission) whether or not Danish collective agreements would suffice as implementation instruments. Danish officials debated this matter very openly with Commission members.

Swedish social partners as far as possible (see Chapter 12). After it had become clear that the European Commission would not accept this way of implementation, the Swedish government readily agreed to adapt its rules. This process was still underway when we concluded our empirical analysis. In the Pregnant Workers case, Sweden openly refused to introduce the required compulsory maternity leave. It seems that the government considered the Swedish protection level more than equivalent to the EU rules and did not want to build statutory barriers that would prevent women from participating in the labour market. This breach of the Directive was also remedied rather swiftly after the Commission had initiated an infringement procedure.

Finland very much resembles Sweden and Denmark in terms of striving for good compliance, although our empirical sample includes two cases with untypical transposition problems. One example underlining the (in principle) good compliance culture is the Parental Leave Directive, where timely transposition was ensured by separation of the transposition process from a related broader reform process. While in other countries transposition was sometimes delayed due to issue linkage with an associated domestic reform process, Finland in this case did not wait until the broader discussion had come to an end, but decoupled the transposition of the Directive from the national reform. While, without a doubt, we have noticed a relatively large number of transposition omissions in Finland, most of these can be explained by inadvertence or interpretation problems (the Young Workers case, for example) or they were of minor importance. The fact that the Pregnant Workers Directive has not been implemented correctly, since Finnish law does not grant breastfeeding women the necessary health and safety protection, is due to administrative sloppiness. National experts explained this transposition shortcoming, which has so far not been detected by the Commission, by the fact that breastfeeding women in Finland usually do not go to work, but take advantage of the attractive parental leave scheme. After Commission intervention, Finland has meanwhile implemented another aspect, albeit this requirement (the need to create a two weeks' compulsory maternity leave) was considered superfluous as well.[10]

Our analysis of the way member states have organised the area of law enforcement has revealed that in Denmark, Sweden and Finland, compliance is also the dominant logic when it comes to enforcement. According to our information, the three countries all seem to have fairly

---

[10] Although it might seem to be a bit over-critical that we classified this case as not having reached the stage of 'essential correctness' until the time of writing (see Chapter 5), we deemed the protection of women not only during pregnancy, but also during the time of breastfeeding to be one of the essential features of the Directive.

well-organised enforcement systems to ensure that EU legislation does not merely make its way onto the statute books, but is also respected in practice (see Chapter 13). They may thus be assigned to the world of law observance with regard to both transposition and enforcement.

Our findings on the three member states that belong to the world of law observance are confirmed by Ulf Sverdrup's data (2003), which suggests that these countries experience fewer infringement proceedings and that they submit to complaints by the European Commission faster than other countries.

15.5.2   The world of domestic politics

Germany is a very clear example of the world of domestic politics, for party political considerations played a major role in almost all German cases observed. If the Directives concerned did not correspond to the preferences of (one of) the parties in government, resistance and long delays were the typical reaction. This was usually the case under centre-right government coalitions. Conversely, if the goals of the Directives matched the partisan preferences of the government, adaptation was swift and often went beyond the minimum requirements. This regularly happened under the red-green coalition of recent years (see Chapters 4 to 9 and Treib 2004).

The fact that compliance with EU law is not a very high-ranking political goal in Austria is clearly indicated by our empirical analysis. In particular the cases of the Working Time, Young Workers and Parental Leave Directives show that concerns relating to domestic politics frequently override the requirements arising from EU law (see Chapter 7 and Leiber 2005). The search for a compromise with and between the social partners was in these cases given clear priority over the timely implementation of the Directives. Altogether, four of the six example Directives were implemented with major transposition problems (i.e. more than six months' delay until the stage of essential correctness was reached); the other two cases were implemented on time but lacked correctness in specific details.

The UK clearly belongs to the world of domestic politics since different party political orientations of government mattered very much. For ideological reasons, the Conservative government fought hard against the Directives at the EU level. The transposition process was then frequently used as a 'continuation of decision-making by other means', i.e. as an opportunity to continue combating Directives that were already adopted against the will of the UK government. The only significant exception was the Pregnant Workers Directive which the Conservative government obviously did not dislike on ideological grounds as much as, for instance, the Working Time or Young Workers Directives (see Chapters 5, 6 and 7). The resistance of the Conservatives could be overcome easily after Labour had assumed power, for the latter is ideologically more disposed to EU social policy. Under Labour, however, differences between both sides of industry became increasingly critical since the Labour government was willing to involve employers and unions much more thoroughly in the preparation of transposition laws (see especially Chapters 8 and 9). Thus, party politics was increasingly supplanted by interest group politics. Nevertheless, concerns of domestic politics were dominant throughout (see also Treib 2004).

The Netherlands has a rather good implementation record, but implementation processes are driven by considerations of domestic politics (rather than by a good compliance culture). Hence, the Netherlands belongs to the world of domestic politics in our typology. The relatively clean record stems from the fact that among the Directives we studied, several cases were unproblematic for the Netherlands, in two cases because the required changes were rather insignificant and no domestic actors had any major stake in these issues (Pregnant Workers, Part-time Work). Two further cases were unproblematic because parallel reform processes were already underway, which made adaptation a relatively easy task (Working Time, Parental Leave). If any country in the world of domestic politics seems close to the borderline towards the world of law observance in our study, it is the Netherlands. However, when domestic reform plans mismatched the thrust of a Directive, the goal of fulfilling EU law was set aside in favour of realising these domestic aspirations. This was very clearly visible in the Young Workers case, where the Dutch government had a deregulatory agenda and thus violated the Directive's partly higher standards (see Chapter 7 and Treib 2004).[11]

In terms of our Directives, Belgium's implementation record is rather poor. The main problems were caused by controversies between the social partners and the state over who should be responsible for implementation (especially in the transposition of the Working Time and Part-time Work Directives). Additionally, compromises between both sides of industry as well as between the social partners and the government on tricky issues took a long time to mature in the Belgian consensus culture (especially

---

[11] There are indeed indications that the rather good performance of the Netherlands in our sample does not hold for other cases. Hence, Ellen Mastenbroek's (2003) quantitative study on the timeliness of transposition of 229 Directives in the Netherlands revealed that almost 60 per cent of the Directives were transposed late, some with a delay of several years. And the picture would become even worse if substantive correctness of transposition were taken into account (which Mastenbroek does not since her data allows no conclusions about the correctness of transposition).

in the Working Time and Young Workers cases). In the light of this, there seems to have been a couple of aggravating factors at work, but no facilitating ones. At any rate, all of these factors are typical of the world of domestic politics. In only one out of six Directives (the Employment Contract Information Directive) were there any signs of neglect. Still, the implementation process here was set in motion, and only after experiencing difficulties did it come to a standstill (see Chapter 4). At least in the field of labour law, it seems that this country merely needs a lot of time to bring its laws into line with EU requirements, as a result of cumbersome internal policy-making patterns (Hartlapp 2005).

In Spain, the administration functions very well with regard to transposing the EU's social policy Directives. Transposition was almost always initiated in good time. If transposition was significantly late, substantively incorrect or partially neglected in Spain, this was due either to political unwillingness as a result of ideological resistance (for instance, the PSOE government disliked the Employment Contract Information Directive), or to political controversies caused by over-implementation or to a genuine lack of awareness (see Chapter 4 and Hartlapp 2005). Our conclusion is therefore that Spain belongs to the world of domestic politics as well.

If we turn our attention to domestic enforcement, our empirical investigations have revealed that the systems of monitoring practical compliance in these countries, as far as the field of labour law is concerned, are not characterised by systematic and severe shortcomings.[12] Hence, the assignment of Germany, Austria, the UK, the Netherlands, Belgium and Spain to the world of domestic politics does not change if we focus on enforcement. We have already seen that, in this world, administrations in general work effectively and dutifully which, however, is counteracted by contestation in the political sphere. As enforcement is above all an administrative task, therefore, this finding fits perfectly to our conceptualisation of the world of domestic politics.

15.5.3 The world of neglect

Among the six countries that belong to the world of neglect, there are three different configurations of factors that account for this classification. In Greece and Portugal, both transposition and enforcement are

---

[12] In Spain, some application problems were noticeable, mainly due to the inefficient decentralisation of responsibilities for enforcement, which lay (mostly) with the Autonomous Regions. Nevertheless, in overall terms Spain does not belong to the countries with ineffective enforcement systems.

characterised by neglect, which makes membership of these two countries in the world of neglect rather obvious. Luxembourg and France are neglectors at the transposition stage, but have rather effective enforcement systems. Since bad transposition cannot be made up for by a dutiful mode of enforcement, both countries also end up in the world of neglect. Italy and Ireland, finally, share features of the world of domestic politics when it comes to transposition, but the enforcement stage in these countries is marked by neglect. In overall terms, therefore, we assigned these two countries to the world of neglect as well.

Neglect is the common feature of all phases of the implementation process in Greece. Transposition normally takes place via ministerial decrees, which often reproduce the text of the underlying Directives in a verbatim way and so an appropriate connection to existing domestic policies is lacking. In general, the transposition process usually remains rather apolitical. The bulk of the Greek administration is considered inefficient (and our cases certainly revealed no evidence to the contrary), while the small percentage of activist politicians at the top of the state hierarchy generally only deal with the most important issues. They do not pay much attention to the transposition of EU policies since the national perception is that no political leeway exists there anyway. In three of our cases (the Employment Contract Information, Pregnant Workers and Young Workers Directives), warning letters from the European Commission were needed to get the transposition process started (see Chapters 7 and 11 as well as Hartlapp 2005). Even trade unions and left-wing governments did not seem to be interested in the EU's labour law Directives. Only the Working Time Directive gave rise to some domestic debate in Greece, due to its coinciding with a national debate. The only piece of EU legislation in our sample that was transposed in time was the Part-time Work Directive. Given the inertia that prevailed in many of the other cases, it looks almost as if it happened by accident. Significant enforcement and application problems also exist in Greece (see above and Hartlapp 2005). Therefore, the pattern of neglect is even more pronounced if all stages of the implementation process are taken into account.[13]

In Portugal, the transposition of Directives is generally seen as an apolitical process of (often verbatim) translation, which is usually carried out

---

[13] It should be noted that these characteristics are not specific to the implementation of EU law in Greece. National regulation processes in Greece also tend to be a rather apolitical affair, relying heavily on decrees that are worked out by administrative, rather than political, actors. Moreover, the application and enforcement of national laws is equally inefficient (maybe even more so because the Commission has lately gone some way towards improving application of EU-related rules via the stimulation of interest group involvement).

through ministerial decrees.[14] It should be pointed out, however, that the specific sample of cases that we studied did not mirror this general picture. Hence, five out of our six Directives were tackled in an atypical fashion. During the second half of the 1990s, a left-wing minority government was in power that sought the political backing of the social partners in order to increase the support for its policies in the parliamentary arena. Hence, it opted for transposition via social dialogue (and thus for laws rather than decrees as instruments). The Pregnant Workers, Working Time, Young Workers and Parental Leave Directives were part of a larger tripartite pact. This led to a 'politicisation' of the transposition process and furthered issue linkage with other topics treated within the social dialogue (see Chapters 7 and 9 as well as Hartlapp 2005). Yet this did not mean timely and correct transposition, but instead imported aspects of a different logic into the transposition process, as opposed to the otherwise typical style of neglect.

During the first half of the 1990s, by contrast, the conservative majority government had typically failed to initiate transposition processes on time. The fact that this was no longer the case in the following phase may also be due to Portugal having become more sensitive to the ever-increasing pressure from the European Commission to improve compliance. What made us still categorise the country as belonging to the world of neglect is that this feature continued to be an important characteristic of the transposition process, at least below the surface. In a number of cases, the government apparently pursued what could be called a 'good-guy policy' of rather swift transposition and prompt notification. Behind this façade, however, a good deal of neglect still prevailed. Thus, several of the legal texts reported to the Commission did not meet all the requirements to be fulfilled.[15] In terms of enforcement and application, furthermore, Portugal is characterised by serious shortcomings (see Chapter 13). Despite Portugal's much publicised efforts to get rid of the image of being an implementation laggard, therefore, the evidence we assembled still points to an overall pattern of neglect. However, these noticeable efforts might lead to an improvement in the future.

[14] Even a high-ranking ministerial official conceived of himself as fulfilling rather apolitical tasks: *'Nous sommes techniciens'* (Interview P1: 1201).
[15] In the case of the Young Workers Directive, a bundle of older provisions without proper transposition were communicated to Brussels to stop the Commission from enforcing the Directive. In the case of the Employment Contract Directive, one provision that is missing in the Portuguese translation of the Directive is also missing in the Portuguese transposition decree. In the case of the Pregnant Workers Directive, a law was notified to the Commission, but proper application of this law was almost impossible since an additional decree specifying the details was still missing (see Chapters 4, 5 and 7, see also Hartlapp 2005).

In Luxembourg, five out of six cases show the typical characteristics of our world of neglect. The implementation process was marked by inertia during the very first phase of administrative preparation in which the implementation measure should be drafted, that is to say before a contentious political process could even have started. The reason given in our interviews was that systematic administrative overload caused the seemingly minor adaptation requirements to be neglected (for more details, see Leiber 2005). At the same time, no adequate efforts were made to rectify the situation of administrative overload in the relevant units of the bureaucracy, while infringement proceedings and even judgments by the ECJ are accepted. By contrast, in the one case in our sample where Luxembourg was confronted with large-scale policy misfit, i.e. the Parental Leave Directive, the transposition process was initiated early on and was able to be completed almost in time (even though the result ultimately turned out to be incorrect in one point). This highly conspicuous case was considered an important project by the Luxembourg government and, given its outstanding character compared with the other tasks to be accomplished, administrative actors also treated it with priority. Hence, the Directive was tackled in a comparatively swift way. Statistical data suggests that Luxembourg's rate of non-compliance in other policy areas is lower than is characteristic of our chosen field of labour law. Further research is thus needed to determine whether our results are atypical across policy areas. With regard to the stages of domestic enforcement and application, our empirical analysis provides no evidence that Luxembourg's enforcement system, though it reveals certain deficiencies,[16] has systematic shortcomings that preclude a reasonable degree of practical compliance. But since a rather well-functioning enforcement system cannot compensate for neglect at the transposition stage (see section 15.3 above), Luxembourg ends up as belonging to the world of neglect in overall terms.

France is the prime example of neglect motivated by a kind of national 'arrogance'. The view that EU social policy was nothing more than a copy of the French system was widespread among our interview partners. Thus a lack of interest in the policies emanating from the EU level, and a tendency to disregard the ensuing adaptation requirements, characterised not only the administration and leading politicians, but also the major interest groups. This attitude thus extended across traditional party-political and ideological splits and usually resulted in inertia. In many cases, implementation took place only after the European Commission had initiated an infringement procedure (for the Employment Contract

---

[16] For example, the number of labour inspectors is comparatively low (see also Ch. 13).

Information, Pregnant Workers, and Young Workers Directives).[17] For the Working Time Directive, not only neglect but also a delaying issue linkage affected good compliance with EU law. Once the EU Commission exerted pressure, however, transposition typically took place rather smoothly. Additionally, application and enforcement function quite well in France. Given that the 'national arrogance' we observed was specifically related to the perceived superiority of the French regulatory model in this field, we would not necessarily expect the same pattern of neglect to prevail in all other policy areas. Official implementation statistics indeed show significant differences between policies, but the French performance across all policy areas is among the worst in Europe.

With regard to transposition, Ireland clearly belongs to the world of domestic politics. The level of conflict among domestic actors, however, was usually lower than in the UK since party political contestation along the left–right continuum is not as strong. Nevertheless, if domestic actors (be it employers' organisations, trade unions or any of the governing parties) developed a strong interest in favour of or against a particular Directive, the ensuing debates then dominated the implementation process. In some cases, consent among the social partners was treated with higher priority than timely adaptation (especially in the case of the Part-time Work Directive; see Chapter 9) and, at times, relatively swift adaptation was only possible due to strong political support on the part of government (but for domestic reasons, as in the Working Time Directive; see Chapter 6). The overall performance of Ireland in terms of transposing our six Directives essentially correctly was comparatively good, with Ireland ranking second of all member states.

However, this picture changes if we turn our attention to enforcement. The Irish enforcement system is marked by considerable shortcomings. The central labour inspectorate has extremely scarce resources and cannot guarantee that employers and workers abide by the laws enacted to a reasonable extent (see Chapter 13). Therefore, the typical mode of dealing with EU law at this stage is marked by neglect. From an overall perspective which takes into account the way of implementing EU law as a whole, we assigned Ireland to the world of neglect.

The same is true for Italy. In terms of transposition, Italy also belongs to the world of domestic politics, although two of the Italian cases (the Employment Contract Information and Pregnant Workers Directives) showed a pattern of neglect, with transposition being significantly delayed due to administrative sloppiness (Leiber 2005). Nevertheless, we include Italy in the world of domestic politics for the transposition stage since, in

---

[17] For more details on this kick-start effect of supranational enforcement, see Ch. 11.

the four other cases, the main reasons for non-compliance were governmental instability and – most importantly – conflicts of interest between political parties and/or both sides of industry, the latter being typical patterns of our world of domestic politics. Admittedly, the case of Italy is less clear than others. It seems that administrative reforms enacted during the 1990s already showed some effect, for administrative inefficiency was not the major problem in the four more recent transposition cases. Italy even managed to implement the Part-time Work Directive without major delay (see Chapters 6, 8 and 9 as well as Leiber 2005). To decide if the overall impression resulting from our study, namely a typical mode of transposition that is subject to considerations of domestic politics, is indeed representative for the country, or if neglect is as crucial a feature at this stage, further qualitative research is needed.[18] While administrative inefficiency is already quite a problem at the transposition stage in Italy, it becomes dominant with regard to enforcement. The serious shortcomings in the organisation of the Italian enforcement system (see Chapter 13) indicate that the Italian way of reacting to EU duties at the enforcement stage follows a logic of neglect. Therefore, Italy was assigned to the world of neglect, in overall terms.

15.6   Outlook

To the best of our knowledge, the typology of three worlds gives a more valid impression of compliance patterns in the fifteen countries covered by our study than the analysis of any of the causal factors presented in earlier research on compliance with EU law. Our typology in fact represents an inductively generated insight from the study of our ninety cases, to be tested and refined in future research. We feel particularly well placed to develop such a heuristically useful grouping on the basis of our detailed empirical work in all member states: 'If it is true that the Owl of Minerva flies only at dusk, it is no less true that we can only offer classificatory wisdom concerning worlds of experience that have been previously observed and analysed' (Castles 2001: 152). Without field work on many individual cases of (non-)compliance, one cannot know whether a case is typical of others and which cases may be subsumed under the heading of a relatively homogenous group. At least, this is true if we are looking for the *causal mechanisms* that are at work in the different member states

---

[18] As already outlined in this chapter, it is not possible to tell the difference between the world of domestic politics and the world of neglect on the basis of quantitative research, since the statistically measurable implementation performance of countries in both worlds may be just the same, in particular in smaller samples of cases. What differs quite systematically is the reason for this (poor) performance.

of national preferences and ideology for the implementation performance of many countries is one major finding of this study.[4] At the same time, some EU member states displayed quite a regular pattern of compliance or non-compliance, regardless of how the specific provisions actually fitted with the relevant national policy legacy and governmental ideology. Therefore, our best point of reference available for predicting the fate of any forthcoming case of policy implementation is in fact the specific national *culture of digesting adaptation requirements*.

We discerned three ideal-typical patterns of how member states handle the duty of complying with EU law. Our intellectual map therefore builds on three different *worlds of compliance* within the fifteen EU member states included in our study: a *world of law observance*, a *world of domestic politics*, and a *world of neglect*. These worlds are not necessarily visible if we look only at the overall implementation performance of member states. Rather, the typology seeks to grasp the most important characteristics of how certain groups of countries usually react to EU Directives in procedural terms (for details, see Chapter 15). We do not claim that the categorisation of three worlds of compliance is able to predict *individual* cases of implementation in the member states. However, we feel confident that it does cover the *typical* patterns of how member states deal with their duty to comply with EU Directives – definitely in the area of social policy, but probably even far beyond that.

16.2   An approximation of the living and working conditions?

What exactly is the effect of the six EU labour law Directives studied here? Did they bring about more equal working conditions? The appropriate answer seems a conditional 'yes, but . . .'.

There is a clearly visible effect, which we operationalised in terms of *the degree of misfit* between earlier national rules and the EU minimum standards (see Chapter 2). It was considered high in ten cases, medium-scale in thirty-three cases, and low in forty-six cases. Among the last group, the reform implications in three cases were of such a minor nature that we considered the pre-existing legislation to fulfil the EU requirements already 'essentially correctly'. And in all of our ninety cases, only one instance occurred in which a country had to enact no changes whatsoever. This indicates that, in an almost negligible group of only four

---

[4] In this sense, our book might come as a timely response to Peter Mair's criticism of the current Europeanisation literature. In a recent review of two of the major contributions to this literature, he argued that 'there is little about strictly political preferences, contestation or mobilization here, and this is to be regretted' (Mair 2004: 344).

cases, the adaptational pressure resulting from an EU Directive was either absent or rather insignificant. For those who believe that national governments strive to protect their national status quo ante, and actually succeed in doing so, this may come as a surprise.[5] In that sense, our findings are at odds both with intergovernmentalist approaches to EU decision-making (see especially Moravcsik 1993) and with extreme neo-institutional arguments stressing that member states above all defend their pre-existing status quo.

Although we observed significant problems with transposition and subsequent application at national level, ultimately the Directives studied did bring about domestic policy change in many cases.

From an overall perspective, therefore, it seems fair to say that EU social policy actually led to a successful approximation of the working conditions in the EU member states *in relative terms*, that is without producing full convergence of the different domestic rules and regulations. Clearly, these EU laws did not give rise to a level playing field for workers and employers across Europe. On the contrary, there are still many divergent rules and standards between the member states. Nevertheless, the diversity of domestic labour law regulations is now less than it would have been without the Directives.

The Directives served as a safety net guaranteeing a lower floor of employment rights. They contained the extent of domestic efforts at deregulation and flexibilisation, requiring some of the previous domestic moves to deregulate the labour market to be revoked (especially in the UK), and they will mark a barrier to any future plans for curtailing employment rights in the areas covered.

In the field of labour law, therefore, the impact of EU intervention is considerable. Meanwhile, only few domestic policies in this area are left untouched by EU Directives, and some of the supranational standards have proven to be rather progressive. For the field of social policy at large, however, the significance of EU standards is eclectic only. Labour law is but one part of national social policy. The most costly fields of national welfare systems are still outside the reach of EU regulation. The determination of wages is explicitly excluded from the sphere of the EU's competences, and progress on social security issues is de facto ruled out by the unanimity requirement. In economic terms, the impact of EU social policy has to be considered minor. The many liberalising measures

---

[5] If defending the domestic status quo had been the dominant strategy of governments, one of our sample Directives should have caused no adaptational pressure at all. However, even the Employment Contract Information Directive, which had to be adopted unanimously, actually entailed medium-range changes in three cases and low degrees of misfit in the remaining twelve cases.

of the single market programme certainly had a much larger effect on the member states. *Therefore, EU social policy still is on an unequal footing with economic integration.*

Despite these limitations, the overall impact of EU social policy and, in particular, labour law should not be underestimated. Beyond the concrete policy effects that we have documented in this book, the Directives may have had a potentially important psychological–political impact on domestic policy-making. They seem to have functioned as 'lighthouses' signalling that the EU is not only a market-making mechanism but active in the domain of social policy as well. In this sense, they might have contributed to a climate in which competitive deregulation appeared to be a less acceptable (and, in the long run, also a less viable) political option. It lies in the nature of this very indirect effect that we cannot present unequivocal empirical evidence for its existence. Nevertheless, we have some indirect indicators. Our empirical studies in the field of labour law did not reveal any significant steps of competitive deregulation. Moreover, the years in which we carried out our research (1999–2003) have not seen much discussion about social dumping in this area. This is in stark contrast to the beginning of the 1990s, when debates about social dumping were still high on the agenda, as in the context of the so-called 'Hoover affair', for instance.[6]

Altogether, we only very rarely observed 'revolutionary' changes that completely transformed existing policy traditions in the areas concerned (for example, in the case of Working Time in the UK). Much more frequent were the gradual (but often still far from insignificant) reforms that did not completely overturn existing policy legacies, but added new elements to what had already been in place before. In the terminology of institutional theory, what we observed most frequently was 'layering' rather than complete transformation. But such revolutionary changes happen only rarely anyway, even in national social policy (Thelen 2003). In other words, EU legislation typically added another 'layer' of new policies to the domestic systems of labour law.

If this is so, does EU social policy satisfy the criterion established in the introduction to this book for a successful combination of 'community and autonomy' (Scharpf 1994) in the European multi-level system? Are 'sufficient degrees of compatibility' secured in order to prevent a competitive devaluation of social standards in the member states? The answer

---

[6] In 1993, the management of Hoover decided to relocate part of its production from a plant in France to another site in Scotland because production costs were significantly lower there, mainly due to lower standards in working conditions. This spurred heated debates about social dumping within the Common European Market (EIRR 230: 14–19).

is again a conditional one. One subfield of social policy seems to have been secured from outright 'social dumping', at least for a couple of years. Very recent developments, particularly in the fields of working time and pay, however, raise doubts as to whether this trend may be sustained. Other subfields have not even been the object of EU regulation (due to the reasons already outlined, this is true, for instance, for wages), and many ongoing reforms in domestic social policy are characterised by spending cuts related to budgetary pressures that were partly induced or aggravated by the EU's Single Market and Monetary Union.[7] We conclude, therefore, that EU labour law harmonisation seems to have been relatively successful but is no panacea for European social standards in general.[8]

16.3   How voluntarist is EU social policy?

For very good reasons, EU social policy has in recent years been called 'neo-voluntarist'. This mode of governance is characterised by its low capacity to impose binding obligations on member states and market participants. Instead, it gives member states ample opportunities to sidestep unwanted adaptations and time and again merely offers a range of non-binding options which member states may or may not choose to accept. Altogether, this is insufficient to prevent effectively the race-to-the-bottom dynamics caused by regime competition among member states in the liberalised single market (Streeck 1995b).

The results of our study confirm this suspicion. At the same time, they offer some interesting qualifications.

16.3.1   *Voluntarist elements in our Directives*

As outlined in the previous chapters, there are many voluntarist (but also many non-voluntarist) elements in the six Directives studied here. In total, we counted fifty-three binding standards, twenty-six non-binding recommendations and forty possibilities for exemption. This equals an average of 8.8 binding provisions, 4.3 non-binding ones and 6.7 exemptions per Directive (see Table 16.1).

Clearly, there are not only non-binding provisions and exemption possibilities but at the same time compulsory elements too, and there are large differences between the individual Directives (see Chapter 3 for recent Directives beyond our sample, including some with again quite detailed

---

[7] On different challenges for the individual EU member states and their options, see Scharpf (2000).

[8] Certainly, such partial intervention cannot replace the action capacity vis-à-vis large economic actors that the European states have lost during recent phases of economic liberalisation (both within and beyond the EU).

Table 16.1 *Voluntarist and non-voluntarist standards contained in the six Directives examined*

Directive	Number of binding standards	Number of non-binding standards	Number of exemption possibilities
Employment Contract Information	6	–	4
Pregnant Workers	14	1	2
Working Time	12	2	14
Young Workers	13	3	11
Parental Leave	7	9	5
Part-time Work	1	11	4
Total numbers	53	26	40
Average across Directives	8.8	4.3	6.7
Cases in 15 member states	795	390	600

binding rules). Therefore, *the basic question* 'Is EU social policy neo-voluntarist?' can indeed be answered in the *affirmative*. Neo-voluntarism is an important feature of recent Directives in the field. The more far-reaching question as to whether this label actually captures the single major trait of EU social policy, or whether it can be used as its *unique descriptor*, however, calls for a *more cautious response* and further arguments.

The domestic impact of these standards has been studied in detail in the previous chapters. As we have argued in Chapter 10, it has not been possible to establish the degree of 'exploitation of voluntarism potentials' for each of the twenty-six soft-law provisions and each of the forty derogation possibilities (adding up to 990 individual cases in the fifteen member states). Nevertheless, the general thrust is clear: our analysis has indicated that there is no logic of minimalism at play, but rather a logic of domestic politics. In other words, member states do not automatically make use of *all* derogation possibilities and disregard *all* non-binding provisions. The exploitation of voluntarist potentials depends rather on a number of specific domestic circumstances, not least on the typical national patterns of reacting to EU standards.

16.3.2 The patchwork character of EU social policy

Notwithstanding the important neo-voluntarist characteristics of EU social policy outlined above, it is vital that we recognise a number of further specifics if we want to do justice to the complexity of dynamics in the field. They are also characteristic of EU social policy since it is, in actual fact, a patchwork-style[9] conglomerate. What Adrienne Héritier (1996) predicted seems to apply in EU social policy as well, namely that the accommodation of diversity in EU policy-making leads to 'regulatory policy as a patchwork'. This is highlighted by a number of features that are outlined below.

Differences between Directives. Table 16.1 above shows that not all Directives are equally neo-voluntarist. The Directives on Employment Contract Information and Pregnant Workers, for example, have few or no non-binding recommendations and a rather small number of exemptions. At the other end of the spectrum are the Directives on Parental Leave and Part-time Work, with rather few binding standards, but many soft-law provisions and also some exemptions. In any case, at least some of our Directives are characterised by clearly specified compulsory standards rather than by optional voluntarism.

Differences between various EU social policy instruments. Chapter 3 revealed that the proliferation of soft governance mechanisms does not crowd out more traditional 'hard' governance. Although the 'open method of co-ordination' very much dominates both the public and academic discourse nowadays on EU-level social affairs, the number of binding legal instruments (Directives and Regulations) has not yet declined, and there is still a surprisingly high number of issues in the legislative pipeline.

Regulations directly affect national standards since there is no need for transposition into national law. As outlined in Chapter 3, the large number of EU Regulations in the field of social security of migrant workers therefore has an immediate effect at the national level. Although derogations are not completely unknown in this area either, the binding character of these measures does not go well with the concept of neo-voluntarism. This is even more extreme when it comes to judgments of the European Court of Justice. They often (re-)interpret Acts adopted in the Council of Ministers in a dramatically far-reaching way and leave the governments no other realistic option than to comply.[10]

---

[9] See the ground-breaking work by Leibfried and Pierson (1995: 63): 'Over the past thirty years a complex patchwork of regulations and court decisions has partially abridged the principle of member-state sovereignty over social policy.'

[10] Theoretically, they could certainly adopt a new Directive or Regulation in order to restore the status quo ante and to prevent the ECJ's ruling from coming into effect. In practice, however, this happens only rarely. First, the judgments have immediate and normally even retroactive effect so that there are already 'sunk costs' when the Council decides on a modification of the provisions in question (which, for procedural reasons, usually happens much later). Second, a large majority or even unanimity is needed to adopt a new piece of EU legislation, but as member states are normally affected unequally by any EU measure, at least some member states may have no interest in taking action against the ECJ's decision.

We conclude that binding EU legislation, supported by the primacy of EU law over national law (an important legal doctrine of the ECJ), is still an important characteristic of EU social policy. In other words, binding and non-binding elements both exist. By no means have voluntary forms completely replaced binding ones.

Differences between subfields of EU social policy. The subfield of industrial relations served as a prime example when the concept of neo-voluntarism was developed.[11] Indeed, both the European Works Councils Directive and the Directive on Employee Participation under the European Enterprise Statute contain a large number of derogations, and basically no unconditionally binding core (Streeck 1997; Keller 2002). The same, however, cannot be said for the labour law Directives studied here. This highlights the fact that it would seem useful to add further concepts (on top of neo-voluntarism) to obtain an exhaustive characterisation of EU social policy.

Not all elements of neo-voluntarism are equally present. Some elements of the concept are less visible in our Directives. A lack of political 'vision' at the higher level of governance,[12] for example, cannot in fact be discerned in our cases. The Directives rather have a clear vision which they actually prescribe legally, i.e. that working hours should have legal limits; that there must be written information on crucial employment aspects; that young and pregnant workers should have special protection; that parental leave should no longer be a female prerogative; and, finally, that part-time workers must not be discriminated against. There are, in particular, clearly visible concepts of life (employees should be able to combine professional and private ambitions), fairness ('atypical' employees should not be treated less favourably than 'typical' employees), and the family (men and women should assume an equal share of childcare responsibilities).

One can certainly imagine even more wide-ranging political goals in the area of social policy. At the same time, one should be aware that sometimes the basic objectives set down by law are even more clearly anchored in EU law than in the ensuing national law. The German government, to give one example, allowed the social partners unlimited derogations

---

[11] See Streeck (1995a, 1995b). The main reason why we did not include a Directive from this area in our sample is that the 1994 European Works Councils Directive, an Act that would have fitted well with our sample in terms of timing, regulated genuinely transnational issues. National regulations on works councils were not under adaptational pressure, which made the case less interesting from the viewpoint of implementation theory.

[12] Streeck warns that observers tend to forget the 'obligation of the "higher level" of governance ... to ensure that the outcomes of self-regulation are compatible with general political objectives and norms of social justice, instead of being merely market outcomes or results of a contingent distribution of power' (Streeck 1995a: 171).

from the basic rules on how to average out weekly working hours. The Working Time Directive, in contrast, set a limit of no more than twelve months to such derogations (see Chapter 6).

On a more general level, i.e. beyond the sphere of the EU's social dimension, however, the reproach seems quite appropriate. As already mentioned, there is no congruence between market liberalisation, on the one hand, and socially motivated EU action to secure 'just' and socially sustainable outcomes, on the other. Peter Lange was right to expect that a 'social democratic... Europe, redistributing to the "losers" as markets become freer, is improbable' (Lange 1992: 256). To be sure, this is not due to the quality of the existing 'social dimension of European integration', but to its limited scope if compared with market integration on a European and global scale ('social non-Europe').[13]

A small *scope of application* is another aspect related to neo-voluntarist policies.[14] Indeed, we found a number of sectors or groups that were excluded from one or the other Directive. At the same time, we were astonished to learn how many derogations exist at the domestic level. It seems that national labour law is in this respect quite voluntarist as well. Our labour law Directives actually required the abolition of several exemptions at member state level and hence extended the scope of application of employment rights. Taking the example of working time, doctors and/or medical personnel (in Austria, Belgium and Germany) as well as agricultural workers (in Germany) were either completely excluded from domestic working time laws or at least refused the same working time limits as other groups of employees. Generally, public sector employees were often treated differently in the member states (as in Belgium or France). Furthermore, some member states tended to exclude small and medium-sized businesses from employment legislation (as did Greece). Finally, some notable national curiosities were eliminated by our Directives. For example, the French law on equal treatment of part-time workers had, by definition, excluded all part-timers working between thirty-two and thirty-nine hours a week.

The impression gained from our empirical studies is that EU law is *not systematically more selective in its scope than national law*. In fact, the source

---

[13] It should be mentioned that a final evaluation of the EU as a social policy actor needs to deal not only with the existing social measures, but also the (potentially) lacking ones. This was, however, not feasible within this study for it amounts to another work-intensive research project in its own right.

[14] This additional criterion stems from our discussions with Wolfgang Streeck. It relates to the number of citizens who are being covered by a legal Act. Among Directives with the same rights, the Directive that excludes the most groups (e.g. shift workers), businesses (e.g. small and medium-sized businesses) or sectors (e.g. the public sector) is the most voluntarist.

of an EU exemption is typically a pre-existing exemption in one of the member states which the relevant government wants to protect. In the cases where this effort succeeds, it is still far from clear whether those governments that do not have the relevant exemption in domestic law will take the occasion to introduce it. Of the forty exemption possibilities offered by our six Directives (creating 600 cases of potential take-up), only 251 cases of actual adoption were reported by our interviewees. 162 of these cases had already existed in national law prior to the Directive and were upheld, so that only a minority of 89 were introduced for the first time. Since we asked specifically for any lowering of pre-existing standards (the rare results are reported in Chapter 10), it seems that the overwhelming majority of these new exemptions concern new rights granted under the Directives.

In conclusion, voluntarist features are indeed frequent in recent EU social law. At the same time, they are not the single overriding characteristic of EU social policy. Rather, they may or may not be a feature of individual Directives, and/or are to a variable degree so. Furthermore, these traits go hand-in-hand with other typical features (such as the enduring importance of binding elements, limiting national exemptions, and the primacy of EU law over national law) that all in all point to a comparatively 'harder' character of EU social law.

In overall terms, the multi-level politics of European social integration leads to a *process of horizontal and vertical layering* (Thelen 2003). There are ever more elements of EU social policy on the supranational level (Regulations, ECJ judgments, spending programmes, Directives, binding and non-binding elements therein, Recommendations and the like, open co-ordination). When it comes to 'downloading' EU social law to the member states, further 'layers' are added to the domestic social policies. The result is a patchwork-style compound form of 'social Europe' consisting of more *and* less voluntaristic, and both EU-induced *and* other elements in social policy, to be witnessed in all parts of the EU's multi-level system.

16.4   How to improve EU social policy?
Some recommendations

Let us finally discuss some possibilities of improving EU social policy in order to mitigate domestic compliance problems. Since going through the individual problems of each member state and identifying possible solutions to these problems would certainly go beyond the scope of this concluding chapter, we focus on those parameters that may be influenced by the actors at the EU level.

16.4.1   Fostering domestic compliance cultures

As we have argued in Chapter 15, the most effective factor to ensure proper transposition, enforcement and application of European legislation is the presence of a culture of good compliance at the domestic level. That said, we must acknowledge that it is far from easy to establish and foster such a culture in the member states, especially for supranational actors with limited capacities and a fragile standing in terms of democratic legitimacy and acceptance by the broader citizenry. As measures that would require only limited resources, one could imagine promotional activities such as conferences or awareness campaigns being carried out by the Commission. Much more ambitious, but probably also more effective, would be the establishment of an 'observatory for compliance' in each member state.[15] These observatories could publicise and report to the EU domestic violations of (a culture of) good compliance (e.g. where interested actors publicly contest the need or usefulness of compliance, or put undue pressure on those who promote law observance). Each observatory might even directly counteract the potential long-term harm done by such statements or campaigns by issuing countervailing press statements and organising public events involving civil society. It could even be considered whether these observatories should be given:

- powers as 'ombudsoffices' that provide information, and potentially also out-of-court arbitration, for citizens who feel that they are being denied certain rights under EU law because the member state did not comply properly with the rules;
- powers to monitor the domestic compliance with EU rules, including a right to investigate individual cases of alleged non-compliance;
- infrastructure and means needed to conduct scientific studies on the state of implementation of EU law in specific geographic or issue areas (on the request of the European Commission, the government or parliament of the relevant member state or any other member state).

16.4.2   Targeting structural obstacles to compliance at the domestic level

Further action to facilitate domestic compliance could target specific national obstacles to effectively fulfilling EU duties and promote those characteristics of the various domestic systems that support good compliance

---

[15] Something similar, although with less focus on fostering domestic compliance cultures, already seems to exist in the area of the internal market: SOLVIT, a network of offices located in the member states that offer assistance when individuals or businesses trying to exercise rights under internal market rules encounter unjustified obstacles within the national administration of their member state (see also Hartlapp 2004).

records. There is a connection between the typical problems in national compliance with EU law on the one hand, and the political and administrative systems of the member states, on the other (see Table 15.2). For example, where the administration is understaffed or badly trained and where policy entrepreneurs are lacking or are systematically not heard by the politico-administrative system, implementation can hardly work properly. There is hence ample room for improvement at these levels. To be sure, such structural reforms require the investment of considerable political and financial resources, and responsibility lies firmly in the hands of the member states. But the European Commission could at least serve as a facilitator of cross-national learning and a communicator of best practice (on differentiated approaches for the different worlds, see section 16.4.4 below).[16]

In addition to such institutional reforms in individual countries, and besides the fostering of a culture of good compliance in the worlds of domestic politics and neglect, a number of improvements seem to be useful for all member states.

16.4.3 Improving the quality of legal texts

Our empirical studies revealed that interpretation problems due to the complex nature of a Directive or its unclear wording may hamper proper implementation even if domestic actors are willing to comply (see Chapter 14). These problems could be alleviated by improving the legal quality of EU legislation. The following three steps would seem to be useful in this context:

- *Improving clarity.* Some of the provisions in our Directives were worded so ambiguously that it was hard for member states to find out what they were expected to do. The Pregnant Workers Directive in particular caused serious interpretation problems. Not only did it contain a number of 'rhetorical' compromises concealing a fundamental clash between two conflicting regulatory philosophies, but it also required member states to attend to the dissemination of guidelines that were

---

[16] A recent 'Commission staff working paper' at least partly points in the same direction. In order to avoid administrative co-ordination problems, the paper proposes that all member states should establish a powerful central administrative unit that would be responsible for co-ordinating the actions of different ministries in incorporating EU law – probably modelled on the British or French examples (CEC 2001a). As this book has shown, however, administrative co-ordination problems are only one institutional obstacle to domestic compliance (and not even a very important one, see Chapter 14). Therefore, the Commission could certainly do more to alleviate the problem of domestic non-compliance by turning its attention to other institutional impediments in the member states as well.

drawn up only many years later (see Chapter 5). But there were also examples in the remaining Directives where unclear wording or insufficient definition of concepts gave rise to implementation problems (notably the lack of specification of central terms such as 'employment conditions' or 'work on a casual basis' in the Part-time Work Directive). These problems could be avoided by improved drafting of the Directives.

- *Avoiding unnecessary complexity.* Many of our interviewees have argued that the Working Time Directive was hard to implement because it was such a byzantine piece of legislation, with many different rules and derogation possibilities for certain sectors and groups of workers. It has to be noted, however, that the convoluted nature of the Directive stems to a large extent from the complex nature of statutory working time regulations in general. Domestic working time laws are usually rather complicated as well. Nevertheless, some of the weaknesses in drafting could have been avoided. For example, the available derogations have been included in one summative Article at the end of the Directive, thereby separating them from the Articles to which they belong substantively. Moreover, some exemptions have been worded in an unnecessarily complicated and convoluted way. For example, the Directive allows derogations from a standard and at the same time specifies exceptions from these derogations under certain conditions (see Article 17 of the Directive).

  Obviously, we are aware of the fact that ambiguous wording and complex phrasing of legislation are often the (more or less unavoidable) outcome of political battles at the decision-making phase. In situations where the negotiating parties have conflicting preferences, vague formulations are often the only way to secure agreement, especially in the Council of Ministers with its high consensus requirements. Nevertheless, it also seems worth considering whether negotiators should not try to rely less on 'rhetorical' compromises, even if this is likely to lengthen the process of finding acceptable solutions. In fact, it should be in the interest of all member states to strive for maximum legal clarity at the decision-making stage since, otherwise, all governments run the risk of being subjected to far-reaching reinterpretations by the European Court of Justice with highly unpredictable policy implications.

- *Optimising communication channels between the Commission and domestic officials.* The Commission should try its utmost to act in a consistent way (difficult though that may be due to its status as a multi-organisation and to evolving legal interpretations). We found a few cases where information reportedly given to national experts in earlier phases of the

European policy process later turned out to be inappropriate, with the result that member states faced unexpected adaptation requirements (most importantly, Luxembourg and Germany in the Pregnant Workers Directive, see Chapter 5). The implementation of the Directive just mentioned was furthermore hindered by the extremely late publication of guidelines which were originally meant to facilitate the application of the complex annexes. Moreover, these guidelines turned out to be much less specific than expected and were thus of little help in coping with the maze of adaptation (again see Chapter 5).

Even if we accept that negotiation situations will sometimes require the use of 'rhetorical' compromises, the way of dealing with them at the implementation stage could be improved. In particular, the Commission could optimise its communication with domestic actors during the phase of implementation. The practice of creating specific working groups, bringing together Commission officials and the national civil servants in charge of transposing a particular Directive, could be extended beyond the present level. Such a working group was set up with regard to the European Works Councils Directive and apparently proved to be a highly useful tool for discussing ambiguous provisions and arriving at mutually accepted interpretations (see, for example, Weber 1997).

16.4.4 Increasing visibility, awareness and enforcement efforts

In terms of the Commission's role as 'guardian of the Treaties', our analysis points to a number of steps through which the Commission's enforcement policy vis-à-vis non-compliant member states could be made more effective. It is true that the Commission has implemented several reforms since the beginning of the 1990s in order to streamline the internal handling of infringement proceedings, increase the use of public 'naming and shaming' by scoreboards and the like, and pay more attention to the substantive correctness of transposition and actual application (see Chapter 11 and Hartlapp 2005). These measures certainly point in the right direction, but the efforts to monitor substantive accuracy and practical compliance will definitely have to be improved. Otherwise, a significant portion of actual non-compliance in the member states will continue to be ignored, since the Commission simply lacks information about these violations of Community law.

In this context, it will not suffice to improve contacts with domestic interest groups that might act as watchdogs, bringing potential violations to the attention of the Commission. While it can indeed be an effective instrument for gathering information about potential infringements, this method has a number of shortcomings. It presupposes the existence of groups that do not only have an interest in the realisation of the EU provision in question, but also know that such a provision in EU law exists in the first place. Yet it is in the area of labour law especially, where it is quite common that rights are provided to weak 'outsider' groups on the labour market such as 'atypical' workers, that these conditions are unlikely to be met. Hence, the Commission should *devote more resources to actively monitoring* whether a Directive's standards are actually fulfilled in the member states. Given that the Commission currently has no more than about 22,000 members of staff (Nugent 2001), which is about the same as the staff working for the administration of a medium-sized city in Germany (Docksey and Williams 1994: 119), the Commission itself will need to be given more resources, which then have to be devoted to implementation rather than policy-making, in order to be able to fulfil adequately the task of ensuring compliance with Community law – not least against the background of Eastern enlargement, which has increased the number of member states from fifteen to twenty-five, with a number of candidate countries and would-be candidates still waiting for EU accession.

In the light of our finding that there are three different *worlds of compliance* at the national level, with very different causes of non-compliance requiring very different remedies, the Commission should differentiate its enforcement policy accordingly. While it is unlikely that much attention will have to be paid to countries in the *world of law observance*, since they normally tend to fulfil their duties arising from Community law, the Commission should focus on the other two worlds more closely. In the *world of domestic politics*, undiscovered violations of European law will tend to be of less importance, as transposition processes are usually highly politicised and there is normally a well-developed system of organised interests that will be keen to see advantageous provisions implemented. As non-compliance usually arises from the unwillingness of governments or the de facto blockage of the transposition process by other political actors, enforcement in these countries is best ensured if the Commission is able to pursue its infringement proceedings quickly so that the opposition may be overcome by mounting pressure 'from above'.

In contrast, the most important problem of supranational enforcement in the *world of neglect* will be undiscovered violations. If administrations disregard the duty to implement EU Directives, while strong and active interest groups either do not exist or are equally uninterested, information about infringements is unlikely to come to the attention of supranational actors unless the Commission itself plays an active part. It is especially with regard to these countries that increased Commission efforts actively to monitor compliance are important. What seems to be even more crucial is an active policy to find out about insufficient enforcement and application, which is rather frequent in this world. Since many of the problems in the countries belonging to this group are caused by administrative inefficiency, 'management' measures should be intensified – for example in the form of supranational training programmes for administrative staff at the national level or Commission guidance on effective organisational reforms.

The Commission could also devote some energy to the exchange of information between domestic bureaucrats and politicians in order to raise awareness among those who belong to the *worlds of domestic politics* and *neglect* of the benefits arising from the type of compliance culture prevailing in the Nordic countries. Just as in the open method of co-ordination, the Commission could identify best practice solutions (in this case, the necessity of taking very seriously the duties arising from Community law) and try to induce domestic actors to learn from each other.

16.4.5 Avoiding misfit in the politics or polity dimension?

Some of our Danish and Swedish cases have revealed that significant implementation problems are likely to arise if compliance with a Directive does not merely require policy change, but actually interferes with established traditions in the politics or polity dimension. In our cases, the issue at stake was a tradition of social partner autonomy in the regulation of employment conditions. This tradition was called into question because collective agreements could not guarantee full coverage of the workforce. Hence, autonomous transposition of Directives by the social partners, even though explicitly provided for in the Treaties, was de facto not a viable solution.

It could be argued that such interference with deeply-entrenched domestic traditions is normatively questionable and thus should best be avoided, especially since they rest on rather legalistic arguments. After all, the old system of autonomous regulation of working conditions, practised especially by the Danish social partners, seems to have worked quite well and, most importantly, without any significant number of complaints from citizens outside the agreements' (theoretical or practical) reach. However, the existing system of autonomous social partnership in effect *prevented a group of workers from being able to take legal action in order to assert their legal rights conferred on them by EU law*. In this sense, the EU's insistence on guaranteeing full coverage of the workforce served the purpose of securing the principle of equal rights for all citizens of the European Union.

It has to be added that social partnership as such was not abolished by EU intervention. Rather, a specific type of social partnership was declared incompatible with the requirements of EU law. The Danish social partners are to all intents and purposes still tightly involved in the preparation of transposition legislation, but their agreements are now backed up by legislation guaranteeing that all can take legal action for their rights. While it might still seem desirable to avoid *unnecessary* interference with such national traditions, in this case interference actually appeared worthwhile in order to ensure the general goal of equal citizenship rights. But if no such principles are at stake, the EU should be very careful to avoid intruding unnecessarily in domestic traditions in the area of state–society relations or in constitutive features of the polity if it wishes to avert the ensuing implementation problems that are very likely to emerge, as well as prevent almost certainly heated debates from occurring at the domestic level.

16.4.6   *Excluding member states that already essentially comply?*

One of the disadvantages of the current approach is that Directives are usually so detailed that even member states whose rules and regulations are already very close to the EU's standards have to initiate a time-consuming reform process in order to comply with the remaining details. A possible solution could be to exclude such countries from the scope of Directives in order to spare them the effort of having to attend to very minor adaptations. So far EU labour law Directives have always been imposed on all member states alike, except for the rather short period where the UK enjoyed its general opt-out from all new social law under the Maastricht Treaty's Social Agreement. To change this situation, however, would be easy since Article 249 TEC provides that Directives are only binding for those member states to which they are addressed.

We found three cases where member states actually complied 'essentially' from the outset. In all cases, the governments (at least officially) were not at all aware of the adaptation requirements and still do not comply today (France with regard to the Parental Leave Directive; Austria and Luxembourg in relation to the Part-time Work Directive). Could these problems be avoided by simply excluding these countries from the relevant Directives? A cursory glance at the specific cases throws new light on the issue: in France, *force majeure* leave for urgent family matters may only be taken for reasons related to a child rather than to any other family member as well. Neither Austria nor Luxembourg comply fully with the 'onion skin model' of comparing workers in discrimination cases. Disregarding these issues would inevitably give rise to discrimination against certain workers vis-à-vis the rest of the EU, which appears unacceptable if we want to preserve the principle of equal rights for all citizens of the Union.

A further very important drawback to this model is that if some states were not bound by EU Directives at all, EU social policy would lose its function as a safety net. A lower floor of standards would no longer be guaranteed across Europe as excluded countries would be free to cut back employment rights, whereas all the other member states would be bound by EU minimum legislation. In sum, therefore, completely excluding certain member states from EU Directives does not appear to be a viable solution even if this means that, sometimes, countries are obliged to initiate cumbersome reform processes in order, in effect, to fine-tune a few minor details.

16.4.7   Less detailed framework directives?

Fritz Scharpf (2002a) has recently proposed that the EU refocus the method of policy-making in EU social policy. Instead of trying to produce very detailed legislation, the EU should go for broader framework Directives, which only define certain general targets while leaving it up to member states to decide how to achieve these goals. In order to avoid giving the Court and the Commission excessive powers of interpretation, he argues, the concrete national solutions should be accompanied by a process modelled after the 'open method of co-ordination', where the Council would issue guidelines, member states would be required to prepare action plans and reports, and the Commission and the Council would periodically assess the member states' progress in achieving the common goals. If a country shows no inclination to follow the guidelines, the Council could adopt binding decisions against this country or authorise the Commission to initiate an infringement procedure. The background to this interesting proposal is the problem of overcoming Council deadlock in areas (such as social security legislation) where national policy legacies are so diverse that agreeing on detailed common standards is highly unfeasible. Against the background of Eastern enlargement in particular, this lack of agreement seems to be a real threat also to further progress in labour law.

At first sight, such a solution could even solve some of the implementation problems we observed. However, the merits as well as the potential dangers require considerable scrutiny. Let us consider, for example, the area of working time regulation. Instead of prescribing that no employee may be required to work more than an average of forty-eight hours per week, the Directive could have merely prescribed that at least 90 per cent of all workers in any country may not work longer than an average of forty-eight hours per week. This solution appears to be quite elegant, as it would have avoided two of the problems associated with the existing regulatory approach, as already discussed in this chapter. First, it would not have interfered with the tradition of autonomous social partner regulation in Denmark and Sweden, as long as the domestic working time rules defined by collective agreements could guarantee that no more than 10 per cent of all workers actually exceed the maximum weekly working time standard.[17] Secondly, it would have spared all countries with generally strict working time rules the effort of having to initiate a time-consuming legislative reform process in order to fulfil the details set down at EU level, without sacrificing the function of EU social policy as a safety net against excessive deregulation, because the commonly-defined threshold would apply to all countries alike.

However, there are also some grave disadvantages to such an approach. To begin with, monitoring compliance would become more difficult because everything would depend on reliable data about the actual weekly working hours of employees (or any other outcome prescribed by EU law). But as we know from unemployment figures, establishing the same methods of calculation and preventing governments from meddling with the underlying criteria is very difficult. In order to guarantee an unprejudiced basis for assessment, the Commission would have to provide for the data collection itself, which would certainly exceed its resources even more than its current task of analysing domestic legislation. This problem might be somewhat diminished by using the existing complaint mechanisms as 'fire alarms', where an examination of the domestic situation by the Commission would be triggered by complaints from domestic interest groups.

The second problem would still remain however. The proposed solution would mean a complete renunciation of the traditional way of policy-making in the area of labour law. Both domestically and at the EU level, labour law has hitherto focused heavily on providing employees with *legally binding rights* that they may invoke in court. If EU legislation would merely define very general goals, especially in the form of certain outcomes to be achieved (such as the 90 per cent threshold already mentioned), workers would no longer have any individual rights. Hence, the decentralised enforcement mechanism of individual court action

---

[17] In order to reach this goal, it would not be necessary to have 90 per cent of the workforce covered by collective agreements. Ensuring that no more than 10 per cent of all workers *actually* exceed the forty-eight-hour week on a regular basis would suffice. In all probability, this outcome could be reached on the basis of the existing system of collective agreements in Denmark and Sweden, which usually also affects non-unionised workers in companies that are covered by collective agreements.

against domestic rules and practices that are not in line with EU law, which has proven to be extremely effective, especially in the area of gender equality, would no longer be available. Moreover, the general principle of equal rights for all citizens of the European Union, which we consider of value in its own right (see section 16.4.5 above), would be thwarted by this type of policy. It is true that the current regime cannot guarantee that all workers have the same level of working conditions, as domestic inspection efforts are uneven and there are differing degrees of openness of the national legal systems to individual complaints. Nevertheless, everybody still has the same legal *entitlements*, irrespective of how they are actually put into practice. In the new model of 'framework Directives' discussed here, this situation would be reversed, as no one could invoke any individual right, but violations would have to prove that the overall situation in the member state in question is not in line with EU goals.

In sum, we would argue that this new type of law-making might have its merits in situations where traditional policy-making by detailed Directives is impeded by irreconcilable differences of interest, which nowadays is in particular true for the area of social security and social protection. In the field of labour law, however, the balance of costs and benefits seems to be negative, as enforcement would become extremely difficult and as the fundamental principle underlying labour law, namely providing individual rights to the entire workforce, would have to be sacrificed.

16.4.8   Can non-binding rules suffice?

The chapter on soft law has revealed that many of the non-binding provisions enshrined in our Directive were actually taken on board by member states. There is no general tendency towards economic minimalism in the implementation of social policy Directives. Hence, soft law may indeed have an impact. In the light of this knowledge, it could be argued that EU social policy should focus more on this non-binding approach, which would also avoid much of the implementation problems associated with detailed Directives. However, our analysis has shown that extremely costly recommendations were almost never taken up. At the same time, there are strong country-specific patterns, with some member states frequently following recommendations (for example Germany), while others almost never do so (for example Denmark or the UK).

This indicates that a purely non-binding approach cannot lead to a level playing field in Europe. It can trigger eclectic improvements of the living and working conditions, but it is not able to guarantee a common floor of minimum standards across all member states systematically. In terms of enforcement and individual rights, moreover, this approach would be plagued by the same problem as the idea of framework Directives that only define broad goals. Much of the existing EU social policy, especially in the field of equal treatment, is about the granting of rights to individuals, which may be invoked in court – ultimately in the European Court of Justice. If the EU only issued non-binding recommendations, this very effective decentralised enforcement mechanism would not work. Soft law, by definition, cannot be invoked in court. In the end, citizens would have to live with what their governments have chosen to implement, but they would not have any leverage on those recommendations that were ignored.

16.4.9   Overall effort should be worthwhile

Transposing a Directive is a significant effort in any case. This is true even where the necessary reforms may be pushed through by issuing an administrative decree without involving parliament to any significant extent. Extreme efforts are required in those countries where legislative reforms usually have to undergo long and intricate decision processes involving ministries, government parties, parliamentary factions, second chambers and interest groups. Initiating these painstaking processes appears to be increasingly unattractive if the required reforms are of little substantive value. This is also true where administrative resources are scarce, as was the case in Luxembourg.

While we found no Directive that seems unjustified,[18] the EU institutions and the member states should still be very careful when deciding whether implementing the Directives that they table or negotiate is really worth the effort in a significant number of these states. After all, resources are scarce in all countries as well as at the EU level. Indeed, our case studies have shown that the logic of neglect, even if it is the typical feature of implementation in some countries, is less likely to prevail if highly visible Directives with significant domestic impact have to be incorporated into

---

[18] A number of our interviewees actually doubted whether the Employment Contract Information Directive was worth the effort. As outlined in Ch. 4, this Directive almost exclusively involved small-scale adaptations in the member states. (On only three occasions was the degree of misfit medium.) However, one should bear in mind that by the time of adoption it was anything but clear that the Posted Workers Directive, which required workers who are sent abroad to provide services to have the same employment conditions as workers in the country in which the work is carried out, would ever be adopted. From an ex ante perspective, therefore, it seemed much more important to have a Directive that at least required employers to issue written statements on the employment conditions of their workers (including those who are sent abroad) since otherwise the control of abuse would have been even more difficult.

national law. In this sense, more ambitious social policy Directives could even increase the chances of domestic compliance.

16.5   Outlook

This book has presented a number of fresh insights into the domestic impact of EU social policy, into the way member states deal with their duty to implement EU legislation, and into the Commission's policy to ensure compliance. To what extent may these results be extended to other policy areas?

There can be no doubt that some of our findings, especially those relating to the implementation performance of individual member states in the six cases studied for each of them, or the impact of our EU Directives on domestic policies or state–society relations, do not hold up beyond the specific policy area studied. However, we are quite confident that the thrust of our arguments relating to implementation theory and to the compliance literature is also relevant for other policy fields, at least in a slightly modified manner. In particular, this is true for our finding that there are multiple *worlds of compliance* in which the process of implementing EU Directives follows very different logics.

Just as this book is published, EU enlargement is becoming a reality that also challenges the policy area discussed here. The Directives that are at the heart of this book are likely to have a substantial impact in the new member states. A recent survey on the working conditions in these countries (EIRR 318, 32–4) shows that weekly working hours are on average much longer than in the former fifteen member states of the EU, with a working week of 44.4 hours compared with 38.2 hours in the 'old' member states. Moreover, night work and shift work are fairly widespread in the new member countries. This indicates that the Working Time Directive, but probably also the other Directives studied here, will indeed make a noticeable difference there.

Only further research can reveal more about compliance with EU law in Eastern Europe. Above all, it will be interesting to see to which of our worlds of compliance the new member states from Central and Eastern Europe will belong or whether they will form a new world functioning according to its own logic.

References

Adinolfi, Adelina 1988. 'The Implementation of Social Policy Directives through Collective Agreements?', *Common Market Law Review* 25(2): 291–316.

Agallopoulou, Pénélope 1999. 'La Réglementation du Temps de Travail en Grèce', in: Yota Kravaritou (ed.), *The Regulation of Working Time in the European Union: Gender Approach*. Brussels: Peter Lang, 255–67.

Almond, Gabriel A., Powell, G. Bingham, Strøm, Kaare and Dalton, Russel J. (eds.) 2000. *Comparative Politics Today: A World View*. New York: Longman.

Alter, Karen J. 2001. *Establishing the Supremacy of European Law. The Making of an International Rule of Law in Europe*. Oxford: Oxford University Press.

Alter, Karen J. and Vargas, Jeannette 2000. 'Explaining Variation in the Use of European Litigation Strategies: European Community Law and British Equality Policy', *Comparative Politics* 33(4): 452–82.

Anderson, Jeffrey J. 2002. 'Europeanization and the Transformation of the Democratic Polity, 1945–2000', *Journal of Common Market Studies* 40(5): 793–822.

ArbuR 1993. 'Keine Einigung über EG-Arbeitszeitrichtlinie', *Arbeit und Recht* 41(3): 79.

Armstrong, Kenneth and Bulmer, Simon 2003. 'The United Kingdom: Between Political Controversy and Administrative Efficiency', in: Wolfgang Wessels, Andreas Maurer and Jürgen Mittag (eds.), *Fifteen into One: The European Union and Its Member States*. Manchester: Manchester University Press, 388–410.

Audretsch, H. A. H. 1986. *Supervision in European Community Law. Observance by the Member States of Their Treaty Obligations – A Treatise on International and Supra-National Supervision*. Amsterdam: Elsevier Science.

Bailey, Ian 2002. 'National Adaptation to European Integration: Institutional Vetoes and Goodness-of-Fit', *Journal of European Public Policy* 9(5): 791–811.

Bailey, Kenneth D. 1992. 'Typologies', in: Edgar F. Borgatta and Marie L. Borgatta (eds.), *Encyclopedia of Sociology*. Vol. IV. New York: Macmillan, 2188–94.

Barnard, Catherine 2000. 'Regulating Competitive Federalism in the European Union? The Case of EC Social Policy', in: Jo Shaw (ed.), *Social Law and Policy in an Evolving European Union*. Oxford: Hart, 49–69.

Barreto, José and Naumann, Reinhard 1998. 'Portugal: Industrial Relations Under Democracy', in: Anthony Ferner and Richard Hyman (eds.), *Changing Industrial Relations in Europe*. Oxford: Blackwell, 395–425.

Belloubet-Frier, Nicole 1995. 'The Case of France', in: Spyros A. Pappas (ed.), *National Administrative Procedures for the Preparation and Implementation of Community Decisions.* Maastricht: European Institute of Public Administration, 227–300.

Bercusson, Brian 1994. 'The Dynamic of European Labour Law after Maastricht', *Industrial Law Journal* 23(1): 1–31.

1995. 'The Collective Labour Law of the European Union', *European Law Journal* 1(2): 157–79.

Berg, Annika 2000. 'Government Backs Down on Expected Working Time Reduction Legislation'. EIROnline Document SE0011173F. Dublin: European Foundation for the Improvement of Living and Working Conditions <http://www.eiro.eurofound.ie/2000/11/feature/SE0011173F.html>.

2001a. 'Government Proposes Legislation to Implement EU Directives on Part-time and Fixed-term Work'. EIROnline Document SE0106104N. Dublin: European Foundation for the Improvement of Living and Working Conditions <http://www.eiro.eurofound.ie/2001/06/inbrief/ SE0106104N. html>.

2001b. 'Working Time Legislation to be Examined Again'. EIROnline Document SE0101176N. Dublin: European Foundation for the Improvement of Living and Working Conditions <http://www.eiro.eurofound.ie/2001/01/ inbrief/ SE0101176N.html>.

2002a. 'Committee Proposes Five More Days of Leave'. EIROnline Document SE0206105F. Dublin: European Foundation for the Improvement of Living and Working Conditions <http://www.eiro.eurofound.ie/2002/06/feature/ SE0206105F.html>.

2002b. 'EU Directives on Part-time and Fixed-term Work Implemented'. EIROnline SE0208102N. Dublin: European Foundation for the Improvement of Living and Working Conditions <http://www.eiro.eurofound.ie/ 2002/08/ inbrief/SE0208102N.html>.

Bergmann, Torbjörn 2000. 'The European Union as the Next Step of Delegation and Accountability', *European Journal of Political Research* 37(3): 415–29.

Beyers, Jan 2002. 'Gaining and Seeking Access: The European Adaptation of Domestic Interest Associations', *European Journal of Political Research* 41(5): 585–612.

Biagi, Marco 1998. 'Italy', in: Roger Blanpain (ed.), *Labour Law and Industrial Relations in the European Union.* Bulletin of Comparative Labour Relations 32. Den Haag: Kluwer, 103–11.

Biering, Peter 2000. 'The Application of EU Law in Denmark: 1986 to 2000', *Common Market Law Review* 37(4): 925–69.

Bilous, Alexandre 1998a. '35-hour Working Week Law Adopted'. EIROnline Document FR9806113F. Dublin: European Foundation for the Improvement of Living and Working Conditions <http://eiro.eurofound. ie/1998/06/ feature/FR9806113F.html>.

1998b. 'Italie. 35 Heures: Une Réduction en Trompe-l'oeil?', *Chronique Internationale de l'IRES* 54(Septembre): 1–7 <http://www.ires-fr.org/files/publicat/ chroint.htm#n54>.

1998c. 'Working time bill soon to become law'. EIROnline Document FR9804103F. Dublin: European Foundation for the Improvement of Living and Working Conditions <http://www.eiro.eurofound.ie/1998/04/Feature/FR9804103F.html>.

Blanpain, Roger and Engels, Chris 1995. *European Labour Law*. Deventer: Kluwer.

1997. 'Belgium', in: Roger Blanpain, Eberhard Köhler and Jacques Rojot (eds.), *Legal and Contractual Limitations to Working Time in the European Union*. Leuven: Peeters Press, 205–37.

Blanpain, Roger, Köhler, Eberhard and Rojot, Jacques (eds.) 1997. *Legal and Contractual Limitations to Working Time in the European Union*. Leuven: Peeters Press.

BMFSFJ 1999. 'Mutterschutzgesetz: Leitfaden zum Mutterschutz'. Bonn: Bundesministerium für Familie, Senioren, Frauen und Jugend.

Borchardt, Klaus-Dieter 1999. 'Der Gerichtshof', in: Carl Otto Lenz (ed.), *EG Vertrag Kommentar*. Köln: Bundesanzeiger, 1612–804.

Börzel, Tanja A. 1999. 'Towards Convergence in Europe? Institutional Adaptation to Europeanization in Germany and Spain', *Journal of Common Market Studies* 37(4): 573–96.

2000. 'Why There Is No "Southern Problem": On Environmental Leaders and Laggards in the European Union', *Journal of European Public Policy* 7(1): 141–62.

2001. 'Non-Compliance in the European Union: Pathology or Statistical Artifact?', *Journal of European Public Policy* 8(5): 803–24.

2002a. 'Pace-Setting, Foot-Dragging, and Fence-Sitting: Member State Responses to Europeanization', *Journal of Common Market Studies* 40(2): 193–214.

2002b. *States and Regions in the European Union: Institutional Adaptation in Germany and Spain*. Cambridge: Cambridge University Press.

2003a. *Environmental Leaders and Laggards in Europe: Why there is (not) a 'Southern Problem'*. Aldershot: Ashgate.

2003b. 'Guarding the Treaty: The Compliance Strategies of the European Commission', in: Tanja A. Börzel and Rachel A. Cichowski (eds.), *The State of the European Union*. Vol. VI: Law, Politics, and Society. Oxford: Oxford University Press, 197–220.

2005. 'How the European Union Interacts with its Member States', in: Simon Bulmer and Christian Lequesne (eds.), *Member States and the European Union*. Oxford: Oxford University Press (forthcoming).

Börzel, Tanja A. and Risse, Thomas 2000. 'When Europe Hits Home: Europeanization and Domestic Change', *European Integration Online Papers* 4(15) <http://eiop.or.at/eiop/texte/2000–015a.htm>.

Broughton, Andrea 2001. 'Temporary Agency Work Talks Break Down'. EIROnline Document EU0106215N. Dublin: European Foundation for the Improvement of Living and Working Conditions <http://www.eiro.eurofound.ie/2001/06/inbrief/EU0106215N.html>.

Bruning, Gwennaële and Plantenga, Janneke 1999. 'Parental Leave and Equal Opportunities: Experiences in Eight European Countries', *Journal of European Social Policy* 9(3): 195–209.

Bruun, Niklas 2002. Die Autonomie von Tarifverträgen. Conference paper, VII

European Regional Congress of the International Society for Labour Law and Social Security, 4–6 September 2002, Stockholm.

Buchholz-Will, Wiebke 1990. 'Kinder erziehen bleibt Privatsache: Elternurlaub in der EG', in: Susanne Schunter-Kleemann (ed.), *EG-Binnenmarkt – EuroPatriarchat oder Aufbruch der Frauen*. Bremen: WE FF Verlag, 158–74.

Bundesarbeitsblatt 1999. 'Teilzeit-Richtlinie wird umgesetzt', *Bundesarbeitsblatt* 1, 1999: 23–24.

Bundeskammer für Arbeiter und Angestellte 1999. *AK aktuell* 1999(2). Wien: Bundeskammer für Arbeiter und Angestellte.

Burchell, Brendan, Deakin, Simon and Honey, Sheila 1999. 'The Employment Status of Individuals in Non-Standard Employment'. Employment Relations Research Series, 6. London: Department of Trade and Industry <http://www.dti.gov.uk/er/emar/emar6.pdf>.

Bursens, Peter 2002. 'Why Denmark and Belgium Have Different Implementation Records: On Transposition Laggards and Leaders in the EU', *Scandinavian Political Studies* 25(2): 173–95.

Caporaso, James and Jupille, Joseph 2001. 'The Europeanization of Gender Equality Policy and Domestic Structural Change', in: Maria Green Cowles, James Caporaso and Thomas Risse (eds.), *Transforming Europe: Europeanization and Domestic Change*. Ithaca: Cornell University Press, 21–43.

Castles, Francis G. (ed.) 1982. *The Impact of Parties: Politics and Policies in Democratic Capitalist States*. London: Sage.

  1993. *Families of Nations: Patterns of Public Policy in Western Democracies*. Aldershot: Dartmouth.

  2001. 'Reflections on the Methodology of Comparative Type Construction: Three Worlds or Real Worlds?' *Acta Politica* 36(2): 140–54.

CEC 1997a. 'Commission to Bring Infringement Proceedings against 14 Member States in the Social Field'. Press Release IP/97/1126. Brussels: Commission of the European Communities.

  1997b. 'Information from the Commission – Method of Calculating the Penalty Payments Provided for Pursuant to Article 171 of the EC Treaty', OJ 1997 No. C63/2–4.

  1999. 'Report on the Implementation of Directive 91/533/EEC on an Employer's Obligation to Inform Employees of the Conditions Applicable to the Contract or Employment Relationship'. Brussels: Commission of the European Communities <http://europa.eu.int/comm/employment_ social/labour_law/implreports_en.htm>.

  2001a. 'Recommendations for the Improvement of the Application of Community Law by the Member States and its Enforcement by the Commission: Commission Staff Working Paper'. Brussels: Commission of the European Communities <http://europa.eu.int/comm/governance/white_paper/ recommendations_en.pdf.>

  2001b. 'Transposal of Directive 33/94/EC Concerning the Protection of Young People in the 15 Member States of the European Union'. Brussels: Commission of the European Communities <http://europa.eu.int/comm/ employment_social/labour_law/ implreports_en.htm>.

  2003. 'Report by the Commission's Services on the Implementation of Council Directive 97/81/EC of 17 December 1997 Concerning the Framework Agreement on Part-Time Work Concluded by UNICE, CEEP and the

ETUC'. Brussels: Commission of the European Communities <http:// europa.eu.int/comm/employment_social/labour_law/implreports_en.htm>.

Centro di Studi Economici Sociali e Sindacali 1997a. 'The government crisis and the reaction of the social partners'. EIROnline Document IT9710136N. Dublin: European Foundation for the Improvement of Living and Working Conditions <http://eiro.eurofound.ie/1997/10/inbrief/IT9710136N.html>.

1997b. 'Government Proposes Reducing the Working Week to 35 Hours'. EIROnline Document IT9710133N. Dublin: European Foundation for the Improvement of Living and Working Conditions <http://www.eiro. eurofound.ie/1997/10/inbrief/IT9710133N.html>.

Chozas Pedrero, Juan 1999. 'The Luxembourg Process and the Spanish Experience', *International Journal of Comparative Labour Law and Industrial Relations* 15(4): 403–18.

Christiansen, Peter Munk, Nørgaard, Asbjørn Sonne and Sidenius, Niels Christian 2001. 'Verbände und Korporatismus auf Dänisch', in: Werner Reutter and Peter Rütters (eds.), *Verbände und Verbandssysteme*. Opladen: Leske + Budrich, 51–74.

Christiansen, Thomas, Jørgensen, Knud Erik and Wiener, Antje 1999. 'The Social Construction of Europe', *Journal of European Public Policy* 6(4): 528–44.

Ciavarini Azzi, Giuseppe (ed.) 1985. *L'application du droit communautaire par les états membres*. Maastricht: European Institute of Public Administration.

1988. 'What Is this New Research into the Implementation of Community Legislation Bringing Us?' in: Heinrich Siedentopf and Jacques Ziller (eds.), *Making European Policies Work: The Implementation of Community Legislation in the Member States*. Vol. I: Comparative Syntheses. London: Sage, 190–201.

2000. 'The Slow March of European Legislation: The Implementation of Directives', in: Karlheinz Neunreither and Antje Wiener (eds.), *European Integration after Amsterdam: Institutional Dynamics and Prospects for Democracy*. Oxford: Oxford University Press, 52–67.

Clauwaert, Stefan and Harger, Sabine 2000. *Analysis of the Implementation of the Parental Leave Directive in the EU Member States*. Brussels: European Trade Union Institute.

Coen, David 1998. 'The European Business Interest and the Nation State: Large-firm Lobbying in the European Union and Member States', *Journal of Public Policy* 18(1): 75–100.

Colchester, Nicholas and Buchan, David 1990. *Europe Relaunched: Truths and Illusions on the Way to 1992*. London: Hutchinson.

Collins, Helen 1994. *The EU Pregnancy Directive: A Guide for Human Resource Managers*. Oxford: Blackwell.

Conant, Lisa 2001. 'Europeanization and the Courts: Variable Patterns of Adaptation among National Judiciaries', in: Maria Green Cowles, James Caporaso and Thomas Risse (eds.), *Transforming Europe: Europeanization and Domestic Change*. Ithaca: Cornell University Press, 97–115.

Cowles, Maria Green 2001. 'The Transatlantic Business Dialogue and Domestic Business–Government Relations', in: Maria Green Cowles, James Caporaso and Thomas Risse (eds.), *Transforming Europe: Europeanization and Domestic Change*. Ithaca: Cornell University Press, 159–79.

Cowles, Maria Green, Caporaso, James and Risse, Thomas (eds.) 2001. *Transforming Europe: Europeanization and Domestic Change*. Ithaca: Cornell University Press.

Cram, Laura 1994. 'The European Commission as a Multi-Organization: Social Policy and IT Policy in the EU', *Journal of European Public Policy* 1(2): 195–217.

Crepaz, Markus M. and Lijphart, Arend 1995. 'Linking and Integrating Corporatism and Consensus Democracy: Theory, Concepts and Evidence', *British Journal of Political Science* 25(2): 281–88.

Cristovam, Maria Luisa 1998a. 'Bargaining on Part-time Work in Portugal'. EIROnline Document PT9803170F. Dublin: European Foundation for the Improvement of Living and Working Conditions <http://www.eiro.eurofound. ie/1998/03/feature/PT9803170F.html>.

1998b. 'Transposition of the Young Workers Directive and the Child Labour Problem'. EIROnline Document PT9807185F. Dublin: European Foundation for the Improvement of Living and Working Conditions <http://www. eiro.eurofound.ie/1998/07/feature/PT9807185F.html>.

2001. 'New Initatives on Gender Equality'. EIROnline Document PT0107158F. Dublin: European Foundation for the Improvement of Living and Working Conditions <http://www.eiro.eurofound.ie/2001/07/feature/PT0107158F. html>.

Damgaard, Erik 2000. 'Denmark: The Life and Death of Government Coalitions', in: Wolfgang C. Müller and Kaare Strøm (eds.), *Coalition Governments in Western Europe*. Oxford: Oxford University Press, 231–63.

de la Porte, Caroline and Pochet, Philippe (eds.) 2002. *Building Social Europe through the Open Method of Co-Ordination*. Brussels: European Interuniversity Press.

Demmke, Christoph 1994. *Die Implementation von EG-Umweltpolitik in den Mitgliedstaaten: Umsetzung und Vollzug der Trinkwasserrichtlinie*. Baden-Baden: Nomos.

1998. 'Nationale Verwaltung und Europäische Umweltpolitik – die Umsetzung und der Vollzug von EG-Umweltrecht', in: Christoph Demmke (ed.), *Europäische Umweltpolitik und nationale Verwaltungen: Rolle und Aufgaben nationaler Verwaltungen im Entscheidungsprozeß*. Maastricht: European Institute of Public Administration, 85–127.

DGB 1991. 'Stellungnahme zu dem Vorschlag für eine Richtlinie des Rates über einen Nachweis von Arbeitsverhältnissen, Kom. (90) 563 vom 8.1.1991'. Düsseldorf: Deutscher Gewerkschaftsbund.

DiMaggio, Paul J. and Powell, Walter W. 1991. 'Introduction', in: Walter W. Powell and Paul J. DiMaggio (eds.), *The New Institutionalism in Organizational Analysis*. Chicago: University of Chicago Press, 1–38.

Dimitrakopoulos, Dionyssis 2001. 'The Transposition of EU Law: "Postdecisional Politics" and Institutional Economy', *European Law Journal* 7(4): 442–58.

DJELR 2002. 'Report of the Working Group on the Review of the Parental Leave Act 1998'. Dublin: Department of Justice, Equality and Law Reform.

Dobbins, Tony 2000. 'Irish Social Partners Endorse New National Agreement'. EIROnline Document IE0003149F. Dublin: European Foundation for the Improvement of Living and Working Conditions <http://www.eiro. eurofound.ie/2000/03/feature/IE0003149F.html>.

2002. 'Part-Time Work Directive Finally Implemented'. EIROnline Document IE0202202F. Dublin: European Foundation for the Improvement of Living and Working Conditions <http://www.eiro.eurofound.ie/2002/02/ feature/IE0202202F.html>.

Docksey, Christopher and Williams, Karen 1994. 'The Commission and the Execution of Community Policy', in: Geoffrey Edwards and David Spence (eds.), *The European Commission*. London: Longman, 117–45.

Douglas, Mary 2001. 'Culture as Explanation: Cultural Concerns', in: Neil J. Smelser and Paul B. Baltes (eds.), *International Encyclopedia of the Social & Behavioral Sciences*. Vol. V. Amsterdam: Elsevier, 3147–51.

DTI 1998. 'Measures to Implement Provisions of the EC Directives on the Organisation of Working Time ("The Working Time Directive") and the Protection of Young People at Work ("The Young Workers Directive")'. London: Department of Trade and Industry.

2000a. 'Part-Time Work: The Law and Best Practice: A Detailed Guide for Employers and Part-Timers'. London: Department of Trade and Industry.

2000b. 'The Part-Time Workers (Prevention of Less Favourable Treatment) Regulations: Regulatory Impact Assessment'. London: Department of Trade and Industry.

Duina, Francesco G. 1997. 'Explaining Legal Implementation in the European Union', *International Journal of the Sociology of Law* 25(2): 155–79.

1999. *Harmonizing Europe: Nation-States within the Common Market*. Albany: State University of New York Press.

Duina, Francesco G. and Blithe, Frank 1999. 'Nation-States and Common Markets: The Institutional Conditions for Acceptance', *Review of International Political Economy* 6(4): 494–530.

Dürmeier, Silvia 1999. 'Teilzeitarbeit im Kontext Europäischer Kollektivvereinbarungen'. DWP 99.01.04. Brussels: European Trade Union Institute <http://www.etuc.org/etui/publications/DWP/Dürmeier2.PDF>.

EASHW 1998. 'Economic Impact of Occupational Safety and Health in the Member States of the European Union'. Report 302. Bilbao: European Agency for Safety and Health at Work <http://agency.osha.eu.int/ publications/reports/302/de/index.htm>.

Edwards, Laura and Burkitt, Nick 2001. 'Wanting More from Work? Expectations and Aspirations of People in Low and Middle Paid Jobs'. DfEE Research Brief RBX 6–01. London: Department for Education and Employment <http://www.dfes.gov.uk/research/data/uploadfiles/RBX06–01.doc>.

Edwards, Paul, Hall, Mark, Hyman, Richard, Marginson, Paul, Sisson, Keith, Waddington, Jeremy and Winchester, David 1999. 'Great Britain: From Partial Collectivism to Neo-Liberalism to Where?' in: Anthony Ferner and Richard Hyman (eds.), *Changing Industrial Relations in Europe*. Oxford: Blackwell, 1–54.

Ehlermann, Claus-Dieter 1987. 'Ein Plädoyer für die dezentrale Kontrolle der Anwendung des Gemeinschaftsrechts durch die Mitgliedstaaten', in: Francesco Capotorti (ed.), *Du droit international au droit de l'intégration. Liber Amicorum Pierre Pescatore*. Baden-Baden: Nomos, 205–26.

Eichener, Volker 1996. 'Die Rückwirkung der Europäischen Integration auf nationale Politikmuster', in: Markus Jachtenfuchs and Beate Kohler-Koch (eds.), *Europäische Integration*. Opladen: Leske + Budrich, 249–80.

  1997. 'Effective European Problem-Solving: Lessons from the Regulation of Occupational Safety and Environmental Protection', *Journal of European Public Policy* 4(4): 591–608.

  2000. *Das Entscheidungssystem der Europäischen Union: Institutionelle Analyse und demokratietheoretische Bewertung*. Opladen: Leske + Budrich.

Eichener, Volker and Voelzkow, Helmut (eds.) 1994. *Europäische Integration und verbandliche Interessenvermittlung*. Marburg: Metropolis.

Eising, Rainer and Kohler-Koch, Beate 1994. 'Inflation und Zerfaserung: Trends der Interessenvermittlung in der Europäischen Gemeinschaft', in: Wolfgang Streeck (ed.), *Staat und Verbände*. Opladen: Westdeutscher Verlag, 175–206.

Elmore, Richard F. 1982. 'Backward Mapping: Implementation Research and Policy Decisions', in: Walter Williams (ed.), *Studying Implementation: Methodological and Administrative Issues*. Chatham, NJ: Chatham House Publishers, 18–35.

Engels, C. and Vanachter, O. 1998. 'Belgium', in: Roger Blanpain (ed.), *Labour Law and Industrial Relations in the European Union*. Bulletin of Comparative Labour Relations 32. Den Haag: Kluwer, 35–53.

Esping-Andersen, Gøsta 1990. *The Three Worlds of Welfare Capitalism*. Cambridge: Polity.

Eurostat 1996. *Labour Force Survey: Results 1995*. Luxembourg: Office for Official Publications of the European Communities.

Ewing, Keith David 1993. 'Swimming with the Tide: Employment Protection and the Implementation of European Labour Law', *Industrial Law Journal* 22(3): 165–80.

Fabbrini, Sergio and Donà, Alessia 2003. 'Europeanisation as Strengthening of Domestic Executive Power? The Italian Experience and the Case of "*Legge Comunitaria*"', *Journal of European Integration* 25: 31–50.

Falkner, Gerda 1998. *EU Social Policy in the 1990s: Towards a Corporatist Policy Community*. London: Routledge.

  2000a. 'The Council or the Social Partners? EC Social Policy between Diplomacy and Collective Bargaining', *Journal of European Public Policy* 7(5): 705–24.

  2000b. 'How Pervasive Are Euro-Politics? Effects of EU Membership on a New Member State', *Journal of Common Market Studies* 38(2): 223–50.

  2000c. 'Policy Networks in a Multi-Level System: Convergence Towards Moderate Diversity?' *West European Politics* 23(4): 94–120.

  2002. 'How Intergovernmental are Intergovernmental Conferences? An Example from the Maastricht Treaty Reform', *Journal of European Public Policy* 9(1): 98–119.

2003a. 'The Interprofessional Social Dialogue at European Level: Past and Future', in: Berndt Keller and Hans-Wolfgang Platzer (eds.), *Industrial Relations and European Integration: Developments and Prospects at EU-level*. Aldershot: Ashgate, 11–29.

2003b. 'Social Policy', in: Michelle Cini (ed.), *European Union Politics*. Oxford: Oxford University Press, 264–77.

Falkner, Gerda, Eder, Martina, Hiller, Karin, Müller, Wolfgang C., Steiner, Gerhard and Trattnigg, Rita 1999. 'The Impact of EU Membership on Policy Networks in Austria: Creeping Change Beneath the Surface', *Journal of European Public Policy* 6(3): 496–516.

Falkner, Gerda, Hartlapp, Miriam, Leiber, Simone and Treib, Oliver 2004. 'Non-Compliance with EU Directives in the Member States: Opposition Through the Backdoor?' *West European Politics* 27(3): 452–73.

2005. 'Sozialpartnerschaftliche Kooperation in der arbeitsrechtlichen Regulierung: ein Europäischer Weg?' in: Beate Kohler-Koch and Rainer Eising (eds.), *Interessendurchsetzung im Mehrebenensystem*. Baden-Baden: Nomos, 341–62.

Featherstone, Kevin and Radaelli, Claudio M. (eds.) 2003. *The Politics of Europeanization*. Oxford: Oxford University Press.

Ferrante, Vincenzo 1998. 'Working Hours Still a Controversial Issue in Italy'. EIROnline Document IT9811238F. Dublin: European Foundation for the Improvement of Living and Working Conditions <http://www.eiro.eurofound.ie/1998/11/features/IT9811238F.html>.

Ferrera, Maurizio 1998. 'The Four "Social Europes": Between Universalism and Selectivity', in: Martin Rhodes and Yves Mény (eds.), *The Future of European Welfare: A New Social Contract?* Houndmills: Macmillan, 79–96.

Feyereisen, Marc 1998. 'Trade Union Proposals for Introduction of Parental Leave'. EIROnline Document LU9802147N. Dublin: European Foundation for the Improvement of Living and Working Conditions <http://www.eiro.eurofound.ie/1998/02/inbrief/LU9802147N.html>.

'Economic and Social Council Proposes its Own Reform'. EIROnline Document LU0103163F. Dublin: European Foundation for the Improvement of Living and Working Conditions <http://www.eiro.eurofound.ie/2001/03/feature/LU0103163F.html>.

Freyssinet, Jacques and Michon, François 2003. 'Overtime in Europe'. EIROnline Document TN0302101S. Dublin: European Foundation for the Improvement of Living and Working Conditions <http://www.eiro.eurofound.ie/2003/02/study/TN0302101S.html>.

Gächter, August 1997. 'Shorter Weekly Rest Periods Possible for Young Workers'. EIROnline Document AT9710137N. Dublin: European Foundation for the Improvement of Living and Working Conditions <http://www.eiro.eurofound.ie/1997/10/inbrief/AT9710137N.html>.

Gallo, Flaminia and Hanny, Birgit 2003. 'Italy: Progress Behind Complexity', in: Wolfgang Wessels, Andreas Maurer and Jürgen Mittag (eds.), *Fifteen into One: The European Union and Its Member States*. Manchester: Manchester University Press, 271–97.

Ganghof, Steffen 2003. 'Promises and Pitfalls of Veto Player Analysis', *Swiss Political Science Review* 9(2): 1–25.

Ganghof, Steffen and Bräuninger, Thomas 2003. 'Government Status and Legislative Behavior: Partisan Veto Players in Australia, Denmark, Finland and Germany'. MPIfG Working Paper 03/11. Cologne: Max Planck Institute for the Study of Societies <http://www.mpi-fg-koeln.mpg.de/pu/workpap/wp03–11/wp03–11.pdf>.

Giuliani, Marco 2003. 'Europeanization in Comparative Perspective: Institutional Fit and Domestic Adaptation', in: Kevin Featherstone and Claudio M. Radaelli (eds.), *The Politics of Europeanization*. Oxford: Oxford University Press, 134–55.

Glaser, Barney G. and Strauss, Anselm L. 1967. *The Discovery of Grounded Theory: Strategies for Qualitative Research*. New York: Aldine.

Goetschy, Janine 1994. 'A Further Comment on Wolfgang Streeck's "European Social Policy after Maastricht"', *Economic and Industrial Democracy* 15: 477–85.

2001. 'The European Employment Strategy from Amsterdam to Stockholm: Has It Reached Its Cruising Speed?' *Industrial Relations Journal* 32(5): 401–18.

Goetz, Klaus H. 2002. Four Worlds of Europeanisation. Conference paper, ECPR Turin Sessions, Workshop 19 on 'Europeanisation and National Political Institutions', 22–27 March 2002, Turin.

Golub, Jonathan 1996. 'Modelling Judicial Dialogue in the European Community: The Quantitative Basis of Preliminary References to the ECJ'. EUI Working Paper RSC 96/58. Florence: European University Institute.

Gorges, Michael J. 1996. *Euro-Corporatism? Interest Intermediation in the European Community*. Lanham/New York/London: University Press of America.

Gray, Margaret 1998. 'A Recalcitrant Partner: The UK Reaction to the Working Time Directive', in: Ami Barav and Derrick A. Wyatt (eds.), *Yearbook of European Law 1997*. Vol. XVII. Oxford: Clarendon, 324–62.

Greenwood, Justin, Grote, Jürgen R. and Ronit, Karsten (eds.) 1992. *Organized Interests and the European Community*. London: Sage.

Günther, Horst 1993. 'Gemeinsamer Standpunkt verabschiedet'. *Bundesarbeitsblatt*. 10/1993: 17–20.

Hall, Mark 1998. 'The EU Parental Leave Agreement and Directive: Implications for National Law and Practice'. EIROnline Document TN98012015. Dublin: European Foundation for the Improvement of Living and Working Conditions. <http://www.eiro.eurofound.ie/1998/01/study/tn98012015.html/>.

2000. 'Commission Reports on Implementation of European Works Councils Directive'. EIROnline Document EU0005248F. Dublin: European Foundation for the Improvement of Living and Working Conditions <http://www.eiro.eurofound.ie/2000/05/feature/EU0005248F.html>.

Ham, Christopher and Hill, Michael 1984. *The Policy Process in the Modern Capitalist State*. Brighton: Harvester Press.

Hanf, Kenneth 1991. The Impact of European Policies on Domestic Institutions and Politics: Observations on the Implementation of Community

Environmental Directives. Conference paper, ECPR Workshop on National Political Systems and the European Community, 22–27 March 1991, Colchester.

Hart, Oliver and Homström, Bengt 1987. 'The Theory of Contracts', in: Truman F. Bewley (ed.), *Advances in Economic Theory: Fifth World Congress*. Cambridge: Cambridge University Press, 71–155.

Hartenberger, Ute 2001. *Europäischer sozialer Dialog nach Maastricht: EU-Sozialpartnerverhandlungen auf dem Prüfstand*. Baden-Baden: Nomos.

Hartfiel, Guenter (ed.) 1982. *Wörterbuch der Soziologie*. Stuttgart: Kröner.

Hartlapp, Miriam 2004. Labour Law Supervision and Enforcement by EU and ILO: Is There One International Implementation Style? Conference paper, ECPR Joint Session of Workshops, 13–18 April 2004, Uppsala.

2005. *Die Kontrolle der nationalen Rechtsdurchsetzung durch die Europäische Kommission*. Politik, Verbände, Recht: Die Umsetzung europäischer Sozialpolitik, Vol. III. Frankfurt/M.: Campus.

Haverland, Markus 2000. 'National Adaptation to European Integration: The Importance of Institutional Veto Points', *Journal of Public Policy* 20(1): 83–103.

Hayes-Renshaw, Fiona and Wallace, Helen 1997. *The Council of Ministers*. Houndmills: Macmillan.

Heinelt, Hubert, Malek, Tanja, Smith, Randall and Töller, Annette E. (eds.) 2001. *European Union Environment Policy and New Forms of Governance: A Study of the Implementation of the Environmental Assessment Directive and the Eco-management and Audit Scheme Regulation in Three Member States*. Aldershot: Ashgate.

Hepple, Bob and Hakim, Catherine 1997. 'United Kingdom', in: Roger Blanpain, Eberhard Köhler and Jacques Rojot (eds.), *Legal and Contractual Limitations to Working Time in the European Union*. Leuven: Peeters Press, 659–93.

Héritier, Adrienne 1996. 'The Accommodation of Diversity in European Policymaking and Its Outcomes: Regulatory Policy as a Patchwork', *Journal of European Public Policy* 3(2): 149–67.

2001a. 'Differential Europe: National Administrative Responses to Community Policy', in: Maria Green Cowles, James Caporaso and Thomas Risse (eds.), *Transforming Europe: Europeanization and Domestic Change*. Ithaca: Cornell University Press, 44–59.

2001b. 'Differential Europe: The European Union Impact on National Policymaking', in: Adrienne Héritier, Dieter Kerwer, Christoph Knill, Dirk Lehmkuhl, Michael Teutsch and Anne-Cécile Douillet (eds.), *Differential Europe: The European Union Impact on National Policymaking*. Lanham: Rowman and Littlefield, 1–21.

2002. 'New Modes of Governance in Europe: Policy-Making without Legislating?' in: Adrienne Héritier (ed.), *Common Goods: Reinventing European and International Governance*. Lanham: Rowman and Littlefield, 185–206.

2003. 'New Modes of Governance in Europe: Increasing Political Capacity and Policy Effectiveness', in: Tanja A. Börzel and Rachel A. Cichowski (eds.),

The State of the European Union. Vol. VI: Law, Politics, and Society. Oxford: Oxford University Press, 105–26.

Héritier, Adrienne, Kerwer, Dieter, Knill, Christoph, Lehmkuhl, Dirk, Teutsch, Michael and Douillet, Anne-Cécile (eds.) 2001. *Differential Europe: The European Union Impact on National Policymaking*. Lanham: Rowman and Littlefield.

Héritier, Adrienne and Knill, Christoph 2001. 'Differential Responses to European Policies: A Comparison', in: Adrienne Héritier, Dieter Kerwer, Christoph Knill, Dirk Lehmkuhl, Michael Teutsch and Anne-Cécile Douillet (eds.), *Differential Europe: The European Union Impact on National Policymaking*. Lanham: Rowman and Littlefield, 257–321.

Héritier, Adrienne, Knill, Christoph and Mingers, Susanne 1996. *Ringing the Changes in Europe: Regulatory Competition and Redefinition of the State*. Berlin: de Gruyter.

Héritier, Adrienne, Mingers, Susanne, Knill, Christoph and Becka, Martina 1994. *Die Veränderung von Staatlichkeit in Europa: Ein regulativer Wettbewerb: Deutschland, Großbritannien, Frankreich*. Opladen: Leske + Budrich.

Hjern, Benny and Porter, David O. 1981. 'Implementation Structures: A New Unit of Administrative Analysis', *Organization Studies* 2(3): 211–27.

Holzinger, Katherina, Knill, Christoph and Schäfer, Ansgar 2002. 'European Environmental Governance in Transition?', Preprints aus der Max-Planck-Projektgruppe Recht der Gemeinschaftsgüter 2002/9. Bonn: Max-Planck-Projektgruppe Recht der Gemeinschaftsgüter.

Hornung-Draus, Renate 1996. 'Abkommen zum Elternurlaub verabschiedet', *Der Arbeitgeber* 48(3): 62–3.

Hoskyns, Catherine 1996. *Integrating Gender: Women, Law and Politics in the European Union*. London: Verso.

HSC 1994. Draft Management of Health and Safety at Work (Amendment) Regulations 199-: Proposals to Implement the Health and Safety Provisions of the EC Directive on Pregnant Workers: Consultation Document, London: Health and Safety Commission.

Hutsebaut, Martin 1999. 'Sécurité sociale et travail atypique – un point de vue syndical européen'. DWP 99.02.02. Brussels: European Trade Union Institute <http://www.etuc.org/etui/publications/DWP/Hutsebaut.PDF>.

Immergut, Ellen M. 1998. 'The Theoretical Core of the New Institutionalism', *Politics and Society* 26(1): 5–34.

Ioannou, Christos A. 2000. 'Social Pacts in Hellenic Industrial Relations: Odysseys or Sisiphus?' in: Guiseppe Fajertag and Philippe Pochet (eds.), *Social Pacts in Europe – New Dynamics*. Brussels: ETUI, 219–36.

Ismayr, Wolfgang (ed.) 2002. *Die politischen Systeme Westeuropas*. Opladen: Leske + Budrich.

Jachtenfuchs, Markus and Strübel, Michael (eds.) 1992. *Environmental Policy in Europe: Assessment, Challenges and Perspectives*. Baden-Baden: Nomos.

Jacobi, Otto 1995. 'Der Soziale Dialog in der Europäischen Union', in: Michael Mesch (ed.), *Sozialpartnerschaft und Arbeitsbeziehungen in Europa*. Wien: Manz, 257–87.

James, Grace 2004. 'Pregnancy Discrimination at Work: A Review'. EOC Working Paper Series 14. London: Equal Opportunities Commission.

James, Phil 1993. 'Occupational Health and Safety', in: Michael Gold (ed.), *The Social Dimension: Employment Policy in the European Community.* London: Macmillan, 135–52.

Jensen, Carsten Strøby 2002. 'Denmark in Historical Perspective: Towards Conflict Based Consensus', in: Stefan Berger and Hugh Compston (eds.), *Policy Concertation and Social Partnership in Western Europe.* New York: Berghahn Books, 77–82.

Jensen, Christian B. 2001. The Unusual Suspects: Why Pro-Integration Member States Have Difficulty Enforcing EU Directives. Conference paper, Annual Meeting of the American Political Science Association, 30 August to 2 September 2001, San Francisco.

Joerges, Christian and Neyer, Jürgen 1997. 'Transforming Strategic Interaction into Deliberative Problem-Solving: European Comitology in the Foodstuffs Sector', *Journal of European Public Policy* 4(4): 609–25.

Joerges, Christian and Vos, Ellen (eds.) 1999. *EU Committees: Social Regulation, Law and Politics.* Oxford: Hart.

Jordan, A. Grant and Richardson, Jeremy J. 1983. 'Policy Communities: The British and European Policy Style', *Policy Studies Journal* 11(4): 603–15.

Jordan, Andrew 2000. 'The Politics of Multilevel Environmental Governance: Subsidiarity and Environmental Policy in the European Union', *Environment and Planning A* 32(7): 1307–24.

Jørgensen, Carsten 1999. 'September Compromise Marks 100th Anniversary'. EIROnline Document DK9908140F. Dublin: European Foundation for the Improvement of Living and Working Conditions <http://www.eiro. eurofound.ie/1999/08/feature/DK9908140F.html>.

2001. 'EU Part-Time Directive Implemented through New Dual Method'. EIROnline Document DK0106125F. Dublin: European Foundation for the Improvement of Living and Working Conditions <http://www.eiro. eurofound.ie/2001/06/feature/DK0106125F.html>.

Jørgensen, Knud Erik 1997. 'Introduction: Approaching European Governance', in: Knud Erik Jørgensen (ed.), *Reflective Approaches to European Governance.* Houndmills: Macmillan, 1–14.

Karlhofer, Ferdinand and Tálos, Emmerich 1996. *Sozialpartnerschaft und EU: Integrationsdynamik und Handlungsrahmen der Österreichischen Sozialpartnerschaft.* Wien: Signum.

Karpenstein, Peter and Karpenstein, Ulrich 1999. 'Der Gerichtshof', in: Eberhard Grabitz and Meinhard Hilf (eds.), *Das Recht der Europäischen Union.* München: C. H. Beck.

Kassim, Hussein 2000. 'The United Kingdom', in: Hussein Kassim, B. Guy Peters and Vincent Wright (eds.), *The National Co-Ordination of EU Policy: The Domestic Level.* Oxford: Oxford University Press, 22–53.

2001. 'Internal Policy Developments', in: John Peterson and Iain Begg (eds.), *The European Union: Annual Review of the EU 2000/2001.* Oxford: Blackwell.

Kassim, Hussein, Menon, Anand, Peters, B. Guy and Wright, Vincent (eds.) 2001a. *The National Co-Ordination of EU Policy: The European Level*. Oxford: Oxford University Press.

Kassim, Hussein, Peters, B. Guy and Wright, Vincent (eds.) 2001b. *The National Co-Ordination of EU Policy: The Domestic Level*. Oxford: Oxford University Press.

Keller, Berndt 1997. *Europäische Arbeits- und Sozialpolitik*. München: Oldenbourg.

2002. 'The European Company Statute: Employee Involvement – and Beyond', *Industrial Relations Journal* 33(5): 424–45.

Keller, Berndt and Sörries, Bernd 1999. 'The New European Social Dialogue: Old Wine in New Bottles?' *Journal of European Social Policy* 9(2): 111–25.

Kiewit, D. Roderick and McCubbins, Matthew D. 1991. *The Logic of Delegation: Congressional Parties and the Appropriation Process*. Chicago: University of Chicago Press.

Kilpatrick, Claire 2001. 'Turning Remedies Round: A Sectoral Analysis of the Court of Justice', in: Gráinne de Búrca and Joseph H. H. Weiler (eds.), *The European Court of Justice*. Oxford: Oxford University Press, 143–76.

2002. 'Emancipation through Law or the Emasculation of Law? The Nation-State, the EU, and Gender Equality at Work', in: Joanne Conaghan, Richard Michael Fischl and Karl Klare (eds.), *Labour Law in the Era of Globalization*. Oxford: Oxford University Press, 487–509.

King, Gary, Keohane, Robert O. and Verba, Sidney 1994. *Designing Social Inquiry: Scientific Inference in Qualitative Research*. Princeton: Princeton University Press.

Kleinfeld, Ralf and Luthardt, Wolfgang (eds.) 1993. *Westliche Demokratien und Interessenvermittlung: Zur aktuellen Entwicklung nationaler Parteien- und Verbändesysteme*. Marburg: Schüren.

Knill, Christoph 1998. 'European Policies: The Impact of National Administrative Traditions', *Journal of Public Policy* 18(1): 1–28.

2001. *The Europeanisation of National Administrations: Patterns of Institutional Change and Persistence*. Cambridge: Cambridge University Press.

Knill, Christoph and Lehmkuhl, Dirk 1999. 'How Europe Matters: Different Mechanisms of Europeanization', *European Integration Online Papers* 3(7) <http://eiop.or.at/eiop/texte/1998-007a.htm>.

2002. 'Private Actors and the State: Internationalization and Changing Patterns of Governance', *Governance* 15(1): 41–63.

Knill, Christoph and Lenschow, Andrea 1997. 'The Impact of National Administrative Traditions on the Implementation of EU Environmental Policy: Preliminary Results of the EUI and EU-Commission Co-Financed "EPIP-Project"'. *Newsletter of the Working Group on Environmental Studies at the European University Institute*. Issue 17.

1998. 'Coping with Europe: The Impact of British and German Administrations on the Implementation of EU Environmental Policy', *Journal of European Public Policy* 5(4): 595–614.

1999. 'Neue Konzepte – alte Probleme? Die institutionellen Grenzen effektiver Implementation', *Politische Vierteljahresschrift* 40(4): 591–617.

2000a. 'Do New Brooms Really Sweep Cleaner? Implementation of New Instruments in EU Environmental Policy', in: Christoph Knill and Andrea Lenschow (eds.), *Implementing EU Environmental Policy. New Directions and Old Problems*. Manchester: Manchester University Press, 251–82.

2000b. *Implementing EU Environmental Policy. New Directions and Old Problems.* Manchester: Manchester University Press.

2001. 'Adjusting to EU Environmental Policy: Change and Persistence of Domestic Administrations', in: Maria Green Cowles, James Caporaso and Thomas Risse (eds.), *Transforming Europe: Europeanization and Domestic Change*. Ithaca: Cornell University Press, 116–36.

Knudsen, Herman and Lind, Jens 1999. 'The Implementation of EU Directives in National Systems: Lessons from the Danish Case', *Transfer* 5(1–2): 136–55.

Kohler-Koch, Beate 1996. 'Die Gestaltungsmacht organisierter Interessen', in: Markus Jachtenfuchs and Beate Kohler-Koch (eds.), *Europäische Integration*. Opladen: Leske + Budrich, 193–224.

2000a. 'Europäisierung: Plädoyer für eine Horizonterweiterung', in: Michèle Knodt and Beate Kohler-Koch (eds.), *Deutschland zwischen Europäisierung und Selbstbehauptung*. Mannheimer Jahrbuch für Europäische Sozialforschung Vol. V. Frankfurt/M.: Campus, 11–31.

2000b. 'Framing: The Bottleneck of Constructing Legitimate Institutions', *Journal of European Public Policy* 7(4): 513–31.

Kohler-Koch, Beate and Edler, Jakob 1998. 'Ideendiskurs und Vergemeinschaftung: Erschließung transnationaler Räume durch europäisches Regieren', in: Beate Kohler-Koch (ed.), *Regieren in entgrenzten Räumen*. PVS-Sonderheft 29. Opladen: Westdeutscher Verlag, 169–206.

Kommission der Europäischen Gemeinschaften 1995. *Arbeitsaufsicht (Sicherheit und Gesundheitsschutz) in der Europäischen Gemeinschaft: Ein Leitfaden*. Brüssel: Kommission der Europäischen Gemeinschaften.

Koniaris, Theodore 2002. *Labour Law in Hellas*. Dordrecht: Kluwer Law International.

Kooiman, Jan, Yntema, Paul and Lintsen, Lucie 1988. 'The Netherlands', in: Heinrich Siedentopf and Jacques Ziller (eds.), *Making European Policies Work: The Implementation of Community Legislation in the Member States*. Vol. II: National Reports. London: Sage, 573–636.

Krislov, Samuel, Ehlermann, Claus-Dieter and Weiler, Jospeh 1986. 'The Political Organs and the Decision-Making Process in the United States and the European Community', in: Mauro Cappelletti, Monica Seccombe and Joseph Weiler (eds.), *Integration Through Law: Methods, Tools and Institutions. Political Organs, Integration Techniques and Judicial Process*. Vol. I. Berlin: Walter De Gruyter, 3–110.

Krück, Hans 1997. 'Der Gerichtshof (Artikel 169)', in: Hans von der Groeben, Jochen Thiesing and Claus-Dieter Ehlermann (eds.), *Kommentar zum EU-/EG-Vertrag*. Vol. IV. Baden-Baden: Nomos, 494–522.

Ladrech, Robert 1994. 'Europeanisation of Domestic Politics and Institutions: The Case of France', *Journal of Common Market Studies* 32(1): 69–88.

Lamers, Josee 1997. 'Complaints about Holiday Jobs'. EIROnline Document NL9707123N. Dublin: European Foundation for the Improvement of Living and Working Conditions <http://eiro.eurofound.ie/1997/07/inbrief/NL9707123N.html>.

Lampinen, Risto and Uusikylä, Petri 1998. 'Implementation Deficit: Why Member States Do Not Comply with EU Directives?' *Scandinavian Political Studies* 21(3): 231–51.

Lange, Peter 1992. 'The Politics of the Social Dimension', in: Alberta M. Sbragia (ed.), *Euro-Politics. Institutions and Policymaking in the 'New' European Community*. Washington, DC: The Brookings Institution, 225–56.

Langewiesche, Renate and Lubyova, Martina 2000. 'Migration, Mobility and the Free Movement of Persons: An Issue for Current and Future EU Members', *Transfer* 6(3): 450–67.

La Spina, Antonio and Sciortino, Giuseppe 1993. 'Common Agenda, Southern Rules: European Integration and Environmental Change in the Mediterranean States', in: J. D. Liefferink, P. D. Lowe and A. P. J. Mol (eds.), *European Integration and Environmental Policy*. London: Belhaven Press, 217–36.

Laursen, Finn 2003. 'Denmark: In Pursuit of Influence and Legitimacy', in: Wolfgang Wessels, Andreas Maurer and Jürgen Mittag (eds.), *Fifteen into One? The European Union and Its Member States*. Manchester: Manchester University Press, 92–114.

Lecher, Wolfgang and Platzer, Hans-Wolfgang 1996. 'Europäische Betriebsräte: Fundament und Instrument Europäischer Arbeitsbeziehungen?' *WSI Mitteilungen* 49(8): 503–12.

Lehmbruch, Gerhard 1985. 'Sozialpartnerschaft in der vergleichenden Politikforschung', in: Peter Gerlich, Edgar Grande and Wolfgang C. Müller (eds.), *Sozialpartnerschaft in der Krise*. Wien: Böhlau, 86–107.

Lehmbruch, Gerhard and Schmitter, Philippe C. (eds.) 1982. *Patterns of Corporatist Policy-Making*. London: Sage.

Lehmkuhl, Dirk 1999. *The Importance of Small Differences: The Impact of European Integration on Road Haulage Associations in Germany and the Netherlands*. Amsterdam: Thela Thesis.

2000. 'Under Stress: Europeanisation and Trade Associations in the Member States', *European Integration Online Papers* 4(14) <http://eiop.or.at/eiop/texte/2000-014a.htm>.

Leiber, Simone 2005. *Europäische Sozialpolitik und nationale Sozialpartnerschaft. Politik, Verbände, Recht: Die Umsetzung europäischer Sozialpolitik*, Vol. II. Frankfurt/M.: Campus.

Leibfried, Stephan and Pierson, Paul 1995. 'Semisovereign Welfare States: Social Policy in a Multitiered Europe', in: Stephan Leibfried and Paul Pierson (eds.), *European Social Policy: Between Fragmentation and Integration*. Washington, DC: The Brookings Institution, 43–77.

2000. 'Social Policy: Left to Court and Markets?' in: Helen Wallace and William Wallace (eds.), *Policy-Making in the European Union*. The New European Union Series. Oxford: Oxford University Press, 267–92.

Lenschow, Andrea 1999. 'Transformation in European Environmental Governance', in: Beate Kohler-Koch and Rainer Eising (eds.), *The Transformation of Governance in the European Union*. London: Routledge, 39–60.

2002. 'New Regulatory Approaches in "Greening" EU Policies', *European Law Journal* 8(1): 19–37.

Levy, Roger 2000. *Implementing European Union Public Policy*. Cheltenham: Elgar.

2001. 'EU Programme Management 1977–1996: A Performance Indicator Analysis', *Public Administration* 79(2): 423–44.

Lewis, Jeffrey 1998. 'Is the "Hard Bargaining" Image of the Council Misleading? The Committee of Permanent Representatives and the Local Elections Directive', *Journal of Common Market Studies* 36(4): 479–504.

2000. 'The Methods of Community in EU Decision-Making and Administrative Rivalry in the Council's Infrastructure', *Journal of European Public Policy* 7(2): 261–89.

Lichbach, Mark I. 2003. *Is Rational Choice Theory All of Social Science?* Ann Arbor: University of Michigan Press.

Lipsky, Michael 1978. 'Standing the Study of Public Policy Implementation on Its Head', in: Walter Burnham and Martha Weinberg (eds.), *American Politics and Public Policy*. Cambridge, MA: MIT Press, 391–401.

1980. *Street-Level Bureaucracy: The Dilemmas of Individuals in the Public Service*. New York: Sage.

Madsen, Jørgen Steen 2000. '"Danish Model" Maintained by Implementation of EU Directives through Collective Agreements'. EIROnline Document DK0001164F. Dublin: European Foundation for the Improvement of Living and Working Conditions <http://www.eiro.eurofound.ie/about/2000/01/feature/DK0001164F.html>.

Mair, Peter 2001. 'The Limited Impact of Europe on National Party Systems', in: Klaus H. Goetz and Simon Hix (eds.), *Europeanised Politics? European Integration and National Political Systems*. London: Frank Cass, 27–51.

2004. 'The Europeanization Dimension', *Journal of European Public Policy* 11(2): 337–48.

Majone, Giandomenico and Wildavsky, Aaron 1978. 'Implementation as Evolution', in: H. Freeman (ed.), *Policy Studies Review Annual 1978*. Beverly Hills: Sage, 103–17.

Malderie, Marjan 1997. 'L'Union Européenne et le Congé Parental'. *Revue du Travail* (janvier, mars): 43–5.

March, James G. and Olsen, Johan P. 1989. *Rediscovering Institutions. The Organizational Basis of Politics*. New York: Free Press.

Marks, Gary, Hooghe, Liesbet and Blank, Kermit 1996. 'European Integration from the 1980s: State-Centric v. Multi-Level Governance', *Journal of Common Market Studies* 34(3): 341–78.

Marsh, David and Rhodes, R. A. W. (eds.) 1992. *Policy Networks in British Government*. Oxford: Clarendon Press.

Mastenbroek, Ellen 2003. 'Surviving the Deadline: The Transposition of EU Directives in the Netherlands', *European Union Politics* 4(4): 371–95.

Maurer, Andreas and Wessels, Wolfgang (eds.) 2001. *National Parliaments on their Ways to Europe: Losers or Latecomers?* Baden-Baden: Nomos.

Mayntz, Renate 1983. *Implementation politischer Programme II: Ansätze zur Theoriebildung.* Opladen: Westdeutscher Verlag.

Mazey, Sonia 1998. 'The European Union and Women's Rights: From the Europeanization of National Agendas to the Nationalization of a European Agenda?' *Journal of European Public Policy* 5(1): 131–52.

Mazmanian, Daniel A. and Sabatier, Paul A. 1983. *Implementation and Public Policy.* Glenview: Scott.

Mbaye, Heather A. D. 2001. 'Why National States Comply with Supranational Law: Explaining Implementation Infringements in the European Union 1972–1993', *European Union Politics* 2(3): 259–81.

Mendrinou, Maria 1996. 'Non-Compliance and the European Commission's Role in Integration', *Journal of European Public Policy* 3(1): 1–22.

Mény, Yves 1988. 'France', in: Heinrich Siedentopf and Jacques Ziller (eds.), *Making European Policies Work: The Implementation of Community Legislation in the Member States.* Vol. II: National Reports. London: Sage, 277–373.

Miguélez Lobo, Faustino 2001. 'Government Introduces New Labour Market Reform'. EIROnline Document ES0103237F. Dublin: European Foundation for the Improvement of Living and Working Conditions <http://www.eiro.eurofound.ie/2001/03/feature/ES0103237F.html>.

Miles, Lee 2001. 'Developments in the Member States', *Journal of Common Market Studies* 39(Annual Review): 139–56.

Ministère Fédéral de l'Emploi et du Travail 2000. 'Clés pour . . . le travail à temps partiel'. Bruxelles: Ministère Fédéral de l'Emploi et du Travail.

Ministerrat 1994. 'Vermerk des Vorsitzes für den Rat (Arbeit und Sozialfragen) (Tagung am 22 September 1994). Betr.: Geänderter Vorschlag für eine Richtlinie über Elternurlaub'. Brüssel: Rat der Europäischen Gemeinschaften.

1996. 'Entwurf eines Protokolls über die 1914. Tagung des Rates (Arbeit und Sozialfragen) am 29 März 1996 in Brüssel'. Brüssel: Rat der Europäischen Union.

Moravcsik, Andrew 1993. 'Preferences and Power in the European Community: A Liberal Intergovernmentalist Approach', *Journal of Common Market Studies* 31(4): 473–523.

1994. Why the European Community Strengthens the State: Domestic Politics and International Cooperation. Conference paper, Annual Meeting of the American Political Science Association, 1–4 September 1994, New York.

Morlino, Leonardo 2002. Europeanization and the Reshaping of Representation in Southern Europe. Conference paper, EUSA Eighth Biennial International Conference, 27–29 March, Nashville, TN, USA.

Müller, Wolfgang C. 2000. 'Austria', in: Hussein Kassim, B. Guy Peters and Vincent Wright (eds.), *The National Co-ordination of EU Policy. The Domestic Level.* Oxford: Oxford University Press, 201–18.

Muratore, Livio 2003. 'Government Transposes Working Time Directive'. EIROnline Document IT0305305F. Dublin: European Foundation for the Improvement of Living and Working Conditions <http://www.eiro. eurofound.ie/2003/05/feature/IT0305305F.html>.

NACAB 2000. 'Wish You Were Here?' London: National Association of Citizens Advice Bureaux <http://www.nacab.org.uk/docks/wish.doc>.

Neyer, Jürgen and Zürn, Michael 2001. 'Compliance in Comparative Perspective. The EU and Other International Institutions'. InIIS-Arbeitspapier 23. Bremen: Institut für Interkulturelle und Internationale Studien.

Nugent, Neill 2001. *The European Commission*. Houndmills: Palgrave.

O'Donnell, Rory and Thomas, Damian 1998. 'Partnership and Policy-Making', in: Sean Healy and Brigid Reynolds (eds.), *Social Policy in Ireland: Principles, Practices and Problems*. Dublin: Oak Tree, 117–46.

Pag, Sabine and Wessels, Wolfgang 1988. 'Federal Republic of Germany', in: Heinrich Siedentopf and Jacques Ziller (eds.), *Making European Policies Work: The Implementation of Community Legislation in the Member States*. Vol. II: National Reports. London: Sage, 163–229.

Page, Edward C. and Dimitrakopoulos, Dionyssis 1997. 'The Dynamics of EU Growth: A Cross-Time Analysis', *Journal of Theoretical Politics* 9(3): 365–87.

Paparella, Domenico 1998a. 'Confindustria Opposes the Law on the 35-hour Week and Proposes New Dialogue Rules'. EIROnline Document IT9803158N. Dublin: European Foundation for the Improvement of Living and Working Conditions <http://www.eiro.eurofound.ie/1998/03/inbrief/IT9803158N.html>.

1998b. 'Government Approves Bill on the 35-hour Week'. EIROnline Document IT9803159N. Dublin: European Foundation for the Improvement of Living and Working Conditions <http://www.eiro.eurofound.ie/1998/03/inbrief/IT9803159N.html>.

1998c. 'Parliament Approves Law on Overtime'. EIROnline Document IT9812192N. Dublin: European Foundation for the Improvement of Living and Working Conditions <http://www.eiro.eurofound.ie/1998/12/inbrief/IT9812192N.html>.

Pedersen, Thomas 2000. 'Denmark', in: Hussein Kassim, B. Guy Peters and Vincent Wright (eds.), *The National Co-ordination of EU Policy*. Oxford: Oxford University Press, 220–34.

Pedersini, Roberto 1997. 'Employers React to the Government's Commitment to the 35-hour Week'. EIROnline Document IT9711216F. Dublin: European Foundation for the Improvement of Living and Working Conditions <http://www.eiro.eurofound.ie/1997/11/features/IT9711216F.html>.

2002. 'Government Approves Legislative Decree Transposing EU Directive on Part-time Work'. EIROnline Document IT 0002261F. Dublin: European Foundation for the Improvement of Living and Working Conditions <http://www.eiro.eurofound.ie/2000/02/feature/IT0002261F.html>.

Peters, B. Guy 1993. 'Alternative Modelle des Policy-Prozesses: Die Sicht "Von unten" und die Sicht "von oben"', in: Adrienne Héritier (ed.), *Policy-Analyse:*

Kritik und Neuorientierung. PVS-Sonderheft 24. Opladen: Westdeutscher Verlag, 289–303.

Petersen, Kåre F. V. 1997. 'The Danish Model under Threat?'. EIROnline Document DK9708122F.html. Dublin: European Foundation for the Improvement of Living and Working Conditions <http://www.eiro.eurofound. ie/1997/08/features/DK9708122F.html>.

1998. 'European Commission Questions Danish Implementation of Directives through Collective Agreements'. EIROnline Document DK9807180N. Dublin: European Foundation for the Improvement of Living and Working Conditions <http://www.eiro.eurofound. ie/1998/07/inbrief/DK9807180N. html>.

Petroglou, Panayota 2000. 'Good Practices for Reconciling Family Life and the Career', Athens: KETHI, Research Center for Gender Equality.

Pierson, Paul 1996. 'The Path to European Integration: A Historical Institutionalist Analysis', *Comparative Political Studies* 29(2): 123–63.

2000. 'Increasing Returns, Path Dependence, and the Study of Politics', *American Political Science Review* 94(2): 251–67.

Pierson, Paul and Leibfried, Stephan 1995. 'Multitiered Institutions and the Making of Social Policy', in: Stephan Leibfried and Paul Pierson (eds.), *European Social Policy: Between Fragmentation and Integration*. Washington, DC: The Brookings Institution, 1–40.

Prechal, Sacha 1995. *Directives in European Community Law: A Study of Directives and Their Enforcement in National Courts*. Oxford: Oxford University Press.

Pressman, Jeffrey L. and Wildavsky, Aaron 1973. *Implementation: How Great Expectations in Washington Are Dashed in Oakland: Or, Why It's Amazing that Federal Programs Work at All this Being a Saga of the Economic Development Administration as Told by Two Sympathetic Observers Who Seek to Build Morals on a Foundation of Ruined Hopes*. Berkeley: University of California Press.

Pridham, Geoffrey and Cini, Michelle 1994. 'Environmental Standards in the European Union: Is There a Southern Problem?' in: M. Faure, J. Vervaele and A. Waele (eds.), *Environmental Standards in the EU in an Interdisciplinary Framework*. Antwerpen: Maklu, 251–77.

Prondzynski, Ferdinand von 1999. 'Ireland: Corporatism Revived', in: Anthony Ferner and Richard Hyman (eds.), *Changing Industrial Relations in Europe*. Oxford: Blackwell, 55–73.

Putnam, Robert D. 1993. 'Diplomacy and Domestic Politics: The Logic of Two-Level Games', in: Peter B. Evans, Harold K. Jacobson and Robert D. Putnam (eds.), *Double-Edged Diplomacy: International Bargaining and Domestic Politics*. Berkeley: University of California Press, 431–68.

Putnam, Robert D., Leonardi, Robert and Nanetti, Raffaella 1993. *Making Democracy Work: Civic Traditions in Modern Italy*. Princeton: Princeton University Press.

Radaelli, Claudio M. 2000. 'Whither Europeanization? Concept Stretching and Substantive Change', *European Integration Online Papers* 4(8) <http://eiop.or. at/eiop/texte/2000–008a.htm>.

Ragin, Charles C. 2000. *Fuzzy-Set Social Science*. Chicago: University of Chicago Press.

Rasmussen, Annegrethe and Thune, Christian 1997. 'Dänemark', in: Rudolf Hrbek (ed.), *Die Reform der Europäischen Union. Positionen und Perspektiven anläßlich der Regierungskonferenz.* Baden-Baden: Nomos, 51–8.

Rasmussen, Hjalte 1988. 'Denmark', in: Heinrich Siedentopf and Jacques Ziller (eds.), *Making European Policies Work: The Implementation of Community Legislation in the Member States.* Vol. II: National Reports. London: Sage, 89–162.

Raunio, Tapio and Hix, Simon 2001. 'Backbenchers Learn to Fight Back: European Integration and Parliamentary Government', in: Klaus H. Goetz and Simon Hix (eds.), *Europeanised Politics? European Integration and National Political Systems.* London: Frank Cass, 142–68.

Regalia, Ida and Regini, Marino 1999. 'Italy: The Dual Character of Industrial Relations', in: Anthony Ferner and Richard Hyman (eds.), *Changing Industrial Relations in Europe.* Oxford: Blackwell Publishers.

Rhodes, Martin 1992. 'The Future of the "Social Dimension": Labour Market Regulation in Post-1992 Europe', *Journal of Common Market Studies* 30(1): 24–51.

1995. 'A Regulatory Conundrum: Industrial Relations and the Social Dimension', in: Stephan Leibfried and Paul Pierson (eds.), *European Social Policy. Between Fragmentation and Integration.* Washington, DC: The Brookings Institution, 78–122.

1997. 'Southern European Welfare States: Identity, Problems and Prospects for Reform', in: Martin Rhodes (ed.), *Southern European Welfare States: Between Crisis and Reform.* London/Portland: Frank Cass, 1–22.

Rhodes, R. A. W. and Marsh, David 1992. 'New Directions in the Study of Policy Networks', *European Journal of Political Research* 21(1/2): 181–205.

Richardson, Jeremy J. 1982a. 'Convergent Policy Styles in Europe?' in: Jeremy J. Richardson (ed.), *Policy Styles in Western Europe.* London: Allen & Unwin, 197–209.

1982b. *Policy Styles in Western Europe.* London: Allen & Unwin.

1996. 'Eroding EU Policies: Implementation Gaps, Cheating and Re-Steering', in: Jeremy J. Richardson (ed.), *European Union: Power and Policy-Making.* London: Routledge, 278–94.

Richardson, Jeremy J., Gustafsson, Gunnel and Jordan, Grant 1982. 'The Concept of Policy Style', in: Jeremy J. Richardson (ed.), *Policy Styles in Western Europe.* London: Allen & Unwin, 1–16.

Richthofen, Wolfgang Freiherr von 2002. *Labour Inspection. A Guide to the Profession.* Geneva: International Labour Organization.

Risse, Thomas 2001. 'A European Identity? Europeanization and the Evolution of Nation-State Identities', in: Maria Green Cowles, James Caporaso and Thomas Risse (eds.), *Transforming Europe: Europeanization and Domestic Change.* Ithaca: Cornell University Press, 198–216.

Risse, Thomas, Cowles, Maria Green and Caporaso, James 2001. 'Europeanization and Domestic Change: Introduction', in: Maria Green Cowles, James Caporaso and Thomas Risse (eds.), *Transforming Europe: Europeanization and Domestic Change.* Ithaca: Cornell University Press, 1–20.

Ross, George 1994. 'On Half-Full Glasses, Europe and the Left: Comments on Wolfgang Streeck's "European Social Policy after Maastricht"', *Economic and Industrial Democracy* 15(3): 486–96.

Sabatier, Paul A. 1986. 'What Can We Learn from Implementation Research?' in: Franz-Xaver Kaufmann, Giandomenico Majone and Vincent Ostrom (eds.), *Guidance, Control, and Evaluation in the Public Sector: The Bielefeld Interdisciplinary Project*. Berlin: De Gruyter, 313–26.

Sabatier, Paul A. and Mazmanian, Daniel A. 1979. 'Conditions of Effective Implementation: A Guide to Accomplishing Policy Objectives', *Policy Analysis* 5(4): 481–504.

1981. 'The Implementation of Public Policy: A Framework of Analysis', in: Daniel A. Mazmanian and Paul A. Sabatier (eds.), *Effective Policy Implementation*. Lexington: Lexington Books, 3–35.

Scharpf, Fritz W. 1988. 'The Joint-Decision Trap: Lessons From German Federalism and European Integration', *Public Administration* 66(3): 239–78.

1994. 'Community and Autonomy: Multi-Level Policy-Making in the European Union', *Journal of European Public Policy* 1(2): 219–39.

1999. *Governing in Europe: Effective and Democratic?* Oxford: Oxford University Press.

2000. 'Economic Changes, Vulnerabilities, and Institutional Capabilities', in: Fritz W. Scharpf and Vivien A. Schmidt (eds.), *Welfare and Work in the Open Economy*. Vol. I: From Vulnerability to Competitiveness. Oxford: Oxford University Press, 21–124.

2002a. 'The European Social Model: Coping with the Challenges of Diversity', *Journal of Common Market Studies* 40(4): 645–70.

2002b. 'Kontingente Generalisierung in der Politikforschung', in: Renate Mayntz (ed.), *Akteure – Mechanismen – Modelle. Zur Theoriefähigkeit makrosozialer Analysen*. Frankfurt a.M.: Campus, 213–35.

Scheuer, Steen 1999. 'Denmark: A Less Regulated Model', in: Anthony Ferner and Richard Hyman (eds.), *Changing Industrial Relations in Europe*. Oxford: Blackwell, 146–70.

Schlüter, Jürgen 1997. 'Jugendarbeitsschutz: EU-Richtlinie umgesetzt', *Arbeit und Recht* 45(4): 17–19.

Schmidt, Manfred G. 1996a. 'The Parties-Do-Matter-Hypothesis and the Case of the Federal Republic of Germany', *German Politics* 4(3): 1–21.

1996b. 'When Parties Matter: A Review of the Possibilities and Limits of Partisan Influence on Public Policy', *European Journal of Political Research* 30(2): 155–83.

2000. *Demokratietheorien*. Opladen: Leske + Budrich.

Schmidt, Marlene 1997. 'Parental Leave: Contested Procedure, Creditable Results', *International Journal of Comparative Labour Law and Industrial Relations* 13(2): 113–26.

Schmidt, Vivien A. 1996. 'Loosening the Ties that Bind: The Impact of European Integration on French Government and its Relationship to Business', *Journal of Common Market Studies* 34(2): 224–54.

1999. 'National Patterns of Governance under Siege: The Impact of European Integration', in: Reiner Eising and Beate Kohler-Koch (eds.), *The*

Transformation of Governance in the European Union. London: Routledge, 155–72.

2000. 'Democracy and Discourse in an Integrating Europe and a Globalizing World', *European Law Journal* 6(3): 277–300.

2002. 'The Effects of European Integration on National Forms of Governance: Reconstructing Practices and Reconceptualizing Democracy', in: Jürgen R. Grote and Bernard Gbikpi (eds.), *Participatory Governance.* Opladen: Leske + Budrich, 141–76.

Schmidt, Vivien A., Tsebelis, George, Risse, Thomas and Scharpf, Fritz W. 1999. 'Approaches to the Study of European Politics', *ECSA Review* 12(2): 2–9.

Schmitter, Philippe C. 1981. 'Interest Intermediation and Regime Governability in Contemporary Western Europe and North America', in: Suzanne Berger (ed.), *Organising Interests in Western Europe: Pluralism, Corporatism, and the Transformation of Politics.* Cambridge: Cambridge University Press, 287–327.

Schmitter, Philippe C. and Lehmbruch, Gerhard (eds.) 1979. *Trends Towards Corporatist Intermediation.* London: Sage.

Schneider, Volker 2003. 'Komplexität und Policy-Forschung: Über die Angemessenheit von Erklärungsstrategien', in: Renate Mayntz and Wolfgang Streeck (eds.), *Die Reformierbarkeit der Demokratie: Innovationen und Blockaden. Festschrift für Fritz W. Scharpf.* Frankfurt a.M.: Campus, 291–317.

Scholl, Bruno and Hansen, Troels Bo 2002. 'Europeanization and Domestic Parliamentary Adaptation: A Comparative Analysis of the Bundestag and the House of Commons', *European Integration Online Papers* 6(15) <http://eiop.or.at/eiop/texte/2002–015a.htm>.

Schroen, Michael 2001. 'Luxemburg: Interessenvermittlung in einem Kleinstaat', in: Werner Reutter and Peter Rütters (eds.), *Verbände und Verbandssysteme.* Opladen: Leske + Budrich, 241–62.

Schuster, Thomas 2000. 'Die Entwicklung von Sozialstandards am Beispiel des Mutterschaftsurlaubes und Mutterschaftsgeldes: Ein Europäischer Vergleich', in: Hilmar Schneider (ed.), *Europas Zukunft als Sozialstaat: Herausforderungen der Integration.* Baden-Baden: Nomos, 125–44.

Schwarze, Jürgen, Becker, Ulrich and Pollack, Christina 1991. *The 1992 Challenge at National Level: A Community-Wide Joint Research Project on the Realization and Implementation by National Governments and Business of the Internal Market Programme: Reports and Conference Proceedings 1990.* Baden-Baden: Nomos.

1993a. *The 1992 Challenge at National Level: A Community-Wide Joint Research Project on the Realization and Implementation by National Governments and Business of the Internal Market Programme: Reports and Conference Proceedings 1991/92.* Baden-Baden: Nomos.

1993b. *Die Implementation von Gemeinschaftsrecht: Untersuchungen zur Gesetzgebungs- und Verwaltungspolitik der Europäischen Gemeinschaft und ihrer Mitgliedstaaten.* Baden-Baden: Nomos.

Schwarze, Jürgen, Govaere, Inge, Helin, Frederique and Bossche, Peter van den 1990. *The 1992 Challenge at National Level: A Community-Wide Joint Research Project on the Realization and Implementation by National Governments and Business of the Internal Market Programme: Reports and Conference Proceedings 1989.* Baden-Baden: Nomos.

Sciarra, Silvana (ed.) 2001. *Labour Law in the Courts*. Oxford: Hart.

Secretaria Confederal de la Mujer CCOO 1999. 'Valoraciones y Propuestad Sindicales a la Ley 39/1999 de 5 de Noviembre para Promover la Conciliación de la Vida Familiar y Laboral de las Personas Trabajadoras (BOE 6–11–1999)'. Madrid: Comisiones Obreras.

Sécretariat Général 1993a. 'Note à l'Attention des Directeurs Généraux'. SEC(93) 216/7. Bruxelles: Commission Européenne.

——— 1993b. 'Note à l'Attention des Directeurs Généraux et Chefs de Service'. SEC(93) 1288. Bruxelles: Commission Européenne.

——— 1996. 'Note à l'Attention de Mesdames et Messieurs les Directeurs Généraux'. SEC(96) 1785. Bruxelles: Commission Européenne.

——— 1998. 'Amélioration des méthodes de travail de la Commission relatives aux procédures d'infraction'. SEC(98) 1733. Bruxelles: Commission Européenne.

——— 2001. 'Rapport sur l'Application du Droit Communautaire par les Etats membres sur le Contrôle de celle-ci par la Commission, contenant des Recommandations en vue de les Améliorer du point de vue de la Gouvernance Démocratique Européenne'. Bruxelles: Commission Européenne <http://europa.eu.int/comm/governance/areas/studies/index_en.htm>.

Seeleib-Kaiser, Martin 2002. 'Neubeginn oder Ende der Sozialdemokratie? Eine Untersuchung zur programmatischen Reform sozialdemokratischer Parteien und ihrer Auswirkung auf die Parteiendifferenzthese', *Politische Vierteljahresschrift* 43(3): 478–96.

Sepe, Onorato 1995. 'The Case of Italy', in: Spyros A. Pappas (ed.), *National Administrative Procedures for the Preparation and Implementation of Community Decisions*. Maastricht: European Institute of Public Administration, 315–57.

Shaw, Jo (ed.) 2000. *Social Law and Policy in an Evolving European Union*. Oxford: Hart.

Siaroff, Alan 1999. 'Corporatism in 24 Industrial Democracies: Meaning and Measurement', *European Journal of Political Research* 36(2): 175–205.

Siedentopf, Heinrich and Ziller, Jacques (eds.) 1988a. *Making European Policies Work: The Implementation of Community Legislation in the Member States*. Vol. I: Comparative Syntheses. London: Sage.

——— 1988b. *Making European Policies Work: The Implementation of Community Legislation in the Member States*. Vol. II: National Reports. London: Sage.

Spanou, Caliope 1998. 'European Integration in Administrative Terms: A Framework for Analysis and the Greek Case', *Journal of European Public Policy* 5(3): 467–84.

STAR 1992. 'Richtlijn Informatieverplichting Arbeidsverhouding'. Advies 4/92. Den Haag: Stichting van de Arbeid.

Steinkühler, Franz (ed.) 1989. *Europa '92 – Industriestandort oder sozialer Lebensraum*. Hamburg: VSA-Verlag.

Stone Sweet, Alec and Brunell, Thomas L. 1998. 'Constructing a Supranational Constitution: Dispute Resolution and Governance in the European Community', *American Political Science Review* 92(1): 63–81.

Strauss, Anselm and Corbin, Juliet 1990. *Basics of Qualitative Research: Grounded Theory Procedures and Techniques.* London: Sage.

1997. *Grounded Theory in Practice.* London: Sage.

Streeck, Wolfgang 1995a. 'From Market Making to State Building? Reflections on the Political Economy of European Social Policy', in: Stephan Leibfried and Paul Pierson (eds.), *European Social Policy: Between Fragmentation and Integration.* Washington, DC: The Brookings Institution, 389–431.

1995b. 'Neo-Voluntarism: A New European Social Policy Regime?' *European Law Journal* 1(1): 31–59.

1997. 'Industrial Citizenship under Regime Competition: The Case of the European Works Councils', *Journal of European Public Policy* 4(4): 643–64.

2000. 'Competitive Solidarity: Rethinking the "European Social Model"', in: Karl Hinrichs, Herbert Kitschelt and Helmut Wiesenthal (eds.), *Kontingenz und Krise. Institutionenpolitik in Kapitalistischen und Postsozialistischen Gesellschaften. Claus Offe zu seinem 60. Geburtstag.* Frankfurt/M.: Campus, 245–62.

2001. 'International Competition, Supranational Integration, National Solidarity. The Emerging Constitution of "Social Europe"', in: Martin Kohli and Mojca Novak (eds.), *Will Europe Work? Integration, Employment and the Social Order.* London: Routledge, 21–34.

Streeck, Wolfgang and Schmitter, Philipp C. 1994. 'From National Corporatism To Transnational Pluralism: Organized Interests in the Single European Market', in: Volker Eichener and Helmut Voelzkow (eds.), *Europäische Integration und verbandliche Interessenvermittlung.* Marburg: Metropolis, 181–215.

Strøm, Kaare 2003. Parliamentary Democracy as Delegation and Accountability. Conference paper, Workshop on Delegation in Contemporary Democracies, ECPR Joint Session of Workshops, 28 March–2 April 2003, Edinburgh.

Sverdrup, Ulf 2002a. Compliance and Conflict Resolution in the European Union. Conference paper, EGPA Annual Conference, 4–7 September 2002, Potsdam.

2000b. Europeanization and Implementation of Community Legislation – A Nordic Model? Conference paper, ECPR Joint Sessions of Workshops, 22–27 March 2002, Turin.

2003. 'Compliance and Styles of Conflict Management'. ARENA Working Paper 08/3. Oslo: University of Oslo.

Swidler, Ann 2001. 'Cultural Expression and Action', in: Neil J. Smelser and Paul B. Baltes (eds.), *International Encyclopedia of the Social & Behavioral Sciences.* Vol. V. Amsterdam: Elsevier, 3063–9.

Szukala, Andrea 2002. 'Das Implementationssystem europäischer Politik: Eine Analyse föderaler Konvergenz in den Mitgliedstaaten der Europäischen Union'. Talk delivered to the graduate seminar of Prof. Wolfgang Wessels, 20 March 2002. Cologne: University of Cologne.

2003. 'France: The European Transformation of the French Model', in: Wolfgang Wessels, Andreas Maurer and Jürgen Mittag (eds.), *Fifteen into One: The European Union and Its Member States.* Manchester: Manchester University Press, 216–47.

Tallberg, Jonas 1999. *Making States Comply. The European Commission, the European Court of Justice and the Enforcement of the Internal Market*. Lund: Lund University.

— 2002. 'Paths to Compliance: Enforcement, Management, and the European Union', *International Organization* 56(3): 609–43.

Tálos, Emmerich and Kittel, Bernhard 2001. *Gesetzgebung in Österreich. Netzwerke, Akteure und Interaktionen in politischen Entscheidungsprozessen*. Wien: WUV.

Tesoka, Sabrina 1999. 'Judicial Politics in the European Union: Its Impact on National Opportunity Structures for Gender Equality'. MPIfG Discussion Paper 99/2. Cologne: Max Planck Institute for the Study of Societies.

Thelen, Kathleen 1999. 'Historical Institutionalism in Comparative Politics', *Annual Review of Political Science* 2(1): 369–404.

— 2003. 'How Institutions Evolve: Insights from Comparative Historical Analysis', in: James Mahoney and Dietrich Rueschemeyer (eds.), *Comparative Historical Analysis in the Social Sciences*. Cambridge: Cambridge University Press, 208–40.

Thelen, Kathleen and Steinmo, Sven 1992. 'Historical Institutionalism in Comparative Politics', in: Sven Steinmo, Kathleen Thelen and Frank Longstreth (eds.), *Structuring Politics: Historical Institutionalism in Comparative Analysis*. Cambridge: Cambridge University Press, 1–32.

Thörnqvist, Christer 1999. 'The Decentralization of Industrial Relations: The Swedish Case in Comparative Persepctive', *European Journal of Industrial Relations* 5(1): 71–87.

Treib, Oliver 2004. *Die Bedeutung der nationalen Parteipolitik für die Umsetzung europäischer Sozialrichtlinien*. Politik, Verbände, Recht: Die Umsetzung europäischer Sozialpolitik, Vol. I. Frankfurt/M.: Campus.

Trentini, Marco 1997. 'Unions and Employers Agree on Application of EU Working Time Directive'. EIROnline Document IT9711140N. Dublin: European Foundation for the Improvement of Living and Working Conditions <http://www.eiro.eurofound.ie/1997/11/inbrief/IT9711140N.html>.

Treu, Tiziano 1998. *Labour Law and Industrial Relations in Italy*. The Hague: Kluwer.

Tsebelis, George 1995. 'Decision Making in Political Systems: Veto Players in Presidentialism, Parliamentarism, Multicameralism and Multipartism', *British Journal of Political Science* 25: 289–325.

— 2002. *Veto Players: How Political Institutions Work*. New York: Sage.

TUC 2000. 'Response to DTI Consultation on Implementation of Part-Time Work Directive'. London: Trades Union Congress.

UNICE 1991. UNICE Comments on the Proposal for a Council Directive on a Form of Proof of an Employment Relationship (COM (90) 563 final), Brussels: Union of Industrial and Employers' Federations of Europe.

Valdeolivas García, Yolanda 1999. 'Las Directivas como instrumento de política social y su relación con el ordenamiento laboral espanol'. *Revista del Ministerio de Trabajo y Asuntos Sociales* 17: 53–110.

Van den Bossche, Peter 1996. 'In Search of Remedies for Non-Compliance: The Experience of the European Community', *Maastricht Journal of European and Comparative Law* 3(4): 371–98.

Vanderhallen, Peter 1998. 'Boom in Sabbatical Leave Applications in Belgium'. EIROnline Document BE9810248N. Dublin: European Foundation for the Improvement of Living and Working Conditions <http://www.eiro. eurofound.ie/1998/10/inbrief/BE9810248N.html>.

Vascovics, Laszlo A. and Rost, Horst 1999. *Väter und Erziehungsurlaub*. Schriftenreihe des Bundesministeriums für Familie, Senioren, Frauen und Jugend. Vol. 179. Stuttgart: Kohlhammer.

Verzichelli, Luca and Cotta, Maurizio 2000. 'Italy: From "Constrained" Coalitions to Alternating Governments?' in: Wolfgang C. Müller and Kaare Strøm (eds.), *Coalition Governments in Western Europe*. Oxford: Oxford University Press, 433–97.

Vogel, Laurent 1994. *Prevention at the Workplace: An Initial Review of How the 1989 Community Framework Directive Is Being Implemented*. Brussels: European Trade Union Technical Bureau for Health and Safety.

  1997. 'The Transposition of Directive 92/85/EEC on the Safety and Health of Pregnant Workers, and Workers Who Have Recently Given Birth or Are Breastfeeding (I)'. *European Trade Union Technical Bureau for Health and Safety Newsletter* 6: 8–13 <http://www.etuc.org/tutb/uk/pdf/1997-06-p08–13.pdf>.

Vos, Ellen 1999. *Institutional Frameworks of Community Health and Safety Legislation. Committees, Agencies and Private Bodies*. Oxford: Hart.

Waarden, Frans van 1999. 'European Harmonization of National Regulatory Styles', in: J. A. E. Vervaele (ed.), *Compliance and Enforcement of Community Law*. Den Haag: Kluwer, 95–124.

Warner, Harriet 1984. 'EC Social Policy in Practice: Community Action on Behalf of Women and Its Impact in the Member States', *Journal of Common Market Studies* 23(2): 141–67.

Weber, Tina 1997. 'European Works Councils: One Year after the Transposition Deadline'. EIROnline Document EU9708142F. Dublin: European Foundation for the Improvement of Living and Working Conditions <http://www.eiro.eurofound.ie/about/1997/08/feature/EU9708142F.html>.

Weiler, Joseph H. H. 1988. 'The White Paper and the Application of Community Law', in: Roland Bieber, Renaud Dehousse, John Pinder and Joseph H. H. Weiler (eds.), *1992: One European Market? A Critical Analysis of the Commission's Internal Market Strategy*. Baden-Baden: Nomos, 337–58.

Weiler, Joseph H. H. 1991. 'The Transformation of Europe', *Yale Law Journal* 108(8): 2403–83.

Wessels, Wolfgang, Maurer, Andreas and Mittag, Jürgen (eds.) 2003. *Fifteen into One: The European Union and Its Member States*. Manchester: Manchester University Press.

Wessels, Wolfgang and Rometsch, Dietrich (eds.) 1996. *The European Union and Member States. Towards Institutional Fusion?* Manchester: Manchester University Press.

Williamson, Oliver E. 1985. *The Economic Institutions of Capitalism*. New York: Free Press.

Wilts, Arnold 2001. 'Europeanization and Means of Interest Representation by National Business Associations', *European Journal of Industrial Relations* 7(3): 269–86.

Windhoff-Héritier, Adrienne 1980. *Politikimplementation: Ziel und Wirklichkeit politischer Entscheidungen*. Königstein/Ts.: Anton Hain.

Yannakourou, Matina 2003. 'OKE Examines Social Dialogue'. EIROnline Document GR0301102F. Dublin: European Foundation for the Improvement of Living and Working Conditions <http://www.eiro.eurofound.ie/2003/01/feature/GR0301102F.html>.

Zervakis, Peter 1999. 'Das politische System Griechenlands', in: Wolfgang Ismayr (ed.), *Die politischen Systeme Westeuropas*. Opladen: Leske + Budrich, 637–72.

Zohlnhöfer, Reimut 2001. *Die Wirtschaftspolitik der Ära Kohl: Eine Analyse der Schlüsselentscheidungen in den Politikfeldern Finanzen, Arbeit und Entstaatlichung, 1982–1998*. Opladen: Leske + Budrich.

Index

Administrative co-ordination deficits
  as reason for (non-)compliance, 14–15,
    24, 62–64, 85, 132, 298–299,
    323–324, 355
Administrative overload
  as reason for (non-)compliance, 14–15,
    24, 64–65, 83–86, 107, 128–129, 132,
    166–169, 302–303, 323–324
Administrative watchdog units,
  as reason for (non-)compliance, 24,
    301–302, 355
Agency loss
  see EU decision-making process;
  principal–agent theory
Austria
  and Employment Contract Information
    Directive, 60–62, 66–68, 70–71, 190,
    270–271, 300, 314–315
  and Parental Leave Directive, 145–147,
    152–158, 182–184, 192–193,
    270–271, 292–293, 305, 333
  and Part-time Work Directive,
    164–166, 171–175, 184, 270–271,
    360–361
  and Pregnant Workers Directive, 77–80,
    83–84, 88–93, 180–181, 270–271,
    278, 292, 302–303, 305, 308
  and Working Time Directive, 99–103,
    110–112, 114–117, 181, 194–199,
    270–271, 278, 287, 305, 333,
    352–353
  and worlds of compliance, 333
  and Young Workers Directive, 123–127,
    130, 133–134, 137–139, 181–182,
    197–199, 270–271, 286–288,
    305–306, 333
  application of Directives in, 114,
    155–158, 172–174, 272–276
  enforcement system in, 67–70, 89–91,
    153–155, 272–276, 335
  infringement procedures initiated
    against, 209

lowering of standards in, 130, 137–139,
  197–199
misfit in, 60–62, 77–80, 83–84, 99–103,
  123–127, 130, 145–147, 164–166,
  262–265, 278, 287, 290–293,
  360–361
national public–private relations in,
  229–230, 237–240, 249–250,
  284–286
transposition performance of, 62,
  66–68, 83–84, 88–89, 110–112, 130,
  133–134, 152–153, 171–172,
  194–196, 270–271, 285–286,
  290–293, 296–297, 300, 306, 333
voluntary reforms in, 181–184, 190,
  192–196

Belgium
  and Employment Contract Information
    Directive, 59–63, 66–68, 70–71, 220,
    270–271, 298–299, 334–335
  and Parental Leave Directive, 142,
    145–147, 149–150, 152–158,
    192–194, 270–271
  and Part-time Work Directive, 164–166,
    171–175, 270–271, 286–288,
    302–303, 305–307, 334–335
  and Pregnant Workers Directive, 77–80,
    88–93, 180–181, 270–271, 298–299
  and Working Time Directive, 97–103,
    110–112, 114, 191, 220, 270–271,
    284–288, 305, 334–335, 352–353
  and worlds of compliance, 334–335
  and Young Workers Directive, 123–127,
    133–134, 181–182, 270–271,
    302–303, 315, 334–335
  application of Directives in, 89–91, 114,
    153–158, 272–276
  enforcement system in, 67–70, 89–91,
    153–155, 172–174, 272–276, 335
  infringement procedures initiated
    against, 62–63, 209

Belgium (*cont.*)
  misfit in, 60–63, 77–80, 99–103,
    123–127, 142, 145–147, 149–150,
    164–166, 262–265, 290–291
  national public–private relations in, 234,
    237–241, 284–285, 306–307
  transposition performance of, 62–63,
    66–68, 88–89, 110–112, 133–134,
    149–150, 152–153, 171–172, 220,
    270–271, 284–285, 290–291,
    296–299, 306–307, 334–335
  voluntary reforms in, 149–150,
    155–158, 180–186, 191–194

Compliance
  definition of, 4, 12
  forms of, 12–13, 17, 203
  hypotheses on reasons for lack of, 23–26
  improvement of, 288–289, 353–365
  literature on, 14–20, 201–205, 323,
    344–345
  measurement of, 12, 17, 19–20, 29–30,
    33–34, 201–205, 267–269, 276, 287,
    323
  national application and, 4, 11–12,
    29–30, 33–34, 272–276
  national enforcement and, 4, 11–12,
    272–276, 323
  national transposition and, 4, 11–12
  pluri-theoretical approach to, 22–26
  stages of, 4–6, 12, 203, 326–328
  see also worlds of compliance; national
    enforcement
Constructivism, 280–283
Corporatism
  see national public–private relations

Denmark
  and Employment Contract Information
    Directive, 60–62, 66–68, 70–71, 190,
    244, 270–271, 300, 331
  and Parental Leave Directive, 145–147,
    152–155, 182, 245–246, 270–271,
    331
  and Part-time Work Directive, 161–166,
    171–172, 174–175, 184, 194–196,
    246–247, 270–271, 292–293, 300,
    305–307, 331
  and Pregnant Workers Directive,
    77–80, 88–93, 244, 270–271, 300,
    331
  and Working Time Directive, 28,
    99–103, 110–112, 212, 244–245,
    270–271, 282, 292–293, 331
  and worlds of compliance, 328, 331

and Young Workers Directive, 122–128,
    133–134, 137–139, 181–182, 244,
    270–271, 279–280, 284, 294, 300,
    309–311, 331
application of Directives in, 67–70,
    272–276
enforcement system in, 67–70,
    89–91, 153–155, 272–276,
    332–333
infringement procedures initiated
    against, 209, 212, 244–246
misfit in, 28, 60–62, 77–80, 99–103,
    123–128, 145–147, 164–166,
    242–245, 247, 262–265, 290–294
national public–private relations in, 61,
    80, 102, 127, 146–147, 164–165,
    229–230, 232, 234, 237–247,
    257–259, 262–265, 282, 284,
    292–293, 306–307, 344, 359–360
transposition performance of, 66–68,
    88–89, 110–112, 127–128, 133–134,
    152–153, 171–172, 242–247,
    270–271, 290–294, 296–297, 300,
    331
voluntary reforms in, 181–182,
    187–188, 190, 193–196, 363–364

Employment Contract Information
    Directive
  aim and content of, 56–58, 70
  and EU-level negotiations, 58–59, 70
  and misfit in the member states, 60–62,
    70, 260, 265
  and national application and
    enforcement, 39–40, 67–70
  and transposition in the member states,
    62–68, 70, 269–271
  and voluntary reforms, 190, 193
  general assessment of effects of, 70–71
  infringement proceedings initiated
    against breaches of, 62–63, 209–210
  see also individual countries
EU decision-making process,
  as reason for (non-)compliance,
    103–106, 128–129, 224, 277–283,
    286
EU social policy
  as a combination of community and
    autonomy, 1–3, 347–348
  concept of minimum harmonisation in,
    2, 360–361
  development of binding legislation in,
    45–49, 54–55, 342
  development of competences and
    decision modes in, 41–45

development of non-binding acts in, 49–55
improvement of, 353–365
overall impact of, 5, 345–348
overall implementation of, 4, 265–271, 276, 343
overall misfit and costs of, 4, 260–265, 342, 345–346
social dumping and, 1–5, 65, 178–179, 345–348
see also neo-voluntarism
European Commission
and reinterpretation of Directives, 81–83, 91–93, 221, 281–283, 286–288
competences and role in supranational enforcement, 6, 205–208
improvement of enforcement policy of, 357–359
literature on enforcement policy of, 18–20, 201–205
quality of enforcement policy of, 4–5, 215–219, 267, 327–328, 343–344
reasons for enforcement policy of, 20, 219–225
see also infringement procedures; European Court of Justice
European Court of Justice
and infringement procedure, 6, 69, 102, 107–110, 132–133, 148–150, 203, 205–214, 221, 232, 245, 251, 267, 288, 330
and preliminary ruling procedure, 25, 29, 48, 63–65, 69, 84, 87, 99, 102, 104–108, 116–117, 147–148, 165–166, 176, 195, 202, 221, 281, 288, 355–357, 364
and reinterpretation of Directives, 25, 29, 93, 99, 102, 104–106, 116–117, 195, 267–268, 281–283, 287, 350, 356
Europeanisation
and EU social policy Directives, 70–71, 91–93, 115–117, 137–139, 155–158, 174–177, 345–348
definition of, 11
literature on, 11, 15–17, 27, 230–231
see also national public–private relations; compliance

Finland
and Employment Contract Information Directive, 60–62, 66–68, 70, 271, 300

and Parental Leave Directive, 145–147, 152–158, 182, 270–271, 300, 316, 332–333
and Part-time Work Directive, 161–166, 171–172, 174–175, 184–186, 270–271, 305
and Pregnant Workers Directive, 77–80, 88–93, 270–271, 332–333
and Working Time Directive, 99–103, 110–112, 270–271, 300
and worlds of compliance, 332–333
and Young Workers Directive, 123–127, 133–134, 181–182, 270–271, 286–288, 332–333
application of Directives in, 155–158, 272–276
enforcement system in, 67–70, 89–91, 153–155, 272–276, 332–333
infringement procedures initiated against, 209, 226
misfit in, 60–62, 77–80, 99–103, 123–127, 145–147, 164–166, 262–265, 290–291
national public–private relations in, 237–240, 284
transposition performance of, 66–68, 88–89, 110–112, 133–134, 152–153, 171–172, 270–271, 290–291, 296–297, 300, 332–333
voluntary reforms in, 181–182, 184–186, 193–194
France
and Employment Contract Information Directive, 60–62, 66–68, 70–71, 210, 270–271, 300, 338–339
and Parental Leave Directive, 145–147, 151–155, 182, 270–271, 360–361
and Part-time Work Directive, 161–166, 171–175, 184, 270–271, 279, 300, 352–353
and Pregnant Workers Directive, 77–80, 84–85, 88–93, 180–181, 190–191, 227, 270–271, 314, 316, 338–339
and Working Time Directive, 97–103, 107–108, 110–112, 115–117, 191, 194–196, 211–212, 270–271, 314, 338–339
and worlds of compliance, 325, 328
and Young Workers Directive, 122–127, 132–134, 191–192, 212–213, 226, 270–271, 300, 338–339
application of Directives in, 67–70, 89–91, 272–276

France (*cont.*)
  enforcement system in, 67–70, 89–91,
    153–155, 172–174, 272–276,
    338–339
  infringement procedures initiated
    against, 84–85, 107–108, 132–133,
    209–213, 223–224, 226–227,
    338–339
  misfit in, 60–62, 77–80, 84–85, 99–103,
    107–108, 123–127, 132–133,
    145–147, 151, 164–166, 262–265,
    290–291, 360–361
  national public–private relations in,
    237–241, 284
  transposition performance of,
    66–68, 84–85, 88–89, 107–108,
    110–112, 132–134, 151–153,
    171–172, 194–196, 222, 270–271,
    290–291, 296–297, 299–301,
    338–339
  voluntary reforms in, 187–188, 190–194

Germany
  and Employment Contract Information
    Directive, 60–64, 66–68, 70–71,
    270–271, 298–299, 309–311
  and Parental Leave Directive, 142,
    145–147, 150–158, 182–184,
    192–193, 213, 270–271, 293,
    309–311
  and Part-time Work Directive, 161–166,
    169, 171–172, 174–177, 184–186,
    270–271, 279, 298–300, 309–311,
    315
  and Pregnant Workers Directive, 77–83,
    88–93, 180–181, 194–196, 270–271,
    282, 286–288, 292, 309–311, 314,
    357
  and Working Time Directive, 99–104,
    110–112, 114–117, 181, 191,
    194–199, 224, 270–271, 277–278,
    287, 309–311, 351–353
  and worlds of compliance, 333
  and Young Workers Directive, 123–127,
    129–130, 133–139, 181–182,
    191–192, 197–199, 270–271, 305,
    309–311
  application of Directives in, 67–70, 114,
    135–137, 155–158, 272–276
  enforcement system in, 67–70, 89–91,
    135–137, 153–155, 272–276, 335
  infringement procedures initiated
    against, 150–151, 209, 213, 223–224
  lowering of standards in, 129–130,
    135–139, 197–199

  misfit in, 60–64, 77–83, 99–104,
    123–127, 129–130, 142, 145–147,
    150–151, 164–166, 169, 262–265,
    287, 290–293
  national public–private relations in,
    237–240
  transposition performance of, 63–64,
    66–68, 81–83, 88–89, 103–104,
    110–112, 129–130, 133–134,
    150–153, 169, 171–172, 194–196,
    270–271, 277–278, 286–288,
    290–293, 296–300, 333
  voluntary reforms in, 150–151, 169,
    175–176, 180–188, 191–196, 293,
    363–364
Gold plating
  see voluntary reforms
Greece
  and Employment Contract Information
    Directive, 60–62, 66–68, 70–71, 222,
    270–271, 302–303, 335–336
  and Parental Leave Directive, 145–147,
    151–158, 182, 213, 270–271,
    286–288, 315–316
  and Part-time Work Directive, 161–166,
    171–175, 184–186, 193, 270–271,
    300, 315–316, 335–336
  and Pregnant Workers Directive, 77–80,
    88–93, 180–181, 210–211, 222,
    270–271, 298–300, 302–303,
    335–336
  and Working Time Directive, 97–103,
    110–112, 115, 191, 194–196, 211,
    270–271, 286–288, 300, 302–303,
    305, 335–336
  and worlds of compliance,
    335–336
  and Young Workers Directive,
    122–127, 133–134, 191–192, 222,
    270–271, 298–299, 302–303,
    335–336
  application of Directives in, 67–70,
    89–91, 153–155, 172–174, 272–276,
    335–336
  enforcement system in, 67–70, 89–91,
    153–155, 172–174, 272–276,
    335–336
  infringement procedures initiated
    against, 110, 209–211, 213, 222–224,
    226, 335–336
  misfit in, 60–62, 77–80, 99–103, 110,
    123–127, 145–147, 151–152,
    164–166, 262–265, 290–291
  national public–private relations in,
    237–241, 249, 256–258, 284

transposition performance of, 66–68, 88–89, 110–112, 133–134, 151–153, 171–172, 194–196, 222, 270–271, 290–291, 296–301, 335–336
voluntary reforms in, 180–181, 184–189, 191–194
Grounded theory, 23, 318–319

Historical institutionalism, 16, 55, 258, 280–283, 289–296, 345–347, 353

Implementation
see compliance
Infringement procedure
domestic impact of, 225–228, 323–324
literature on, 18–20, 201–205
social policy Directives and, 62–63, 84–87, 104–110, 129–130, 132–133, 147–151, 209–214, 244–246, 343
stages of, 205–208
see also individual countries and Directives; European Commission; European Court of Justice
Interest groups
see social partners (EU level, national level); national public–private relations
Intergovernmentalism,14, 277–280, 345–346
Interpretation problems
as reason for (non-)compliance, 14–15, 24, 26, 77, 81–87, 91–93, 104–106, 147–148, 166–169, 285–289
Ireland
and Employment Contract Information Directive, 59–62, 64, 66–68, 70, 270–271, 302–303
and Parental Leave Directive, 144–148, 152–158, 182–184, 192–193, 213, 270–271, 279–280, 286–288, 305, 308
and Part-time Work Directive, 164–168, 171–172, 174–175, 184–186, 247, 270–271, 286–288, 302–303, 305, 339
and Pregnant Workers Directive, 75–80, 88–93, 190–191, 270–271, 302–303
and Working Time Directive, 97–103, 106–107, 110–112, 114–115, 181, 194–196, 270–271, 279–280, 287, 302–303, 309–311, 314, 339
and worlds of compliance, 327, 339
and Young Workers Directive, 123–127, 133–137, 181–182, 191–192, 270–271, 302–303

application of Directives in, 67–70, 114–115, 135–137, 153–158, 272–276
enforcement system in, 67–70, 89–91, 135–137, 153–155, 272–276, 339
infringement procedures initiated against, 129–130, 147–148, 209, 213, 223–224
misfit in, 45, 59–62, 64, 77–80, 97–103, 106–107, 123–127, 145–148, 164–168, 287, 290–291
national public–private relations in, 167–168, 237–240, 242–244, 247
transposition performance of, 64, 66–68, 88–89, 106–107, 110–112, 133–134, 147–148, 152–153, 167–168, 171–172, 194–196, 270–271, 288, 290–291, 296–297, 308, 339
voluntary reforms in, 106–107, 181–186, 190–194
Issue linkage
as reason for (non-)compliance, 62–64, 81–84, 107–110, 129–131, 150, 313–316, 323–324
Italy
and Employment Contract Information Directive, 60–62, 64, 66–68, 70, 210, 222, 270–271, 298–300, 339–340
and European Works Councils Directive, 256
and Parental Leave Directive, 145–147, 150, 152–155, 182–184, 192–193, 213, 222, 255, 270–271, 294, 298–299, 305, 339–340
and Part-time Work Directive, 164–166, 171–172, 174–177, 184–186, 255–256, 270–271, 294, 298–299, 339–340
and Pregnant Workers Directive, 77–80, 85, 88–93, 180–181, 222, 270–271, 277–278, 292, 298–300, 339–340
and Working Time Directive, 99–103, 108–112, 211–212, 222, 270–271, 298–299, 305, 309–314, 339–340
and worlds of compliance, 325, 327
and Young Workers Directive, 122–127, 133–134, 181–182, 194–196, 215–219, 222, 270–271, 279, 300, 305, 339–340
application of Directives in, 272–276
enforcement system in, 67–70, 89–91, 153–155, 272–276, 339–340

Italy (*cont.*)
  infringement procedures initiated
    against, 108–110, 150, 209–213,
    222–224, 343
  misfit in, 60–62, 64, 77–80, 85, 99–103,
    108–110, 123–127, 145–147, 150,
    164–166, 171, 262–265, 290–292,
    294
  national public–private relations in,
    237–241, 249, 292
  transposition performance of, 64,
    66–68, 85, 88–89, 108–112, 133–134,
    150, 152–153, 171–172, 222,
    270–271, 290–292, 294, 296–301,
    339–340, 343
  voluntary reforms in, 150, 171,
    175–176, 181–188, 192–196, 294

Joint-decision trap, 43

Lowering of standards,129–132, 135–139,
    197–199
  see also neo-voluntarism
Luxembourg
  and Employment Contract Information
    Directive, 59–62, 64–68, 70, 190,
    270–271, 302–303, 337–338
  and Parental Leave Directive, 145–149,
    152–158, 182–184, 192–193, 213,
    248–249, 270–271, 279–280,
    286–288, 305–307, 315, 337–338
  and Part-time Work Directive, 161–166,
    171–172, 174–175, 184, 248–249,
    270–271, 337–338, 360–361
  and Pregnant Workers Directive, 77–80,
    85–86, 88–93, 180–181, 190–191,
    210–211, 270–271, 286–288, 292,
    302–303, 337–338, 357
  and Working Time Directive, 99–103,
    110–112, 115, 194–196, 270–271,
    302–303, 337–338
  and worlds of compliance, 325, 328,
    337–338
  and Young Workers Directive, 122–127,
    132–134, 181–182, 191–192,
    212–213, 270–271, 302–303,
    337–338
  application of Directives in, 67–70, 115,
    155–158, 272–276
  enforcement system in, 67–70,
    89–91, 153–155, 272–276,
    337–338
  infringement procedures initiated
    against, 85–86, 132, 148–149,
    209–213, 223–224, 292

  misfit in, 60–62, 64–65, 77–80, 85–86,
    99–103, 123–127, 132, 145–149,
    164–166, 262–265, 290–292,
    360–361
  national public–private relations in,
    237–244, 248–249, 257–258,
    306
  transposition performance of, 64–68,
    84–85, 88–89, 110–112, 132–134,
    148–149, 152–153, 171–172,
    194–196, 222, 248–249, 270–271,
    286–288, 290–292, 296–297, 307,
    337–338
  voluntary reforms in, 148–149,
    155–158, 181–184, 190–194

Methodology, 6–7, 9, 12, 17, 19–20, 23,
    26–30, 32–40, 194, 196–197, 199,
    216–219, 234, 237, 267–269, 276,
    287, 317–321
  and case selection, 7–9, 351
Misfit
  aggregation of, 31–32
  and overall compliance in the member
    states, 25
  as determinant of supranational voting
    behaviour, 279–280, 342, 345–346
  as a reason for (non-)compliance,
    15–16, 27, 81–88, 103–107, 289–296,
    364–365
  as a theoretical concept, 15–16, 27,
    230–231, 289–296
  cost dimension of, 30–31, 61–62, 80,
    102–103, 127, 147, 165–166,
    260–262
  definition and operationalisation of,
    27–32
  dimensions of, 15–16, 27–31
  policy dimension of, 27–28, 60–61,
    77–80, 99–102, 123–127, 145–146,
    164
  politics and polity dimension of, 29–30,
    61, 80, 102, 127, 146–147, 164–165,
    263–264, 359–360

National application
  see compliance, see also individual
    countries and Directives
National enforcement
  literature on, 17–20
  measurement of, 12, 34–40, 272–276
  problems with, 272–276, 335–337,
    339–340, 343–344
  requirements for adequate performance
    in, 34–40, 272–276

see also compliance; individual countries
and Directives
National public–private relations
actual Europeanisation of, 236–259, 344
EU decision-making process and,
237–242
EU impulses for change of, 29–30,
33–34, 231–233
forms of, 233–236
implementation process and, 242–257
literature on Europeanisation of, 15–16,
21–22, 230–231
see also individual countries; social
partners (national level)
National transposition
see compliance, see also individual
countries and Directives
Neo-functionalism,14
Neo-voluntarism
and development of EU social policy
over time, 54–55, 350–351
and EU social policy Directives, 161,
348–353
as a theoretical concept, 3, 349
domestic policies and, 352–353
impact in the member states of, 5,
178–200, 349, 352–353
see also voluntary reforms; lowering of
standards

Open method of co-ordination, 9, 41, 45,
50–51, 54, 55, 178, 350, 359–361,
363–364
Over-implementation,
see voluntary reforms

Parental Leave Directive,
aim and content of, 140–142, 148–150,
156
and EU-level negotiations, 140, 142,
148–150, 156
and misfit in the member states,
145–150, 156, 260, 265
and national application and
enforcement, 39–40, 153–155
and transposition in the member states,
147–150, 153, 156, 269–271
and voluntary reforms, 155–158,
182–184, 186–187, 189, 192–193
general assessment of effects of,
155–158
infringement proceedings initiated
against breaches of, 147–151, 209,
213
see also individual countries

Part-time Work Directive
aim and content of, 159–161, 165–166,
176
and EU-level negotiations, 159,
161–166, 176
and misfit in the member states,
164–166, 176, 260, 265
and national application and
enforcement, 39–40, 172–174
and transposition in the member states,
165–172, 176, 269–271
and voluntary reforms, 169–171,
175–176, 184–187, 189, 194–196
general assessment of effects of,
174–177
infringement proceedings initiated
against breaches of, 209, 213–214
see also individual countries
Party politics
as determinant for supranational voting
behaviour, 279–280, 310, 328–332
as reason for (non-)compliance, 25,
63–66, 81–83, 103–107, 127–131,
146–147, 150–151, 164–165, 169,
293–294, 298–299, 309–313,
322–323, 344–345
Pluralism
see national public–private relations
Portugal
and Employment Contract Information
Directive, 59–62, 65–68, 70–71, 190,
270–271, 336–337
and Parental Leave Directive, 145–147,
152–158, 182–184, 192–193, 213,
270–271, 305, 336–337
and Part-time Work Directive,
161–166, 170–177, 184–186,
270–271, 294
and Pregnant Workers Directive, 77–80,
87–93, 180–181, 190–191, 270–271,
292, 305, 336–337
and Working Time Directive, 99–103,
110–112, 115, 211, 270–271,
302–303, 305, 336–337
and worlds of compliance, 336–337
and Young Workers Directive, 123–127,
133–139, 181–182, 191–192,
197–199, 220, 270–271, 305,
336–337
application of Directives in, 67–70,
89–91, 115, 135–137, 153–158,
272–276, 336–337
enforcement system in, 67–70, 89–91,
135–137, 153–155, 172–174,
272–276, 336–337

Portugal (*cont.*)
  infringement procedures initiated
    against, 209, 211, 213, 223–224
  lowering of standards in, 131–132,
    137–139, 197–199
  misfit in, 60–62, 65, 77–80, 87, 99–103,
    123–127, 145–147, 164–166,
    170–171, 262–265, 290–292, 294
  national public–private relations in, 87,
    237–240
  transposition performance of, 65–68,
    87–89, 110–112, 133–134, 152–153,
    170–172, 220, 270–271, 290–292,
    294, 296–297, 336–337
  voluntary reforms in, 155–158,
    170–171, 175–176, 181–186,
    190–194, 294
Pregnant Workers Directive
  aim and content of, 73–75, 92
  and EU-level negotiations, 75–77, 92
  and misfit in the member states, 77–80,
    92, 260, 265
  and national application and
    enforcement, 39–40, 89–91
  and transposition in the member states,
    81–89, 92, 269–271, 286–288
  and voluntary reforms, 180–181,
    186–187, 189–191, 193–196
  general assessment of effects of,
    91–93
  infringement proceedings initiated
    against breaches of, 84–87, 209–211,
    292
  see also individual countries
Principal–agent theory, 280–283,
  286

Regulatory procedures
  as reason for (non-)compliance,
    14–15

Social partners (EU level), 2, 7, 26, 58–59,
  140, 142, 147–148, 159, 161–164,
  229, 232, 285–289, 344
Social partners (national level),
  as reason for (non-)compliance, 14–16,
    20–22, 24–25, 87, 104–106, 108–110,
    128–129, 147–150, 166–169,
    284–286, 288, 303–309, 323,
    344
  see also national public–private relations
Sociological institutionalism, 16, 325–326
Soft law
  see voluntary reforms; open method of
    co-ordination

Spain
  and Employment Contract Information
    Directive, 60–62, 64, 66–68, 70–71,
    270–271, 335
  and Parental Leave Directive, 145–147,
    152–155, 182–184, 254–255,
    270–271, 286–288
  and Part-time Work Directive, 164–166,
    169–177, 184–186, 188, 197–199,
    270–271, 309–313
  and Pregnant Workers Directive, 75–80,
    86–93, 180–181, 270–271, 286–288
  and Working Time Directive, 99–103,
    110–112, 115–117, 194–196,
    270–271, 287, 300, 315
  and worlds of compliance, 335
  and Young Workers Directive, 122–127,
    133–134, 181–182, 270–271, 279,
    300, 314–315
  application of Directives in, 67–70,
    89–91, 115, 272–276
  enforcement system in, 67–70, 89–91,
    153–155, 172–174, 272–276, 335
  infringement procedures initiated
    against, 86–87, 209, 223–224,
    343
  lowering of standards in, 197–199
  misfit in, 60–62, 64, 77–80, 86–87,
    99–103, 123–127, 145–147, 164–166,
    169–170, 262–265, 287, 290–291
  national public–private relations in,
    237–241, 249, 254–255
  transposition performance of, 64,
    66–68, 86–89, 110–112, 133–134,
    152–153, 169–172, 194–196, 202,
    270–271, 286–288, 290–291,
    296–297, 300, 335, 343
  voluntary reforms in, 169–170,
    175–176, 180–186, 188–189,
    193–194
Statism
  see national public–private relations
Sweden
  and Employment Contract Information
    Directive, 60–62, 66–68, 70–71,
    270–271, 300
  and Parental Leave Directive, 145–147,
    152–158, 182, 270–271, 300,
    331–332
  and Part-time Work Directive, 161–166,
    171–172, 174–175, 184, 252–253,
    270–271, 305–306, 314–315,
    331–332
  and Pregnant Workers Directive,
    161–166, 171–172, 174–175, 184,

252–253, 270–271, 305–306,
  314–315, 331–332
and Working Time Directive, 99–103,
  110–113, 250–252, 270–271, 278,
  292–293, 305–306, 314–315,
  331–332
and worlds of compliance, 331–332
and Young Workers Directive, 123–127,
  133–134, 181–182, 212–213,
  270–271
application of Directives in, 113,
  153–158, 172–174, 250–252,
  272–276
enforcement system in, 67–70, 89–91,
  153–155, 272–276, 332–333
infringement procedures initiated
  against, 209, 212–213, 226, 292
lowering of standards in,
misfit in, 60–62, 77–80, 87–88, 99–103,
  123–127, 145–147, 164–166,
  250–253, 262–265, 278, 290–293,
  359–360
national public–private relations in, 61,
  80, 102, 127, 229–230, 234, 237–240,
  249–253, 258–259, 278, 284,
  292–293, 306, 344, 359–360
transposition performance of, 66–68,
  87–89, 110–112, 133–134, 152–153,
  171–172, 250–253, 270–271,
  290–293, 296–297, 300, 331–332
voluntary reforms in, 181–182,
  187–188, 193–194

The Netherlands
  and Employment Contract Information
    Directive, 60–62, 66–68, 70, 190,
    270–271, 300, 305
  and Parental Leave Directive, 145–147,
    152–155, 182–184, 270–271, 300,
    334
  and Part-time Work Directive, 161–166,
    171–175, 184–186, 270–271, 334
  and Pregnant Workers Directive, 75–80,
    88–93, 270–271, 334
  and Working Time Directive, 97–103,
    110–112, 115–117, 181, 191,
    194–199, 270–271, 287, 300, 315,
    334
  and worlds of compliance, 334
  and Young Workers Directive, 123–127,
    130–131, 133–139, 197–199,
    270–271, 305, 309–312, 314,
    334
  application of Directives in, 67–70,
    89–91, 135–137, 272–276

enforcement system in, 67–70, 89–91,
  135–137, 153–155, 172–174,
  272–276, 335
infringement procedures initiated
  against, 209
lowering of standards in, 130–131,
  137–139, 197–199
misfit in, 60–62, 77–80, 99–103,
  123–127, 130–131, 145–147,
  164–166, 262–265, 287,
  290–291
transposition performance of, 66–68,
  88–89, 110–112, 130–131, 133–134,
  152–153, 171–172, 194–196,
  270–271, 290–291, 296–297, 300,
  334
voluntary reforms in, 182–186,
  188–190, 193–194

Unintended consequences
  see EU decision-making process
United Kingdom
  and Employment Contract Information
    Directive, 59–62, 65–68, 70–71,
    270–271, 295, 300, 309–311
  and Parental Leave Directive, 142,
    145–147, 152–158, 182–184, 213,
    253–254, 270–271, 286–288, 295,
    300, 305, 308, 333–334
  and Part-time Work Directive, 161–169,
    171–175, 184, 193, 253–254,
    270–271, 295, 302–303, 333–334
  and Pregnant Workers Directive, 75–81,
    88–93, 270–271, 295, 333–334
  and Working Time Directive, 97–106,
    110–113, 115–117, 181, 194–196,
    211, 270–271, 277–278, 286–288,
    295, 300, 302–303, 305, 308–311,
    333–334
  and worlds of compliance, 321, 325,
    333–334
  and Young Workers Directive, 122–129,
    133–139, 181–182, 270–271,
    277–279, 295, 300, 302–303,
    309–311, 333–334
  application of Directives in, 89–91, 113,
    135–137, 155–158, 172–174
  enforcement system in, 67–70, 89–91,
    135–137, 153–155, 272–276, 335
  infringement procedures initiated
    against, 104–106, 147–148, 209, 211,
    213, 223–224
  misfit in, 59–62, 65–66, 75–81, 97–106,
    122–129, 145–147, 164–169,
    262–265, 290–291, 295

United Kingdom (*cont.*)
  national public–private relations in,
    229–230, 237–240, 249, 253–254,
    257–258, 284
  transposition performance of, 65–68,
    81, 88–89, 104–106, 110–112,
    128–129, 133–134, 147, 152–153,
    166–169, 171–172, 194–196,
    270–271, 277–278, 290–291,
    295–297, 300, 308, 333–334
  voluntary reforms in, 166–169,
    181–184, 187–189, 193–194,
    363–364

Veto players
  as reason for (non-)compliance, 16–17,
    25, 296–297, 310–311
Voluntary reforms
  as adaptation to soft law, 150–151,
    155–158, 169–171, 175–176,
    179–189, 315, 363–364
  as over-implementation of binding
    standards, 106–107, 148–150,
    155–158, 166–169, 189–194, 315
  patterns across countries and Directives,
    186–188, 193–194, 328
  theoretical views on, 178–179
  see also individual countries and
    Directives; neo-voluntarism,

Working Time Directive
  aim and content of, 94–96, 116
  and EU-level negotiations, 97–99, 116
  and misfit in the member states, 99–103,
    116, 260, 265
  and national application and
    enforcement, 112–115
  and transposition in the member states,
    103–112, 116, 194–196, 269–271,
    286–288
  and voluntary reforms, 181, 186–187,
    189, 191, 193–196
  general assessment of effects of, 115–117
  infringement proceedings initiated
    against breaches of, 104–110, 209,
    211–212, 244–246

  see also individual countries
World of domestic politics
  countries belonging to, 333–335,
    342–343
  definition of, 322–323
  see also worlds of compliance
World of law observance
  and compliance culture, 328–329, 354
  countries belonging to, 331–333
  definition of, 321–323
  see also worlds of compliance
World of neglect
  countries belonging to, 335–340
  definition of, 323–324
  see also worlds of compliance
Worlds of compliance
  and culture versus interests, 325–326
  and law-abidingness of administrative
    and political systems, 324–325
  and method of building typologies,
    317–321
  and scope of typology, 328, 340–341,
    344–345
  and stages of implementation, 326–328
  and transition between worlds, 329–330,
    354–355
  concept of, 328–332, 344–345

Young Workers Directive
  aim and content of, 118–121, 137
  and EU-level negotiations, 122–123,
    137
  and misfit in the member states,
    123–127, 137, 260, 265
  and national application and
    enforcement, 39–40, 135–137
  and transposition in the member states,
    127–134, 137, 269–271
  and voluntary reforms, 181–182,
    186–187, 189, 191–196
  general assessment of effects of,
    137–139
  infringement proceedings initiated
    against breaches of, 129–130,
    132–133, 209, 212–213
  see also individual countries